*To the men and women of five nations who served in the
Economic Section, Strategic Effects, MNF-I, Baghdad
and in C-9, MNC-I, Camp Liberty, Iraq*

The Political Economy of Iraq

The Political Economy of Iraq

Restoring Balance in a Post-Conflict Society

Frank R. Gunter

Lehigh University, USA

Edward Elgar

Cheltenham, UK • Northampton, MA, USA

Published by
Edward Elgar Publishing Limited
The Lypiatts
15 Lansdown Road
Cheltenham
Glos GL50 2JA
UK

Edward Elgar Publishing, Inc.
William Pratt House
9 Dewey Court
Northampton
Massachusetts 01060
USA

Reprinted 2014

A catalogue record for this book
is available from the British Library

Library of Congress Control Number: 2012949784

This book is available electronically in theElgarOnline.com
Economics Subject Collection, E-ISBN 978 1 84980 989 4

ISBN 978 1 84980 988 7 (cased)

Typeset by Servis Filmsetting Ltd, Stockport, Cheshire
Printed and bound in Great Britain by TJ International Ltd, Padstow, Cornwall

Contents

Preface

This is an attempt to write the book that I wish I had read before getting off the plane in Iraq in 2005. By that time, I had read or at least scanned several hundred books, journal articles, and research studies on the post-1955 political economy of Iraq. What I was not able to find was a single recent work that attempted to provide an integrated study of the entire political economy. The books by Lord Salter (1955), Abbas Alnasrawi (1994; 2002), Kamil Mahdi (2000; 2002), and unpublished studies by the World Bank and the International Monetary Fund were excellent and generously repaid a close reading. But these and the other similar works were either outdated or included only some of the key sectors and challenges facing post-2003 Iraq. What I needed was a recent work written, not for my colleagues at the University, but for the intelligent layman and women that I worked with for a total of 25 months in Iraq. I needed a work that attempted – in an integrated fashion – to describe, analyze, and make policy recommendations for almost the entire political economy of Iraq. The reader must judge whether I was successful.

My thinking on the most important challenges facing Iraq has evolved significantly. If I had been asked just before the Air Force transport made its nighttime "corkscrew landing" into Baghdad International Airport in May 2005 then I would have said that increasing oil exports and restoring agriculture production were the most important economic challenges facing the country. However, when I left Iraq for the last time in June 2009 as a business class passenger on a daylight flight in a comfortable commercial jet airliner, I was convinced that, as important as the petroleum and agricultural sectors are, the greatest barriers to accelerating Iraqi economic development are corruption and regulatory hostility towards private business. As a result, I consider Chapter 4 (Corruption) and Chapter 10 (Entrepreneurship) to provide the most value added.

The arrangement of the book is as follows. Chapters 2 and 3 provide overviews of Iraq's real growth, unemployment, and inflation followed by discussions of health, poverty, education, and gender issues. Chapters 4 through 6 are devoted to the three dominant characteristics of the political economy of Iraq: corruption, political instability, and petroleum. Chapters 7 through 12 each focus on a sector of the Iraq economy:

agriculture; financial intermediation; state-owned enterprises; entrepreneurship; infrastructure and essential services; and international trade and finance. Chapter 13 discusses fiscal, monetary, and exchange rate policy. The last chapter (Chapter 14) tries to isolate the major trends that will determine the characteristics of Iraq in 2025. This chapter ends with seven policy recommendations.

Several disparate groups have shaped my thinking. Most importantly, I am indebted to the military, diplomatic, consultant men and women with whom I shared 70 hour work weeks in Iraq for 25 months in 2005–2006 and 2008–2009. During the same period, the Iraqi businessmen, academics, and government officials that I had the opportunity to converse with provided valuable insights and their patience was gratefully appreciated. I am also grateful to those friends and acquaintances that work in academics or for the government who provided valuable comments on earlier drafts of parts of this book. Finally, the Lehigh University undergraduates who enrolled in my "Political Economy of Iraq" course were a tremendous help in organizing the material for optimal presentation.

If I tried to list all the names of those that provided useful insights into the political economy of Iraq then I would greatly exceed the publisher's word limit and probably accidently leave someone out. However, I am especially indebted to Karen Puschus, Wendy Polhemus, Kat Woolford, Paul Savello, June Reed, Brian Moore, Andrew Gough, Kevin Darnell, Glenn Goddard, Larry Milam, Terry Kelly, Samee Desai, Frank Mulcahy, Ian Furgerson, Tony Meyer, Chris Canniff, Tim Kane, Scott Chando, John Holmes, Jeffrey Butcher, Pat Carroll, Frederick Alegre, Karl Schwartz, Miriam Lutz, Tony Daza, Martin Sierra, Seung-gu Weon, Sam Korab, Janet Rudasil-Allen, Sandy MacMurtrie, Ali Bachani, Tim Fawcett, Tim Curran, Susan Maybaumwisniewski, Jeff Peterson, Robert Looney, Joe Banavige, Keith Crane, Mercedes Fitchett, Andrew Wallen, Anderson Warner, Nancy Blacker, Kim Faithfull, Terry Kelly, General Paul Lefebvre, and many others.

I am also indebted to General Austin and General Lynch, both of the US Army, for permitting me to join their Staffs in Iraq. I have not listed the names of many of the Iraqis who were extremely helpful. Some asked for confidentiality and I am concerned that others may be endangered because of their frankness about corruption and mismanagement. Tara Gorvine, Alison Hornbeck, and Christine Gowen of Edward Elgar Publishing have been extremely helpful, professional, and patient. The Lehigh University's College of Business and Economics funded valuable research support by Zaozao He, Jingyi Ye, Mengcen Qian, and Ye Ye. And I can honestly say that the book would not have been written without the extensive knowledge and unfailing patience of the Economics

Department Administrative Coordinator, Rene Hollinger. In addition, I am especially indebted to four colleagues who aggressively pushed me to finish this book on schedule: Eli Schwartz (now deceased), Nicolas Balabkins, Wight Martindale, and Anthony O'Brien. Finally, as always, I am grateful to my wife for continuing to smile whenever I bring up "salt poisoning of soil in Ninawa province" as a topic for dinner conversation.

A note on spelling. There is no standard transliteration of Arabic into English. Even Government of Iraq publications will use different spellings of the same Arabic word, sometimes in the same document. For example, the province and city in Northern Iraq can be rendered as Arbil, Arbīl, Erbil, Irbil, and so on. For the names of geographic locations – provinces, cities, rivers, and so on – I have tried to consistently use the spelling of the National Geographic Society. This usage is primarily a matter of convenience since I have made constant use of their maps.

1.   Iraq's lost decades

> Iraq has an altogether exceptional opportunity of achieving a
> development which within a few years would substantially increase
> her economic resources and raise her general standard of living. For
> she now has advantages which are rarely found in combination.
> (Lord Salter 1955, p. 1)

> Iraq in the years prior to its invasion of Kuwait was at the top of the
> per capita GDP ladder of developing countries. By 1993, real monthly
> earnings were lower than the monthly earnings of unskilled agricultural
> workers in India – [then] one of the poorest countries in the world.
> What happened to an economy noted for the wealth of its oil reserves,
> agricultural potential, water resources, relatively high rates of literacy
> and skills, vast access to foreign technology and expertise, an enviable
> balance-of-payments surplus and foreign reserves, and a long history of
> determined effort to develop and diversify the economy?
> (Abbas Alnasrawi 1994, p. xv)

In Iraq, history is repeating itself. In 1955, Lord Salter argued that an
objective analysis of Iraq's political economy showed that the country
would have a bright future of peace and prosperity. His vision was wrong
or very premature as conflict, corruption, and mismanagement devastated the country. A military coup in 1958 overthrew King Faisal II and
imposed a socialist republic. A leader of the Arab Ba'athist Socialist
Party, Saddam Hussein, became president in 1979, purged his enemies and
launched on a 24-year absolutist reign that combined severe oppression at
home, brutal wars with two of Iraq's regional neighbors, and the building
of an extremely corrupt and bureaucratic economy. After Saddam's overthrow by a US-led coalition in 2003, Iraq was politically, economically,
and physically in ruins and teetering on the edge of a civil war.

Now in 2012, there is once again a resurgence of optimism. Violence
has dropped sharply since 2006. Oil prices are higher than expected while
oil export volumes are increasing. And, as a result of what Fouad Ajami
(2006) referred to as the "foreigner's gift", Iraq has a nascent democracy.
Iraq once again has the potential to achieve a bright future for its people.
Whether that potential will be realized depends on the ability of the
Iraqi people and their leadership. For in choosing the best route for their
country to travel upstream into the future, they must not only steer clear

of the wreckage of previous voyages but also deal with new threats only faintly seen in the morning fog.

However, Iraq's response to these old and new challenges must reflect the changed political, economic, and social reality of Iraq at the beginning of the twenty-first century. This chapter provides a basic introduction to Iraq's geography, history, political structure, and economy as well as a discussion of the major trends and challenges. It is intended as a foundation for the rest of this book but readers who already possess knowledge of Iraq are invited to skim the rest of this chapter or skip it entirely.

Mesopotamia – a common name for Iraq – means: "the land between the two rivers": the Euphrates and Tigris. Both rivers originate in the mountains of Turkey. The Euphrates detours through Syria before entering Iraq from the west. The Tigris enters Iraq from the north and the two rivers flow roughly parallel through Iraq before they merge into the Shatt al-Arab waterway just north of the city of Basrah before flowing into the Persian Gulf. Most of Iraq's 32 million people live near the Euphrates or Tigris rivers with the three of the four largest Iraqi cities – the capital of Baghdad, the major port city of Basrah in the south, and Mosul in the north – located on the Tigris. The fourth largest city, Arbil, is in the mountainous region of northeast Iraq. These two rivers have provided transportation, irrigation for agriculture, and drinking water for almost a dozen great civilizations for ten millennia.

Iraq has three climate regions. The southwest of the country is a flat, very arid desert. At the other extreme, the northeast is mountainous with sufficient precipitation for rain-fed agriculture. In between is a band of semi-arid climate that stretches from the Syrian and Turkish borders in the northwest to the Persian Gulf in the southeast. The climate of central Iraq has hot summers, cool winters, and an agreeable spring and autumn.

Politically, Iraq is divided into 18 provinces, three of which – Dahuk, Arbil, and Sulaymaniyah – have joined together into a regional government, the Kurdish Regional Government (KRG). While Iraq is a federal system according to its 2005 constitution, only in the KRG are sub-national entities active. For the rest of the country, the national government in Baghdad makes almost all decisions.

Following the violence of 2006–2007, there is a tendency for outsiders to overly emphasize ethnic and religious differences in Iraq. These differences are important but there are other factors that may have as much or more influence on the future of the country. With respect to ethnicity and religion, the population of southeast Iraq is mostly Arab and Shi'a Muslim; the northeast are generally Kurds and Sunni Muslims; while the west is largely Arab and Sunni Muslim. However, there are members of every ethnic and religious group in every province of Iraq and there are cities

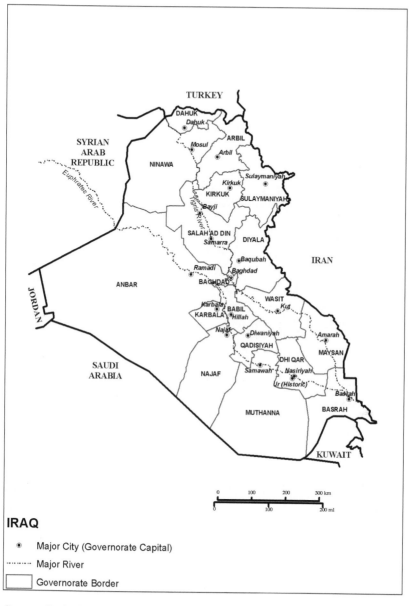

Source: Professional Maps of Houston, Texas (2012).

Figure 1.1 Political map of Iraq

and provinces where it is not clear whether the majority of the population is Shi'a or Sunni Muslim, Arab or Kurd.

As is well known, Iraq was almost torn apart by conflict following the 2003 invasion by the US-led coalition. From about 7300 civilian deaths in 2003, violence increased sharply especially after the 2006 insurgent bombing of the Golden Mosque. The worst year was 2006 when an estimated 34 500 Iraqi civilians were killed – almost 100 a day. As killing accelerated it led to large number of Iraqis becoming refugees either inside their own country or fleeing to Syria, Jordan, and other neighboring countries. Less noted is how concentrated the killing was. Most of the civilian fatalities were in five provinces while at the other extreme there were an equal number of provinces with few violent civilian deaths even during the worst periods. And to the surprise of many commentators both inside and outside Iraq, the killing began to slow in 2007 and by 2011 the number of civilian violence-related fatalities was less than 5 percent of those in 2006. This drop in civilian fatalities was not the result of one group obtaining a complete victory nor was it imposed from outside. Apparently, the Iraqi people looked into the abyss of an unending civil war and backed away. The diminution of violence has shifted emphasis back to economic development – which in Iraq means oil.

Iraq is an island floating on a sea of oil. It is generally considered to have the fourth largest petroleum reserves in the world but ongoing surveys may boost it to first place in front of its neighbor Saudi Arabia. Oil export earnings are the source of almost all government revenues and account for over two-thirds of the country's GDP. However, the Iraqi oil industry employs only a small fraction of the country's labor force. One of the continuing challenges facing the Iraqi government is dealing with oil price volatility. Oil production and export volumes tend to change gradually but oil prices are subject to rapid changes. As a result, government revenues are on a roller coaster. For example, these revenues fell 33 percent in 2009 before increasing 21 percent in the next year.

For thirty years, Iraq's oil legacy was squandered by conflict, corruption, and mismanagement. In fact, it is only recently that oil export earnings approached the levels previously achieved in 1979. But living standards for the average Iraqi are much lower than three decades ago because of the high rate of population growth. As a result of having one of the highest fertility rates in the world, Iraq has a young, rapidly growing population. Combined with the destruction of the recent conflicts, rapid population growth has severely challenged the ability of the government to provide universal elementary education and basic essential services. In addition, every year hundreds of thousands of Iraqis join the labor force and start looking for work in an economy characterized by high unemployment and underemployment. If these young people are unable to find useful work then it will be politically destabilizing. Meeting these challenges is made more difficult by the widespread corruption and mismanagement of a government in transition.

Now that Saddam's socialist central planning model has been abandoned, it is not clear which form of capitalism will be most effective at raising living standards rapidly. In 2012, Iraq might best be described as having partially evolved from central planning to state-guided capitalism in which government tries to guide the market by supporting particular industries that it expects to become "winners" or that are important sources of employment. But, if current political and economic trends continue, then there is a real danger that Iraq's state-guided capitalism is only a way station to becoming an oligarchic capitalistic state – like most of the other countries in the Arab Middle East – in which the bulk of the power and wealth is held by a small group of individuals and families. Despite wealth from natural resources, such oligarchic capitalistic states tend to have: great income inequality, sluggish growth, large informal or underground sectors, and massive corruption.

Iraq is facing many of the same types of political, economic, and social challenges that it failed to overcome five decades ago; now Iraq has to face these same challenges with a larger population, a less innovative economy, more hostile relations with its regional neighbors, a recent history of sectarian violence, and probably greater cynicism about the competency and honesty of the nation's leaders. While its petroleum wealth is a cause for optimism, the major determinant of Iraq's future will be the choices that Iraqis make over the next decade. If the Iraqi people and their leadership choose once again to take counsel of their fears and pursue short-term political and economic advantage as opposed to establishing a framework for long-term balanced prosperity and a solid democracy then Iraq will probably fail again. To paraphrase Toynbee (1972, p. 161): countries generally die from suicide, not by murder.

However, there is another route. If Iraq could restore balance in its political economy by combining reduced economic dependency on oil with reduced governmental corruption and bureaucracy in a more responsive political system, then the future could be very different. Its huge oil wealth could finance a more sustainable economic future with a better life not only for the current population of Iraq but also for generations to come. The many difficulties of following this alternative route are the subjects of the rest of this book.

2. Population and key macroeconomic variables

> It has been suggested that during the period of Abbasid rule (A.D. 754–1258), when Baghdad was the centre of the civilized world, the present state of Iraq may have supported a population of some 20 million people . . . [However] in the middle of the nineteenth century it has been estimated that the population numbered only 1.28 million.
> (R.I. Lawless 1972, p. 97)

DATA QUALITY

There is no shortage of data on Iraq's macroeconomy. The problem is that the data available is often inconsistent. When it comes to the size of the country's population, Gross Domestic Product (GDP), unemployment, and inflation, not only do different sources provide very different numbers but also the trend of a single variable from a single source is often unreliable. The latter problem is often caused by unannounced changes in the composition of a variable or the method of its estimation.

The three decades of internal and external conflict have made it difficult and often dangerous to gather data. For example, during post-1991 periods of severe internal conflict, markets in many areas of Iraq were split; it was dangerous or impossible for workers, customers, or products to travel even short distances. Iraq, for periods of time, ceased to be a national market rendering data on trade, manufacturing, agriculture, employment, and so on difficult to gather and interpret. Also, since 2003, the Government of Iraq (GoI) has been engaged in a difficult transition from socialist accounting to that of a modern market economy. As shown in Eastern Europe after the collapse of the Soviet Union, this transition can lead to serious gaps in data as definitions and collection methods change. In addition, the GoI continues attempts to conceal unfavorable data in order to put its operations in the best possible light.

In addition, as will be discussed in Chapter 4, Iraq suffers from serious corruption including large-scale smuggling across its borders with Iran, Syria, and Turkey. This distorts its international trade and investment data. Also, corruption combined with an extremely hostile regulatory environment has resulted in a large and growing informal (underground) economy. Production, consumption, and employment in the informal economy is only partially reported in the official statistics resulting in a wide gap between economic activity reported in official statistics and the reality on the ground. In recognition of severe problems with the GoIs statistical methodology, the World Bank ranks 2011 Iraq's Statistical Capacity Index as 46 percent – almost tied with Afghanistan and the Sudan. The world average is 68 percent (World Bank 2012a).

There are also policy implications. Low-quality data makes it more difficult to avoid waste. Major reconstruction decisions must either be delayed until better data is available, often at the cost of continued suffering among the population, or these decisions must be based on educated guesses based on inadequate or contradictory information. It is ironic that once these educated guesses are used to make policy, they take on a life of their own and are treated as being more credible than they actually deserve to be.

In Baghdad in 2006, I was instructed to provide a provincial breakdown of a certain political economic variable. Having wrestled with this data previously, I immediately responded that none of the existing data sources for this variable covered all 18 provinces and, in the few provinces where more than one source was available, they contradicted each other. I immediately received a response that Washington really did not care about my concerns about data quality; they wanted the provincial breakdown submitted within 48 hours. After making a large number of plausible – at least to me – assumptions, I finally produced the data and assuaged my conscience by attaching a note detailing the weaknesses. Of course, this caveat was stripped out before Washington apparently used the data to make a small revision in US reconstruction policy. Maybe my numbers were actually fairly correct but I still cringe when I run across references to this data as being from an authoritative US Government source.

POPULATION

Population data should be much more reliable than that for GDP, inflation, unemployment, and so on. It is easier to count people than to estimate these other variables. However, in Iraq even population data is very uncertain. The last nationwide census was in 1987; the 1997 census only covered the 15 non-Kurdish provinces and was probably contaminated by political considerations. Iraq was under UN sanctions and it was important to Saddam that the census revealed not only the high humanitarian cost of the sanctions but also robust growth among groups that supported the Saddam regime. An example of the latter was the importance of showing a growing Arab population in Kirkuk compared to earlier censuses that showed the city and province were mostly Kurdish. Further complicating estimates of population are the devastating effects of the post-1980 violence which has also resulted in large numbers of internal and external refugees.

During the 1980–1988 Iran–Iraq War – the deadliest war ever waged between developing nations – Iraq suffered an estimated 250 000–500 000 people killed or wounded. The Iraq invasion of Kuwait in 1990 and Saddam's reprisals against his own people followed. The true number of dead or wounded from this period will probably never be known but it is estimated at about 300 000. Finally, there were the casualties suffered following the invasion of Iraq by the US-led coalition in 2003. Estimates of deaths during this period range from 50 000 to the controversial figure of 650 000 deaths by *The Lancet*. Probably the most reliable estimate is the 160 000 deaths of the Iraq Body Count organization. Not only were a large number of Iraqis killed over the last three decades but also the violence was accompanied by large-scale population displacement.

The breakdown of government authority during the worst of the insurgent violence in 2005–2007 raises questions about the accuracy of official estimates of the number of refugees. However, for the 15 non-Kurdish provinces, the GoI estimated that there were 250 000 displaced families (approximately 1.7 million persons) at the end of 2008. With the decrease in violence, there is evidence that many refugees are beginning to return. In fact, by the end of 2010, the GoI estimated that the number of displaced had fallen by roughly 20 percent to 200 000 families (approximately 1.3 million persons) (COSIT 2012, Table 20/14). With the additional motivation of the civil conflict in Syria, improving conditions in Iraq appear to have accelerated the rate of return of displaced persons although no reliable data is available (SIGIR 2012, pp. 71–2).

In the absence of a recent census, current population estimates – regardless of the source – are based on multi-decade extrapolations of old census data adjusted by estimates of deaths, international refugees, the results of a variety of smaller surveys, and rules of thumb. Due to the uncertainty about birth, death (especially violent deaths), and migration rates during a period of severe internal and external conflict combined with deliberate distortions introduced to data so as to favor a particular ethnic or religious group; estimates of Iraq's current population therefore should be considered as no more than educated guesses. This has resulted in a divergence of estimates, while the IMF estimated that the country's population was 31 million in 2011, the GoI estimated a population of 33 million in the same year (COSIT 2012, Table 1/2). It is probably better to think of estimates of Iraq's population not as a point – say 32 million persons in 2011 – but as a range – maybe 32 million persons plus or minus 10 percent. In other words, if a professional census had been performed in that year, it would not have been terribly surprising if the census results showed Iraq's population to be as low as 29 million or as great as 35 million.

Uncertainty about the actual population of Iraq reduces the usefulness of most other data for Iraq. For example, consider the estimated per capita GDP purchasing power parity (PPP) basis of $3900 in 2011. It would not be surprising to discover that income per person was as high as $4300 if the population was only 29 million or as low as $3600 if the population was 35 million. The impact of this difference on the quality of life of the average Iraqi would be great since it is the difference between trying to live on $12 a day as opposed to only $10 a day.

It is unlikely that more accurate population data will be available in the near future. The 2005 Constitution called for a periodic census but as in previous years, the 2012 GoI budget provides no funding for planning or executing a census. One reason for the delay, as discussed in Chapter 5, is that the results of a census may cause a major political shift in the oil-rich Kirkuk province. If a census were to show a majority Kurdish population in Kirkuk then this would strengthen the movement to have Kirkuk join the Kurdish Regional Government (KRG). As a result, the GoI may prefer to live with population uncertainty rather than permit a census that might weaken the national government's authority.

Although all of the population data is based on educated guesses, there are at least four population characteristics that are so prominent that one can be reasonably certain that the data reflects reality and not statistical artifacts.

First, Iraq is a land of large households. Although it appears that the average household size has shrunk over the last several decades, the average household size was still 6.7 persons in 2009. Among the 31 percent of the population that live in rural areas (COSIT 2012, Table 2/2), the typical Iraqi family has four or five children, with two or three adults in each household. With the exception of agricultural work, relatively few women or elderly people are in the labor force; the typical Iraqi household has a single male wage earner supporting six or seven dependents. Women, mostly widows, head an estimated 11 percent of all households.

Second, Iraq – as a result of a high fertility rate – is a very youthful country. Iraqis aged less than 15 years account for almost 43 percent of the population. This is a substantially greater proportion of young people in Iraq than in neighboring countries: Saudi Arabia (30 percent of the population is younger than 15), Kuwait (27 percent), Turkey (26 percent), and Iran (23 percent) (US Census 2012).

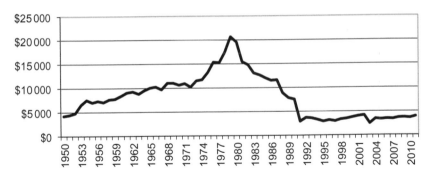

Source: Maddison (2003), adjusted and extended by author.

Figure 2.1   Iraq real per capita GDP

Third, providing productive employment for each cohort of young persons is the most important challenge facing Iraq. Each year about 850 000 Iraqis become old enough to work. Adjusting for each year's retirements and deaths among the working population as well as the very low labor force participation rate among women means that the nation must create about 250 000 additional jobs each year. In other words, in any year when the country fails to create a quarter of a million net new jobs, there will be an increase in the pool of mostly male, mostly uneducated, unemployed. This growing pool of unemployed discouraged young men without any expectation of finding a good job – and therefore supporting a family – is a major source of instability.

Finally, Iraq's population is increasing at a fairly rapid rate by international standards. With about 2.8 percent annual population growth, the Iraqi population will double in about 25 years. Contrast this to the average 1.6 percent population growth rate among other Middle East and North Africa (MENA) countries (their populations will double in about 44 years) and the 1.4 percent population growth among other Low-Middle Income Counties (LMIC) (their populations will double in about 50 years). Thus any year in which real GDP growth is less than 2.8 percent will be a year of decreasing per capita incomes.

GROSS DOMESTIC PRODUCT

The pattern of real per capita income shown in Figure 2.1 is based on data from several sources and depends upon some fairly controversial assumptions. However, it provides a rough guide to changes in inflation-adjusted

Iraqi per capita income. While real GDP per capita is now greater than immediately following Saddam's 1990 invasion of Kuwait, it is only about a fifth of what it was in 1979. Over the last sixty years, year-to-year changes in per capita income were primarily driven by three variables: the value of oil exports, conflict, and population growth.

From 1950 through 1979, there was a steady rise in per capita incomes as a result of increased oil export volume combined with higher world oil prices. The latter year was distinguished not only by the highest living standards ever achieved by the Iraqi people but also by Saddam seizing absolute power. The decade long collapse in per capita income that followed was caused both by an almost 65 percent drop in real oil prices as well as the incredible waste of blood and treasure of the eight-year long war that followed Saddam's September 1980 invasion of Iran. A gradual recovery in oil export revenues following the end of that war was aborted by Saddam's August 1990 invasion of Kuwait followed by his military defeat, UN sanctions, and the invasion of Iraq by a US-led coalition in March 2003. However, in 2003, world oil prices began to march upward until they reached almost the same real level in 2008 as during OPECs glory year of 1979.

If oil prices were as high in 2008 as in the halcyon days of 1979 then why were Iraqi per capita income and living standards so much lower in 2008? Two reasons explain this. First, as a result of conflict including deliberate attacks against the country's oil infrastructure combined with serious mismanagement, the volume of oil exports was about 1.8 million barrels per day (mbpd) production – almost 40 percent less – in 2008 than in 1979. But the second reason is more important – rapid population growth. Iraq's population was less than 13 million in 1979 compared to an estimated 31 million in 2008 – a 140 percent increase (COSIT 2012, Table 1/2). Even if the volumes of both oil exports and world oil prices were to return to 1979 levels, the average Iraqi would only have about 40 percent of the real income and living standards that his or her parents had three decades before.

As shown on Table 2.1, the IMF estimates that the 2011 per capita GDP was about $3000 (converting Iraqi dinars (ID) to dollars at an exchange rate of 1170 dinars/dollar). However, the average Iraqi's share of GDP provides little insight into the quality of life of the average Iraqi because it fails to consider the cost of living. Since Iraq is a relatively low-cost country, especially for services, the $3000 has an estimated PPP value of about $3900 (US CIA 2012). In other words, an Iraqi who earned the average income in his or her country would have approximately the same living standard as a resident of the USA whose total spending for all purposes – food, rent, clothing, medical care, and so on – equaled $3900. Multiplied by the country's estimated population, this results in a 2011 GDP (PPP) of $127.2 billion (62nd largest in world) (US CIA 2012).

Table 2.1 Key macroeconomic variables

	2004	2005	2006	2007	2008	2009	2010	2011
Real GDP growth	46.5%	−0.7%	6.2%	1.5%	9.5%	4.2%	0.8%	9.6%
Non-oil real GDP growth	14.9%	12.0%	7.5%	−2.0%	5.4%	4.0%	4.5%	5.0%
GDP per capita	$951	$1124	$1720	$1926	$2845	$2087	$2340	$2983
Oil production (mbpd)	2.00	1.90	2.00	2.04	2.29	2.38	2.35	2.75
Oil exports (mbpd)	1.40	1.40	1.40	1.59	1.82	1.88	1.85	2.17
Oil prices	$31.60	$43.90	$55.60	$63.00	$91.50	$55.60	$74.20	$76.50
Inflation consumer prices	31.7%	31.6%	64.8%	4.7%	6.8%	−4.4%	2.4%	6.0%
Inflation core price				12.3%	11.7%	6.1%	3.3%	5.0%
Exchange rate ID per $	1453	1469	1467	1255	1193	1170	1170	1170

Source: IMF (2011a).

Iraq's national income is more dependent on the export of a single natural resource than the population of any other country. In 2010, natural resources accounted for about 69 percent of Iraq's GDP. The Congo Republic, in second place, was more than five percentage points less. Among other major oil exporting nations, natural resources only contributed 54 percent of Saudi Arabia's GDP, 43 percent in Kuwait, 32 percent in Iran, and about 20 percent in the United Arab Emirates (UAE) and Venezuela (World Bank 2012b, Table 3.18, pp. 204–7). As a result, in the short run, the health of Iraq's economy is determined to a great extent by the value of its petroleum exports.

The percentages for non-petroleum sectors of GDP tend to change substantially year to year even though the actual production of these sectors is relatively stable. For example, oil prices fell from $91.50 per barrel (pb) in 2008 to $55.60 pb in 2009. Despite a small increase in the volume of oil exports, the 40 percent drop in oil prices led to sharp declines in oil export earnings and therefore the proportion of GDP accounted for by petroleum.

It might be more useful to think of Iraq as two economies – oil and non-oil. In the non-oil economy: services (mostly provided by the national government) accounts for about 76 percent; manufacturing accounts for 13 percent; and agricultural accounts for about 11 percent. The non-oil economy accounts for about 98 percent of the labor force; with only about 2 percent of the labor force working in the oil economy. Growth in the non-oil economy is relatively stable.

When oil prices change, the GoI tends to adjust by cutting government investment. For example, between 2007 and 2008, public sector investment in fixed capital increased by 234 percent to about 18.0 trillion ID (about $15.4 billion) before decreasing by 32 percent to approximately 12.2 trillion ID (about $10.5 billion) in 2008 (COSIT 2012, Table 14/11). These large year-to-year funding changes in multi-year infrastructure projects are a source of great inefficiency. When a project's funds are exhausted for the year, construction sites are essentially abandoned until the new fiscal year allows projects to be restarted. This abandonment permits degradation of materials if not outright theft. Often, workers continue to receive their salaries even though there is no work to be done. As a result, the total cost of each interrupted project is substantially increased.

UNEMPLOYMENT

There are various surveys that show that Iraqis consider unemployment the most important issue for the GoI to address. In fact, to the average Iraqi, unemployment is a more serious problem than lack of essential services, corruption, or security (SIGIR 2012, Figure 4.12, p. 84). As I found when looking at data for populations and GDP, there are no shortages of estimates of unemployment in Iraq with current estimates ranging from 15 percent to 40 percent. But again, one should have little confidence in the accuracy of any given estimate.

There are several possible explanations for this wide divergence in unemployment estimates. First, both in official reports and news stories, there is confusion about the different employment concepts or a failure to make it clear exactly which concept is under discussion. Reports of unemployment (no job but currently looking for work) will often include estimates of: underemployment (working but in a job that does not use a person's skills, education, or working part-time when full-time employment is desired); or discouraged workers (wants a job but not working and no longer looking for a job).

Since, of course, the unemployment rate is the percentage of the labor force – not the population – that is unemployed; estimates of unemployment rates require estimates of a nation's labor force. The labor force is defined as people aged 15 years and older either employed or unemployed but actively seeking work. Estimates of the size of the Iraq labor force in 2010 ranged from 7.5 million to 9 million persons. Iraq's labor force is only about 25 percent of the population and that is below the average MENA country. The low proportion of the population in the labor force is caused by the large proportion of the population that is less than 15 years old, almost 43 percent, and the fact that relatively few females either work or are looking for work.

A second reason for the wide range of unemployment estimates is the difficulty of including employment in the Iraq informal (underground) economy in the national employment estimates. Since the Iraq government is bureaucratic and corrupt, private businesses find it difficult and expensive to legally hire a worker. As a result, many businesses in the private sector hire workers "off the books" which excludes them from the official employment statistics. Some of the higher unemployment estimates by Iraqi ministries appear to assume that if a person is neither working for the government nor a farmer then that person must be unemployed.

Finally, "ghost workers" and unreported immigrant workers may also distort unemployment and employment statistics. Many state-owned enterprises (SOE) and ministries have workers who receive pay each month from the government for working full-time but, in reality, do little work and may not even show up at the workplace except on payday. For some SOE, the proportion of these "ghost workers" is believed to exceed 25 percent of total employment. A proportion of these ghosts have jobs elsewhere, maybe even with another SOE. As a result, the number of employed in the

Table 2.2   Employment and underemployment (%)

2009 estimates	Iraq	Baghdad	Age 15–19
Employed full-time (30 hours or more)	36	40	20
Employed part-time (less than 30 hours)	12	9	8
Employed seasonally or irregular	15	12	30
Self-employed	37	39	42
Total employed	100	100	100
Unemployed (% of labor force)	18	18	27
Underemployed (% of labor force)	33	31	55

Sources: COSIT (2008), Tables 5.1 and 5.27; Johnson (2007); and author's estimates.

economy is exaggerated. Another bias in the data is from the employment of large numbers of undocumented workers from Egypt and other poor countries. To make up for the large proportion of the male population that was drafted into the army during the 1980–1988 War with Iran, Saddam encouraged large numbers of foreign workers to come to Iraq to work in its factories and on its farms. Most of these economic immigrants were forced to leave Iraq during the sanctions period. But since 2003, there has been increasing anecdotal evidence that undocumented workers are returning to Iraq in large numbers especially to the southern provinces. Employers claim that hiring Iraqis to do certain jobs not only costs more but also Iraqi workers are more difficult to manage and to motivate.

All of the above distort the official data; like the data for population and real GDP, the best that can be hoped for is an educated guess at the true pattern of employment and unemployment in Iraq. Table 2.2 is such an educated guess based primarily on extrapolations of a 2007 COSIT survey (COSIT 2008) modified by a variety of other sources and the author's prejudices.

As shown in Table 2.2, young persons are more likely to be seasonally or irregularly employed. The latter category includes day laborers. The data for self-employment conceals more than it reveals. As in most developing countries, there is a bi-modal – "bedpost" – distribution of the self-employed. At one extreme of the self-employed, there are skilled workers (carpenters, plumbers, and so on) or educated individuals (merchants, medical personnel, and so on) who are relatively well compensated, tend to have employees, and are self-employed by choice. However, at the other extreme of the self-employed are persons engaged in small-scale service activities, who work alone, and are self-employed as a matter of survival until they can obtain any other job.

Due to missing or defective data, estimates of underemployment are even more uncertain than those of unemployment. Table 2.2 reports the result of a standard rule of thumb that underemployment equals the sum of part-time workers and seasonal–irregular workers plus half of those listed as self-employed, all divided by the labor force (underemployed = (part-time + seasonal–irregular + half of self-employed)/labor force).

What can be concluded from Table 2.2? Consistent with Johnson's study of 2006 unemployment and underemployment in Iraq (see Johnson 2007), there are two important conclusions. First, underemployment is a serious problem in Iraq. While the national unemployment rate was 18 percent, the combined unemployment and underemployment rate was 51 percent – more than half of the labor force. Second, the young (aged 15–19 years) are experiencing much higher rates of both unemployment and underemployment with the combined rate at an estimated 82 percent! A major cause of the much higher rates of unemployment and underemployment of the young is the GoIs reliance on the public sector to provide employment for young people just entering the job market. In other words, the government is the "employer of first resort".

Below is a 2008 attempt to "follow the money" to determine the actual sources of funds used to pay Iraq's labor force of 7.5 million people. Since oil export earnings account for approximately two-thirds of GDP and over 90 percent of GoI revenues, one would expect that oil export earnings fund a large proportion of the jobs in Iraq, but it is interesting to delineate the routes that these funds took. While roughly 50 percent of the Iraqi labor force is paid with oil money, actual employment in the oil industry is small – maybe 2 percent of the labor force.

Oil-funded employment ~50%
    Oil industry ~2%
    Ministerial employment ~33%
    State-owned enterprises ~8%
    Grant or loan generated ~1%
    Grain agriculture ~6%
Non-oil-funded employment ~32%
    Non-grain agriculture ~6%
    Large-scale non-SOE Iraqi firms ~3%
    Foreign direct investment ~1%
    International organization, non-governmental organization, and so on ~2%
    Informal economy ~20%
Unemployed ~18%

The largest numbers of recipients are ministerial employees that account for about one-third of the labor force. This reflects not only the government workers involved in provision of a large range of public and merit goods but also the government's role as the "employer of first resort". As will be discussed further in Chapter 9, the SOE (even those that are only an empty shell with zero production) are encouraged to maintain their employment levels. These accounted for an estimated 8 percent of the labor force. In addition, about 1 percent of the labor force is paid from GoI grants or loans. It is difficult to determine whether this is actually productive employment or another form of transfer payments based on political connections.

Agricultural employment, about 12 percent of the labor force, can be roughly divided into two categories. Farmers who grow grain are government employees in everything but name. As will be discussed in Chapter 7, the GoI owns much of the land, supplies most of the inputs – seed, fertilizer, fuel, and so on – and sets the prices at which the grain crops can be sold. On the other hand, farmers of non-grain crops, although subject to detailed and arbitrary government regulations and policies, might be more accurately described as self-employed.

About 6 percent of the nation's labor force are employed in the nation's small formal economy either by the relatively rare Iraqi-owned large-scale private firms, foreign investors especially in construction and hotel industries, or by foreign government, international organizations, and non-governmental organizations. Another 20 percent of the labor force is employed in the informal or underground economy. Iraq has an extremely hostile regulatory environment (see Chapter 10) that discourages small businesses from operating openly. They would rather avoid government regulation and demands for bribes by operating in the informal economy despite the associated inefficiencies. Some of these activities are clearly illegal such as prostitution or serving alcohol but others are activities that would be legal if the small business owner was willing to pay the necessary fees and bribes. It is not uncommon for officials to count Iraqis working in the informal economy as unemployed.

Female and Male Employment

In 2010, while an estimated 69 percent of Iraqi males 15 years or older were in the labor force, the estimate for females was about 14 percent (World Bank 2012b, Tables 2.1 and 2.2, pp. 42–8). Iraq's female labor force participation is low compared to the average MENA country that has a female rate of 20 percent while the rate among LMIC is 37 percent. Female participation in Iraq's labor force continues to be severely constrained by religious and cultural strictures. Saddam's Arab Ba'athist Socialist Party strongly supported female equality in government employment although there was substantial backsliding from this ideal during the sanctions period. However, females still fill an estimated 30 percent of government jobs compared to only an estimated 5 percent of jobs in private sector.

Of course, the unusually low labor force participation rate of women in Iraq tends to slow the country's economic growth. In 1920, Weber wrote of the importance of the "protestant work ethic" as a major cause of economic development in the West (Weber [1920] 2002). A more recent study concluded that Muslims ranked even higher than Protestants with respect to pride in work and willingness to sacrifice to make a better future (Zulfikar 2012). Therefore, it is ironic that the great benefit of this strong religion-based "work ethic" is more than offset by an unwillingness to allow one-half of the population to fully participate in building a better Iraq.

Not only is there a wide gap in the labor force participation rates of men and women but also they tend to be employed in different professions. Most working educated women are engaged in teaching at the primary or secondary levels (33 percent of all female employment) while the major source of employment for uneducated women is agricultural work (31 percent). There is a big gap until the next most important profession; about 5 percent of women are employed in the financial sector. Male employment is much more diverse. To reach two-thirds of male employment, one must include retail and wholesale trade (19 percent), building and construction (14 percent), farming (13 percent), communication and transport (12 percent) as well as public administration and military (11 percent) (COSIT 2008, Table 5-20A, p. 324).

As expected, not only do Iraqi women have a lower labor-force participation rate combined with fewer employment options for those women who do seek employment; the average Iraqi woman earns a much lower wage than her male counterpart. In fact, among agricultural workers, 85 percent of women aged 15–19 years and 34 percent of those aged 20–29 years reported zero wages. The corresponding non-wage employment for men in agricultural employment was 20 percent and 8 percent (COSIT 2008, Table 5-17A, p. 316). Many rural women are expected to work on the family farm as part of their family duties.

The "Five Iraqs": Primary Sources of Provincial Employment

Each of the major categories of employment is represented in every one of the 18 provinces although the range is wide. To take agriculture for example, at one extreme, an estimated 39 percent of the employed in Salah ad Din province are farmers while, at the other extreme, only 4 percent of the residents of Basrah province till the soil. However, based on the major sources of employment in each province, one can roughly divide the country into "five Iraqs" – each defined by its dominant source of employment and income. (Data is from COSIT 2008, Table 5-20A, pp. 324–5 but the division is by the author.) The "Five Iraqs" are:

1. Oil Iraq: Basrah and Kirkuk
    While oil and gas reserves have been discovered in almost every Iraqi province, Basrah and Kirkuk accounted for almost 94 percent of the nation's production in 2010. As a result, while the oil industry accounts for only 2 percent of national employment, it is the most important category of employment in these provinces.
2. Farming Iraq: Salah ad Din, Babil, Anbar, and Qadisiyah
    These provinces tend to be more agricultural as either the Euphrates or Tigris river flows through each of these provinces providing water for irrigation. While only 31 percent of the total Iraqi population lives in rural areas, in these four provinces a majority of the population lives in rural areas (51 percent).
3. Business Iraq: Ninawa, Baghdad, Karbala, and Najaf (and Basrah again)
    Since the days of the Ottoman Empire, the three most important trading and manufacturing cities in Iraq have been Mosul (Ninawa province), Baghdad, and Basrah. As will be discussed in Chapter 12, several million religious tourists annually visit Najaf and Karbala provinces. Tourism-related construction and services for these mostly Iranian tourists are major businesses.
4. Government job Iraq: Dahuk, Arbil, and Diyala
    Dahuk and Arbil (along with Sulaymaniyah) comprise the KRG in northern Iraq. Diyala is south of the KRG on the Iranian border. Over 30 percent of the labor forces in these three provinces work for the government in public administration, military service, or education. The average for the rest of the country is 19 percent.
5. Balanced Iraq: Sulaymaniyah, Wasit, Muthanna, Dhi Qar, and Maysan
    In these provinces there is no single dominant employment sector.

The existence of the "Five Iraqs" is as a reminder that policy initiatives or unexpected shocks will probably have very different impacts on the various provinces. For example, if religious tourism increases sharply while agriculture stagnates then not only will there be a net overall effect – positive or negative – on Iraq's GDP and unemployment but also there will be some provinces that will boom while others decline. It is also unlikely that large-scale labor migration will substantially mitigate these differences. For cultural and historical reasons, it is unlikely that large numbers of the unemployed or underemployed from a province with slower real growth will permanently move to a province with a better economy. For example, according to the GoI, Dhi Qar province had the highest unemployment rate in 2008 while Sulaymaniyah province had the lowest. However, it is unlikely that an Arab Shi'a from Dhi Qar province would move his family to Sulaymaniyah province that, being mostly Kurdish and Sunni, has a different language and follows a different form of Islam.

INFLATION

As shown in Table 2.1, inflation – according to official sources – has experienced large year-to-year changes, from about 32 percent in 2004 and 2005, the rate of price increases almost doubled to almost 65 percent in 2006 before falling to less than 5 percent in 2007 and 7 percent in 2008. According to these same sources, there was deflation of about 4 percent in 2009 before achieving a positive 2 percent increase in prices in 2010 and 6 percent in 2011. Like unemployment, estimates of Iraqi inflation are subject to severe definitional as well as data problems. These problems are so severe that I think that the reported pre-2008 inflation figures are essentially meaningless. The data from 2008 and later are also question-able. They may provide a rough guide to the direction of inflation change, for example "inflation is getting worse", but the published data does not provide a reliable guide to actual price changes. There are at least five reasons for price uncertainty, which provide insight into the difficulties of developing sound macroeconomic policies in Iraq.

First, inflation – a rise in the average price level – is measured by estimating changes in the number of ID that it costs to buy a "basket" of goods and services. As long as these goods and services are sold in markets, the biggest challenges in estimating inflation are determining which items should be in the basket and periodically gathering price data for each of the goods and services. But markets in the formal sector do not provide many of the goods and services consumed by the average Iraqi. Instead these goods and services are either provided by the GoI or are pro-duced in the informal (black market) sector. This makes determining the "price" of a particular good or services an arbitrary and, often, a political exercise. The GoI is the sole or dominant supplier of essential services such as electricity, water, fuel, food rations, and so on. The GoI generally provides these essential items at zero or very low cost – substantially less than any market clearing price for these items. As expected, provision at below market prices leads to shortages and rationing. But what is the relevant price of a rationed good?

Electricity is a good example of the problem. Even today, it is rare for a family or business in Iraq to have 24 hour a day access to grid electricity. When the grid is "dark", a family or business must purchase electricity from an entrepreneur operating a community generator, buy black market fuel to operate a private generator, or wait through the heat and the dark until the grid is on again. (See Chapter 11 this book, Table 11.1 for the use of backup sources of electrical power.)

Under these conditions, what is the true price of electricity? According to the October 2010 electricity pricing guidelines, a family receives its first 1000 kilowatt hours (kWh) a month for free and pays only 50 ID per kWh (about 4.3 US cents per kWh) for the next thousand. But what is the price of electricity when the grid is dark? One might argue that it is the price of electricity from the alternative – probably black market – source. Obviously, reliable pricing data on such a source is difficult for government officials to obtain. What if a family is forced to sit in the heat and dark and wait until the grid is back on because an alternative source is not available? It seems deceptive to argue that the relevant price is 50 ID per kWh if one cannot buy electricity at any price. In theory, one might try to estimate the highest price that the family would be willing to pay for electricity if it was available but, as can be imagined, any such estimate would be extremely arbitrary. The GoI does not seem to use either of these options, rather they use the official price for government supplied goods and services even when these goods and services are not available!

This leads to a severe distortion of inflation data when the GoI raises official prices. One of the drivers of the sharp rise in inflation in 2005 and 2006 was the increase in official fuel prices. In order to reduce smuggling and under pressure from the IMF, the GoI raised the official price of diesel fuel from about one US cent per liter in 2004 to six cents per liter in 2005, and 11 cents in 2006 – over a 1000 percent increase in a two-year period in the price of a basic consumer item. But, in reality, did fuel prices actually increase? In 2004, there was a severe shortage of diesel fuel at official prices due, primarily, to the illegal diversion of such fuel into the black market. Consumers and businesses were forced to buy diesel fuel in the black market at a price that was ten to 20 times the official price. When official fuel prices started to be raised in 2005, consumers were able to obtain more fuel from legal sources at the official price because of a decline in the profitability of illegally diverting fuel into the black market. Thus actual fuel prices paid by consumers and private firms generally grew much slower than reported in the official inflation statistics. In some provinces, actual fuel prices may actually have declined. By focusing on official prices, the official inflation statistics exaggerated actual price increases.

Second, one of the continuing characteristics of the Iraq economy is the large-scale smuggling of consumer products from neighboring countries. This smuggling of everything from frozen chickens to fuel to refrigerators both distorts Iraq's trade data and further complicates the GoIs attempts to estimate changes in domestic prices. In addition to shortages brought about by artificially low official prices, smuggling was also encouraged by the GoIs complex and expensive trade regulations. As will be discussed in Chapter 12, although it has a low tariff – 5 percent on most products – Iraq has some of the most restrictive trade regulations in the MENA countries. Therefore, for most products, it is more profitable for a merchant to pay a bribe to the appropriate official to look the other way when an item is smuggled into the country than to legally import it.

Third, from 1980 through at least the end of 2007, Iraq suffered from severe internal and external conflict. As a result, through much of this period, Iraq was not a single market. The same products sold for different prices (differences much greater than the costs of transportation) not only in different provinces but also in different towns within the same province. The gathering and analysis of this data proved extremely difficult.

Fourth, there was a strong incentive for elements of the GoI to exaggerate inflation. The real wages of government employees had declined substantially during the sanctions period. As a result, during the initial years of the US-led coalition occupation of Iraq there was continuing requests that the coalition permit substantial increases in government employee wages in order to restore living standards of government employees to reasonable levels. In particular, the 65 percent official inflation rate in 2006 was used to justify a substantial increase in both the salary and pension benefits of government employees. In retrospect, the adjustments were probably excessive since the average government employee is now believed to earn about 50 percent more than someone in the private sector with similar skills. Finally, the ubiquitous corruption in Iraq that is the subject of Chapter 4 means that, for many goods and services, a price has two parts. The consumer or firm must not only pay for the product itself but also pay a bribe to a government official to allow the purchase. This two-part purchase both raises the true price of obtaining a product and – since there is no reason to think that the amount of the bribe is either constant or even closely related to the price of the purchase – the failure to report the actual amount paid in the bribe is another wedge between actual price changes and the official inflation rates.

Raising government salaries and benefits was not the only policy response to the perceived acceleration of inflation. The Central Bank of Iraq (CBI) began a deliberate appreciation of the ID that resulted in the exchange rate increasing from 1467 ID/$ in 2006 to 1170 ID/$ in 2009 – about a 20 percent appreciation of the ID. This was intended to reduce the rate of inflation by decreasing the prices of imported goods. Of course, as will be discussed in Chapters 12 and 13, this appreciation also reduced the competitiveness of non-oil exports from Iraq – the "Dutch Disease".

IMPROVING THE QUALITY OF MACROECONOMIC DATA

The primary statistical authority of Iraq, the Central Organization for Statistics and Information Technology (COSIT), is an invaluable source of data not only on the Iraqi economy but also on its society. This book makes extensive use of COSITs (2012) *Annual Abstract of Statistics: 2010–2011* as well as COSITs (2008) *Iraq Household Socio-Economic Survey: 2007.* As an example of the careful preparation of these publications, in Volume III of the *Iraq Household Socio-Economic Survey: 2007,* COSIT lists not only standard errors for the data (pp. 780–795) but also the exact questions asked during the survey (pp. 799–986). However, better data results are always necessary for better policy (see IMF 2011a, Annex III, pp. 12–15). However there are at least three challenges facing the publication of timely accurate data concerning Iraq by COSIT and other Iraqi organizations with statistical responsibilities.

First, COSIT staffing is inadequate and many employees lack the necessary training. It is important that COSIT is adequately funded to allow it to hire and train the best people for this important job.

Second, in most cases, COSIT must rely upon the various government ministries to submit reasonably accurate data on a timely basis. But the degree of cooperation differs greatly among ministries. For example, the Ministry of Finance and also the Ministry of Industry and Mineral Resources generally provide quality data on a timely basis. At the other extreme, the Ministries of Health and Trade are considered to be particularly opaque. It is apparent that some ministries consider the provision of data to be of little importance or seek to hide unfavorable data. The prime example is the unwillingness of some ministries to cooperate in the ongoing census of government employees. This census, which was supposed to have been completed in 2006, is still in progress six years later. The census results are expected to support accusations of either mismanagement or corruption especially with respect to ghost workers, and some ministries have gone beyond failing to cooperate and have actually physically threatened census takers. In addition, COSIT access to KRG data is also limited.

The third and potentially the most serious challenge to data collection that is both timely and useful, is the universal temptation of all government departments to restrict or distort data that puts the government in a bad light or that might have adverse political consequences. This of course is another example of "Goodhart's Law" that states that whenever a reliable variable becomes important for policy then it ceases to be reliable. The prime example is the continuing delay in performing a rigorous national census. As noted above, the last census of all 18 provinces was in 1987. Aside from its importance in developing economic policy and furthering the progress towards a stronger democracy in Iraq, the results of this census should provide a valuable assessment of the accuracy of the more limited surveys that have been performed since 2003.

SUMMARY

This summary of Iraq's recent GDP, employment, and inflation data is intended to provide a framework for the rest of this book. It should be kept in mind that there is no shortage of data about this economy. The challenge is determining which data most accurately describes what is actually happening in Iraq. While data challenges exist in most all developing countries, Iraq's combination of recent conflict, socialist-market transition, and massive corruption make its economic data more questionable than most.

3. Health, poverty, education, and gender issues

> Health conditions in Iraq are considered some of the worst
> in the region. Indicators over the past twenty years show that
> the health of the population has seriously deteriorated.
> (GoI 2010, p. 119)

> In the past two decades, the entirety of the educational system has
> deteriorated. A serious effort is required to heal the wounds and hasten
> the reforms that will achieve the larger aims of economic reform.
> (GoI 2010, p. 114)

Good health, low poverty levels, and access to education are important determinants of the quality of life. Prior to the initiation of 30 years of conflict in 1980, Iraq had made dramatic progress in all three areas. In fact, in the late 1970s, Iraq was considered by many to be the leading Arab country with respect to equitable social development. However, the physical and moral destruction of the wars initiated by Saddam with Iran and Kuwait followed by defeat by the US-led coalition, the UN imposed sanctions, Saddam's overthrow in 2003 by a second US-led coalition, widespread corruption, and the vicious fight with an insurgency that brought the country to the edge of civil war in 2006 tore the fabric of Iraqi society apart.

As a result, it is surprising that, with the exception of variables related to gender equality, Iraq's key social indicators of development are reasonably close to the average of the MENA countries as well as that of the LMIC. In other words, Iraq lost its position of primacy in social development but it did not fall to the bottom; it is now close to the average of countries who have roughly the same level of per capita income.

The UN 2000 Millennium Development Goals program provided development goals in eight areas to be achieved by the year 2015. Iraq's progress towards these goals is monitored both by Iraq's COSIT (2012, Section 19) and the World Bank (2012b, pp. 1–33). Unfortunately, for some of the same reasons discussed in the previous chapter, COSIT and the World Bank often report different data for Iraq for the same indicators. However, the trends are similar. Table 3.1 provides the World Bank 2010 data for Iraq with respect to the key social indicators of development

Table 3.1   Social indicators of development

2010 data	Iraq	MENA	LMIC
Per capita income (PPP)	$3 400	$2 600	$3 600
Life expectancy male/female	65/72	70/74	64/67
Malnutrition (less than 5 years old)	7%	8%	25%
Child mortality (per 1000 births)	39	34	69
Maternal mortality (per 100 000 live births)	75	88	300
Tuberculosis (per 100 000 persons)	64	42	174
Access to improved sanitation	73%	88%	47%
Universal primary education	65%	88%	88%
Gender equality	81%	93%	93%
Contraception (among married women)	50%	62%	50%

Sources: World Bank (2012b): per capita income WDI Table 1.1, pp. 20–22; life expectancy WDI Table 1.5, pp. 34–7; malnutrition, education, gender equality, mortality WDI Table 1.2, pp. 24–7; contraception, TB, improved sanitation WDI Table 1.3, pp. 28–31.

listed in the Millennium Development Goals. Iraq's results are compared to those of MENA countries as well as those of the LMIC. The LMIC have a national income (2010 GNI per capita) between $1006 and $3975. Iraq's 2010 per capita GNI was $2340. This is less than the country's 2010 per capita income (PPP) of $3400 that includes an adjustment for cost of living.

ABSOLUTE AND RELATIVE POVERTY

By international standards, absolute poverty is high in Iraq but relative poverty is low. Absolute poverty measures whether persons are able to obtain the essentials of life while relative poverty measures the gap between the poor and the well off in a country. The usual measure of absolute poverty is the proportion of the population that earns less than $1.25 or $2 per day adjusting for differences in cost of living (PPP). Trying to live on less than $1.25 (PPP) a day probably means insufficient food, little access to education or medical care, and a shortened lifespan. Earning more than $1.25 but less than $2 (PPP) is not as bad in that one has the potential of maintaining long-term health. Of course, if an individual is alone and very young, pregnant, or very old then life is difficult on even $2 (PPP) a day. It is a precarious life in that a single error or accident has the potential to plunge an individual or family into desperate – sub $1.25 – poverty.

Absolute poverty is high in Iraq. In 2007, about 930 000 persons, 3 percent of the Iraqi population, were living on less than $1.25 a day, which is almost as the same proportion as the average for all of the MENA countries. However, in Iraq almost 6.5 million persons, 21 percent of the population, were living on less than $2 a day compared to only 14 percent of the MENA countries population (World Bank 2012b, pp. 69–72).

The major determinant of absolute poverty is personal income. Iraq's per capita GDP (PPP) was an estimated $3400 in 2010, $3900 in 2011, and if early real growth estimates are correct, may reach $4200 in 2012. If this trend, driven by high oil prices and increasing oil export volumes, continues then one would eventually expect a substantial drop in the country's absolute poverty.

Relative poverty looks at the distribution of income or consumption across a country's population. A Gini Index usually measures this distribution. If everyone in a country has the same income then the Gini Index would be zero. At the other extreme, if one person received all of the income in the country and everyone else received nothing then the Gini Index would be 100.

Surprisingly, relative poverty in Iraq is low. Iraq's 2005 Gini Index was an estimated 31, about the same as Egypt and the Netherlands. This is a more even distribution of income than most of Iraq's neighbors. For example, Iran had a Gini Index of 38 while Jordan's was 35. In fact, of the 155 countries whose Gini Indices are reported by the World Bank, 86 percent had a more uneven distribution of income than Iraq. The low relative poverty in Iraq is driven, in part, by the large proportion of the population that are government employees where the range of salaries tends to be less than in the private sector. This is not to deny that there are large income differentials in Iraq. The bottom 20 percent of the population received only about 9 percent of the national income while the top 20 percent of the population received almost 40 percent of the national income (World Bank 2012b, pp. 74–6).

Will Iraq's low Gini Index – relatively low-income inequality – continue? The "Kuznets Curve" predicts that the trend of income inequality is shaped like the letter "U". Initially, economic growth leads to a worsening of income inequality. It is only when the country achieves high levels of per capita income that income inequality begins to fall again. In other words, low and high-income countries tend to have lower Gini Indices than middle income countries. Note that an increase in income inequality does not necessarily mean that incomes of the bottom 20 percent of the population are actually declining. All that is required is that the incomes of the bottom 20 percent of the population grow at a slower rate than incomes at the top of the income pyramid. Like many developing countries, Iraq may face a poverty choice. If the GoI continues to play a dominant role in the economy then Iraq will probably experience slower real growth and therefore higher absolute but lower relative poverty. On the other hand, more rapid growth from a liberalized economy will probably result in lower absolute but higher relative poverty. Lower absolute poverty is usually accompanied by better health.

HEALTH

Life Expectancy

A primary measure of health is life expectancy. As can be seen in Table 3.1, the average life expectancy from birth in Iraq is better than the average in the LMIC but worse than in MENA countries. But the gap between male and female life expectancies is larger in Iraq than in either MENA countries or LMIC. In fact, of the 155 countries for which data is available, only 11 have a larger gap between male and female life expectancies than Iraq (World Bank 2012b, pp. 34–7). According to the last Iraqi census of 1997 – which excluded the KRG – more boys are born each year than girls. Up to approximately age ten girls actually die at a more rapid rate than boys. However, beginning at age ten, the death rate of males substantially surpasses that of females so that by the age 15–19 cohort, the number of females exceeds that of males. This trend continues so that among Iraqis older than 65 years, the number of females exceeds that of males by 27 percent (COSIT 2012, Table 2/7).

While the violent death of countless males is a major contributing factor to the gap in life expectancies, there are also differences between the genders in life choices. Many young men in Iraq are addicted to painkillers that are readily available without a prescription. Despite the injunctions contained in the Qur'an, alcohol abuse is not uncommon. Possibly associated with substance abuse among young males, there is a disproportionate rate of automobile accident fatalities. According to the latest data, males accounted for 80 percent of automobile-related fatalities. Fatalities and serious injuries are common in workplaces and, since the labor force is mostly male, this also has a disproportionate impact on life expectancies. Finally, about 42 percent of men are smokers compared to less than 7 percent of women (COSIT 2012, Tables 6/11 and 19/22).

Malnutrition and Child Mortality

Malnutrition is measured as the percentage of children less than five years of age whose weight is less than two standard deviations below the average weight for that age. It is estimated that 333 000 Iraqi children, about 7 percent, of those aged 0–5 years are malnourished. Malnourishment at this age often leads to stunting and lifelong health problems. Considering the social and economic disruptions of the last few decades, one would expect severe malnutrition among the Iraqi young. However, the rate of malnutrition in Iraq is only about one-third that of a typical LMIC nation. There are three explanations generally given to describe why Iraq has less malnutrition than other counties with roughly the same income. First, the official data for Iraq severely underestimates actual cases of malnutrition. Second, the Public Distribution System (PDS), discussed in detail in Chapter 7, attempts to provide a basket of food to everyone in Iraq. While, the baskets are often short one or more items (COSIT 2012, Table 15/71) and it can be difficult to add an additional person to a family's allocation; these baskets do supply food essentials – at very low cost – that can provide a foundation for a reasonable diet. Third, although there are not enough quality orphanages and there is a continuing tragedy of abandoned children living on the streets of major cities; most orphaned children are not abandoned but rather end up being cared for by someone in their extended family.

Comparisons of child mortality rates among different countries are almost meaningless since countries use different standards for a "live" birth. Many countries require at least a 26 week gestation. If a child has not been carried until at least the end of the second trimester of pregnancy then, if the child dies, it is not counted as a death in the nation's child mortality data. Other nations require a certain minimum length or weight to be considered a live birth. Some governments do not count any child's death that occurs within the first 24 hours after birth while, at the other extreme, the USA counts it as a live birth if the child shows any signs of life regardless of gestation, length, weight, or time of death. These different definitions greatly complicate cross-country comparisons of child mortality. It is more meaningful to focus not on the level of a country's child mortality but on the trend.

Between 1990 and 1999, according to GoI statistics, Iraq experienced a doubling of infant mortality to 101 deaths per 1000 live births. This sharp deterioration is generally blamed on shortages of food and medicine as a result of the UN sanctions. However, as revealed by investigations into the oil-for-food scandal, even when funds were available and imports of food and medicine were allowed; Saddam diverted a large portion to his family, the army, and his supporters. It is also likely that Saddam exaggerated the official rate of infant mortality in his attempt to make a moral argument that the UN was engaged in a crime against humanity. Since, the fall of Saddam in 2003, infant mortality estimates decreased rapidly to about 35 deaths per 1000 live births in 2006 and about 24 deaths per 1000 live births in 2009 (COSIT 2012, Table 19/7). Iraq's 2015 Millennium Development Goal for infant mortality is 17 deaths per 1000 live births and if current trends continue then Iraq should achieve this goal.

Maternal Mortality

Maternal mortality followed a similar path as infant mortality. From 117 maternal deaths per 100 000 live births in 1990, these deaths rose 150 percent to 291 maternal deaths in 1999. Following the invasion of Iraq, maternal deaths fell to 84 per 100 000 live births in 2006 and an estimated 75 maternal deaths in 2010 (COSIT 2012, Table 19/9). As Table 3.1 shows, this compares favorably to the averages in both MENA countries and LMIC. The 2015 Millennium Development Goal goal for Iraq is 29 maternal deaths per 100 000 live births. It is unlikely that Iraq will achieve this goal.

A contributing factor to the failure to rapidly reduce maternal mortality is a shortage of female doctors and midwives especially in rural areas. For cultural reasons, many Iraqis consider it unacceptable for a male doctor to examine or attend a woman during childbirth. As a result, not only do many women fail to receive optimal pre-natal care but, during childbirth, there is a one in eight chance that she will not be attended by a skilled health professional (COSIT 2012, Table 19/10). The GoI is attempting to increase the number of female health professionals but the more difficult challenge may be to provide incentives for such professionals to settle in rural areas that tend to impose restrictions on how single women should live.

The decline in violence in Iraq since 2007 has had two favorable effects. First, there are signs that some of the medical professionals who fled the country during the period 2004–2007 are beginning to return. This return may also be motivated by a deterioration of security or economic conditions in other Middle Eastern countries that provided sanctuary for Iraqi medical professionals. A second favorable result of the decrease in violence in Iraq is that it has become safer for a woman, such as a health professional, to travel a distance to see her patient. Both of these changes should contribute to a reduction in the proportion of unattended child-births – 12 percent in 2006 – thereby reducing maternal mortality. The 2015 Millennium Development Goal for for attendance at childbirth by a health professional is 100 percent. Meeting this goal will be difficult in such a short period of time but, if the GoI is determined, it should be possible.

Tuberculosis (TB), Human Immunodeficiency Virus (HIV), and Sanitation

TB is a common infectious disease that attacks the lungs and is often fatal. It is spread through the air when a person with active TB coughs or sneezes. About one-third of the world's population is thought to have TB. While data on TB in Iraq is difficult to obtain, it is estimated that 31 out of every 100 000 Iraqis – about 10 000 persons in total – had the disease in 2010. But only about one-third of these people were receiving medical care (COSIT 2012, Tables 19/1 and 19/12).

Antibiotics are used to kill the TB bacteria but these antibiotics in pill form must be taken daily for six months according to a very strict regimen. I tested positive for TB and was instructed that if I missed taking my pill for one day then I could double up on the next but that if I missed two days in a row – even in the final week – then I must restart the six-month regimen. And no alcohol for the entire six months! Not only will failing to follow the strict TB antibiotic regimen reduce the probability of curing the infection but it also increases the likelihood of developing a strain of TB resistant to standard antibiotics. As a result, the preferred treatment option requires that a TB patient take his or her daily pill under the direct observation of a medical professional. Only about 86 percent of Iraq's TB patients are currently taking medication under direct observation while the country's 2015 Millennium Development Goal for directly observed treatment is 100 percent. Due to the difficulty of getting direct observation of treatment in rural areas, it is unlikely that Iraq will achieve this goal.

Persons with HIV are particularly vulnerable to TB since HIV weakens resistance to disease. HIV first came to Iraq in a shipment of contaminated blood in 1985. Under Saddam, those infected were forcibly segregated. Since Saddam's fall, the GoI has opened over two dozen clinics nationwide to provide free HIV testing and treatment. However, there is widespread ignorance and fear of HIV. Families often abandon infected members and there are rumors that religious fanatics are murdering those believed to be HIV positive on the grounds that the infection is proof of sin. While the GoI reported in 2009 that there were only 44 infected Iraqis, it is believed that many cases are not reported because of fear that victims will be ostracized (IRIN 2009). Although there is no reliable data, it has been estimated that the actual number of HIV infected Iraqis might be as great as 500. While the GoI has begun a program to educate the population about HIV, they are proceeding tentatively for fear of sparking a panic and possible reprisals against the infected. In 2009, only 79 percent of males aged 15–30 and 70 percent of females in the same age cohort knew that HIV could be sexually transmitted (COSIT 2012, Table 11/12).

Of course, as a LMIC with substantial poverty that has just passed through a near civil war, the Iraqi people are at risk for a large variety of health problems in addition to TB and HIV. But research over the last several decades has shown that as long as the average person can obtain sufficient amounts of potable water and has access to improved sanitation facilities, he or she can either avoid most other diseases or at least have a reasonable chance of recovery if he or she becomes sick.

According to the World Health Organization (WHO) (WHO and UNICEF 2006), an estimated 50 percent of Iraq's rural population had access to sufficient water from an improved source in 2004. Access is defined as at least 20 liters (5.3 gallons) per person per day from a source within one kilometer (0.6 mile) of the person's dwelling. About one-third of rural households obtained their water from a household connection, the remainder obtained their water from from a public tap, protected well, rain water, or water tanker truck. Urban access to potable water was 97 percent with almost all urban residents obtaining their water from a household connection. This access is not dependable with 22 percent of rural residents and 32 percent of urban residents reporting that their water supply was interrupted daily. With respect to the quality of water, 14 percent of Iraqis report that they boil, filter, or chemically treat their water before drinking (COSIT 2008, Table 2-00, p. 56).

How does access to potable water in Iraq compare to other countries? Rural access in Iraq is much less than that of its regional neighbors who average 79 percent access but almost exactly the same for urban residents at 97 percent (WHO and UNICEF 2006, p. 32). The GoI reports little progress over the last few years in increasing either rural or urban access to potable water. It is unlikely that the country will reach its 2015 Millennium Development Goal of 100 percent urban and 89 percent rural access (COSIT 2012, Table 19/1).

Increasing access to sufficient amounts of potable water is less a problem of inadequate infrastructure than of political will. Despite the fact that published water tariffs are quite low, fees for water usage are rarely collected due, in part, to a lack of metering. As a result, almost all users currently pay a zero price for their water and there is little incentive for consumers to conserve or for the Ministry of Municipalities and Public Works to aggressively strive to ensure that every Iraqi has access to potable water. Despite these inefficiencies, raising water tariffs or even collecting the existing low tariffs is extremely unpopular and expected to reduce support for any politician that proposes it. The impact of such perverse pricing of essential services will be discussed at greater length in Chapter 11.

Improved access to potable water and access to improved sanitation are closely related since ad hoc sanitation measures often lead to water contamination. If improved sanitation means that the population has ready access to facilities that prevent human, animal, or insect contact with excreta then only about 76 percent of Iraq's urban population and 67 percent of its rural population have access to such facilities. As can be seen in Table 3.1, while the Iraqi population has better access to improved sanitation facilities than the average LMIC (urban 66 percent, rural 34 percent); the average MENA country does much better. An estimated 94 percent of their urban populations and 80 percent of their rural populations have access to improved facilities (World Bank 2012b, Table 3.13, pp. 186–9). Due primarily to definitional issues, the GoI reports higher levels of both urban (90 percent) and rural (70 percent) access to improved sanitation. Surprisingly, the GoI data shows a drop in access over the last several years. It is not clear whether this reflects a real drop in access or results from a change in the wording of the relevant survey questions.

Hospitals and Clinics

From 2002 to 2010, the number of hospitals had increased to 235 while the number of clinics had decreased to 315 (COSIT 2012, Table 10/1A). This relatively low number of medical facilities as well as a low ratio of clinics to hospitals is not uncommon in countries at a similar level of economic development as Iraq. It is caused, in part, by a severe shortage of doctors and nurses. There are only 0.7 doctors per 1000 persons in Iraq and only 1.4 nurses and midwives per 1000 persons. The average MENA country has doctor and nurse ratios of 1.4 and 2.3 respectively (World Bank 2012b, pp. 100–103).

The shortage of skilled medical professionals was caused primarily by large-scale emigration since 2003. Some of these emigrants were attracted by better economic opportunities abroad (known as "brain drain") while others fled the sharp rise in violence in the middle of the decade especially since some insurgent groups deliberately targeted medical and other professionals. Exacerbating the impact of the loss of medical professionals was a deterioration in the quality of medical education and a shortage of medical supplies. Beginning in the early 1990s with the UN imposed sanctions and continuing until at least the reduction of violence in 2007, medical training in Iraq suffered from both shortages of laboratory and other teaching materials as well as increased corruption. As a result, poorly trained physicians and nurses were able to obtain certification. While the GoI is executing a complex plan to increase the proportion of the population that has ready access to medical care, ensuring the quality of that care by improving medical education will be very difficult. Educating future doctors and nurses is not the only educational challenge facing the country.

EDUCATION: CURRENT STATUS

In 2010–2011, approximately 4.9 million Iraqis attended primary school – about 54 percent of which were boys. Primary school teaching staff was about 260 000 for a teacher–student ratio of about 1 to 19 (COSIT 2012, Table 9/3). In the same year, there were almost 2.0 million secondary students with boys accounting for 58 percent. Since there were about 140 000 secondary teachers, the teacher–student ratio was about 1 to 14 (COSIT 2012, Table 9/8). While the quality of primary and secondary schools varies greatly, it is generally poor. Teachers are often unskilled, unmotivated, or absent. The curriculum is generally outdated and there is often a shortage of textbooks and other educational material. Facilities are limited – sometimes requiring multiple shifts – and often requiring long commutes by even young children. Many school buildings are rundown, lacking adequate lighting, running water, and sanitation facilities. In fact, an estimated 15 percent of all schools are in danger of collapse (GoI 2010, p. 115). While the GoI and international organizations have built many schools in the post-Saddam era, it is not uncommon the find the new buildings not in use, looted, or confiscated by a government or non-government organization for non-educational uses.

While progress is being made, the illiteracy rate in Iraq among persons who are ten years or older is still high – about 19 percent. This high rate of illiteracy not only has adverse economic impact but also reduces the ability to effectively participate in commercial and political activities. Corruption also tends to thrive in societies with high levels of illiteracy. If you cannot read then you are an easy target for every government official who can wave papers in your face.

As can be seen in Table 3.2, in 2007, more than twice as many females as males are considered illiterate by IMF standards. The IMF definition of literacy is being able to both read and write, with understanding, a short statement about their daily life. Illiteracy is much worse in rural areas where 28 percent of the total population (ten years and older) is considered illiterate compared to 17 percent in urban areas. There are also great differences between the genders. In rural areas, over 40 percent of the female population is illiterate, compared to only 16 percent of males. There is also a strong correlation with age. For example, while only about 16 percent of women aged 10–14 are unable to read and write, this proportion rises to almost 70 percent among women who are 50 years old and older (COSIT 2008, Table 3-1, p. 222). There has been some progress, a decade ago, total illiteracy was over 25 percent including half of rural females (COSIT 2012, Table 19/20). Iraq's 2007 illiteracy rate was about twice that of the average MENA country (World Bank 2012b, Table 2.14, pp. 95–6).

Table 3.2   Education and gender (%)

Maximum education achievement in 2007	Males	Females	All
Illiterate	12	26	19
Read and write	24	24	24
Primary (6–11 years)	30	28	29
Secondary (15–17 years)	23	15	19
Post-secondary	11	7	9

Source: COSIT (2012), Table 19/20.

Why are so many Iraqis – especially females – either illiterate or have only limited ability to read and write? Table 3.3 gives the results of a survey that asked families across Iraq for the reasons that their children (both male and female) had never attended primary, intermediate, or secondary school. Lack of family or individual interest was the most common answer. It is difficult to deconstruct this answer but it may be a function of both culture and economic opportunities. Many Iraqi families think that it is inappropriate to have a daughter instructed by a male teacher at any age but especially after she reaches puberty. Thus if there are an insufficient number of female teachers at the primary and especially at the intermediate level then parents will withdraw their daughters from school. The shortage of female teachers in rural areas is especially acute since these generally more religious communities can impose restrictions on the freedom of women to fully participate in community life or, in some cases, to even move about without being accompanied by a male relative. As a result, it is difficult to persuade educated women to accept teaching assignments in rural areas. If they are unmarried then their lives might

Table 3.3   Reasons for never attending school (%)

	Family not interested	No school	Disability or disease	Not interested	Cannot afford	Other reasons
Primary	32	14	9	9	5	37
Intermediate	39	18	12	9	8	18
Secondary	41	13	11	13	6	18

Source: COSIT (2008), Table 3.8, p. 233.

be severely constrained. If they are married then there is the difficulty of finding employment for their spouse in a rural community that probably does not provide a great variety of employment opportunities.

According to a survey, 15 percent of Iraqi families say that they either kept their child (both male and female) out of primary school or curtailed their attendance because of the expense (COSIT 2008, Table 3-13, p. 240). While education is technically free, there are three types of costs that must be paid by students or their families. First, the average annual out-of-pocket costs range from an estimated 93 000 ID ($74) to attend a primary school to 300 000 ID ($240) for secondary school (COSIT 2008, Table 3-16, p. 244). If a family has two or three children of school age then the out-of-pocket costs alone might equal as much as 25 percent of household income. Often families choose to continue the education of their male children while saving money by curtailing female schooling.

Second, like most public institutions in Iraq, there is corruption in the educational system. Families must be willing to pay a succession of small bribes to ensure that their children actually receive the promised instruction.

Finally, the opportunity cost of having a child in school might be high especially for families engaged in farming or small commercial activities where children can contribute productively even at a very young age. For example, a family might decide that their ten year old might be better engaged in herding the family's goats or doing chores in the family shop than in a classroom. This may be especially true for females where, as shown in Table 3.4, higher education levels are associated with *higher* unemployment. The unemployment rate for females who complete intermediate schooling is almost three times greater than for those who are illiterate. As mentioned in the previous chapter, female employment in Iraq is limited with almost two-thirds employed in either farming or teaching. The traditional labor-intensive farming that is practiced throughout much of Iraq tends to reward experience more than education. In addition, although the legal minimum age for marriage is 15 years, there are cases of girls as young as age 12 getting married. Girls and women almost invariably leave school upon marriage.

EDUCATION: LESSONS LEARNED

Research on education in Iraq is in its infancy and it will probably be a decade before it can provide a solid foundation for an Iraq specific education policy. One could look to other countries' experiences with educational policy but it may not be applicable. One of the challenges

Table 3.4   More education does not always lead to lower unemployment (%)

Education level completed	Male unemployment rate	Female unemployment rate
Illiterate	13–19	4–10
Read and write	14–20	5–11
Primary	12–18	9–15
Intermediate	12–18	24–30
Secondary/Votech	9–15	13–19
Bachelors	11–17	20–26
Total	12–18	12–18

Source: COSIT (2008), Table 5.3, p. 289.

of developing a sound educational policy is that the same policy will often have different results in developing countries – such as Iraq – than in developed countries. However, among developing countries, research has discovered four initiatives that will probably improve education in Iraq.

First, returns on education decline by the level of schooling. In other words, investment in primary education tends to produce greater returns to a society than investment in secondary education, which produce greater returns than investment in university education (Psacharopoulos and Patrinos 2002, Tables 1 and 5, pp. 12, 15). Therefore, if human and financial resources are constrained then the GoI should concentrate on primary and secondary education before funding university education. While it is difficult to obtain and interpret the cost of education data in Iraq, it is estimated that, in 2008, the cost per student of the GoI providing one year of elementary or secondary education was at least 500 000 ID ($420) while a university education cost at least ten times that amount. This multiple of ten seems very low by international standards and better data on overhead costs of university education will probably increase the multiple.

Second, research shows that the more general the curriculum, the higher returns to education. This is a surprising result since it is often thought that vocational training is more practical and useful than general education. However, teaching a general curriculum costs less than vocational training. Classes tend to be larger and there is less of a requirement for specialized equipment. In addition, whether or not they have a higher unemployment rate, general curriculum graduates tend to spend less time unemployed possibly because they have more job flexibility (Psacharopoulos 1991, pp. 190–191). One of the many challenges facing vocational training in Iraq is the inflexibility of the educational bureaucracy. For example, rather than teach students to maintain and repair the modern imported tractors that Iraqi farmers prefer, teachers will instead instruct them on obsolete Iraqi tractors because that is what they know.

Third, there are many initiatives that are being sold to improve educational quality but only some have been shown to be successful. The successes include reducing home–school distance and increasing the availability of textbooks. About 11 percent of Iraqi families state that excessive distance to school is why their children are not attending (COSIT 2008, Table 3-13, p. 240). This non-attendance could be reduced either by constructing and staffing more local schools or by improving transportation to existing schools. Greater availability of textbooks tends to significantly reduce the number of students held over for another year. One estimate was that for every $1 spent on textbooks resulted in a $12 saving in education expense by speeding students through school. Iraq should seek to have at least one textbook for every five students for every subject. It should also be noted that at the secondary level, low-quality teachers significantly impair learning. Countries that require teachers to specialize at the secondary level tend to have better results for example mathematics majors rather than education majors teaching mathematics classes.

However, popular (and expensive!) ideas such as decreasing class size and providing computers to students do not often lead to significant improvements in education quality. While smaller classes with high-quality instruction are better than larger classes with the same quality of instruction, this is not the usual choice. Instead, because of a shortage of skilled teachers, developing countries like Iraq often have to choose between large classes with high-quality instruction or smaller classes with lower quality teachers. The former tends to lead to better education (Hanushek 2005, pp. 201–5).

Finally, it is an error to attempt to use education to solve problems that are not really educational in nature. In Iraq, there is a continuing push to increase the number of university seats in order to train doctors and other skilled professionals to replace those that are leaving the country – the so called "brain drain". This is a common error in developing countries exemplified by India that trains some of its brightest people at great expense to be outstanding medical professionals in Canadian and US hospitals. It is more efficient to improve the pay and working conditions of Iraqi physicians and other skilled professions so as to decrease their motivation to migrate than to train additional new doctors to replace them for several years until they migrate as well.

Excessive Post-Secondary Education

The unemployment rates shown in Table 3.4 are roughly the same for Iraqis whose final education was at the intermediate level and those that received more advance degrees is evidence that Iraq has either an excess of highly educated persons or is providing education in the wrong fields. Further evidence is found in the constant pressure on the GoI to hire college graduates to do jobs that do not really require advanced education, and the high rate of "brain drain" in the technical fields. These results support a decrease in the number of Iraqis obtaining higher education until a falling unemployment rate for college educated Iraqis shows that there is no longer an excess of highly educated Iraqis. However, shifting educational priorities away from universities is an uncomfortable recommendation for the Iraqi elite who do not want to reduce the chances of their own children obtaining a university education as a stepping stone to a high pay, high status job. In other words, the private benefits of higher education to the student or the student's family is greater than the benefit of one more college educated person to the entire Iraqi society. Not least is that having an advanced degree improves the chances of a young man making an advantageous marriage.

MARRIAGE CULTURE

One of the most controversial issues involving the Iraqi population is the culture of marriage. It includes religious, historical, and tribal aspects of marriage that are widely accepted – if not widely practiced – among some groups in Iraq and yet harshly disparaged by members of other groups. As a result, these aspects often cause confusion among foreigners trying to understand the country and its people. These controversial aspects include early marriage, cousin marriage, wife discipline, fertility decisions, polygyny, temporary marriages, and honor killings. It is true that Islam generally provided greater rights for women in the seventh century AD than they possessed in Christian lands during the same period. It is also widely accepted that women's rights are stated in the Qur'an and that women control the private space in Islamic life (Allawi 2009, p. 204). But these truths are insufficient to justify the harsh or unfair treatment inflicted on married and unmarried women in Iraq and other Islamic countries.

Early Marriage

Although the current legal minimum age of marriage in Iraq is 18, exceptions can be made to allow marriage as early as 15 years with the approval
of a judge and the minor's guardian. Before this approval is given, the
judge must evaluate the minor's physical capacity for marriage as well as
overall fitness. And if the judge decides that an objection by the minor's
guardian is unreasonable then the judge can overrule the objection and
allow the marriage to take place without the guardian's approval. About
17 percent of all Iraqi women were married before age 18. Despite the
legal minimum age of 15 – with a judge's approval – in about 3 percent of
all marriages, the bride is younger than 15 years old (UNICEF 2012). In
these cases, since tribal or religious traditions allow earlier marriages, the
national law is ignored. A number of the girls that married below the age
of 15 were found to have given birth to one or more children before they
turned 15 years of age (COSIT 2008, Table 4-13, p. 276). As expected,
there are often substantial long-term adverse health effects from young
girls experiencing intercourse and childbirth.

Cousin Marriage

Iraq also has one of the highest levels of cousin marriage in the world.
Marrying a first or second cousin is not only permitted but, among some
groups in Iraq, actually encouraged. It is estimated that one-third of all marriages in Iraq are between cousins while in certain rural areas the ratio rises
to about half of all marriages. Cousin marriage increases the importance
of family over other loyalties; after all, your uncle is your father-in-law. As
discussed in the next chapter, this belief that nothing is more important than
one's family encourages nepotism and other activities generally considered
to be corruption. In addition, some women's rights advocates that cousin
marriage tends to facilitate wife abuse since an abused woman cannot flee
to a female relative for sanctuary. It is likely that an abused woman's sister
is not only married to the brother of the abusive husband but also lives
next door. With respect to the health consequences, surveys show that only
about one-third of women and men aged 12–30 are concerned that marriage
to a close relative might affect their child's intelligence, spread genetic diseases, or lead to deformities (COSIT 2012, Tables 11/13 and 11/14).

Wife Discipline

According to a 2006 GoI survey, a husband's right to physically discipline
his wife is widely accepted among Iraqi women. Almost 60 percent of all

Iraqi women believe that a husband may physically discipline his wife for a variety of reasons. The most commonly stated justifications are: if a wife leaves her home without telling her husband; if the wife is neglecting the children; if she argues with her husband; if she abstains from sexual relations; or burns a family meal. The right of a husband to beat his wife is most accepted among rural, married, and uneducated Iraqi women. But, even among urban, unmarried, and educated women, at least 46 percent of women believe that a husband is within his rights to strike his wife under certain circumstances (COSIT 2012, Table 19/26).

This widespread acceptance of an Iraqi husband physically disciplining his wife is based, at least in part, on a statement in the Qur'an. Whether the Qur'an can be accurately understood in translation rather than in the original Arabic is often debated. However, a standard translation states:

> Men are in charge of women, because Allah hath made the one of them to excel the other, and because they spend of their property (for the support of women). So good women are the obedient, guarding in secret that which Allah has guarded. As for those from whom ye fear rebellion, admonish them and banish them to beds apart, and scourge them. (Pickthall [1930] 1992, Sura 4:34, p. 97)

In another widely read translation, the critical words are given as: "beat them (lightly)" (Ali 1985, p. 220). The text in parentheses within this quote represents clarifying remarks by Ali that other translators do not include. Some commentators argue that the "beating" should be primarily symbolic rather than a severe infliction of pain or injury, possibly a husband spanking his wife. Others say that the critical words in question can also mean: "go away from them". Regardless of the disagreements among translators, commentators, and religious thinkers, it is widely believed in Iraq that a husband may physically discipline his wife. It is unlikely that an Iraqi husband will be sanctioned by the courts or even disparaged by his neighbors for beating his wife unless he kills her or causes serious injury.

Fertility Decisions

One of the most important decisions for a married couple is how many children to have. This is usually measured as the total fertility rate, the number of children that would be born to the average woman through her entire child bearing years. If a country has a fertility rate of about 2.1 children per woman, then its long-run population will stabilize. If the fertility rate is below 2.1 then the country's population will continue to grow for a period of time (population momentum) but the average age will increase and, eventually, the population will begin to decline in size. Based on its total fertility rate, Iraq is an outlier with a substantially higher fertility rate than its regional neighbors. In 2010, Iraq's fertility rate was 4.7 compared to a 2.7 average for MENA countries and 2.9 for the LMIC. Iraq also has a high adolescent fertility rate with 91 births per 1000 women aged 15–19. The MENA country rate for adolescent fertility is 37 births per 1000 women and it is 68 births for LMIC (World Bank 2012b, pp. 112–15).

Iraq's fertility rate has declined over the last two decades due, in part, to increased use of contraceptives by married couples. As shown in Table 3.1, about half of married women use some form of contraception. While Iraq's fertility rate is falling, it is decreasing at a much slower rate than among its regional neighbors. For example, Iraq's fertility rate fell from 6.0 children per woman in 1990 to 4.7 in 2010 – a decrease of 1.3 while, during the same period, Iran's fertility rate fell from 4.8 children per woman to 1.7 – a decrease of 3.1 (World Bank 2012b, Table 2.19, pp. 112–15).

Polygyny

Among the more controversial aspects of Islam are the possibility of marrying up to four wives simultaneously, the divorce procedure, and temporary marriage. Although accepted in some groups in Iraq, all three are atypical of the whole nation. The average Iraqi marries one woman, does not divorce her, and does not engage in temporary marriages. However, the Qur'an permits a man to have up to four wives simultaneously, polygyny, but a woman is forbidden to have more than one husband at the same time. Since the Qur'an also requires that a husband with multiple wives must be willing to divide his time and wealth equally among his wives, polygyny is not common except among tribal leaders in rural areas. A husband can divorce his wife simply by publicly stating three times: "I divorce you." The wife may not divorce her husband in this way.

Temporary Marriage

The Shi'a branch of Islam accepts temporary marriage where a man and woman agree to be married for a set period of time – possibly as short as one night. The temporary marriage contract sets out the conditions of the marriage including any cash gift that the man will provide the woman. It is possible that the contract may even forbid any physical contact between the temporary husband and wife. There is no divorce, the marriage ends on the contracted date. Temporary marriages can be negotiated for a variety of reasons. While in Iraq, I heard that four school teachers had temporarily married their van driver. The marriage contract forbade physical contact and required the four teachers to periodically pay their "husband" for driving and maintaining the van. The marriage had two advantages for the teachers. It freed them from following the strict clothing requirements, the "hijab", in the evenings when they shared a house with their driver. More importantly, the presence of their "husband" reduced the restrictions on activities faced by unmarried women in more traditional communities. At the other extreme, temporary marriage is condemned as a form of legal prostitution especially when very young women or girls receive cash to temporarily marry older strangers in Basrah and some other major cities.

Honor Killings

Honor killing is the murder of a family member, usually a girl or woman, for having brought dishonor on the family. The dishonor is usually sexual in nature. A girl or woman might be murdered by her family for being a rape victim, engaging in adultery, or even talking to a boy in public in the absence of proper supervision. There have also been honor killings on the basis that a family member engaged in homosexual activity. It is difficult for a girl or woman to defend herself against accusations of a sexual offense since it is unlikely that she will receive an opportunity to defend herself in any kind of open forum. Even if a religious court decided to hear her case, her testimony is worth half that of a man (Ali 1985, Sura 2:282, pp. 128–30; Pickthall [1930] 1992, p. 63). While there is no reliable data, there are probably at least 200 honor killings each year in Iraq. While such murders are against the law, sentences are often lenient. During one year in Anbar province, the typical sentence for a man convicted of an honor killing of his daughter, wife, or sister was six months in prison.

FEMALE POLITICAL PARTICIPATION

As required by the 2005 Constitution, 25 percent of the members in the Iraqi Council of Representatives are women. The 2015 Millennium Development Goal is that women will hold 50 percent of all seats in Iraq's national parliament (COSIT 2012, Table 19/1). It is extremely unlikely that Iraq will achieve this goal even within a generation. At the provincial level, there is substantial female representation among the upper and middle management members of provincial governments. In 2010, 22 percent of these positions were held by women but with a wide range among provinces. In the more religiously conservative provinces female representation is low, only 9 percent of the upper and middle management positions in Najaf province are held by women while in Anbar province, the ratio is 13 percent. At the other extreme, provinces with large Kurdish populations tend to have more females in senior positions. In Kirkuk province, women hold 30 percent of the senior positions while they hold 35 percent of these positions in Sulaymaniyah province (COSIT 2012, Tables 19/23 and 19/28).

Some research on developing countries shows that female elected representatives tend to have different budgetary priorities than males. Female representatives are more concerned with spending for essential services especially drinking water and better roads and less interested in funding large-scale economic development projects or – surprisingly – education (Chattopadhyay and Duflo 2005, pp. 290–291). But there is little evidence that female government officials are less corrupt than their male counterparts. Will an increase in female representation in national and provincial governments lead to greater opportunities for women in Iraqi society? The evidence is mixed. In some MENA countries, the women who are chosen by the various parties to run for parliamentary seats tend to be very traditional concerning gender issues.

WHAT SHOULD BE DONE?

In its *National Development Plan: 2010–2014*, the GoI (2010) provides a long list of detailed recommendations for improving health and education (Chapter 8 of the plan) as well as another chapter devoted solely to rectifying what the GoI sees as a "noticeable deficiency in attitudes toward women" (Chapter 9 of the plan). But of these many valuable recommendations, which is the most important? Ensuring that 100 percent of the population receives at least an elementary school education is not only a desirable goal in itself but also can be expected to have favorable impacts on other important social goals.

Currently, almost one million Iraqi children aged 6–11 years are not receiving an elementary education. In addition, there are a large number of Iraqis – especially women – older than 11 years of age who have not received an elementary education and, in fact, many are illiterate. There are strong positive externalities for literacy/primary education – we all benefit when more of our neighbors can read, write, and count. In addition, compared to the illiterate, men and women with a primary education not only are more economically productive but also tend to have better health, raise healthier families, and live longer. Politically, illiterate or uneducated voters are dangerous to democracy. They tend to be more ignorant of the issues and more easily led by demagogues.

Ensuring that 100 percent of those girls and boys aged 6–11 years are enrolled in elementary schools will require not only more local schools but also – more importantly – changing incentives for teachers and potential teachers so that they are willing both to locate to where the students are and to provide a quality education. Educational circumstances differ dramatically across Iraq. For example, rural families who are engaged in agriculture may require their school age children to work in the fields during planting and harvest; the periods of planting and harvest are different for different crops. Urban families might require their children to work in a family business during key events such as religious holidays, and so on. The difficult challenge of achieving a quality elementary education without excessively burdening families so that they withdraw their children might be best achieved through a division of responsibility. The national Ministry of Education could set national standards such as for subject matter and number of required hours of education per year while delegating the actual operation of schools to provincial or even local governments. One possibility would be for the GoI to annually transfer to each province a sum to educate all of the province's school age population. Provinces would then have the flexibility to spend these funds to achieve the goal of 100 percent quality elementary education.

More difficult will be eliminating illiteracy among older Iraqis. Adult illiteracy has an adverse impact on economic development, reduces democratic stability, and impairs progress towards an improved status for women. Yet reducing this illiteracy raises difficult challenges of organization to ensure adequate incentives for both instructors to teach older Iraqis and for illiterate Iraqis to participate. Again, there is no template or blueprint for reducing adult illiteracy that can confidently be applied nationwide. But if Iraq can achieve 100 percent primary education among the young and 100 percent literacy among all Iraqis then it should have a strong favorable effect on health, political stability, and the general quality of life.

4. Corruption

> Iraq has a history of massive corruption. The previous regime
> bankrupted the country through massive embezzlement of
> public funds for personal palaces and other conspicuous and
> wasteful consumption at the expense of the average citizen.
> (GoI 2005b, p. 36)

Like sand after a desert storm, corruption permeates every corner of Iraqi society. According to the report by Transparency International (2011), Iraq is not the most corrupt country on earth – that dubious honor belongs to a tie between Somalia and North Korea – but Iraq is in ninth-to-last place ranking 175th out of the 183 countries evaluated. Corruption in Iraq extends from the ministries in Baghdad to police stations and food distribution centers in every small town. (For an excellent overview of the range and challenges of corruption in Iraq, see Looney 2008.) While academics may argue that small amounts of corruption act as a "lubricant" for government activities, the large scale of corruption in Iraq undermines private and public attempts to achieve a better life for the average Iraqi. The former Iraqi Minister of Finance and the Governor of the Central Bank stated that the deleterious impact of corruption was worse than that of the insurgency (Minister of Finance 2005). This is consistent with the Knack and Keefer study (1995, Table 3) that showed that corruption has a greater adverse impact on economic growth than political violence.

Corruption is the abuse of public power for private benefit. Corruption occurs if a government official has the power to grant or withhold something of value and – contrary to laws and publicized procedures – trades this something of value for a gift or reward. Corruption is a form of rent-seeking. Among corrupt acts, bribery gets the most attention, but corruption can also include nepotism, official theft, fraud, certain patron-client relationships, or extortion (Bardhan 1997, pp. 1320–1322; Gunter 2008b). Private corruption, such as insider trading, is not considered in this chapter.

One of the challenges of studying corruption in Iraq is that the word "corruption" is both descriptive and pejorative. Societies that have long cultural traditions of patron-client relationships or giving "gifts" to officials tend to object strongly to describing such behavior as corruption. It is often argued that calling such cultural traditions corruption is a distortion, an attempt to apply Western standards to non-Western societies. It would be useful if there were a separate word to describe corrupt behavior in a neutral fashion and another to refer to such behavior critically such as the distinction between "killing" and "murder".

However, in this chapter, corruption is intended to describe a particular form of behavior not to make a pejorative statement. However, an adverse connotation may be deserved since corruption tends to adversely affect economic development regardless of cultures. The correlation between corruption (Transparency International rankings) and per capita income adjusted for cost of living (IMF World Development Indicators, GDP per capita adjusted for PPP) is strongly negative. Regardless of culture or geographic location, there are no (very) corrupt rich countries and few honest poor countries.

To maintain a reasonable size, this chapter focuses on corruption of Iraqi officials and institutions. Therefore it excludes the rapidly increasing number of studies on the corruption of international institutions such as the United Nations during the sanctions period as well as evidence of corrupt acts on the part of representatives of other nations, such as the USA, that have played major roles in Iraq's recent history.

CORRUPTION UNDER SADDAM

Under Saddam (1979–2003), corruption was controlled from the top in a classic case of "state capture". With Arab Ba'athist Socialist Party control, almost all of the Iraqi economy was nationalized. Positions of power in the economy were assigned to members of Saddam's family and his loyal supporters. As was expected, this elite received a dominant share of the benefits from any economic activity. This pattern is consistent with that of most socialist developing countries. In fact, according to Gordon Tullock (2005b, p. 29): "what is called socialism in much of the backward world is simply an elaborate mechanism for transferring rents to friends and close supporters of the dictator".

But corruption under Saddam's dictatorship differed in two fundamental ways from the corruption that exists during the current Iraqi transition to full democracy. First, Saddam's family and his immediate ring of supporters captured a large proportion of the bribes and other gains from corruption (Marr 2004, pp. 208–9). Consequently, those at the base of the governmental pyramid captured relatively small amounts of the gains from corruption. In contrast, current Iraqi corruption is more "democratic" with corrupt gains more widely distributed.

Second, under Saddam corruption was more "honest" – honest in the ironic sense that one refers to an "honest judge" as one who, once bribed, stays bought. Since corruption under Saddam tended to be more structured, when bribes were paid to a public official, there was a high degree of confidence that the promised favor would be rendered. Current Iraqi corruption is more entrepreneurial. Government officials are engaged in sometimes cooperative, sometimes competitive efforts to extract the maximum rents from not only private citizens but also from other branches of the state bureaucracy. As a result, it is difficult to discover the proper person to bribe in order to obtain a specific favor and there is less confidence that that favor will be provided even if the bribe is paid. (This is a not-uncommon phenomenon. See Rose-Ackermann 1999, p. 32.)

It is likely that, although Saddam, his family, and supporters were able to capture a larger proportion of the nation's economic income through their well organized corruption; current entrepreneurial de-centralized corruption imposes a more serious burden on Iraq because of increased uncertainty (Bardhan 1997, p. 1324).

EXTENT OF CORRUPTION AFTER SADDAM

Estimating the amount of corruption in Iraq is difficult for several reasons. First, this offense is often perceived as lacking a victim. Iraqi private citizens may find themselves excluded from business opportunities because of the length of time, expense, or complex procedures required to pursue the opportunity legally. If, in order to speed up the bureaucratic process, citizens either offer bribes or agree to public officials' demands then the citizens often see the officials as doing favors – not imposing burdens. Even if Iraqi bribe paying citizens feel victimized, they hesitate to report corruption for fear of retaliation or legal sanction. Second, conflict with a variety of insurgent groups following the 2003 invasion, increases both the opportunities for corruption and makes it easier to conceal it. This symbiotic relationship between corruption and the insurgency is discussed in greater detail below.

Victims in Iraq rarely report the crime of corruption, so almost all information on corruption is obtained from investigative reporting including publicized corruption investigations or surveys. In Iraq as elsewhere, publicized investigation reports tend to grossly underestimate actual levels of corruption because only a fraction of corruption cases are investigated and the results of some investigations are often not released to the public. Further complicating the analysis is the fact that decisions to initiate corruption investigations in Iraq are often political in nature. However, reported investigations help reveal the scale of the corruption problem in Iraq.

Corruption in Iraq extends from the top to the bottom of official Iraq. Allawi (2007, pp. 348–68) in his excellent discussion of Iraqi corruption went as far as to state that corruption had turned the GoI into a "Potemkin State". Ministers responsible for Defense, Trade, Electricity, Oil, and Interior (the police) have been investigated for corruption and several have fled the country with hundreds of millions of dollars. It has been estimated that one-third or more of some agencies budgets are lost to corruption (see Al-Rahdi 2007; Rubin 2008; Sattar 2012). At the other extreme, there is evidence that the official village grain merchants who are responsible for distributing the monthly food baskets (PDS) are substituting lower quality items in the baskets and selling the higher quality products. The ubiquitousness of Iraqi corruption is exemplified by the findings of the Inspector General of the Higher Education Ministry that as many as 4000 of the almost 14 000 candidates in the January 2009 elections had forged university degrees (Al-Jawari 2009).

At the individual level, corrupt acts are inequitable. They allow some to avoid laws, regulations, and practices that others must follow. Thus, corruption undermines the average Iraqi's confidence that success results from individual effort, rather than from bribery or political connections. Further exacerbating the impact of corruption in Iraq is the symbiotic relationship between corruption and the insurgency. In addition, there is a growing body of research that corruption tends to have an adverse impact on a country's economy (Bardhan 1997, pp. 1322–4).

Corruption continues to be good for the insurgency. Terrorist groups in Iraq finance their operations, in part, with the proceeds from corruption. Some state factories, including an oil refinery, were taken over by insurgent groups or by groups that are willing to pay the insurgent groups for security. Organizations and ratlines that handle smuggled or other black-market goods provide terrorists with routes into and out of the country as well as safe houses for the terrorists, their weapons, and the making of improvised explosive devices (IED) (Gunter 2007; Looney 2006). Not only is corruption good for the insurgency but also the insurgency facilitates corruption because it justifies bypassing accounting and regulatory procedures. It also increases the urgency of getting things done regardless of the cost and provides an acceptable excuse for corruption-related losses.

Corruption also directly undermines the GoIs anti-insurgency efforts in Iraq. One of the key elements of a successful counterinsurgency endeavor is to immediately begin the restoration of essential services in order to build confidence and support for the government and counterinsurgent forces (Gunter 2007; US Army 2006, p. 272). Since 2003, massive corruption has restricted or delayed the provision of food, electricity, water, medical care, and so on to the Iraqi population.

In addition to its impact on the GoIs anti-insurgency campaign, corruption adversely affects the Iraqi economy. In fact, there are two economies in Iraq; an oil-funded public sector economy (about 50 percent of Iraq's labor force – author's estimate) and a non-oil-funded economy with an informal sector. Both sectors are burdened by corruption although employees in the public sector often have the opportunity to accept bribes as well as pay them. The weak performance of the non-oil Iraqi economy is one factor in undermining support for the government among the Iraqi public. This reduces the Iraqi people's confidence in the future and their willingness to support the GoI.

It should be noted that while many economists believe that corruption tends to reduce economic growth (Mauro 1995), others state that the results are not conclusive (Svensson 2005). In Iraq, the burden on private businesses is substantial. When asked about the impact of corruption on business, a 2011 survey of about 900 in nine Iraqi provinces showed that it is prevalent in such "basic business transactions as business registration, banking and even garbage collection" (CIPE 2011, p. 29). With respect to the costs of corruption compared to the overall costs of doing business 51 percent thought that corruption increased costs by more than 20 percent.

In addition to increased costs for businesses, Iraqi markets for goods and services tend to be inefficient because of the uncertainty and risk associated with corrupt activities. Firms deliberately stay inefficiently small and organize their activities in complex manners to avoid coming to the attention of those in authority who will seek payoffs. The amount of directly unproductive economic activity – labor and resources used not to produce or trade but to "get around" artificial barriers to production and trade – is large. Since the Iraqi banking system rarely lends to firms in the informal economy, less efficient high-interest money lenders or more prosperous family members are asked to provide financing.

Not only does corruption in Iraq lead to slower real growth but also it worsens the distribution of income. The poor in Iraq must pay bribes but rarely receive them. The impact of corruption also leads to an expansion of the budget deficit, reduced services for the money spent and a waste of needed investment spending. Because of corruption, the Iraqi national government has to spend much to get little.

For example, an estimated 10 percent – 25 percent of Iraqi government workers are "ghosts" who receive a paycheck but rarely show up for work. Instead, these "ghosts" give a portion of their pay to their supervisor to ignore their absence while the ghosts stay home or work at another government or private sector job. Other government workers use their government office, equipment, staff, and so on for private businesses. The completion of a census of all government employees would allow the identification of ghost workers, but this census has been delayed for over six years (IMF 2011a, p. 12). Census takers have been bribed, threatened, and beaten in government offices to prevent them from providing an accurate list of government workers.

Of those employees who do show up for work, many of them may not be actually qualified for the job they are employed to do. According to the 2010 investigation by the Iraqi Integrity Commission and the Ministry of Justice, between 20 000 and 50 000 government employees obtained their positions with forged education documents (*Niqash* 2011a).

Finally, the widespread perception of corruption tends to discourage legitimate foreign entities from trading, lending, or investing in Iraq. Outside of the oil sector, corruption costs will be a major part of a foreign firm's decision to which country to trade with or invest in (Cheung 1996; Thede and Gustafson 2010).

Corruption in Iraq is not static; in the absence of an effective anti-corruption strategy, it tends to worsen over time. Corrupt officials are motivated to increase the inclusiveness and complexity of laws, maintain monopolies, and otherwise restrict legal, economic, or social activities in order to be able to extract even larger bribes or favors in the future. Perhaps the most damaging aspect of corruption is that it increases the level of uncertainty and forces individuals and organizations to expend a great deal of effort in attempts to reduce this uncertainty. Investors have to worry not only about changing market conditions but also whether various unknown officials in Baghdad will seek to block their investment in order to extract additional bribes. Reducing corruption is critical to Iraq's long-term economic development. But in order to develop an effective anti-corruption strategy, it is necessary to first determine the causes of corruption in Iraq.

WHY IS IRAQ CORRUPT?

The determinants of corruption in Iraq can be divided into two general categories. Long-term demographic, environmental, and cultural aspects may be important causes of corruption but are difficult to change. On the other hand, there may be economic or political incentives for corruption in Iraq that, optimistically, may be subject to short-term policy solutions. Dependency on a single natural resource, petroleum in the case of Iraq, does not fit neatly into either category and, somewhat arbitrarily, will be discussed under policy.

Table 4.1   Long-term institutional and environmental causes of corruption

	References	Applicable to Iraq
Low levels of literacy	Glaeser et al. (2004)	Yes – literacy: 74%
Inhospitable climate	Acemoglu et al. (2001)	Yes
History of French or socialist legal system	La Porta et al. (1999) and Djankov et al. (2002)	Yes – socialist
Catholic or Muslim	Treisman (2000) and Landes (1998)	Yes – 97% Muslim
Cousin marriage		Yes – 33% or more

Long-Term Determinates of Corruption

There is an extensive literature on the long-term causes of corruption. In Table 4.1, five of these determinants are listed along with their applicability to Iraq.

Low levels of literacy provide a fertile soil for corruption. An illiterate population is not only vulnerable to exploitation by low-level government officials but also is unable to effectively monitor its government. While the quality of the data on literacy in Iraq is questionable, it is believed that about 88 percent of the male population is at least basically literate compared to 74 percent of Iraqi females (COSIT 2008, Table 3-1, p. 222). Iraq's 2007 illiteracy rate of 19 percent was about twice that of the average MENA country (World Bank 2012b, Table 2.14, pp. 95–6).

Acemoglu et al. (2001) found a correlation between high mortality rates for Europeans during the colonial period and the type of institutions that were established in the colonized countries. Countries with climates friendly to Western Europeans tended to get better quality colonial administrators who tended to bring their families and stay for extended periods of time. Therefore, these countries tended to receive better quality administration as colonial administrators attempted to establish "neo-Europes" with institutions that protected private property and checked government power. Such institutions tended to constrain corruption.

Countries with climates hostile to Europeans because of heat or disease tended to get lower quality administrators who left their families at home and lived in the colony as little as possible. There was a tendency for these administrators to have a short-term focus and establish "extractive" institutions in order to make as much as they could and get out while they still had their health (Acemoglu et al. 2001, p. 1370). However, this colonial influence on corruption was limited in Iraq. While commercial interests continued, the British mandate lasted only three decades from about 1918 (with the conquest of Mosul) to about 1948 (the Treaty of Portsmouth) (see Marr 2004, Chapters 2–4).

If during the colonial or post-colonial period, countries adopted French or Socialist legal systems then they tend to be more corrupt (La Porta et al. 1999). Napoleonic code or socialist legal systems tend to be extremely bureaucratic with complex regulations covering every aspect of life. Corruption becomes a way of life in such societies as a way of dealing with the bureaucracy. The Arab Ba'athist Socialist Party that dominated Iraq from 1968 through 2003 imposed an extensive bureaucratic socialism on the country with most of the important economic decisions made by party members in the ministries in Baghdad.

More controversial is the finding by Treisman (2000) and Landes (1998, Chapter 24) that countries with large Catholic or Muslim populations tend to be more corrupt than Protestant ones. Possibly this is because Protestants tend to be more distrustful of any authority – including the state – and therefore more aggressively monitor it. Also, both Catholics and Muslims may place less emphasis on education. Of course, Iraq is almost 97 percent Muslim. While there is a great deal of respect for religious leaders in Iraq, there are limits. Several analysts state that the significant losses sustained by religious parties in the January 2009 provincial elections were caused, in part, by the public losing confidence in the administrative competence or honesty of religious parties' officials (Arraf 2009; *The Economist* 2009b).

A demographic characteristic that may also be related to Iraqi corruption is cousin marriage. While the marriage of first and second cousins is not uncommon in Arab society, in Iraq it is estimated that about one-third of all marriages are within this degree of consanguinity with the rate of cousin marriage rising to about 50 percent in rural areas (Bobroff-Hajal 2006; COSIT 2008). In fact, Iraq may have the third highest rates of cousin marriage in the world after Pakistan and Nigeria. Such marriages tend to strengthen the influence of families and clans because not only do they multiply the relationships between any two members (your father-in-law is also your uncle) but also they reduce interactions between different clans. With widespread cousin marriage, it is clear why nepotism is not seen as an act of corruption but rather as a positive virtue – caring for a member of your tight-knit family and clan.

Short-Term Determinates of Corruption

While a society can possibly break its ties to its socialist past, it is difficult or impossible to change a country's physical environment, history, or culture. However, there are other determinants of corruption that

Table 4.2   Policy-related causes of corruption

	References	Applicable to Iraq
Dominant natural resource	Ades and Di Tella (1999) and Leite and Weidemann (1999)	Yes – petroleum is two-thirds of GDP
Lack of market competition	Ades and Di Tella (1999), Djankov et al. (2002), and Bliss and Di Tella (1997)	Yes
Weak free press	Brunetti et al. (2003)	Yes – 1979 to 2003 No – 2004 to present
Lack of political competition	Persson and Tabellini (2004)	Yes – 1979 to 2005 Partial – 2006 to 2008 No – 2009 to present
Large-scale subsidies		Yes
Lack of legal sanctions		Yes
Inadequate public sector salaries	Rose-Ackerman (1999), Mookherjee and Png (1995), and Krueger (1974)	No – but problems with excessive public sector salaries

are more of a function of policy error and therefore can potentially be improved in a reasonable period of time. Table 4.2 lists seven policy-related causes of corruption and their applicability to Iraq.

Oil is the curse of Iraq

In Leite and Weidemann's study (1999, pp. 22, 24), it was shown that export dominance by a single natural resource such as petroleum tends to be associated with greater corruption. Natural resources tend to have high economic rents – a large gap between the cost of production and the export price. This results in large incentives for corrupt behavior to capture these rents (Rose-Ackerman 1999, p. 19). Oil accounts for almost 95 percent of Iraq's export revenues and over two-thirds of its GDP. In fact, Iraq has the highest level of natural resource dependence in the world (World Bank 2012b, pp. 204–7).

In Iraq, the Baghdad ministries control the massive revenues from oil exports. Since the revenues from oil exports account for over 90 percent of total government revenues in Iraq, the ministries are not dependent on taxpayer voters. The Baghdad ministries use the oil funds primarily to maintain the salary and benefits of their employees including both those who are directly employed by the ministries as well as those employed by

SOE associated with many of the ministries. The perverse but predictable priorities of the ministries were dramatically revealed during the unexpected revenue shortfall in the first half of 2006. Maintenance and capital expenditures were slashed while government employment actually increased. The ministries and the associated SOE are, to a great extent, a welfare program providing generous salary and benefits in return for little work.

In addition, the independence that the Baghdad ministries enjoy as a result of oil export revenues, allows them to follow economic and social policies that block or undermine the economic liberalization goals set forth in the National Development Plan or Strategy (GoI 2005b; 2007; 2010).

Lack of market competition
Lack of market competition is associated with corruption for at least two reasons. First, the possibility that the government may allow the creation or maintenance of monopolies tends to provide strong incentives for corruption. Individuals or groups would be willing to pay bribes or otherwise favor certain government officials in order to capture monopoly profits. Second, Iraqi firms will try to influence officials to reduce or eliminate competition from imports (Ades and Di Tella 1999; Djankov et al. 2002).

Under Saddam, detailed planning was done in Baghdad by dozens of ministries. These plans determined in exhaustive detail almost all economic activities from fertilizer consumption by farmers to setting the price for imported automobiles. Almost all of the manufacturing entities were combined into around 200 SOE. Although these SOE were generally low-quality high-cost producers, they served at least three purposes. First, they reinforced Saddam's Arab Ba'athist Socialist Party control of the political levers of power. Or to be more precise, political and economic power was joined. Second, control of the ministries and the SOE provided a means for Saddam to reward his supporters and, by exclusion, punish those who were less than enthusiastic. Finally, the SOE provided multiple opportunities for government officials to extract bribes and divert funding for their personal benefit.

Since 2003, there has been no discernable progress in reducing the dominance of the SOE in the domestic economy. As will be discussed in Chapter 9, this dominance has been maintained both by continuing to provide large direct and indirect subsidies as well as by discouraging the private business sector. The burdens placed on private businesses in Iraq are onerous even by regional standards.

Table 4.3, adapted from the 2012 World Bank's "Doing Business" series (see World Bank 2012a), compares the bureaucratic burden of legally

Table 4.3   Relative ease of doing business in Iraq, MENA, and the USA

2012 Relative Ranks (183rd is the worst)	Iraq	MENA range	USA
Starting a business	176th	12th to 176th	13th
Getting credit	174th	48th to 177th	4th
Trading across borders	180th	5th to 180th	20th
Closing a business	183rd	25th to 183rd	15th

Source: World Bank (2012a).

performing common business transactions in Iraq to those of 182 other nations. The same data for the MENA countries and the USA is included for comparison purposes. Not only does Iraq possess one of the most hostile regulatory environments for private business in the world but also there has been little progress over the last six years.

Legally starting a business, obtaining credit, engaging in foreign or domestic trade, or going bankrupt are extremely complex and expensive processes. The bureaucratic complexities that tie Iraqi businesses into knots are not random or unloved artifacts of earlier days. Government ministries continue to expend a great deal of influence to preserve these complex procedures for a very simple reason. The more complex, illogical, and time-consuming the procedures are – the greater the number and size of bribes that can be extorted from businessmen (Cheung 1996, p. 3; Tanzi 1998).

Weak free press
A free press reduces the potential for corruption both by increasing the likelihood that corrupt acts will be uncovered and providing a mechanism with which public opinion against corruption can be marshaled and expressed (Brunetti and Weder 2003). Iraq has made a rapid transition from an extremely restrictive media environment before 2003 to a media free for all with a sharp rise in the number of media outlets (Brookings Institution 2009, p. 45). This increase in outlets was accompanied by increased variety of views and opinions. Stories about corruption are increasingly common. A few are careful investigative pieces but most make undocumented claims of responsibility combined with calls for action. Based on a sample of stories, letters to the editor, and the call-ins to radio shows in the Arabic media, there appears to be little patience with the notion that corruption is part of Arab or Iraqi culture. The more common view is outrage at corrupt government officials.

Unfortunately, there is substantial continuing opposition to the newly freed media. The government offers cash bonuses, subsidized apartments, and, in some cases, free land to a select list of journalists. The government states that these benefits recognize the courage of these journalists and are not an attempt to purchase favorable coverage. Other media outlets have been constrained by a flood of lawsuits requiring, in some cases, that editors spend one-third or more of each month in court defending their coverage of the news (Al-Ansary 2011).

Lack of political competition

Political competition serves a similar role as a free press in reducing the prevalence of corruption (Persson and Tabellini 2004). From 1979 through 2004, Iraqis did not have a realistic chance to express themselves politically but since then there have been four nationwide votes, most recently, provincial elections in January 2009 and the national elections in March 2010. These elections were important steps forward for democracy in Iraq especially since the provincial voters retained few incumbents. News stories in both the Arabic and English language press emphasized that perceived corruption was an important determinant in the repudiation of previously dominant parties (see Black 2009; Crisis Group 2009, p. 27; Parker and Redha 2009).

However, there is little worldwide experience of this sort of transition to help in predicting whether future elections will continue to focus on corruption. Studies of transitional political systems show that while democracy tends to reduce corruption, it is a long-term process (Lambsdorff 2006, p. 10). In addition, it appears that some of the first-time Iraqi candidates are also troubled by corruption.

Large-scale subsidies

The greater the value of the good or service controlled by the government official, the greater the value and possibly number of bribes that he or she can extract. In other words, the existence of large government subsidies leads to increased corruption since the maximum bribe – the difference between the official and market prices – is greater.

Under Saddam, gasoline, kerosene, diesel, and other fuels were almost free and the post-Saddam governments continued this policy although the size of the subsidy was reduced beginning in December 2005. For example, while the average price of premium gasoline in the Gulf in September 2005 was $1.06 per gallon (28 cents/liter), in Iraq the same fuel sold for 13 cents per gallon (3 cents/liter). This gap provided tremendous profits for corruption. If a single tanker truck of premium gasoline was diverted from the official market and its cargo sold in the Iraqi black market or smuggled

The political economy of Iraq

to a neighboring country, a profit of $6000–$7000 was possible. A poorly paid customs official or border guard could easily double his annual income by accepting a cash bribe to turn a blind-eye to such diversions. Surprisingly, in the face of political opposition and street protests, the GoI has raised the official fuel prices to approximately equal to the prices in neighboring countries. However, this leaves the official price below the market-clearing price and there are still large profits to be earned from diverting fuel from official channels into the black market. For example, in one month in 2011, 120 fuel tankers that were headed to Samarra and 260 Baghdad-bound tankers went missing and were believed to have delivered their fuel to the black market (Faruqi 2011).

Similar situations exist with other essential goods and services such as water, electricity, or food. There is widespread divergence from official channels into the black markets. For example, food is heavily subsidized through the system of monthly food baskets for every Iraqi family. One survey showed that in some provinces almost 82 percent of the food rations (PDS) were illegally diverted between the seaports (most of the subsidized food is imported) and the village or town food distribution centers. In an effort to reduce this corrupt diversion of food funds, the GoI has canceled direct cash purchases of food, which may reduce corruption but will certainly increase the transaction costs in this market (*Khaleej Times Online* 2011).

Weak legal sanctions

Of course, there are disincentives to accepting a bribe. In Iraq, although laws may call for severe punishment for bribery, the chances of being caught and convicted are practically zero. In 2008, the GoI charged only 300 persons with corruption (out of a total of over 2.3 million government employees) and convicted 86. Not only is this believed to be only a small fraction of the corrupt but also the convicted were low-level employees charged with selling fake passports (US Department of State 2008). While the number of investigations has increased substantially, it is still extremely unlikely that a corrupt act will be discovered, investigated, prosecuted, adjudicated, and punished.

Inadequate public sector salaries

A more controversial possible cause of Iraqi corruption is that inadequate public sector salaries motivate government employees to seek and accept bribes. In theory, raising the compensation of government employees will tend to discourage corruption although the pattern of incentives can be complex (Mookherjee and Png 1995, p. 154). Examining whether public sector compensation in Iraq is adequate is especially complicated. If one looks at average salaries alone then the typical government employee is better compensated than a worker in the private sector. Combined with benefits, protection against dismissal, a less intense – some would say relaxed – pace of work; government employment is eagerly sought after. There are multiple applicants for each government service opening.

However, once anyone has obtained a government position, the financial rewards for advancement in Iraq tend to be meager. For example, a senior enlisted member of the US Army would earn almost 300 percent more than a Private even before adjusting for time in service raises. This is not true in the Iraqi Army, Iraqi Police, or in almost any other Iraqi institution. A senior enlisted member of the Iraqi Army earns only about 20 percent more than a Private.

The existence of generous compensation for entry-level positions combined with meager raises for seniority provides strong incentives for accepting bribes. New employees are expected to "purchase" their entry into government employment by bribing senior officials (classic rent-seeking; see Krueger 1974). The payment is usually some combination of an initial bribe – possibly financed by borrowing – and a monthly cash "contribution" to one's supervisor. Of course, each level of management is expected to make a "contribution" to the next most senior level of management. As a result, it is believed that the actual paycheck received by many senior members of the bureaucracy accounts for a small fraction of their compensation. Many seek bureaucratic advancement primarily to increase their ability to extract larger bribes.

REDUCING CORRUPTION

Over the last fifty years, many countries have attempted to eradicate corruption in their economies. However, not only have there been no successful eradications of corruption but also most attempts to reduce it to tolerable levels have failed. Some of the failures were not surprising. Anti-corruption policies that are comprised entirely of exhortations to virtue and a spurt of well-publicized investigations tend to have little long-term effect. In addition, various political factions will often usurp anti-corruption campaigns to settle scores with their opponents and, as a result, anti-corruption efforts often collapse in mutual recriminations.

Pessimism is especially a realistic perspective when considering anti-corruption in Iraq. Looney (2008, pp. 429–35) argues that reducing Iraqi corruption will require dealing with the growth of the informal economy, the deterioration of social capital and the relationship among tribes, criminal gangs, and the insurgency. But is this list too demanding?

Successful anti-corruption campaigns, such as Hong Kong's (Speville 1997), do take into account each country's cultural, social, political, historical, and economic situation. These campaigns include institutional changes to reduce the economic incentives for corruption combined with improved governance, transparency, and an aggressive effort to communicate the purpose and progress of the campaign to the public. Successful anti-corruption campaigns must have widespread support to enable them to move forward in the face of tenacious covert opposition. Finally, for lasting results, there must be a serious effort to change the culture of corruption. In summary, successful anti-corruption campaigns tend to be complicated, difficult, politically risky, and expensive. (Klitgaard 1988, Chapter 8; Rose-Ackerman 1999, Chapter 1).

In view of the costs of a possibly ineffective Iraqi anti-corruption campaign, is the game worth the candle? In view of the other security, political, and economic challenges facing the new Iraqi government, should an anti-corruption campaign be put aside until a certain degree of stability is achieved? There are two contrary arguments.

First, the current cost of corruption is probably unsustainable. Corruption finances the remaining insurgency. It slows economic growth and worsens income distribution. Corruption hurts Iraq's budget situation from both sides. Oil revenues and other government revenues are lower because of corruption while as much as one-third of government expenditures are diverted from their assigned purposes. Second, in the absence of an aggressive anti-corruption campaign, corruption tends to worsen.

The government of Iraq has long been aware of the criticality of the corruption fight although its emphasis has shifted. In Iraq's original *National Development Strategy: 2005–2007* (GoI 2005b), one of the primary goals was to eradicate corruption. This theme is continued in the revised *National Development Strategy: 2007–2010* that states: "Corruption – the abuse of public office for private gain – is arguably the most critical component of governance in a natural resource rich country like Iraq" (GoI 2007, pp. vi, 92). However, the *National Development Plan: 2010–2014* reduced the statement on fighting corruption to a single paragraph (GoI 2010, p. 178).

Despite public statements of the importance of the anti-corruption effort in Iraq, follow-through on these statements has been weak and confused. For example, in January 2008, the Iraqi Prime Minister declared that 2008 would be: "The Year of Anti-Corruption" and published an 18 point plan to fight corruption. However, by the end of the year only three or four of the points had been acted on and government spokesmen seemed unaware that that the original declaration had ever been made. The GoI did join the Extractive Industry Transparency Initiative in 2010 and, in March 2008, signed the United Nations Convention Against Corruption (UNCAC) with its more than 160 provisions. However, the required implementing legislation for both of these agreements is progressing slowly. In Iraq's defense, the UNCAC is a very complex document that combines broad coverage – corruption in the private sector is included (Article 12, pp. 14–15) – as well as strange lacunae (it lacks a specific definition of corruption) (UN 2004). The UNCAC concentrates on improved governance and rule of law (UN 2004). What is missing from the GoI anti-corruption strategy are initiatives to attack corruption directly by changing the economic incentives.

MICROECONOMICS OF ANTI-CORRUPTION

There is a market for corrupt acts and the size of the payment (bribe) tends to rise or fall until the amount of corrupt acts demanded is equal to the amount supplied. For example, officials control the necessary licenses to produce a product and, without corruption, it will require an extended period of time, such as six months, to obtain a license. Citizens will pay a bribe to speed up the licensing process if the bribe is not excessive compared to the net benefit that results from more rapid approval. The officials will be willing to accept a bribe if it is great enough compared to the net cost of speeding up the approval.

Viewed as an economic decision, the willingness of an Iraqi official to accept or solicit bribes is a function not only of the size of the bribe but also of the consequences of being caught. The size of the bribe is related to the scale of the benefit sought by the bribe payer, whether the official must share the bribe with colleagues, and whether other officials might provide competition by offering to provide the same illegal benefit for a smaller bribe. The consequences of being caught accepting a bribe are a function of the likelihood of being discovered, investigated, prosecuted, and convicted as well as the seriousness of the punishment if convicted. In the entrepreneurial corruption that is occurring in Iraq today, there are not only multiple demanders of corrupt acts but also multiple suppliers as well.

So an anti-corruption policy could reduce corruption in three ways. First, a policy may reduce the demand for corruption by reducing the net benefit to the bribe payer. In our example, a revision of procedures may reduce either the wait for the necessary licenses (for example from six to one month) or by reducing the number of regulations or licenses required. Second, a policy may decrease the supply of corruption by increasing the net cost to the official accepting the bribe. One method of increasing the net cost would be to increase the likelihood of the official being investigated and punished for accepting a bribe. Finally, increasing the transaction costs involved with the bribe transaction may reduce corruption. This transaction cost involves the cost/difficulty of searching for someone to bribe (or pay a bribe), negotiating terms for the corrupt transaction, and if necessary enforcing the agreement.

Even well-designed anti-corruption campaigns tend to stall because of unexpected consequences. In Iraq, there has been a strong push to change government administrative procedures in order to make corrupt acts more difficult to perform or conceal. However, such changes are not costless. Requiring a ministry's senior leadership to approve all expenditures may or may not reduce corruption but it certainly increases bureaucratic delay. It is currently required that the national cabinet approve the construction of new factories (*Arab News* 2011). When multiple bureaucracies are involved in each decision as a form of checks and balances, inefficiencies can grow sharply. For example, administrative delays, driven in part by concerns about corruption, have resulted in a half a year's delay between when the National Council of Representatives approves expenditures and when the funds are actually available to be spent by a beladiya – a local office of the Ministry of Municipalities and Public Works.

In addition, corrupt officials may also attempt to "capture" a new anti-corruption campaign and turn it into just another means of extracting bribes from the guilty (or the innocent). It is not clear whether the new Iraqi government is willing to expend the political capital necessary to substantially reduce corruption. If it does summon the political will then gradually the perception of reduced corruption will increase public support for the effort. However, if the anti-corruption efforts falter then public cynicism will make any future attempt more difficult.

ANTI-CORRUPTION STRATEGIES: IRAQ AND USA

One method of reducing the demand for corruption is to reduce the economic incentives to the bribe payer. Reducing economic incentives for corruption are not directly addressed in the *National Development Strategy: 2007–2010* (GoI 2007). However, most of the components of an incentives strategy are listed under other headings including: reducing oil subsides (16), reducing agricultural subsidies (41), reforming electrical pricing (46), and privatizing SOE (53) (GoI 2007). One economic initiative that could be expected to also reduce the supply of corruption has dropped off the priority list. Reducing the subsidy for potable water was included in the *National Development Strategy: 2005–2007* (GoI 2005b, p. 29) but was not included in the *National Development Strategy: 2007–2010* (GoI 2007, p. 72).

As mentioned above, one of the few recent success stories in the fight against corruption in Iraq is the sharp reduction in direct fuel subsidies. The large gap between official and market prices provided a sizeable rent to be captured by any corrupt official who could obtain fuel at the official price and divert it to the black market. The increase in official fuel prices reduced the profit for diverting fuel from official sources into the domestic or foreign black market. In economic terms, raising the official fuel prices simultaneously reduced both the demand and supply for corrupt acts. The black market premium over official prices fell from 400 percent in the First Quarter of 2006 to 47 percent a year later (Grigorian and Kock 2010, p. 8).

Another possible means of reducing the demand for corrupt acts would be to eliminate or simplify the incredibly complex and ambiguous regulatory environment for private businesses in Iraq. As discussed above, Iraq has one of the most hostile business regulatory environments in the world (166th out of 183). Simply adopting the commercial code of the UAE would move Iraq to 33rd place in the world (World Bank 2012b) and sharply reduce the willingness of Iraqi businesses to pay bribes.

The second prong of the anti-corruption strategy is better governance especially the investigation, prosecution, and punishment of corruption. These efforts can be viewed as attempting to increase the cost to the bribe taker of engaging in corrupt acts or increase the transaction costs of engaging in a corrupt transaction (both can be represented as upward shifts in the supply curve of corrupt acts).

There are three national governmental organizations that are expected to play important roles in raising the costs of supplying corrupt acts. The Board of Supreme Audit is the Iraqi equivalent of the US Government Accountability Office (US GAO). The Inspector Generals are a post-Saddam creation but these inspectors are not independent – they report to the head of their ministry. The final leg of the anti-corruption tripod is the Commission of Public Integrity, the Iraqi equivalent of the US Federal Bureau of Investigation (FBI).

All three organizations are slowly growing in size and proficiency but there have been relatively few top-level prosecutions for corruption. The Iraqi anti-corruption tripod currently suffers from four weaknesses: insufficient funding, lack of training, out of date equipment and facilities, and a serious lack of high-level political support. The weaknesses of funding, training, and modernization are gradually being overcome but little progress is being made with respect to the problem of the lack of high-level political support in the fight against corruption.

Until May 2009, senior ministers, including Prime Minister Maliki, were able to block corruption investigations using Article 136B of the Criminal Code. This Saddam-era article, which was suspended under the Coalition Provisional Authority (CPA) and then later restored, requires investigators to get the permission of the minister of an agency before it can take any case involving that agency to court. Judge Rahdi Hamza al-Radhi, the former head of the Commission of Public Integrity who has the well-deserved reputation of being both brave and honest, testified that the use of Article 136B as well as repeated threats and acts of violence against corruption investigators have stalled most high-level anti-corruption investigations in Iraq (Al-Rahdi 2007). It was only in April 2011 that Article 136B was finally canceled in the midst of a confused debate over constitutional powers (Visser 2011). The cancelation of Article 136B has made it more complicated for ministers to block corruption investigations but there have been some creative responses. One is aggressive "cooperation" such as burying poorly staffed investigatory agencies with mountains of irrelevant documentation.

Associated with the need for improved governance, the *National Development Strategy: 2005–2007* (GoI 2005b, p. 36) called for "establishing e-government to increase transparency and modernize governmental business processes". E-government means that everything that the government does, from the prices and quantities of daily oil exports to a trial testimony, will be accessible online almost immediately. It is hoped that e-government will lead to not only a better informed citizenry but also make government officials more careful about what they do (or at least what they report). Despite the logic of reducing corruption by improved governance and transparency, empirical evidence of its efficacy is still weak. According to Svensson (2005, p. 35): "little evidence exists that devoting additional resources to the existing legal and financial monitoring institutions will reduce corruption".

The final prong of the anti-corruption plan is to reduce the cultural tolerance of corruption. Through media campaigns, it is hoped that corruption will cease to be perceived as "business as usual" and become increasingly seen as un-Iraqi like behavior. Despite surveys that show that religious leaders are the most credible Iraqi authority figures when it comes to changing the climate of corruption, elected officials and bureaucrats still take the lead. For example, at a two day December 2008 "Day of Integrity" event, most of the conference was devoted to political speeches and academic papers. Probably more effective at changing public attitudes are some theatrical initiatives. In 2008, the GoI sponsored a series of plays with anti-corruption themes starring well-known Iraqi actors and actresses. The performances were well attended and enthusiastically

Table 4.4   Components of anti-corruption strategies

	GoI 2008 initiatives	US Government 2009 initiatives
Reduce economic incentives of corruption	None	None
Improve governance	1, 2, 4, 6, 8, 17, 18	1, 4, 6, 7, 22
Increase likelihood of punishment	5, 7, 9, 10, 11, 12, 13, 14	2, 5, 8, 10, 11, 14, 15, 16, 20, 21, 23, 25
Change culture of corruption	15	3, 9, 12, 13, 17, 18, 19, 24
Sign international anti-corruption agreements	3, 16	None

received and pre- and post-performance surveys revealed a stronger anti-corruption attitude (Pearson 2009).

Do recent GoI and US Government anti-corruption strategies incorporate the best anti-corruption practices? In Table 4.4, I sort the specific initiatives of the, as yet, unpublished GoI 2008 and US Government 2009 anti-corruption strategies among the five categories discussed above. Even by this crude analysis, it is clear that improved governance and law enforcement continue to dominate the GoI anti-corruption strategy. There is only a single initiative that will attempt to change the culture of corruption in the country. In addition, Iraq has signed two international anti-corruption agreements: the Extractive Industry Transparency Initiative to reduce corruption in the petroleum industry and the UNCAC. But it is expected to be several years before significant execution of these agreements can begin.

However, the GoI and US Government anti-corruption strategies do not contain any initiatives that are directly intended to weaken the strong economic incentives favoring corruption. As was discussed above, some economic initiatives that should reduce corruption incentives are included in the 2005 and 2007 National Development Strategies but were excluded from the higher priority anti-corruption strategies.

As a result, any reduction in corruption in Iraq can be expected to be temporary. Even if many corrupt officials are removed from office, their successors will face the same temptations with probably the same results. As they say in the New York Police Department Internal Affairs: getting rid of the rotten apple without getting rid of the rotten barrel means that you'll have to do it all over again next year. By not directly attacking the economic incentives that favor corruption, Iraq continues to ignore the elephant in the room. Under Saddam, the salient characteristic of the Iraqi economy was its centrally planned, large, and intrusive state sector. As long as its influence remains, incentives for corruption will remain strong.

One way to deal with this problem would have been to reduce the influence of the ministries over the national economy either by transferring their powers to provincial entities or trusting to the embryonic market economy. Competition between provinces or markets would act to reduce the expected profitability of corrupt acts. While the 2008 Provincial Powers Law – still awaiting approval – was intended to shift power from Baghdad to regional and provincial governments; the current Iraqi government has failed to significantly curb ministerial powers. Instead, the Iraqi government and its international advisors have focused on increasing ministerial capacity to carry out their socialist responsibilities rather than shift these tasks to other entities or eliminating them entirely. But, as shown by the experience of many nations, any anti-corruption strategy that fails to change institutions so as to reduce the economic incentives for corruption will fail.

5. Political stability and economic development

> A dynasty rarely establishes itself firmly in lands
> with many different tribes and groups.
> (Ibn Khaldun [1384] 1967)

Will political instability condemn Iraq to economic collapse, foreign dominance, or even a rupture into three or more states? Or having looked into the abyss of civil war in 2006–2007, will Iraqis find a way to create a peaceful multi-region, multi-religion, multi-ethnic state while peaceably resolving its regional disputes?

These political and social challenges have been the subject of several excellent books (see Barkey et al. 2011; Haddad 2011; Visser and Stansfield 2008) as well as a wide range of studies by various governmental, non-governmental, and international organizations (for example, see Cordesman and Khazai 2012). In view of the complexities involved, it is impossible to do complete justice to them in a small space. Therefore this chapter will be limited to a few key issues related to the relationship between internal politics, external relations, and the Iraqi economy.

ANYTHING THAT YOU SAY ABOUT IRAQ IS TRUE SOMEWHERE

Many media and government reports on the potential for instability in Iraq simplify their analysis by focusing on a single characteristic – such as religion – along with an explicit or implicit claim that this characteristic is the only one that matters. This treatment is related to the idea that Iraq is an artificial construct, an artifact of British imperial arrogance. If the Iraqi state is an illegitimate construct imposed by foreigners – the argument goes – then one must look to religious or ethnic affiliations to understand the "real" Iraq. Such a view ignores the strong historical, political, economic, and social ties connecting the major urban areas along the Tigris and Euphrates rivers: Mosul, Baghdad, and Basrah. Therefore it is important to remember several truths about Iraq.

First, categories such as Arab, Kurd, Chaldo-Assyrian (Christian),

Sunni, Shi'a, Southerner, or Baghdadi conceal as much as they reveal. Each ethnic, religious, or regional group in Iraq generally encompasses a wide variety of attitudes and beliefs. For example, in an attempt to understand the politics of Iraq's large Shi'a population, one study divided them into five categories based on how the Shi'a define themselves.

1. Non-sectarian Shi'a, often highly educated.
2. Arabic Shi'a, who define themselves primarily by Arab language and culture.
3. Religious Shi'a, who define themselves primarily by their religion.
4. Pro-Iranian Shi'a, who see Iran as a cultural center or big brother.
5. Nationalist Shi'a, who identify themselves with the Iraqi state and generally oppose closer relations with Iran.

Of course, on some issues such as outrage over the 2006 attack on the Golden Mosque – all Shi'a agree. But on many matters such as federalism, female education, attitudes towards Iran or Saudi Arabia, budget priorities, and so on there is deep disagreement within the Shi'a community; but also a willingness to make certain issues a "common cause" with members of other groups that have a similar stance on these concerns. One discovers a similar complex reality of differing motivations, beliefs, and policy recommendations in Iraq's Sunni, Christian, Arab, Kurd, regional, and other communities.

Second, for a thousand years, there have been extended periods of relatively peaceful economic, political, social, and religious contacts among the various ethnic and religious groups in Iraq. Sometimes these contacts were associated with simple commercial transactions. Others reflect long historical connections. For example, of the five major tribes of Iraq, three have both Shi'a and Sunni branches.

In part this reflects the tendency of people to build closer relationships with people of the same village or region than with co-ethnic or co-religious persons who live further away. This tends to lead to loyalties that are primarily geographic. For example, people of southern Iraq often think of themselves as Southerners or 'Basrawis' (residents of Basrah) rather than Shi'as, Sunnis, Arabs, and so on. Regions might provide a better framework for understanding Iraq since they have an "historical depth" (Visser 2008, pp. 2–4) that may gradually produce greater loyalty than ethnic or religious affiliations. Another example of forming a common cause is the coming together of various ethnic, religious, and regional groups in opposition to Saddam. (See Al-Bayati 2011, especially Chapter 5, for an insider's account of the difficult efforts to form a united opposition to Saddam.) However, like almost everything else is Iraq, the degree of regional identification differs dramatically across the country.

Finally, political instability-short-of-conflict is not always a bad thing; it can have a favorable impact on long-term economic development by providing an outlet for social frustration arising from uneven development. Instability-short-of-conflict can take the form of regime change – for example from an autocratic government to a bureaucratic or parliamentarian one – as well as changes in dominate parties without a change in regime; or there may be changes in party leadership.

One of the difficulties of writing on political instability in Iraq is the rapidity of change in the policies and persons involved. Even if there is an impression of stability since the same policies and persons continue to resurface again and again, there are sometimes subtle, sometimes dramatic, changes in the likelihood that a particular policy will be executed or that a particular person's political career will be strengthened. Analysis of these changes is the subject of the diplomatic cables that every country's Baghdad representative constantly sends to his or her national capitals. Due to publication schedules and the shifting state of affairs in Iraq, it is almost certain that any statement about the current political situation in Iraq will be seriously outdated by the time this book is read. Therefore, this chapter will concentrate on long-term domestic and foreign trends concerning political instability and their impact on Iraqi economic development.

POLITICAL INSTABILITY AND ECONOMIC DEVELOPMENT

Samuel Huntington's (1968) hypothesis of the relationships among modernization, economic development, and political stability has been described as the last great attempt to integrate social, economic, and political causes of instability (Fukuyama 2011, p. ix). There are more elaborate recent models of the relationships between economic and political change but Huntington's hypothesis provides a solid framework for examining the challenges facing countries at Iraq's stage of political and economic development. (For an alternative model, see Acemoglu and Robinson 2006, pp. 673–92.)

Huntington (1968, p. 41) attempted to explain an oft-observed phenomenon that: "Modernity breeds stability but modernization breeds instability." In other words, high-income countries generally experience less political instability or conflict. However, low-income countries that undergo an acceleration of economic growth tend to experience *more* political instability or conflict. Huntington sought to explain this counterintuitive result by looking at the rates of change of modernization, economic

Huntington hypothesis

Source: Huntington (1968), p. 55.

Figure 5.1   Economic development and political instability

development, opportunities for mobility, and political institutions.
Huntington's explanation is shown in Figure 5.1.

Urbanization, increases in literacy and education, and increased exposure to media all lead to social mobilization. People who live in in low-
income countries begin to realize that there are better ways of living in
other countries. Thus social mobilization leads to expanded aspirations.
People begin to believe that progress is possible and they want a better
life for themselves and their children. Iraq has a relatively well-educated
population – by Middle Eastern standards – and following the fall of
Saddam's regime, there was not only a sharp increase in access to the rest
of the world through communication and travel but also a widespread
perception that living standards in Iraq were going to rapidly improve.
In Huntington's (1968) terms, since 2003, social mobilization increased
rapidly in Iraq leading to expanded aspirations.

Economic development increases a society's capacity to satisfy those
aspirations. It does not have to be immediate or complete, for example
farmers may be aware that others have trucks but if they are able to buy
motorbikes then this may partially satisfy their new-borne aspirations – at
least for a while. However, if economic development lags too far behind in
fulfilling the growing aspirations created by social mobilization then social
frustration – a growing dissatisfaction with current circumstances – will
increase.

Unfortunately, economic development in Iraq has generally proceeded
slowly and, in some sectors, stalled completely. This was not caused

by a lack of overall economic growth defined as increases in per capita GDP. As discussed in Chapters 2 and 6, Iraq has experienced fairly rapid economic growth primarily as a result of increased petroleum prices. However, as a result of conflict, government mismanagement, and corruption the average Iraqi has yet to see substantial qualitative improvements in quality of life or employment opportunities. The result of increased social mobilization in Iraq combined with slow economic development is increased social frustration.

Social frustration tends to increase most rapidly in countries that have a youth bulge, where the young – usually defined as 15–24 year olds – are an increasing proportion of the population (Urdal 2012, pp. 121–2, 125). This definition describes Iraq where 15–24 year olds account for 20 percent of the population, the highest proportion in the Middle East. One of the major sources of social frustration among the Iraqi young is the inability to obtain a good job. As discussed in Chapter 2, the combined unemployment and underemployment rate may exceed 80 percent for those new to the labor force (see Chapter 2, Table 2.2).

Social frustration can be dissipated if the society allows sufficient opportunities for mobility. This mobility can be geographic (people moving from one province to another or from rural areas to urban), occupational (moving to a higher paying/higher status job/profession), or international (migrating to another country – "brain drain").

Unfortunately, opportunities for economic or social mobility are limited in Iraq. Rural to urban migration has been going on for decades and, as a result, the urban population now accounts for almost two-thirds of Iraq's population. This has resulted in severe shortages of essential services and housing in urban areas.

In addition, there is evidence that increased education is no longer a sure route to higher income or status in Iraq. For both males and females, unemployment rates are higher for educated Iraqis with a Bachelor's degree than for persons with only a secondary school diploma. The gap is especially serious for females with a Bachelor's degree who have a greater chance of unemployment than a female with only a primary education (COSIT 2008, Table 5.3). International mobility is also constrained. The worldwide recession that began in 2008 has not only reduced employment opportunities in the more economically developed countries but also has resulted in higher legal barriers to foreign workers. In addition, the perceived decline in the quality of education at an Iraqi university has also reduced the likelihood of successful migration.

If social frustration grows faster than can be dissipated by improved mobility then people will want increased political participation in order to demand that the government either accelerate economic development or increase mobility. People will seek to either join existing political organizations or create new ones in order to give voice to their demands.

Demands for expanded political participation often collide with rigid or closed political institutions that are intended to protect the interests of those currently in or have previously been in positions of power. Such institutions restrict incorporating new political participants in any meaningful way. This exclusion tends to lead to a worsening of political instability or, if the situation continues to deteriorate, conflict (Urdal 2012, p. 123). This collision between demands for expanded political participation and closed political institutions is one of the major causes of the political instability that began in Egypt early in 2011 and has now spread across many nations in the Middle East and North Africa. Democracies tend to be more open to increased political participation than autocratic governments. As a result, democracies tend to have more "micro-instability" with new parties or factions constantly jostling for power but less "macro-instability" such as regime change. However, even democracies with widespread support tend to have difficulty incorporating a rapidly growing youth population. Urdal (2012, p. 127) reports that for each one percentage point increase in the proportion of youth there is a four percentage point increase in the risk of conflict. Of course, these are only probabilities, each country is unique and may adopt policies that increase or decrease the likelihood that political instability will occur.

As Figure 5.1 illustrates, according to the Huntington (1968) hypothesis, there are three ways that Iraq can forestall political instability or conflict: by accelerating economic development; by increasing opportunities for geographic, occupational, or international mobility; or by increasing the flexibility of political institutions when confronted with new demands for political participation. As will be argued in the next six chapters of the book, accelerating economic development and increasing mobility will require major changes in the political economy of Iraq. However, while making these changes will be both controversial and difficult, the failure to radically restructure Iraq's political economy will increase the likelihood that increasing political instability will lead to a return to civil conflict.

VIOLENCE IN IRAQ

As is well known, Iraq not only has a long history of internal conflict but also has been involved in large-scale wars with several of its neighbors. What is not as well known is that Iraq is an extreme outlier among the nations of the world with respect to conflict. Adam Szirmai (2005, p. 448)

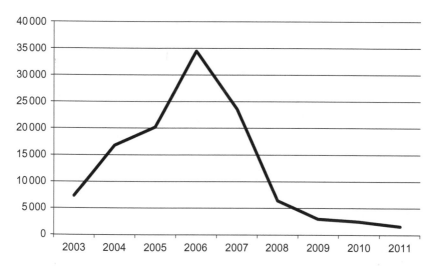

Source: Brookings Institution (2012), Iraq Index. July. 3.

Figure 5.2 Total estimated Iraqi civilian fatalities

argues that Iraq was the most conflict-ridden nation in the world between 1945–2003. During this period Iraq experienced 48 years of civil conflict (resulting in an estimated 181 000 Iraqi casualties) and seven years of international wars (resulting in around 116 500 casualties). As shown by Figure 5.2, the violence continued after 2003 with Iraq descending into what many analysts saw as a full-fledged civil war in 2006–2007.

It should be noted that even during the worst periods of 2006–2007, violence was concentrated into relatively few provinces. While five provinces had terribly high levels of violence (Ninawa, Baghdad, Babil, Anbar, and Basrah); six provinces experienced relatively low levels of violence against either police or civilians (Dahuk, Arbil, Sulaymaniyah, Qadisiyah, Maysan, and Muthanna) (Brookings Institution 2007, July, p. 22; Gunter 2007). The differences in the levels of violence among villages and cities were equally dramatic with atrocities occurring in one village while on the same day another village, only several hours away, enjoyed a market day with various groups mixing peacefully.

In view of the complexity of the situation, what can be said about the likelihood of further conflict in Iraq? There is no shortage of literature about the causes and implications of ethnic, religious, or regional differences on political stability in Iraq. Optimistically, there are many anecdotes about military, business, political, and personnel relationships that cut across religious, ethnic, and regional lines. Even during the worst of sectarian violence in 2006–2007 there were examples of heroic members of all groups risking their lives to protect their neighbors who were members of another ethnic or religious group. Of course, at the other extreme, there were the horrible atrocities involving murder and mutilation both of adults and children. So which picture reveals the true Iraq? Some researchers such as Haddad in his 2011 book *Sectarianism in Iraq: Antagonistic Visions of Unity* advocate a more nuanced understanding of the origin and possible outcome of Shi'a–Sunni relations. While Haddad (2011) focuses on Shi'a–Sunni relations, his analysis also sheds light on the other fault lines in Iraqi society including Arab–Kurd, Muslim–Christian, and regional disputes.

Haddad lists three major points. First, "The social and political relevance of sectarian identity advances and recedes according to wider socioeconomic and political conditions" (2011, p. 2). Two examples were the crushing by the GoI of the mostly Shi'a revolt in the southern provinces in 1991 and the routing of the GoI by the US-led coalition in 2003 that reduced the status of many Sunnis. These shocks led both communities to emphasize religious affiliations to a greater degree. The initial efforts by the US-led coalition to establish a post-invasion Iraqi government strengthened sectarian loyalties by making sectarian affiliation synonymous with representation. For example, rather than seek regional balance, the 25 member Iraqi Governing Council established in 2003 was deliberately composed of 13 Shi'a Arabs, five Sunni Arabs, five Kurds, a Turkman, and a Christian (Haddad 2011, pp. 150–151).

Second, even during the worst periods of conflict, relatively few of the leadership of any of the warring groups sought to break away from the Iraqi state. Their efforts were not to destroy the state as much as have the state better represent their interests and reflect their ideals. It is ironic that while well-meaning foreigners based on large-scale maps were recommending that the country be broken into four states – Sunni, Shi'a, Kurd, and Baghdad; the Iraqi leadership of the disputing groups generally sought to reform rather than eliminate the GoI. The desired reforms were both real and symbolic. As an example of the former, there was a demand that government services and employment be "fairly" distributed across ethnic, religious, and regional lines. Almost as important was the demand that the symbolism of the Iraqi state not be too closely associated with that of any of the disputing parties – that the GoI at least appear to be neutral and inclusive (Haddad 2011, pp. 36–7).

Third, the defeats inflicted during the 1990–1991 Persian Gulf War and the 2003 US-led invasion caused a retreat of the Iraqi state both in reality – it was no longer able to provide security and essential services throughout the country – and symbolically – the state was perceived to represent only a fraction of the population. This created a vacuum in post-Saddam Iraq. This vacuum was filled by an expansion of the influence of religious, ethnic, regional, tribal, and other groups that not only tried to provide various social services but also provided a sense of community with which people could identify during an extended period of social, political, and economic disruptions (Haddad 2011, pp. 87–116, 145–7).

If Haddad's analysis is correct then what are the implications? Optimistically, an increase in the GoIs capacity to effectively maintain order and efficiently should ensure that essential services are available to the population; which in turn should lead to a gradual reduction of the intensity of an individual's identification with a religious, ethnic, or regional group. An Iraqi may still look to his or her religious leader for spiritual guidance and, maybe, advice on which politician to vote for but, as the state returns to fill the vacuum, Iraqis will no longer rely on non-government groups for security from gangs or access to essential services. Pessimistically, certain groups will resist the GoI attempts to restore the influence of the state.

KIRKUK AND THE KRG

The reaction to the post-1991 vacuum in national authority that has the greatest potential to become a permanent part of Iraq's political future is the semi-independent KRG. The KRG is still part of Iraq. However, since the USA and UK established a no-fly zone over the region in 1991, the KRG has maintained its own army – the Peshmerga – and its own international oil trade and investment policies. The KRG has diverged from the rest of Iraq in several ways. The KRG is generally considered to be less sectarian than provincial governments in the rest of Iraq. It might also be considered the only federal part of Iraq with authority divided between the GoI in Baghdad and the KRG; in the rest of Iraq, federalism is in its infancy with important decisions made in Baghdad. Even with respect to corruption – the special sin of Iraq – there has been some apparent progress in the KRG. In the 2009 provincial elections, the anti-corruption Gorran Party was surprisingly successful (Barkey 2011, p. 55).

The KRG is generally considered to have three possible futures. Most pessimistically for a united Iraq, the KRG might seek, at some undefined time in the future, to separate itself from the rest of Iraq in order to form an independent Kurdish state possibly including parts of Syria, Turkey, and Iran that have large Kurdish majorities. Some believers see the creation of an independent Kurdish state as a correction of a historical error when the Kurds were left out in the early twentieth century great-power delineation of borders that created states for Arabs, Persians, and Turks (Stansfield and Ahmadzadeh 2008, pp. 129–30). However, the separation of the KRG into an independent state is extremely unlikely for several practical reasons. Any attempt to form such a state will face strong and probably violent opposition not only from the GoI but also from Turkey and other neighboring countries concerned about possible insurgencies among their own Kurdish populations. In addition, one of the current advantages of the land-locked KRG is that it can play off the Iraqi and the Turkish governments against each other especially with respect to oil production and exports. If an independent Kurdish state fails to obtain reliable access to pipelines in either Iraq or Turkey then its population will experience a substantial decline in living standards. Finally, over the last century, the Kurdish communities in Iraq, Turkey, Syria, and Iraq have gradually grown apart and now possess substantially different attitudes and loyalties. They may be "one people" in theory but any attempt to create a Kurdish state will require the reconciliation of fundamentally different visions of what such a state represents.

Another, less threatening although still destabilizing, vision of the future of the KRG is that it will continue to be a sanctuary region for Kurds within Iraq with a loyal Peshmerga to offset any threat from the Arab majority. Protection for Kurds would not only be limited to the KRG but would also include Kirkuk and other areas that have a large Kurdish population or are important to Kurdish history and culture. As an example, in 2011, Peshmerga forces moved into Kirkuk province to provide security around the provincial capital, also called Kirkuk. While these forces were withdrawn a month later under pressure from both the GoI and the US Government, the KRG leadership has reserved the right to intervene outside the KRG if Kurdish interests are threatened. This version of the future of the KRG will be fundamentally a continuation of the present.

But there is a more optimistic future. The leadership of the KRG have spoken about a regional government that will represent the interests of all of the residents of an Iraqi region: not just Kurds but also Arabs whether Sunni or Shi'a, Chaldo-Assyrian Christians, and Turkmen (Stansfield and Ahmadzadeh 2008, pp. 123–5). In other words, in the KRG there would be less emphasis on the "K", Kurdistan, and more emphasis on the "R", Regional. Critics see such statements by the KRG leadership as cynical political ploys intended to disguise their real goal of independence. However, there have been attempts to incorporate non-Kurdish groups such as Chaldo-Assyrian Christians, and Turkmen into positions of responsibility in the KRG government while attempting to reduce their loyalty to entities outside the KRG. There is a long tradition of Chaldo-Assyrian Christians joining the Peshmerga. Which vision of the future will actually occur depends in large part on whether or not there is a success-ful resolution of the three issues dividing the KRG and the GoI: oil, the Kirkuk referendum, and the 17 percent rule.

Kirkuk, although not legally in the KRG, is important for two reasons. First, Kirkuk province contains most of one of the largest "supergiant" oilfields in Iraq (and the world) with an estimated 8.6 billion barrels in reserves. This huge field extends into two KRG provinces, Arbil and Sulaymaniyah, but the primary pumping stations and other facilities are in Kirkuk province. Production from this oilfield is about 600 thousand barrels per day (bpd) making it – after Basrah – the second most produc-tive province in Iraq. As can be seen in Chapter 6, Figure 6.1, the oil from the Kirkuk oilfield is pumped southwest to Bayji in the province of Salah ad Din before splitting into three streams. The largest amount is pumped north for export through Turkey; an estimated 400 000 bpd in April 2012. Smaller amounts are either refined at the Baiji refinery – one of the largest in Iraq – or shipped south for refining or export through the Persian Gulf. If the KRG is cut off from Kirkuk then its ability to control oil exports will be severely constrained.

Second, Kirkuk province previously had a large non-Arab population primarily Kurds. However, beginning in the 1980s, Saddam instituted a policy of ruthless Arabization of Kirkuk city; forcing Kurds to flee, giving their jobs and homes to Arabs who received incentives to move into the city. Following the 2003 collapse of the Saddam regime, the process of ethnic change has reversed with the return of the Kurds and the departure – sometimes forced departure – of Arabs. The current Arab/Kurd population ratio is unknown since the last reliable census of Kirkuk province was 25 years ago. However, both Arabs and Kurds claim to be a majority.

Article 140 of the Constitution was intended to resolve the status of Kirkuk province through a two-step process of a census followed by a referendum to determine residents' preferences for the future of the city: affiliation with the KRG or continuation as the capital of an independ-ent province. Over the seven years since the approval of the Constitution, there has been much discussion and posturing by the parties involved but no census and, therefore, no referendum. Initially, the KRG sought to delay the census pending the "return" of Kurds who claim that they were forced out by Saddam. More recently, the GoI appears to be delaying the census believing that ambiguity over the Arab/Kurd population ratio is better than a possible KRG victory. It should be noted that Turkey opposes Kirkuk province joining the KRG since it believes that it would increase the likelihood of an attempt at KRG independence (Barkey et al. 2011, pp. 22–3).

In addition to Kirkuk province, the GoI and the KRG continue to feud over contracting with foreign oil companies and the KRGs share of national budget expenditures. As discussed in Chapter 6, the GoI has yet to pass the National Oil Law written in 2007. This Oil Law was required by the 2005 Constitution and was intended to delineate national, regional, and provincial responsibilities for oil and gas exploration and production especially where foreign oil companies are involved. While the passage of the National Oil Law was delayed, the KRG signed contracts directly with foreign oil companies. When oil produced by the KRG is exported, the payments are deposited in the GoIs Development Fund for Iraq account at the New York Federal Reserve. The KRG then expects a portion of these funds to be transferred back to the regional government.

The GoI sees these KRG contracts with foreign oil companies as violating its authority over the exploitation of Iraq's oil reserves but lacks a means to force the KRG to comply. If the GoI delays or restricts payments to the KRG for "illegal" oil exports then the KRG responds by reducing such exports which not only cuts the GoIs export income but also decreases confidence in Iraq as a reliable trading partner. The GoI has also attempted to constrain the KRG by banning foreign oil companies that contract with the KRG from participating in oil production in the rest of the country. However, some major foreign oil companies, such as Exxon Mobil, have been willing to run the risks of signing contracts with the KRG. These oil companies appear to think either that the GoI is bluffing about excluding such companies from contracts in the south (especially where the foreign companies are already engaged in production activities) and/or the foreign companies believe that they can negotiate more favorable agreements with the KRG and therefore would be willing to forego doing business in the south of the country.

The third and final contretemp between the GoI and the KRG concerns national budget expenditures. Currently, 17 percent of the national budget is spent in the KRG based on their supposed proportion of the nation's population. But since it has been decades since a complete national census, the true population ratio is unknown. Based on a 2007 sample of about 127000 persons, COSIT estimated that the KRG population was roughly 3.9 million or about 13 percent of the estimated national population (COSIT 2008, Table 1-3, p. 39). However, these estimates are not considered reliable due to the composition of the sample. As discussed above, holding a new national census is controversial since it would probably also provide evidence on the relative Sunni–Shi'a populations. While the Shi'a believe that they account for about two-thirds of the population; the

Sunnis think that the true populations of the two sects are closer to parity. It is expected that the census that has already been delayed for six years will continue to be rescheduled.

These disputes between the GoI and the KRG are unlikely to be resolved in the near future. Prime Minister Maliki's government depends on the support of both the KRG and Shi'a representatives to remain in power, which puts him on the horns of a dilemma: favor the KRG in the disputes and he will face weakened support from the southern Shi'a that are the largest component of his coalition; but, if he attempts to rein in the KRG then their representatives will withdraw their support and his government will probably fall. As a result, the most likely outcome is that the GoI and KRG will continue to muddle through without any clear-cut resolution. Recriminations and accusations will continue, accompanied by a series of short-term political and economic compromises. Of course, both the GoI and the KRG have to be aware of the ambitions of other nations with respect to this dispute.

EXTERNAL TENSIONS

Kenneth Pollack, of the Brookings Institution, half-humorously stated at a 2012 Middle East Institute discussion that Machiavelli's *Florentine Histories* (written in the sixteenth century) might be the best guide to understanding the complex relations between Iraq and its six neighbors. The Florentine reference was to the fact that each of the countries contains several official or private groups that directly or indirectly engage with foreign governments or organizations often in opposition to the official policy of their governments. For example, with respect to Syria, one might think of at least four Iraqi foreign policies: the official policy of the GoI; the policy of the Shi'a groups that – although members of the current Iraqi government – are more supportive of the Syrian authorities; the policy of the Sunnis that favor the Syrian rebels; and, finally, the KRG who see the conflict in Syria as leading to closer KRG–Turkey relations.

This "Florentine" complexity originates from a combination of weak governments with country borders that cut across ethnic and religious divisions. Iraq is primarily ethnically Arab – speakers of Arabic – and an estimated two-thirds of the population is Shi'a. To the east, Iran is mostly Shi'a but not Arab – the primary language is Persian. To the west, Saudi Arabia, Kuwait, Syria, and Jordan are Arab but mostly Sunni. In Syria, the minority Shi'a controlled the government at least through the end of 2012. Finally, Turkey is neither Arab nor Shi'a; its primary language is Turkish while most of its Islamic population is Sunni. There is also a large

Table 5.1   Living in an interesting neighborhood

	Corruption 2011	Government 2011	Population 2010 (Ages 0–14)
Iraq	175 (1.8)	Hybrid (4.0)	32 million (43%)
Iran	120 (2.7)	Authoritarian (2.0)	74 million (23%)
Turkey	61 (4.2)	Hybrid (5.7)	73 million (26%)
Syria	129 (2.6)	Authoritarian (2.0)	20 million (37%)
Saudi Arabia	57 (4.4)	Authoritarian (1.8)	27 million (30%)
Jordan	56 (4.5)	Authoritarian (3.9)	6 million (38%)
Kuwait	54 (4.6)	Authoritarian (3.7)	3 million (27%)

Sources: Corruption – Transparency International (2011); government – Economist Intelligence Unit (2012); population – World Bank (2012b), Table 2.1, pp. 42–4.

population of ethnic Kurds that are mostly Sunni in Turkey (Kurds are an estimated 18 percent of the Turkish population; in Iraq 17 percent of the population; in Syria 8 percent of the population; and in Iran 7 percent of the population).

In addition to the complexity of intersecting national, ethnic, and religious interests; countries in the region vary greatly in their degree of corruption, type of government, and proportion of youth. As can be seen in Table 5.1, Turkey seems to have the healthiest political economy in the region with a reasonably honest and somewhat democratic government as well as a good age distribution. At the other extreme is Syria, which has a corrupt and authoritarian government and a large youth bulge. In 2012, Syria is suffering from large-scale government inflicted violence. The other countries have combinations of internal strengths and weaknesses that – along with ethnic and religious divisions – influence their disputes and misunderstandings with Iraq and their other regional neighbors.

Among the many cross-border disputes, there are seven that are particularly troubling to the stability of Iraq. First, as discussed above, there are groups in the KRG that support an independent state uniting the Kurds of Iraq, Turkey, Iran, and Syria.

Second, both Iran and Turkey have made post-2003 cross-border military incursions into Iraq. Iran temporarily seized certain Iraqi oilfields on or near the border. Iran's incursion was possibly in response to Iranian domestic political pressures to demonstrate dominance towards Iraq or to improve Iranian negotiating positions with respect to the exploitation of these fields. Turkish military forces have attacked towns in the KRG with artillery and ground forces. The Turkish government claims these towns were harboring anti-Turkey Kurdish terrorist groups. Both of these incursions raise the issue of the US role in the future defense of Iraq. Will it be limited to selling advanced military equipment to the Iraqi military or will the USA, in a crisis, act in the defense of Iraqi sovereignty?

Third, as will be discussed in detail in Chapter 7, there have been dramatic decreases in the water flow of the Euphrates river as a result of the diversion of water for agriculture in both Turkey and Syria. In the absence of treaties guaranteeing a minimum flow, Iraq faces the potential of further accelerated desertification and salinization of agricultural land in the western and southern parts of the country. Without a substantial increase in the efficiency of Iraqi water use combined with treaty guarantees of future water flows from its neighbors, this will lead both to a reduction in Iraqi agriculture and further migration of poor farmers into urban areas.

Fourth, as a result of extremely confusing negotiations in the late nineteenth and early twentieth centuries among the UK, Russia, the ailing Ottoman Empire, and Persia; Iraq was left with limited access to the Persian Gulf. To the east, the Shatt al-Arab waterway that connects Basrah with the Gulf is shared with Iran for much of its length while traffic from the Gulf to Iraq's other major port in the west, Umm Qasr, must travel in the Khawr Abd Allah waterway that is shared with Kuwait. (For a detailed discussion of the negotiations that limited Iraq's access to the Gulf see Chapter 8.) As Iraqi export and import trade increases, it can be expected that both Kuwait and Iran will become less compromising with respect to the use of water routes that they share with Iraq. In fact, Kuwait has already announced plans to build a port on one of the major water routes from the Persian Gulf to Basrah while Iran has made threats that it will close the Persian Gulf to oil tankers in response to increasing pressure from the west.

Fifth, major disputes related to the 1990–1991 Iraqi invasion of Kuwait continue to fester. Kuwait currently receives 5 percent of Iraq's oil export revenues to compensate for the human and physical damages of the invasion. Iraqi authorities tend to see these reparations as temporary – when approximately $53 billion in estimated damages are paid then the reparations will end. On the other hand, several prominent Kuwaiti leaders see invasion losses as being much larger. As a result, they expect the reparations payments to continue almost indefinitely. At the same time, Iraq and Kuwait are engaged in complex negotiations over the exploitation of oilfields that are located under the border.

Sixth, there is widespread cross-border smuggling between Iraq and all of its neighbors but particularly with Iran and Syria. This smuggling is facilitated by tribal relationships such as the close relations between Iraqi and Syrian branches of the same tribe (Visser 2008, p. 23). Smuggling undermines the GoIs management of the economy. For example, in 2012, sanctions in Iran and political turmoil in Syria have greatly restricted trade and investment leading to severe dollar shortages in both countries. As a result, intermediaries are exchanging ID for dollars at the CBI and smuggling the dollars to Syria or Iran. As will be discussed in greater detail in Chapter 13, in order to prevent a destabilizing loss of its dollar reserves, the CBI has been forced to restrict access to its currency exchange window.

Finally, both Syria and Iran appear to be entering long-term periods of internal political instability. With respect to Syria, Iraq may seek to be a destabilizing force to weaken a Sunni neighbor that was a major source or transit station for foreign fighters as well as financial and logistical support for the insurgency in Iraq. With respect to Iran, the flow of instability is likely to go the other way. Surprisingly, Iran is also undergoing a period of unprecedented demographic collapse that will affect its long-term influence in Iraq and the region.

Demographic Divergence

Possibly related to the religious and ethnic differences between Iraq and its neighbors, there is evidence of a substantial divergence in fertility – the number of children that a woman is expected to bear. While almost all countries experience a decline in fertility rates in the initial stages of economic development, Iran is experiencing a collapse in fertility rates almost unprecedented in recent world history.

As can be seen in Table 5.2, Iraq's fertility rate (number of children born to the average woman in her child-bearing years) declined from approximately 7.3 in 1950 to 6.4 in 1980 and to 4.5 in 2010. It should be noted that a 4.5 fertility rate is still well above the 2.1 rate needed for the population of a country to gradually stabilize with zero population growth. Also, Iraq currently has a higher fertility rate than any of its neighbors. During the same period, the fertility rate of women in Turkey decreased to 2.0 while fertility in Iran fell from 6.9 in 1950 to only 1.6 in 2010. Iran is an extreme world outlier with respect to the rapid drop in fertility. While Turkey and Kuwait are now on a gradual path to zero population growth, Iran is actually experiencing a demographic collapse.

Table 5.2   Total fertility rate and population

	2010 fertility	1980 fertility	1950 fertility	2010 population
Iran	1.6	6.5	6.9	74 000 000
Turkey	2.0	4.2	6.3	72 800 000
Kuwait	2.3	5.1	7.2	2 700 000
Saudi Arabia	2.6	7.0	7.2	27 400 000
Syria	2.8	6.8	7.2	20 400 000
Jordan	2.9	7.1	7.4	6 200 000
Iraq	4.5	6.4	7.3	31 700 000

Source: United Nations (2012).

If the rest of the world is any guide then it is unlikely that Iran will be able to reverse its unprecedented drop in fertility. Of the 155 countries whose total fertility rates were tracked by the World Bank over the last three decades, 145 experienced fertility declines, two were stable (the USA and Ireland) and for the eight countries that experienced an increase in fertility (Belgium, Finland, France, Greece, Israel, Italy, Spain, and the UK) none were developing countries and the average fertility increase for these eight countries was just 0.12 additional children per woman (data from World Bank 2012b, Table 2.19, pp. 106–8).

Why are fertility rates falling? Possible explanations range from increased availability of contraceptives that allow women greater control over their fertility to a hypothesis that such a sharp drop in fertility means that a people have lost faith in the future. If the future is hopeless then why have children? The usual examples given to support this hypothesis of despair is the sharp drop in fertility – and life expectancy – in Russia after the collapse of the Soviet Union and the depopulation of Italy in the later Roman Empire. In a controversial analysis, Goldman (2011, pp. 1–7) argues that fertility falls when women become educated AND their religious fervor decreases. One of these causes is not sufficient to bring about a sharp fertility reduction. For example, the USA – which has the highest fertility rate among high-income countries – has a female population that is both highly educated and highly religious; about two-thirds of women say religion is important (Gallup 2010, p. 3).

The Goldman (2011) hypothesis appears consistent with Iran's demographic collapse. Female education has increased substantially with 94 percent reaching the last grade of primary education in 2008 compared to only 67 percent in 1991 (World Bank 2012b, Table 2.13, p. 85). At the same time, there is anecdotal evidence of a decline in religious fervor among Iranian women shown by a substantial decrease in voluntary attendance in Friday mosque services. More broadly, one survey revealed that only about 25 percent of literate Iranians (male and female) now attend mosque (Goldman 2011, pp. 6–7).

What will be the impact on Iraq of the demographic collapse in Iran? While Iran's situation is almost unique in modern times, the precedent from ancient history is not favorable. Countries that are strong but expect to substantially weaken in the near future tend to be dangerous to their neighbors. There is a temptation to strike while they still have strong hopes of obtaining advantages that will prevent or at least delay their decline (Goldman 2011, p. xi).

The complexity of Iraq's external challenges might be a reason for optimism. If Iraq's only point of contention with Turkey was the divergence of water from the Euphrates and the Tigris rivers then it is a zero-sum game where the only way that one country can win is if the other country loses. However, Iraq and Turkey have a variety of other issues besides water. In addition to the Turkish desire that elements in the KRG be constrained in their independence movement, Turkey is a major oil and natural gas importer and there is interest in obtaining natural gas from Iraqi fields for transshipment across Turkey to the European market (the Nabucco pipeline) (Barkey et al. 2011, pp. 57–8). Further in the future, rail transportation from Basrah city to Rabiya (on the Syrian border) has the potential of becoming a major transit corridor for container shipments from the Persian Gulf to eastern Turkey. Similar webs of complex relationships exist between Iraq and each of its neighbors. These complex relationships could provide a framework for mutually beneficial compromises. But who will negotiate for Iraq? In view of the many complex internal and external challenges to the GoI, can another regime change be avoided?

WILL IRAQ'S DEMOCRACY ENDURE?

What is the likelihood that increased political instability in Iraq will lead to a reversion to an authoritarian state? Attempts to answer this question have taken two approaches. First, one can look at the probability of a democracy surviving under various economic conditions. Surprisingly, this research is fairly optimistic about the future of Iraqi democracy. Second, one can compare the capacity of the Iraqi government to the expected pressures imposed on it by internal and external shocks. A weak government may survive if it is never tested and a strong government may fail if pressures are too great. This second approach is more pessimistic.

Economic Growth and Democracy

If "democracy is a regime in which government offices are filled by contested elections" (Przeworski et al. 2000, p. 19) then, after the March 2010 national elections, Iraq should be classified as a democracy. Especially, since this is the second national election therefore breaking the curse of Middle East democracy which often follows the pattern of: "one man, one vote, once". Some have argued that the meaning of democracy is broader than just contested elections and, in fact, the Economist Intelligence Unit (2012) classifies Iraq as a "hybrid" regime containing both democratic and authoritarian elements. Regardless of definitions, Iraq has made dramatic progress in both civil and political rights since Saddam was overthrown. But how vulnerable is Iraq to a reversion to an authoritarian state run by another strong man?

Iraq's growing per capita income (see Chapter 2, Table 2.1) favors the survivability of its democracy. Democracies with a per capita income of less than $1000 (PPP) tend to survive an average of about eight years before being replaced by an authoritarian regime; while those with a per capita income between $3001 and $4000 (PPP) tend to survive an average of 36 years. There are no cases of a democracy with a per capita income of over $7000 (PPP) ever being replaced by an authoritarian regime (Przeworski et al. 2000, Table 2.3, p. 93). According to this study, a democratic nation with Iraq's current per capita (PPP) income of about $3900 would be expected to survive an average of about 36 years.

The survival of democracies is also sensitive to economic growth. When democracies experience economic growth, their odds of being replaced by an authoritarian regime in any given year are only one in 66 but income declines reduce these odds of regime survival to one in 20: "most deaths of democracy are accompanied by some economic crisis" (Przeworski et al. 2000, pp. 109, 117). As discussed in Chapters 2 and 6, Iraq's economic growth is dominated by the price of oil and this results in sharp year-to-year changes. But if some combination of higher export volume and higher oil prices results in continued real growth then this will increase the likelihood that Iraq's democracy will survive.

Another characteristic that tends to be associated with a higher rate of regime change is income inequality. Research suggests that democracies are more stable in egalitarian societies but the effect is not strong (Przeworski et al. 2000, p. 120). As discussed in Chapter 3, relative poverty is low in Iraq. The 10 percent of the population with the lowest incomes receive an estimated 4 percent of the national income. While far from equality, this proportion of national income received by the poorest Iraqis compares favorably with income distribution in most developing countries. Of course, substantial increases in per capita income are unlikely to have a stabilizing influence if most of the increase is diverted by corruption or wasted by internal conflict.

To the extent that the results of these studies of a large number of developed and developing countries are applicable to Iraq, the nation can expect its nascent democracy to survive as long as economic growth continues and the rise in average per capita income is not accompanied by a substantial deterioration in income shares of the poorest Iraqis. But statistical results across a large sample of countries can only provide limited comfort. What can be said about Iraq's specific situation?

Governmental Capacity and Pressures

A more complex method of examining Iraq's political stability is to compare the strength or capacity of the country's state institutions and civil society to the adverse pressures or forces faced by the country. The Fund for Peace has estimated such a comparison for 177 countries. The results for Iraq are mixed. Although, it is currently rated as one of the ten worst countries due to high pressure combined with moderate capacity; its vulnerability is decreasing rapidly. Between 2007 and 2012, Iraq was one of four most improved nations in the sample (Fund for Peace 2012, p. 34).

Iraq received a poor or weak rating for each of the 12 measures of adverse pressures. Iraq's worst scores are for the quality of its "Security Apparatus", the existence of "Fractionalized Elites", and the high likelihood of "External Interventions" (Fund for Peace 2012, p. 37). These results point to severe pressures on the GoI. In fact, there are only eight countries in the world that face greater internal and external pressures on their government: Somalia, Chad, Sudan, the Democratic Republic of Congo, Afghanistan, Haiti, the Central African Republic, and Zimbabwe (Fund for Peace 2012, p. 4).

Fortunately, evaluations of Iraq's governmental capacity – ability to resist pressure – are not as grim, In fact, of the 14 countries in the highest pressure category (100–120), Iraq ranks highest. Of the seven capacity categories, Iraq is rated highest in the vibrancy of its "Civil Society" and – surprisingly – the competency of its "Military" (Fund for Peace 2012, p. 44). Furthermore, as mentioned previously, Iraq's governmental capacity is rapidly improving.

Political stability in Iraq is threatened by many internal and external challenges. At the same time, the capacity of the government to meet these challenges is limited. Iraq faces high threats to its political stability combined with a low capacity to deal with these threats. As a result Iraq remains extremely vulnerable. However, if the economy continues to achieve real growth, accompanied by increasing employment oppor-tunities, without a worsening of income distribution, then the internal pressure leading to serious political instability should diminish. If, at the same time, the GoI can reduce corruption and improve governance then its capacity to deal with existing and new challenges will rise. In terms of the Huntington (1968) hypothesis, Iraq must simultaneously accelerate economic development, facilitate mobility, and ensure that the political process is open to new participants. If Iraq succeeds in these very diffi-cult tasks then the odds improve that it can avoid another authoritarian government – another Saddam.

6. Oil and gas

A place called Ardericca [near Babylon] . . . forty [furlongs]
from the well which yields produce of three different kinds.
For from this well they get bitumen, salt, and oil . . .
(Herodotus 420 BC, in Godolphin 1942, Book VI, Paragraph 119, p. 380)

Iraq possesses large reserves of low-cost crude oil that are so great so as
to not only dramatically impact the nation's economy but also to substantially shift the worldwide balance of demand and supply of oil. It is a
tremendous opportunity but if the ongoing oil boom is to provide more
than a temporary boost to Iraq's economy then serious engineering, management, economic, political, and social problems must be solved. Out of
these, the engineering problems might be the easiest to remedy.

EXPLORATION, PRODUCTION, AND EXPORT

Oil

Iraq is afloat on a sea of oil.

Despite large-scale production beginning in 1927, its proven reserves are
still huge. Reflecting a controversy over the best metric to estimate proven
reserves (Cordesman and Al-Rodhan 2006, p. 229), Iraq is believed to have
between 115 and 146 billion barrels. At 115 billion barrels, Iraq is in fourth
place in the world behind Saudi Arabia (proven reserves of 260 billion
barrels), Venezuela (206 billion barrels), and Iran (140 billion barrels) and
ahead of Kuwait (100 billion barrels). If the 146 billion barrels estimate is
correct then Iraq is in third place. At current rates of production, Iraq's oil
will last for almost 50 years.

By 2005, only about 10 percent of the country has been explored for
oil or gas. In addition, the existing estimates of oil and gas reserves are
outdated; based on obsolete technology. Ongoing attempts to more accurately estimate Iraq's reserves may result in a 50 to 250 billion barrels
increase in the country's proven reserves. If the adjustment adds over
140 billion barrels to Iraq's proven reserves then Iraq will supplant Saudi
Arabia as the country with the largest proven petroleum reserves.

Iraq's crude is relatively inexpensive to get out of the ground. It is not only near the surface but also generally concentrated in large fields. Iraq has nine "supergiant" (over 5 billion barrels) fields and 22 "giant" (between 1 and 5 billion barrels) fields. As a result, along with Saudi Arabia, Iraq has some of the lowest production costs in the world. With reasonable efficiency, Iraq can break-even exporting oil at a world price of only $10 per barrel.

Crude oils are compared and described by density and sulfur content with the most desirable crudes having a low density (light) as well as low sulfur content (sweet). Light crudes are cheaper to distill into more valuable fuels while excess sulfur must be removed to prevent pollution and equipment corrosion. As a result, the market pays a significant premium for light-sweet crudes. The standard for density is that of the American Petroleum Institute (API) which lists light crudes as °API 35 to 45, and average crudes as 25 to 35. With respect to sulfur, sweet crudes have less than 1 percent sulfur by weight (Hyne 2001, pp. 4–5).

Iraq's two major export crudes are both somewhat sour but they are on the border between average and the desirable light density. Basrah light crude is listed at °API 34 while Kirkuk crude has a density of °API 36. Both have about 2 percent sulfur contamination.

This is important because many of the world's sources of light crudes such as those of Norway, the UK, and Algeria have already been substantially exhausted while new discoveries such as those of Brazil and Canada tend to be very heavy and very sour. Iraq is therefore in an enviable position of not only having the potential of dramatically increasing its petroleum production and exports but also having a relatively desirable crude to sell.

This desirable product is unevenly distributed across Iraq. In fact, one can describe much of Iraq's troubled past and possible future in two data laden figures: the map of Iraq's oil and gas infrastructure in Figure 6.1; and the relationship among Iraq's production, exports, and world oil prices in Figure 6.2. These figures provide insights not only into the country's economy but also its politics. Both deserve close study.

As we can see in Figure 6.1, the currently most productive oilfields are primarily in two provinces: Kirkuk and Basrah. The greatest reserves include the supergiant Kirkuk oilfield (estimated 8.6 billion barrels in reserves) with Iraq's other supergiant oilfields in Basrah province which include the Rumaila field (over 17 billion barrels) and West Qumac (8.7 billion barrels). In fact, Basrah and Kirkuk provinces account for almost 94 percent of the nation's petroleum production. Of the remaining 16 provinces, six provinces produced less than 40000 bpd in 2010 while ten provinces produced zero or insignificant amounts.

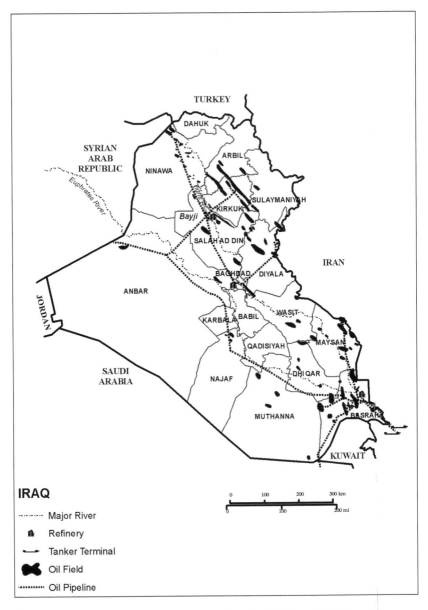

Source: Professional Maps of Houston, Texas, based on US CIA (2012) data.

Figure 6.1   Oil and gas

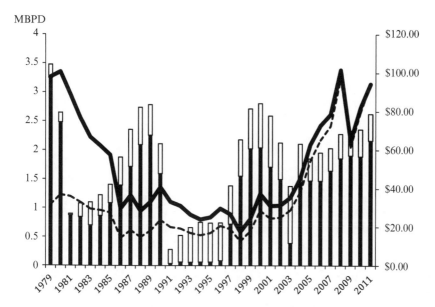

Notes: Columns represent total annual oil production in millions of barrels of oil per day (mbpd – left axis). The black lower portion of each column shows exports; the white upper potion shows oil processed within Iraq. Lines represent the Brent Blend oil price ($ per barrel – right axis). The heavy solid line is the real – inflation adjusted – price of oil while the dashed line is the nominal price.

Sources: Oil production, exports, and nominal Brent Blend oil price: EIA (2012). Real oil price calculation by author.

Figure 6.2   Iraq oil production, exports, and world oil prices

While the developed oil reserves with currently producing wells are concentrated in two provinces, undeveloped reserves are much more widely distributed throughout Iraq. There are substantial undeveloped reserves in Maysan province (estimated 8.5 billion barrels), Baghdad province (6.5 billion barrels), and Dhi Qar province (5.1 billion barrels). In fact only six provinces have less than 100 million barrels each of undeveloped petroleum reserves.

The country's earnings from crude oil exports are dependent, of course, on both the world price of oil and the volume of oil exported. In Figure 6.2, the lines show the real (solid line) and nominal (dashed line) Brent Blend index of oil prices (Iraq earns about 90 percent of the Brent Blend price) and the columns show the total volume of oil either exported or processed domestically. Note that the solid line shows oil prices in 2011 dollars – adjusted for inflation. When both prices and export volumes are high such as in 1979 and 2008, the nation's crude oil export earnings account for a very large proportion of GDP. For example, in 2008, with average crude exports of 1.82 mbpd and an average price of $91.50 pb, Iraq earned almost $74 billion – equal to almost 86 percent of GDP. However, in 2009, although export volumes increased to 1.88 mbpd, the drop in world oil prices to $55.60 pb resulted in a drop of oil earnings to $45.6 billion which contributed to a 25 percent fall in real GDP (IMF 2011a, p. 8 and Table 1, p. 16).

Unlike most oil exporting nations, Iraq will not reach its "peak oil" point for at least three decades. Therefore, one would expect that improvements of technology and increased infrastructure investment would have led to a steady increase in the volume of the nation's crude exports. But as Figure 6.2 illustrates, the volume of Iraq's crude production and exports since 1979 were extremely uneven since it was determined by conflict – not technology or investment. Following the "golden year" of 1979, crude oil production and exports collapsed in the early 1980s as a result of the Iran–Iraq War, in the 1990s as a result of Saddam's invasion of Kuwait, and in the 2000s as a result of the invasion by the US-led coalition and the accompanying insurgency. It is only with the drop of violence in 2007 that Iraq's oil production and exports returned to "normal" times.

This illustrates the key insight into Iraq's oil revenues. In the long term, Iraq's oil revenues will be determined by the increase in export volume. The country has developed an aggressive plan to rapidly expand its oil production and exports even though, as is argued below, a rapid increase in oil production may not be optimal. *However, in the short run, Iraq's national income is driven by changes in world oil prices – not increases in oil production and export volumes.*

Oil Infrastructure

Extracting and processing oil for either export or domestic refining requires an extremely complex infrastructure. After the crude oil is extracted from the wells, it is pumped to a gas–oil separating plant to remove any associated gas, water, and salts from the crude. Much of the associated natural gas is wastefully burnt – flared off – since most Iraqi fields lack the infrastructure to process, store, or transport the gas. The water may be either the result of a natural water migration into an oilfield as field pressure drops or it may result from water deliberately forced into a field to facilitate oil recovery. The salts must be removed to avoid excessive corrosion of pipes, pumps, and so on. The next step depends on whether the oil has measurable amounts of the very corrosive and poisonous gas hydrogen sulfide (H_2S). If the oil contains this dangerous gas with its rotten egg smell then it must be sent to a stabilization plant to remove the H_2S before it can be delivered to a pipeline. Finally, the crude will be pumped either to an Iraqi refinery, to Turkey through the Kirkuk–Ceyhan pipeline, or to crude carriers at the oil terminals on the Persian Gulf (EIA 2010, pp. 6–7; Hyne 2001, pp. 10–11, 409–10; SIGIR 2009c, pp. 1–2).

The major links in oil production, refining, and exports can be seen in Figure 6.1. Most of Iraq's oil exports come from the oilfields in the southeast of the country and are pumped aboard crude carriers in the ports south of Basrah city to be shipped through the Persian Gulf. The second highest export capacity is through the Kirkuk–Ceyhan pipeline from the supergiant oilfield in Kirkuk province to Turkey. In the first five months of 2012, oil exports from southern Iraq averaged 1.9 mbpd (83 percent of total oil exports) while the northern pipeline carried the remaining 0.4 mbpd (17 percent) (Ministry of Oil 2012). Also important is the strategic pipeline from Basrah to Kirkuk that allows crude from the southeast to be exported to Turkey or crude from Kirkuk to be exported from Basrah. The other major pipelines to Syria and Kuwait are currently not in commission as a result of lack of maintenance, sabotage, and political disputes.

While the process from oil production to refining or export is not as time sensitive as that of electricity generation (see Chapter 11), any "break" in the process can lead to shutdowns up and down the supply chain. This supply chain fragility is illustrated with three examples from recent Iraqi history. First, storms in the Persian Gulf can substantially slow or stop the loading of crude carriers and result in rapidly filling onshore storage facilities. If the Basrah–Kirkuk and Kirkuk–Ceyhan pipelines are near capacity, it is necessary to cease pumping oil at the wells in the Basrah fields until the storms end and loading can resume. Second, Iraqi refineries are relatively inefficient and produce more heavy fuel oil (HFO) than can be used domestically. Too thick to be transported by pipeline, this HFO is usually removed from the refineries by truck. When the HFO cannot be removed rapidly enough, storage tanks reach their capacity and it is necessary to suspend refining. This often requires an increase in imported fuels. Finally, there are continuing difficulties coordinating the activities of the Ministries of Oil and Electricity. The Ministry of Electricity argues that inadequate fuel quality and quantity reduce electrical generation while the Ministry of Oil states that inadequate electrical quality (frequency drops) and quantity reduce refinery productivity.

Based on oil viscosity, the permeability of the reservoir, and pressure, only a fraction of the oil in a field can be recovered under normal conditions. This is referred to as the recovery factor (Hyne 2001, pp. 431–2). In Iraq, these conditions limit the quantity of oil that can actually be recovered from oilfields to 50 percent to 70 percent of the total reserves. In addition, there is an optimal range of oilfield exploitation that maximizes the recovery factor. If the rate of production of a field is above this range then it is likely that there will be a permanent decrease in the total quantity of oil that can be extracted without the use of aggressive techniques to increase oil flow.

Unfortunately for Iraq's ability to extract the maximum amount of oil, it has had to alternate periods of aggressive exploitation of its primary oilfields with periods of sub-optimal production. The story is shown on Figure 6.2. Actual oil production peaked in 1979 before declining sharply during Saddam's war with Iran (1980–1988). During this conflict, Iraq was forced to abandon production from oilfields in southeast Iraq and many of these oilfields were not properly prepared for shutdown or the surface equipment was destroyed. At the same time, Iraq attempted to maximize short-term production from those oilfields that were more distant from the Iranian front. The destruction sustained in the Desert Shield/Desert Storm operations of the early 1990s combined with the lack of an export market during the pre-UN Oil for Food program, and the post-2003 looting, sabotage, mismanagement, and corruption have all kept production from some oilfields low while others were pumped at rates high enough to reduce the long-term recovery rates, especially at the older oilfields near the Iraq–Iran border (Cordesman and Al-Rodhan 2006, pp. 225–7).

In addition, the oil and gas infrastructure in Iraq, from wellhead to sea terminal or cross-border pipeline was in a bad state of repair when the violence finally diminished in 2007. The remaining infrastructure will require massive investment to restore production from existing oilfields much less to begin production at new oilfields. Restoring reasonable levels of efficiency will be difficult and may take decades.

In the short term, the binding constraint on substantially increasing Iraq's oil exports is the limited capacity of oil pipelines and storage facilities in Basrah province. The GoI has proposed an $8.4 billion project to build new storage facilities on the Faw peninsula, three new pipelines to the water's edge, and four floating terminals in the Gulf to speed the filling of large oil tankers (Hafidh 2011). As expected, this attempt to rapidly expand the oil infrastructure in the south has led to severe bottlenecks as sharply increased imports of equipment and supplies overwhelm existing port facilities. In addition, political groups, unions, tribes, and government officials have sought to profit from the urgent activities by demanding "cooperation payments" or bribes.

In the long term, the most serious challenge to expanding oil production is the water shortage. Depending on the viscosity of the oil and the nature of the oil reservoir; it can require two to eight barrels of water to produce each barrel of oil. Most of this water is injected into Iraqi oilfields in order to maintain pressure and therefore production levels. Depending on the oilfield, most of this water might be recovered during oil production and reused. However, there remains a large net demand for water to maintain – much less increase – oil production. This water has to be filtered and de-oxygenated before it is used to reduce pipe and pump corrosion. If water from the Persian Gulf is to be used then it must also be desalinated. The cost of filtering, de-oxygenating, or desalination depends on how pure the water was originally. Therefore, oilfield operators prefer to use clean – potable – water to reduce their costs.

A related issue is the disposal of contaminated water. Water used in oil recovery is often severely contaminated and will pollute river or ground water if it is dumped.

As discussed in Chapter 7, official water prices in Iraq are low or zero and, as a result, water is distributed by political fiat rather than by a market. At the same time, existing environmental laws are poorly written and rarely enforced. The national oil companies have taken advantage of this situation by diverting clean water for the use in the oilfields and casually disposing of contaminated water. In view of the growing shortage of clean water for family use and agriculture; increased water demand for oil production can be expected to lead to pitting the oil industry against households, agriculture, and other industries.

Natural Gas

In addition to oil, Iraq also has huge reserves of natural gas. Natural gas is mostly methane and, unless treated, is odorless and invisible. About 12 percent of Iraq's gas (5.6 trillion cubic feet or tcf) is found in four major fields while the remaining 88 percent (42.2 tcf) is associated gas. Associated gas is mixed with crude oil and when the oil is pumped to the surface, the associated gas evaporates. Since this vapor is explosive, it must be either captured or flared off – that is, wastefully burned. As expected, the proportion of flared gas from strictly gas fields is relatively low, most of the flared gas is associated with oil production. As recently as May 2012, an estimated 65 percent of all associated gas was flared with much of the remainder re-injected into oil wells to maintain the pressure needed to force the oil to the surface (COSIT 2012, Table 18/2; Ministry of Oil 2012). There are only two options to reduce the wasteful flaring of natural gas.

The first option is to take the gas to the user. Because of its characteristics, there are only two reasonably inexpensive methods of transporting gas: by pipeline or by ship. Pipelines must be dedicated to gas transportation; one cannot use a fuel or crude oil pipeline without extensive modification. Prior to the 1990–1991 Gulf War, Iraq exported natural gas to Kuwait through a 170 km (105 mile) long pipeline to Ahmadi, Kuwait. However, this gas pipeline is currently shutdown due to damage from conflict, sabotage, and looting. In addition, renewed gas exports would also require the passage of a petroleum law. There has also been discussion of an Arab Gas Pipeline project that would transport gas from the Akkas field (a 2.1 tcf field in Anbar province) to Syria. However, because of the severe 2012 conflict in Syria, this project is stalled. Exporting gas by ship requires special port equipment as well as specialized ships since to liquefy gas requires a temperature of −162°C (−259°F).

The alternative option is to take the user to the gas, that is, locate large users of natural gas near the fields. Since almost two-thirds of the associated gas is being flared off, the shadow price of energy from gas is almost zero. This would provide a strong comparative advantage for the production of products such as electricity, aluminum, or cement that are energy intensive. To take cement as an example, its manufacture requires the heating of raw materials (limestone, clay, additives) to about 980°C (1800°F). In Western Europe, energy accounts for almost one-third of the total cost of cement production. Unfortunately, there have been few successful attempts to locate energy using factories near where gas is flared. When in Iraq, I saw a cement plant using refined fuel as an energy source while, across the road, gas was wastefully flared off.

OIL LAW CONTROVERSIES

Production, transportation, domestic refining, or export of petroleum products is complicated by the absence of governing laws and regulations for the oil and gas industries. In the continuing controversy over Iraq's proposed Oil Law, much attention has been paid to constitutional ambiguities over both the right to sign oil contracts with foreign companies and the divisions of oil export revenues between national and provincial governments. However, the debate over the oil clauses of the Constitution is more important than simply resolving textual uncertainties. To the provincial, regional, and national governments, decisions about control of production, contracts with foreign companies, and the division of oil revenues are existential – critical and irrevocable determinants of the future welfare and political power of the negotiating parties. Provinces or regions that "win" the negotiations can look forward to increasing prosperity for the foreseeable future. "Losers" will increasingly fall behind. It has become a battle that is too important for any party to even consider substantial compromise.

Any paraphrase of the relevant portions of the 2005 Constitution (GoI 2005a) would add to the distortion caused by translation. The key articles are in Section Four, Powers of the Federal Government: Articles 111, 112, and 115.

Article 111: Oil and gas are owned by all the people of Iraq in all the regions and governorates.

Article 112: First: The federal government, with the producing governorates and regional governments, shall undertake the management of oil and gas extracted from present fields, provided that it distributes its revenues in a fair manner in proportion to the population distribution in all parts of the country, specifying an allotment for a specified period for the damaged regions which were unjustly deprived of them by the former regime, and the regions that were damaged afterwards in a way that ensures balanced development in different areas of the country, and this shall be regulated by a law.

Second: The federal government, with the producing regional and governorate governments, shall together formulate the necessary strategic policies to develop the oil and gas wealth in a way that achieves the highest benefit to the Iraqi people using the most advanced techniques of the market principles and encouraging investment.

Article 115: All the powers not stipulated in the exclusive powers of the federal government belong to the authorities of the regions and governorates that are not organized in a region. With regard to other powers shared between the federal government and the regional government, priority shall be given to the law of the regions and governorates not organized in a region in case of dispute.

With respect to Article 111, "governorate" means the same as "province" while regions reflects the constitutional right for two or more governorates/provinces to join together as a governing body (see GoI 2005a, Section Five, Articles 117 and 119). As of mid-2012, only three of Iraq's 18 provinces have agreed to form a region. This is, of course, the Kurdish region in northern Iraq. The importance of Article 111 is in the statement that it refers to "all of the regions and governorates" not just those that are currently producing oil or gas or are expected to produce them in the future. This is in contrast to Sections 112 and 115 that explicitly (Article 112) or implicitly (Article 115) refer to producing regions and governorates.

Among the ambiguities of Articles 111, 112, and 115 are the following. Both the producing regions/provinces and the federal government are assigned responsibility for the "management" of existing fields. But the incentives of sub-national political bodies differ greatly from those of the national government with respect to sequencing of production, expense reimbursement, and contracting. Sub-national authorities generally want the production from their areas to be first in line for development, they want generous definitions of allowable costs that would be subtracted from export earnings before the remainder would be transferred to the national treasury, and they want the authority to negotiate directly with foreign companies. The national government wants a national oil and gas development strategy, a narrow definition of allowable costs, and national negotiation of all contracts with foreign entities.

Another conflict exists between oil producing regions/provinces and the other provinces. As noted above, the provinces of Basrah and Kirkuk account for almost 94 percent of the nation's petroleum production. But Article 111 states that: "Oil and gas are owned by all the people of Iraq". Producing provinces want the bulk of domestic and foreign investment – and the accompanying employment – to be concentrated near existing fields, arguing that such a concentration will lead to the most rapid increase in exports and national income. These provinces also argue that efficiency would be increased if the production of supporting infrastructure including everything from cement and pipe manufacturing to training for oil workers was located near the producing fields. Non-producing provinces want a substantial portion of investment to be in new fields to more evenly distribute the gains from petroleum. For the same reason, they want the production of supporting infrastructure to be more widely distributed.

One interpretation is that the management of fields that are currently in production will be shared between producing regions or providences and the national authorities. On the other hand, new fields will be the sole responsibility of the national authorities. As expected this has led to arguments concerning fields that were previously productive but were closed because of conflict or the former oil embargo. If these fields are returned to production then are they considered new fields or not? Also, there are disagreements over whether fields that have been professionally evaluated including the drilling of test wells but have not begun commercial production should be considered as currently producing or new fields.

The final, and probably most serious, dispute concerns the use of the export earnings. While there was some discussion during the writing of the Constitution about establishing a Sovereign Wealth Fund (SWF) – providing annual payments directly to all eligible Iraqis from oil export earnings – this was never really a serious option. Instead, the Constitution in Article 112 states three priorities for the distribution of oil revenues. These are: (1) revenues will be distributed on the basis of population; (2) with a temporary allotment for regions that were severely damaged during Saddam's regime; and (3) another temporary allotment for regions that were damaged during the 2003–2007 insurgency. The intent is to balance development across the nation.

Immediately after the passage of the Constitution, in the absence of any reliable estimates of reconstruction costs or even accurate population figures for each province, the GoI responded to these priorities by budgeting $1 billion to be allocated to provinces on the basis of estimated population – with a 17 percent allotment to the Kurdish region – and an additional $1 billion for reconstruction in the provinces that were perceived to have suffered the most under Saddam and during the insurgency. As expected, this Solomonic decision left all of the provinces complaining that either their population or their reconstruction needs (or both) had been severely underestimated.

In order to resolve (or possibly perpetuate) these conflicts and ambiguities, four major pieces of petroleum legislation have been under consideration by the GoI since 2007. These are: (1) the basic oil and gas framework law; (2) the revenue sharing law; (3) the law reorganizing the Iraqi Ministry of Oil; and (4) the law reconstituting the Iraqi National Oil Company (INOC). (For a detailed discussion of these laws and their extremely complex interactions and implications, see the excellent analysis by Zedalis 2009, especially Chapter 3.)

Pending the final approval of the basic oil and gas framework law, both the KRG and the national government have signed contracts with foreign companies for petroleum exploration and production. Periodically, the GoI has publicly questioned the legality of contracts signed by the KRG. It is widely expected that the final passage of the basic oil and gas framework law will put an end to these controversies. However, a more realistic view is that the national, regional, and provincial governments can be expected to continue to seek advantage by proposing conflicting interpretations of the basic law that will have to be gradually resolved possibly by judicial interpretation but probably by political compromise. The different visions of petroleum development will be reconciled with difficulty and certainly not by the ratification of even all four of the major pieces of petroleum legislation. While the political sector continues these debates, Iraq continues to produce, refine, and sell refined oil products in both the domestic and (illegally) foreign markets.

DOMESTIC REFINING AND FUEL SALES

Once Iraq's oil has been pumped from the ground and, if necessary, excess sulfur removed then there are three possible destinations. As Figure 6.2 shows, much of the country's officially estimated oil production is exported; the remaining crude oil is transported by pipeline or truck to either be burned for electrical generation or to one of the domestic refineries to be processed into more valuable fuels. Little progress has been made in increasing refinery production. Although Iraqi refineries processed 0.6 mbpd of crude oil in 2001, refineries only processed 0.4 mbpd of crude oil in 2009 despite a sharp increase in oil production (COSIT 2012, Table 18/3).

What the official estimates miss is the large-scale divergence of crude oil or refined fuels into the black/underground market. This has made it almost impossible to reconcile physical flows of crude and processed oil with the resulting financial transactions (IMF 2011a, p. 10). The divergence of oil into the black market may occur at many different points between the wellhead and the ultimate consumer. Crude oil is smuggled over the Iranian and Turkish borders by truck as are refined fuels from Iraqi refineries. In addition, some of this refined fuel appears in the domestic black market either directly from the refineries, diverted during transportation, or out the "back door" of official fuel retailers.

The booming business in black market crude and fuel is driven by countrywide fuel shortages and facilitated by a general lack of crude/fuel monitoring and auditing. While the dramatic rise in official fuel prices between 2005 and 2007 severely reduced the profits possible from black market diversion, the political unpopularity of these increases has resulted in an unwillingness of the GoI to allow official prices to rise enough to set amounts demanded of gasoline and diesel (gas oil) equal to amounts supplied in urban markets. This provides profit opportunities to anyone who can redirect fuel from official sources; and consumers are willing to pay a high price for black market fuel when official sources run out.

Diverting crude or fuel is simplified by the common lack of reliable basic metering. Pipeline meters are either missing or miscalibrated while cargoes of fuel trucks are often either estimated or roughly calculated by dipping a marked stick into the tank. There are common reports of the drivers or others selling fuel and then diluting the remainder to maintain the expected volume. Progress is being made with all exports through the Basrah–Kirkuk and the Kirkuk–Ceyhan pipelines finally being metered by the end of 2010. However, completing the metering of domestic fuel usage is expected to take several more years (IMF 2011a, p. 13). Of course, the supply of crude and fuel to the black market is facilitated by the widespread corruption.

Contributing to the strength of the Iraqi black market is the shortages of fuels as a result of the inefficiency of the nation's refineries. Refineries use heat and chemical processes to break crude into valuable fuels such as gasoline and diesel (gas oil). The residual HFO can be used for fuel but it flows poorly, pollutes excessively, and is not very valuable (Hayes 2005, pp. 175–7). Iraqi refineries tend to produce substantially greater proportions of HFO then foreign refineries using the same crude feedstock. Excessive production of HFO has led to the periodic shutdowns of refineries since it cannot be legally dumped and is difficult to transport. Attempts to burn HFO in electrical generation plants that are not designed for this fuel led to increases in maintenance costs.

In view of the very inefficient public sector refining, transportation, and sale of fuel, should Iraq engage in any of these activities? A 2008 study estimated that while the Iraqi treasury earned – net of costs – approximately $37 per barrel of crude exports, it only received about $2 for each barrel of crude that was refined and either sold to SOE or by official dealers to customers. If these estimates were even roughly accurate then the treasury and the national economy would be better off simply exporting all crude and importing all the fuel that the country needs.

There are two counterarguments. First, the cost estimates were made when Iraq was still recovering from large-scale insurgent attacks on fuel refining and transportation. With a restoration of relative peace, it is expected that security-related costs will decline and refinery efficiency will increase. Second, there are no technical reasons why Iraq cannot dramatically increase its efficiency in refining, transporting, and selling fuel. Like much of the oil industry, refineries suffered from foregone maintenance and severe parts shortages as a result of the wars and insurgencies of 1980–2007. If refineries are repaired and necessary upgrades performed then efficiency should increase.

THE OPTIMAL RATE OF EXPLOITATION

Iraq is the most oil-dependent country in the MENA countries and, in fact, the most natural resource dependent county in the world. Oil accounts for roughly two-thirds of its GDP, which is substantially greater than the oil dependence of its neighbors Kuwait (less than 40 percent) or Saudi Arabia (less than 30 percent). In other words, Iraq is the most vulnerable country in the region to any changes in the price of oil (IMF 2010a, p. 15); yet, the oil industry only accounts for about 2 percent of the country's employment.

The challenge of Iraq's oil future is to exploit its tremendous reserves so as to maximize the long-term benefit to its people. Dealing with this challenge raises theoretical, technical, policy, and legal issues that have dramatically divided Iraq's polity.

Recently, Iraq has experienced increases in total oil revenues as higher

Table 6.1   Medium-term crude oil production scenarios

	2011	2014	2017	2017 GDP*
GoI 2010 proposal	2.75 mbpd	6.20 mbpd	12.20 mbpd	$490 billion
GoI 2011 revised proposal	2.63 mbpd	5.00 mbpd	10.00 mbpd	$410 billion
IMF 2011 estimate	2.63 mbpd	3.95 mbpd	5.35 mbpd	$240 billion

Note: * Assumes $100 pb oil price and 10% annual growth of non-oil economy.

Sources: Arango and Krauss (2012); EIA (2012); IMF (2011a), Box 1, p. 6; and author's estimates.

than expected oil prices have more than offset lower than expected export volumes. For example, in 2011, average oil prices reached $104.90 pb compared to the budgeted price of only $76.50 pb. However, oil exports were slightly less than the budgeted quantity of 2.20 mbpd. This under-estimation of oil prices combined with an over-estimation of export volumes continues a post-2003 trend. In 2011, this combination resulted in total revenues of $83 billion in 2011 compared to the budget forecast of $61 billion (IMF 2011a, p. 5). As a matter of scale, the 2011 oil export revenues were equal to 76 percent of the nation's GDP (US CIA 2012).

In late 2010, the GoI announced an extremely aggressive medium-term production plan for oil. National oil production, which was an estimated 2.63 mbpd in 2011, was planned to increase to 12.20 mbpd by 2017 – a 360 percent increase in six years! The International Monetary Fund (IMF) criticized this plan as overly optimistic and estimated that Iraq might be able to achieve 5.35 mbpd by the end of 2017 (IMF 2011a, Box 1, p. 6). After further review and possibly in response to IMF criticism, in late 2011, the GoI revised the 2017 target for oil production down to 10.0 mbpd. The consequences of these three estimates are shown in Table 6.1.

The impact of these different oil production estimates on Iraq's 2017 GDP is dramatic. If the GoI were to achieve the targets for oil production and exports in its 2011 revised proposal then per capita GDP would reach about $10 300 compared to roughly $6000 in per capita GDP for the more conservative IMF estimate and about $3000 in 2011. Even ignoring the effects of inflation and income distribution, this growth would bring about a striking improvement in the quality of life of the average Iraqi in 2017.

Several unlikely assumptions are necessary to make these predictions of which two are especially problematic. First, all three estimates assume that the world price of oil will be $100 pb in 2017. As is discussed below, it is contradictory to assume that Iraq will be able to substantially increase the world's supply of oil without putting downward pressure on world oil prices. Second, it is assumed that Iraq's non-oil economy will grow at 10 percent per year for the 2012–2017 period. While the country's non-oil economy grew at about 10 percent per year in 2004–2006, more recently real growth was about 5 percent (see Chapter 2, Table 2.1). Why is the impact of growth on the non-oil economy not stronger? The oil industry is extremely capital intensive but conservative in employment. Currently, it is estimated that only 2 percent of the Iraq labor force works in the oil industry. The GDP multiplier is probably low because of the dominance of imports in consumer spending and the tendency to save in non-productive forms. But is the best economic development strategy for Iraq to rapidly increase oil production and exports?

There are two arguments that this aggressive strategy might be inappropriate. First, technical constraints may make it difficult to achieve the GoIs oil production goals at a reasonable cost. These constraints have been the subject of extensive studies. But the second argument, that a slower rate of crude oil production is desirable even if a more rapid rate is technically possible, has received much less attention. These two arguments will be referred to as the technical constraints and market constraints arguments.

Technical Constraints

A fundamental truth of project management is that of the three desirable characteristics – "good, fast, and cheap" – *you can only choose two*. If Iraq seeks to rapidly increase its oil exports then its cost per barrel will rise sharply for several reasons.

First, domestic producers of the necessary equipment and supplies for expanding oil and gas production are either non-existent or are very inefficient. Almost all of this domestic capability is in SOE that, as discussed in Chapter 9, will require substantial improvements in managerial incentives for any substantial efficiency gains to occur. Second, attempts to import necessary equipment and supplies are already running into bottlenecks. The throughput of the Basrah ports is still restricted by damage from conflict, severe mismanagement, and labor disruptions. As a result, Iraq's port of Umm Qasr has been inundated with imports of oil industry equipment and getting needed supplies off ships and onto the roads has become a difficult challenge (*The Economist* 2010, p. 38). There are options for speeding up delivery of needed materials but, consistent with the fundamental truth, such work-around methods tend to be either more expensive or result in lowered quality. For example, some oil companies are attempting to avoid port congestion by transporting equipment overland, by arranging for air transport, or by looking the other way while their agents bribe government officials to speed up processing.

Second, aside from the difficulty of obtaining the necessary equipment and supplies either from domestic producers or as imports, technological constraints must be faced. It takes time to efficiently build pipelines, oil–gas separation plants, or even roads. Iraq combines a high unemployment rate with a severe shortage of skilled labor. There are large numbers of unskilled workers but electricians, plumbers, and other types of skilled workers are in short supply. Iraq must either train the needed skilled workers or hire expatriate electricians, plumbers, and so on.

Finally and most importantly, there is a shortage of necessary managerial human capital. In particular, Iraq has very few (or no) individuals who are currently capable of efficiently managing billion dollar projects. The few individuals qualified to manage smaller projects are severely overtasked. To efficiently manage a billion dollar project requires not only a first-class education but also 12–20 years of "on the job" experience with regularly increasing responsibilities and quality mentoring on complex projects. During the 30 years that Saddam's Iraq was substantially cut off from the world, the quality of higher education particularly in the engineering and management fields deteriorated greatly. The socialist economy of the Saddam era rewarded managers more for their political capability than for their ability to achieve technological or market efficiencies. If a rapid expansion of crude oil production and exports is attempted without possessing quality management to oversee the process then the country can expect huge waste, substantial delays, and severe corruption.

Any attempts to overcome the shortage of domestic big-project managers by a "temporary" reliance on expatriate managers will not only be expensive but raises other issues. Who will manage the managers? There is a principal–agent problem since the motivations of the GoI and expatriate managers are different. It is difficult or impossible to draft large project management contracts for expatriate managers and ensure their compliance with these contracts without substantial technical and management capability. With a few exceptions, these capabilities are lacking at the upper levels of the GoI. Retaining foreign consultants to write and monitor agreements with expatriate managers or breaking the project into easier to understand pieces are options but these just push back the question by one more level. Who has the skills to contract and monitor the consultants who have been hired to contract and monitor the expatriate managers? Or who knows enough about the large project to know how to break it down into manageable pieces?

In view of the technical constraints, how rapid an expansion of the country's crude oil production is possible? The IMF 2011 (2011a) estimate shown in Table 6.1 is probably a reasonable one. However, even this conservative plan will require substantial expansion of the oil industry's infrastructure. These include new single point moorings and pipelines for Basrah, new pipelines to connect the southern fields to Turkey, a new pipeline to Syria, construction of desalinization plants to supply water for oilfield injection, and a great expansion of oil storage facilities (IMF 2011a, Box 1, p. 6). While this conservative scenario would still result in almost a 100 percent increase in 2017 production compared to that of 2011, it will be painful for the Iraqi people to accept the necessity of a reduced rate of increase of crude oil production. The expectation of a sharp oil-driven increase in the living standard of the average Iraqi has both fueled regional disputes and provided a reason for optimism for the average Iraqi. It will be difficult for elected politicians to try to convince the Iraqi public that a slower growth rate is optimal for technical reasons not to mention the impact of a rapid expansion of oil exports on the world oil market.

Market Constraints

Although Iraq was a founding member of the Organization of Petroleum Exporting Countries (OPEC) in 1960, its production quota was suspended in the 1990s. Reinstating a production quota for Iraq is expected to be controversial since by the end of 2011, Iraq was the third largest producer in OPEC. Therefore if OPEC intends to maintain its current overall production ceiling then reinstating Iraq will require substantial and growing cuts in other members' quotas. On the other hand, if these cuts are not made then it will result in about a 10 percent increase in OPEC members' total production. Since, as discussed below, the demand for oil tends to be price inelastic, this production increase will likely lead to a substantial price decline that will result in a decrease in total OPEC earnings. While discussions continue between OPEC and Iraq, serious negotiations will probably not occur until Iraqi production reaches 4 mbpd (Ajrash and Kholaif 2012). This could occur as early as 2013 or as late as 2015.

But even if OPEC decides to increase Iraq's quota or the GoI decides to ignore OPEC decision, the GoI will still have to decide on the optimal rate of expansion of its oil production and exports. In theory, there are three options: leave the oil in the ground as an investment; pump it now and use the funds to establish a SWF; or pump it now and use it as an income stream.

The choice of whether to leave the country's petroleum in the ground or pump and export it depends not only on the current price of crude oil or natural gas but also on the expected risk adjusted prices of crude and gas in the future as well as the expected risk adjusted return on alternative investments. For example, if the inflation adjusted price of oil is expected to rise from its current level of about $100 pb to an inflation adjusted $200 pb in the next decade then this is equivalent to a 7.2 percent annual real return. If the country's next best investment option – say a diversified portfolio of European, Japanese, and American stocks – is only expected to have an annual real return of 5 percent over the next decade then Iraq's best investment strategy is to leave the crude in the ground. Not pumping the oil has a higher expected return. On the other hand, if the next best investment pays a real return of 10 percent then Iraq should pump and export now since it has the option of investing crude export earnings in a higher earning alternative.

The GoI could sell its oil reserves in the ground but this is extremely unlikely. This unwillingness to allow foreigners substantial control over Iraqi oil and gas extends to production sharing agreements (PSA). Under a PSA, a foreign oil company obtains the right to a proportion of a country's future oil production in return for providing needed services. None of the contracts signed by the GoI as a result of the multiple oilfield development auctions includes a PSA option. However, while the exact terms are rarely made public, it appears that some of the oilfield development contracts signed by the KRG with foreign oil companies contain PSA clauses. This discrepancy is one of the major causes of the disputes between the GoI and the KRG over oil exports.

Therefore, if Iraq must finance its needed investment through production and sale of oil and gas then the critical question is choosing the optimal rate of exploitation of its huge oil reserves. Even based on outdated surveys, Iraq possesses almost 11 percent of OPEC proven crude oil reserves; reflecting OPEC dominance of world oil reserves, this is equivalent to an estimated 9 percent of the world crude reserves (OPEC 2009). Since most of the other large producers are already producing at near maximum capacity, there are only two countries – Iraq and Saudi Arabia – that are capable of substantial increases in crude exports over the next decade. Therefore, because of its huge reserves of reasonably good quality oil and the potential of substantial increases in exports over the next decade, Iraq must confront the fact that its production decisions will substantially impact the world price of oil.

In the short run, the demand for crude oil is very inelastic. In fact, a study of 21 countries showed a very inelastic demand for oil with an average short-run elasticity of only 0.05 compared to a long-run elasticity of 0.23 (Cooper 2003, Table 4). Therefore, an increase in total crude oil exports, everything else unchanged, will actually lead to a decline in the total revenues of oil exporting countries. For example, if the long-run elasticity of 0.23 is accurate then a 10 percent increase in total world oil exports will lead to more than a 40 percent drop in oil prices!

The supply of crude oil is also inelastic. A large proportion of the costs of getting crude oil out of the ground and to a market are fixed. Examples are the drilling, oil–gas separation plants, pipelines, and associated pumps. Oil companies and oil exporting nations will require the expectation of high enough prices to provide a profit after accounting for all costs before they will begin investing in increased production. But, once production has begun, lower prices – even dramatically lower prices – will not lead to a substantial reduction in oil production. The fixed costs are sunk and cannot be recovered. As long as the price of oil covers the variable costs of oil production, countries will continue to produce oil.

As a result of the oil market having both inelastic demand and supply, the marginal revenue – additional revenue of exporting one more barrel – will be substantially less than the world price of oil. As a result, a rapid expansion in Iraqi oil exports will not only drive up the cost of producing each barrel but also reduce the net earnings from oil exports. Even if total oil export revenues increase, a rapid expansion of oil exports may injure the production of other export goods and services by reinforcing Iraq's already bad case of the "Dutch disease". "Dutch disease" was first used by *The Economist* business magazine to explain the decline of the manufacturing sector in the Netherlands following the exploitation of a large natural gas field. It occurs when a country has a single dominant export product that leads to a large current account surplus and currency appreciation. This appreciation reduces the competitiveness of the country's exports while encouraging increased imports.

One of the surprising economic policy successes of the GoI since 2003 had been the fact that the ID not only avoided losing its value but also actually appreciated by over 20 percent. The causes and impacts of this phenomenon are discussed at greater length in Chapter 13 but the role of crude oil exports is clear. In addition to receiving large amounts of foreign aid, the steady rise in oil prices from 2003 through 2008 combined with a gradual rise in crude exports (see Figure 6.2) resulted in an unintended current account surplus. It was "unintended" because the GoI had planned large-scale investment projects, especially in the areas of essential services provision, and these investments would have required a large increase in imports pushing the current account into deficit. But, because of limited bureaucratic capacity to execute these investment projects, the GoI was unable to accomplish them and therefore there was no sharp rise in imports. The resulting current account surplus led to a rise of Iraq's international reserves to over $60 billion at the end of 2011 and an increased confidence that the ID would maintain its value or possibly increase.

But the appreciation of the ID has had an adverse impact on non-oil employment in Iraq. Iraq's exports from carpets to dates have become 20 percent more expensive and, as a result, have failed to regain even a fraction of the pre-invasion share of foreign markets. At the same time, imports have flooded the Iraqi market. While in Iraq, I once attempted to find some "made in Iraq" consumer goods to use for a display for visiting VIPs. However, Baghdad shops were filled with imported appliances, tools, canned goods, and household items and few items were made in Iraq.

One option for reducing the adverse impact of the "Dutch Disease" while preserving wealth for future generations of Iraqis is a SWF (IMF 2011a, p. 14). Some of the earnings from petroleum exports would be deposited in the GoI SWF. The SWF would then invest in a diversified portfolio of financial assets from other countries. Since these earnings would not be converted into ID, they would not promote further appreciation. At some future time, the SWF could begin to make periodic payments to Iraqis. Establishing a SWF was one of the eight objectives for the Financial and Monetary Sector in the *National Development Plan: 2010–2014* (GoI 2010, p. 53) However, little progress has been made in making this fund operational.

Opposition to the establishment of an Iraqi SWF is based on two related arguments. First, it is argued that the development needs of Iraqis are so great that the GoI should rapidly expand development expenditures to both reduce poverty and alleviate political instability. Second, the high level of cynicism among Iraqis concerning the honesty of their leadership leads to the widespread fear that the political elite would loot a sovereign fund.

CONCLUSION

The combination of increased oil export volumes and high international oil prices provides Iraq with maybe a decade to build a new country. This time and money could be used to lay the foundation for a diversified economy with reduced dependence on oil exports and gradually replace the GoI as the "employer of first resort". Unfortunately, driven more by political incentives and constraints then economic efficiency, the GoI will most likely seek a rapid expansion of oil exports and then spend the massive earnings on oil infrastructure investment, subsidies of essential services, and improved compensation for government employees. Iraq will not run out of oil for decades but if oil exports continue to dominate Iraq's GDP then the country will be vulnerable to an unexpected drop in the real price of oil. Due to the inelasticity of oil demand discussed above and the trends in world energy demand and supply discussed in Chapter 14, a sharp drop in real oil prices to less than $50 pb cannot be excluded as a possible outcome. If this occurs then Iraq will find itself stuck with an oil economy in a world of low price oil. Despite the current advantages, the long-term economic and political health of the Iraqi people might be better served by a less aggressive petroleum policy that seeks economic diversification over oil export maximization.

7. Agriculture and the public distribution system

> The Tigris and Euphrates rise without warning; are always abrupt; carry five times the sediment of the Nile, have their annual flood in March, April, and May, too late for the winter and too early for the summer crops; traverse a country where the temperature rises to 120 degrees [49 Celsius] in summer and falls to 20 degrees [−7 Celsius] in winter . . . In spite of the many drawbacks, the ancient Babylonians made of the Euphrates delta a country so rich that Alexander the Great conceived the project of making Babylon the capital of the world.
>
> (Lord Salter 1955, p. 40 quoting Sir William Willcocks)

Iraq, along with Turkey, is one of the few countries in the Middle East with sufficient water for large-scale agriculture (Ahmad 2002, p. 170; Savello 2009a, Table 2, p. 2). It is well known that Iraq was an agricultural cornucopia throughout most of its history, so it is surprising that currently Iraq is a large net-importer of agricultural products. This change has more to do with the mismanagement of the agriculture and agribusiness sectors by a succession of regimes than any fundamental change in the Iraqi agricultural environment.

As can be seen in Figure 7.1, Iraq has three different climates. The southwest region is a relatively flat, very arid desert. Mean annual rainfall is only 100 to 170 millimeters (four to seven inches). At the other extreme, the northeast of the country is mountainous with a Mediterranean type climate. Annual precipitation ranges from 760 to 1000 millimeters (30 to 40 inches); sufficient for rain-fed agriculture. In between is a band of semi-arid climate that stretches from the Syrian and Turkish borders in the northwest to the Persian Gulf in the southeast. Out of Iraq's four largest cities, two cities – Baghdad and Basrah – and most of the country's population are in this semi-arid region. In central Iraq, typical temperatures range from 40°C (100°F) in July and August to 17°C (64°F) in the winter, although highs of 48°C (120°F) and lows below freezing have been known. The climate of central Iraq is similar to that of southwestern USA with hot summers, cool winters, and agreeable spring and autumn.

Iraq's total land area is approximately 44 million hectares (440 000 km^2 or 176 million donums (donums being the most common Iraqi

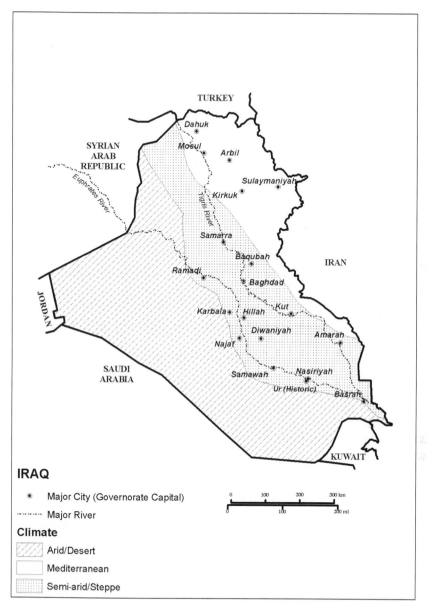

Source: Professional Maps of Houston, Texas (2012).

Figure 7.1   Climate map

measurement of area)). Only about 27 percent (12 million hectares or 48 million donums) of Iraq's total land area is potentially suitable for agriculture. The rest is too dry, salt poisoned, or otherwise unusable. However, only about two-thirds of this potentially suitable land (8 million hectares or 32 million donums) has actually been used for agriculture in the recent past (Omer 2011, p. 16), with much of this land used for meadows and pastures rather than for crops. With respect to crops, grain production accounted for approximately 86 percent of the cultivated area while vegetables accounted for an additional 9 percent. The remainder was for fruits, oil seeds, tubers such as potatoes, legumes, industrial crops such as cotton, and forage crops (COSIT 2012, Table 3/5A; FAO 2012b).

The scale of farming ranges widely in Iraq from extremely large wheat farms to family farms of less than one donum (0.24 hectares or 0.62 acres). The most common farms are small in size – about 15 and 45 donums (4–12 hectares or 10–30 acres). They typically grow a small crop of grains (wheat, barley, rice, and some corn) along with vegetables (tomatoes, cucumbers, melons, eggplant, squash, onions, and potatoes). Often there will be a small flock of sheep (20–30), or a few cattle. Production per hectare is substantially below that of other Middle Eastern countries due to the use of outdated farming techniques, poor quality seed, and old equipment.

Agriculture's share of GDP varies significantly from year to year depending on world oil prices. When oil prices are high as in 2009 then oil's share of Iraq's GDP grows and, consequently, agriculture's share falls. But to provide a sense of scale, from 2003 through 2009, agriculture accounted for between 8.5 percent and 10.0 percent of GDP.

Although, agricultural employment has fallen by almost half since the late 1970s, it is still the largest source of employment in Iraq after government jobs. In 2008, agricultural jobs accounted for 18 percent of all employment. In comparison, trade only accounts for 14 percent of total employment while construction provides another 12 percent. Employment in farming is particularly important in four provinces: Salah ad Din where agriculture accounts for 40 percent of all employment, Babil 39 percent, Anbar 33 percent, and Qadisiyah 28 percent (COSIT 2008, Table 5-20A, p. 325).

Cash income received from agricultural labor is below the national average of all industries. For example, about one-quarter of households that report agriculture, hunting, forestry, or fishing as their major source of income received less than 400 000 ID per month (about \$340 per month). The average rural household has about eight members, of which half are 15 years or older, which is considered adulthood for employment purposes; household income averages for these low-income farmers was about 100 000 ID (or $85) per worker per month (COSIT 2008, Table 1-6, p. 43).

Agricultural employment differs by gender. Among men, agriculture accounts for only 13 percent of all employment, which puts it behind trade at 19 percent and construction at 14 percent. Particularly on smaller farms, males of farming families will seek other employment in nearby semi-urban or urban areas while helping out on the family farm during labor-intensive periods such as planting and harvesting. Since 1990, the number of males engaged in farming has decreased by over 40 percent while the number of females has remained almost unchanged. In fact, agriculture accounts for one-third of the female labor force activity, more than any other industry (COSIT 2008, Table 5-20A, pp. 324–5). The importance of agricultural employment for females is, in part, a function of cultural restrictions on women working outside the home. Despite the fact that about the same number of males and females are currently employed in agriculture, male workers earn 93 percent of all agricultural income. Not only are women paid less than men but also, in many cases, they receive no pay (COSIT 2008, Table 9-11, p. 658).

Water shortages, increased salinization (salt poisoning of soil), ambiguous land ownership, and government policies towards crop prices are the major challenges facing Iraq farmers. If these challenges can be met then Iraqi agribusiness has the potential of becoming not only a significant source of employment but will also help to reduce Iraq's dependency on imported food.

AGRICULTURE PRODUCTION

Iraq's overall agricultural production has decreased about 15 percent over the last two decades although some sectors expanded during this period. The largest drop was in the value of livestock production, which declined by about 35 percent. Fruit production also decreased. Cereal production including wheat, barley, and rice has grown almost 23 percent since 1990 while vegetable production, including tomatoes, increased by over 20 percent (World Bank 2012b, p. 147; FAO 2012a). While productivity has increased, it remains substantially below that of other nations. For example, the 2010 cereal yield in Iraq was approximately 1690 kilograms per hectare (kgph) (about 1500 pounds per acre) compared to an average of about 2380 kgph in the MENA countries and 2720 kgph in other LMIC (World Bank 2012b, Table 3.3, pp. 146–9).

There are several interrelated causes of the stagnation in agricultural growth. Soil fertility continues to decline as a result of salinization, mismanagement, and over use. Multiple revisions in land ownership since 1958 have created great uncertainty and disruption that has encouraged a short-term perspective among cultivators. Bureaucratic interference from the Ministry of Agriculture and six other ministries that impact farming waxes and wanes unpredictably as the price of oil changes (Owen and Pamuk 1999, p. 169). Inadequate maintenance and low levels of new investment have reduced both the volume and, more importantly, the predictability of irrigation flows. Finally, the 2006–2008 appreciation of the ID of about 20 percent combined with (since 2003) open markets for imported agricultural products have substantially increased import competition for domestic production.

Grain production has a millennia long history in Iraq and has dominated Iraq's agricultural production based on both land area and crop value. To a great extent, the dominance of grain production reflects a long-standing Iraqi government policy of encouraging grain self-sufficiency. Much of the concern with grain self-sufficiency is a function of Iraq's history since the beginning of the Iraq–Iran War in September 1980. This war severely constrained food and other imports through Iraq's Persian Gulf ports, especially in 1984 when both sides began to target tankers and merchant ships. The ceasefire in 1988 was followed in 1990 by Iraq's invasion of Kuwait that resulted in an embargo and almost a decade of sanctions. Despite the corrupt UN "Oil for Food" program, there were severe food shortages of basic foods. As a result, the GoI engaged in a complex and extensive program to support grain production.

Cereals, primarily wheat and rice, account for almost two-thirds of the agricultural area and, in 2010, were valued at over $237 million (World Bank 2006b, p. 53; FAO 2012a, Top Production). Both the production and marketing of cereals are heavily influenced by the national government. The Ministry of Agriculture provides heavily subsidized inputs including fertilizer, irrigation water, and electricity. The subsidy of the water supply is particularly important since about 60 percent of wheat and 100 percent of rice fields are irrigated (World Bank 2006b, p. 55). The harvested wheat and rice are purchased by the national government at prices generally below those of imports. In addition, as will be discussed below, the PDS also depresses cereal prices.

Grains continue to have the highest import value and volume. In 2010, wheat imports reached almost 3.0 million metric tons valued at almost $1.2 billion. In the same year, rice was the third largest agricultural import – after sugar – with 0.7 million metric tons at $315 million (FAO 2012a, Top Imports). Grain exports were de minimus. However, as can be seen in Table 7.1, in 2010 despite government subsidies, grain is no longer Iraq's most valuable agricultural product; tomatoes are now in first place.

Table 7.1   2010 Agricultural production

Top 10 by value	Value	Volume (metric ton)
1. Tomatoes	$374 000 000	1 000 000
2. Dates	$235 000 000	567 000
3. Wheat	$195 000 000	2 700 000
4. Cattle meat	$134 000 000	50 000
5. Sheep meat	$130 000 000	47 000
6. Grapes	$122 000 000	212 000
7. Okra	$97 000 000	151 000
8. Cucumbers and gherkins	$86 000 000	433 000
9. Eggplants	$83 000 000	387 000
10. Chicken meat	$70 000 000	578 000

Source: FAO (2012a).

Fruit and vegetable production receive much lower levels of GoI subsidies and enjoy less stringent regulation than grains. Most of the annual production is immediately transported and sold in nearby urban areas. Only a relatively small proportion of fruits and vegetables are processed. Among fruits and vegetables, tomatoes have the highest level of domestic production by value. In 2010, Iraq produced about 1.0 million metric tons with an estimated value of $374 million. This made tomatoes the most valuable commodity crop in front of dates at $235 million, and wheat at $195 million. Tomato production has increased rapidly and Iraq has become the world's twentieth largest producer in 2010. The majority of the tomato crop is consumed domestically and Iraq even imports an additional 110 000 metric tons of tomatoes, its tenth most important commodity import by volume.

Although tomatoes account for a larger volume and value of production, dates have historical importance in Iraqi as well as in Arabic and Islamic cultures. While tomatoes are a relatively recent import to Iraq, dating from the eighteenth century, date production in Iraq/Mesopotamia goes back to the fourth millennia BC. Dates are mentioned multiple times in the Qur'an and, in fact, the peak season for date consumption among Muslims is during the month of Ramadan when most of the entire Muslim community around the world – over 1.5 billion people – celebrate the end of each day's Ramadan fast with dates. Dates are also important to other religions and cultures; date consumption is high during the Christian Christmas and the Hindu festival of lights, Diwali.

Dates are Iraq's single most valuable agricultural export. In 2009, date exports amounted to about 265 000 metric tons valued at $59 million

(FAO 2012a, Top Production and Top Exports). However, decades of conflict, sanctions, and mismanagement have substantially reduced both the volume and the quality of Iraqi dates. The number of date palms decreased from about 16.2 million in 1989 to about 10.0 million in 2007 (GoI 2010, p. 65). In the late 1970s, Iraq provided 80 percent of the world's date exports (Owen and Pamuk 1999, p. 169); but in 2010, Iraq was seventh in world production behind Egypt, Saudi Arabia, Iran, Pakistan, the UAE, and Algeria. However date production is beginning to increase in Iraq, in 2010 production was almost 20 percent greater than in 2008.

It takes 7–10 years for a newly planted date orchard to produce quality fruit. It is a labor-intensive crop since producing quality dates requires cultivators on ladders or on cranes to manually fertilize the female palms. There are a variety of pests that infest date orchards and consume or damage the fruit. These pests are generally controlled either by aerial or ground spraying. The profitability of date orchards is enhanced by the practice of growing complementary citrus crops amongst the date palms. In view of the long period before new orchards bear quality fruit and the severe competition from other date exporting nations, the future of Iraqi date production is mixed. Rehabilitating existing or abandoned orchards will probably be profitable; planting new dates orchards will probably not be.

WATER

Water Demand

The demand for water is still dominated by agriculture although the degree of this dominance is decreasing. In 2000, agriculture used an estimated 52 billion cubic meters per year (m^3/yr) of water or about 79 percent of total water withdrawal. Municipal use totaled roughly 6.5 percent and industrial water withdrawal accounted for the remaining 14.5 percent (FAO 2012b).

Demographic changes are driving the increased municipal demand for water. Not only does the population continue its rapid growth – the population of Iraq has almost doubled in the last three decades – but also this population is increasingly urban. A rise in urbanization tends to increase the volume of water usage. According to one study, in a nomadic society, water use per person per day is an estimated 10–30 liters. In a village, per person water use averages 60–80 liters per day, while in a modern urban area, water use per day might reach 400–800 liters per person (Agnew and Anderson 1992, pp. 276–7).

The increase in industrial water withdrawal has been even more dramatic. Over a period of 15 years, industrial use increased 33 times. Much of this industrial water use is wasted in two ways. First, since water usage fees are extremely low and often not collected, industrial water users have little incentive to avoid using excess amounts of water. Second, environmental standards are rarely enforced in Iraq and it is common for industrial users to dump water contaminated by factory use back into the nearest river. This decreases the quality of river water for downstream users.

In addition to the continuing demand for water for agriculture, industry, and urban uses, there is the complicated issue of the restoration of the large Mesopotamian Marshes located in southeast Iraq between the cities of Nasiriyah and Basrah. These three Marshes covered an estimated 20 000 km² (7800 square miles) and were the home of a large population of, as well as many rare, birds and mammals. Efforts to drain the Marshes in order to create farmland and facilitate oil exploration began in the 1950s but relatively little progress was made until the 1990s. However, following the First Persian Gulf War 1990–1991, Saddam diverted the Euphrates and the Tigris rivers so as to rapidly drain the Marshes in order to punish the Marsh people for supporting opposition to his regime. By 2003, an estimated 90 percent of the Marshes had been drained with great environmental damage and a forcible relocation of many of the Marsh people.

Following the 2003 invasion by the US-led coalition, water has been diverted back into the Marshes and some parts have begun to recover. However, a return to its original size will require substantial water diversion – possibly 10 billion m³/yr – for at least another decade. Even when the Marshes are restored to approximately their original size, the necessity of keeping the Marshes a vibrant living area will require a substantial annual flow of water from the Euphrates and the Tigris rivers. It is not clear whether the water supply will be sufficient.

Water Supply

Mesopotamia is from the Greek for "land between two rivers". For over seven millennia, almost all of Iraq's water has come from the Euphrates and the Tigris rivers. The Euphrates (in the western part of Iraq) accounts for about one-quarter of the nation's usable water while the Tigris accounts for the remainder. Groundwater is a source of less than 1 percent of Iraq's water. Both rivers originate in the mountains of Turkish Anatolia before flowing through Turkey, Syria, and Iraq. The Euphrates receives 100 percent of its flow from Turkey and Syria while the Tigris receives about two-thirds of its flow from Turkey and Iran. The two rivers merge north of Basrah to form the Shatt al-Arab waterway that flows for about 150 km (roughly 90 miles) to the Persian Gulf (World Bank 2006b, p. 12).

The flow of the Euphrates and the Tigris rivers are subject to substantial variances in timing, volume, and quality. The annual peak flow of both rivers occurs in late winter and early spring following the snowmelt and rainy season in Turkey. As a result, almost 50 percent of the flow into the Euphrates and the Tigris occurs in just two months – April and May. This flow is too late for winter crops in Iraq and too early for spring crops. In addition, there is a large year-to-year variance in the volume of water of approximately plus or minus 8 billion m^3/yr (plus or minus 12 percent of average annual water resources) (World Bank 2006b, p. 14; Savello 2009b, Table 1, p. 2). The timing and wide variance in annual flows in both rivers have led to the construction of large water storage facilities (barrages) to not only capture some of the April and May floods and release the water during the main growing seasons but also to store some of the water from years of larger than average flows until they are needed.

Aside from the annual variations, Iraq expects a large reduction in future water volume of the Euphrates and the Tigris rivers as a result of further dam construction and irrigation projects in Turkey, Syria, and Iran. Dams constructed as part of Turkey's Southeastern Anatolia Irrigation Project (the Turkish acronym is GAP) have already resulted in a significant reduction in the volume of the Euphrates. The ongoing GAP calls for the construction of 22 dams and 19 hydroelectric plants on the two rivers (Yilmaz 2003, p. 81).

The completion of the GAP with its expanded irrigation in Turkey and similar, smaller scale projects in Syria will lead to a further decrease in river flow especially in the Euphrates. By the 2020s, Iraq can expect a 50 percent reduction in the volume of water in the Euphrates. From current annual flows of 19–21 billion m^3, the Euphrates is expected to fall to about 9 billion m3 (World Bank 2006b, p. 14). At 9 billion m^3/yr, it is likely that the Euphrates will run dry before it joins with the Tigris north of Basrah (World Bank 2006b, Figure A2.2, p. 51). Not only will this reduce water availability for irrigation and municipal consumption but also there will probably be an adverse impact on electricity generation at the Haditha Dam, the only major Iraqi dam on the Euphrates.

Fortunately, the problem is not as severe for the Tigris river. Although Turkey and Iran contribute almost two-thirds of Tigris water, their planned irrigation projects over the next decade will only reduce flow by about 4 billion m^3/yr or roughly 10 percent. Since the Tigris currently has about 50 percent more water than is required for agriculture, municipal, and industrial use, this reduction will not cause a severe water shortage over the next decade like the Euphrates. However, some analysts believe that by the 2030s, water in both rivers will be insufficient for Iraq's expected agricultural and other needs (Yilmaz 2003, pp. 86–8).

Will the diversion of water by upstream nations for irrigation and power generation lead to conflict? Many commentators have pointed to the competition among Turkey, Syria, Iran, and Iraq for the waters of the Euphrates and Tigris as a sign of impending war.

The counterargument has at two parts. First, upstream developments are not an unalloyed disaster for downstream nations; there is room for cooperation that could make all nations better off. For example, dams built by upstream nations provide a degree of controlled water flow that has alleviated some of the terrible damage done by periodic flooding of the Euphrates. In addition, as discussed in Chapter 5, Turkey, Syria, and Iraq have a variety of other issues of mutual concern such as the Kurdish question. During negotiations, upstream nations have been willing to make concessions on water flow in order to achieve other goals.

There is currently no agreement on the use of the Euphrates or the Tigris rivers like those that govern water relations between Egypt and the Sudan (1959 Agreement) or the 1994 Agreement between Israel and Jordan (Richards and Waterbury 2008, p. 174). However, there are at least two "rules" or norms that Turkey, Syria, and Iraq seem to be following. In July 1987, Turkey and Syria agreed to a Protocol of Economic Cooperation that committed Turkey to maintaining a flow in the Euphrates of at least 15.7 billion m^3/yr at the Turkish–Syrian border (Dolatyar and Gray, 2000). During most months, the flow has greatly exceeded this level and during the filling of the Ataturk Dam reservoir in Turkey that temporarily reduced the flow below the promised level, Turkey provided advance notice to downstream nations and increased flow before and after to bring the multi-month average to promised levels.

The second norm is a result of 1990 negotiations under the Secretariat of the Arab League. It was agreed that Syria could keep up to 42 percent of the Euphrates water received at the Turkish–Syrian border and allow the remaining 58 percent to flow into Iraq. Pessimistically, if Turkey releases the minimum and Syria utilizes the maximum then Iraq will receive 58 percent of 15.7 billion m^3/yr water in the Euphrates or about 9.0 billion m^3/yr. As was mentioned above, this is about half of the current flow and will probably lead to the Euphrates running dry before it joins the Tigris north of Basrah.

The second argument against the thesis that disputes over the Euphrates river will lead to conflict is that all three nations are extremely inefficient in their use of water. Irrigation canals open to the sun allow evaporation, cracked canals permit leakage, and flood irrigation not only wastes water but also often leads to salt poisoning of the soil. As a result, it is estimated that about half of water reserved for agriculture is wasted. In addition, since water is priced substantially below its marginal cost, there is little incentive to conserve water not only in agriculture but also in municipal and industrial uses. Potentially, if water were used more efficiently this would more than offset the expected reduction in the Euphrates and the Tigris flows over the next two decades.

Like many downstream nations in the world, Iraq avoids emphasizing possible efficiency gains in order to avoid weakening its negotiating position. It is thought that if a downstream nation is moving towards increasingly efficient use of water then this will be taken as a sign to upstream nations that it is unnecessary for them to make concessions to maintain existing flows. However, if Iraq can be assured that upstream nations will not abrogate existing norms such as the 15.7 billion m³/yr and 42 percent/58 percent norms discussed above then the incentives to improve water use efficiency will be clear.

Once the water of the Euphrates and the Tigris rivers crosses the borders into Iraq, it flows into a complex irrigation system. Four major dams and two reservoirs are used to control the rate of flow and, in the case of the Haditha Dam, create electricity. There are over 50 large-scale gates and regulators that direct the flow of water to over 200 major irrigation and drainage pump stations with over 1000 pumps. These stations direct the water into an estimated 127 000 km (76 000 miles) of primary and secondary irrigation canals. As a result of over two decades of neglect, the efficiency of this complex system is low. The pumps are generally worn out and obsolete resulting in extensive "down" time for maintenance or repairs. Most of the irrigation canals lose large amounts of water in leaks that not only reduce irrigation flow but also increase salinization by raising the water table.

Because of geology, drainage is generally difficult. Drainage water, contaminated with salts and other agricultural waste, requires its own system to prevent it mixing with river water. This is a more severe problem in the Euphrates watershed and, in response, the GoI constructed the East Euphrates Drain to capture drainage water and move it south of Baghdad where it flows into the Main Outlet Drain (MOD). The drain system is almost a third Iraqi river that sometimes has a greater flow than the Euphrates where the two cross north of Basrah city. The MOD has its own discharge into the Persian Gulf.

Since water is effectively free, the reduction in river flow combined with leaks and evaporation in the irrigation system results in severe water shortages in many parts of irrigated Iraq. Water feuds are not uncommon as farmers associated with various tribes or clans attempt to increase the flow to their fields by reducing the water available to others. In many rural areas, tribes or clans threaten or bribe government officials to divert water flows. Violence is not uncommon. For example, three water officials and their families were murdered because of water disputes near Abu Ghraib in the first half of 2010 (IRIN 2010c).

In addition to the expected reduction in the volume of the two rivers, both rivers are experiencing a fall in water quality as a result of increased irrigation runoff in Turkey, Syria, and Iran. Since irrigation runoff has increased amounts of dissolved salts, the already difficult challenge of reducing salt poisoning of the soil – salinization – in Iraq will only get worse.

SALINIZATION

The most serious challenge facing Iraqi agriculture is salinization with about 75 percent of the nation's irrigated land suffering from various degrees of salt poisoning and an estimated 161 000 donums (39 000 hectares or 100 000 acres) of agricultural land lost annually from production (GoI 2007, p. 36; GoI 2010, p. 63). These salts are natural elements in the soil and all water, even rainwater, contains salts. However, arid regions are especially vulnerable to an excessive buildup of salts near the ground surface and that reduces soil fertility. The major effect of salt poisoning is that it makes it more difficult for plants to absorb water. Plants differ widely in their tolerance of excessive salts; for example, rice is more salt tolerant than other grains. However, even moderate salinization stunts the growth and reduces the productivity of most crops (Abrol et al. 1988, Section 3.1). The evidence of high levels of salt poisoning is obvious even to a casual observer; from a helicopter, one observes plant discoloration, barren spots, and white salt crusts.

Irrigation, unless carefully managed, can accelerate the salinization process. As irrigation water is absorbed by plants or evaporates, most of the salts are left in the soil. Ideally, there would be sufficient additional water to dissolve these salts and adequate drainage to carry this salt-laden water away. This process is most successful when the moisture content of the soil is low and the groundwater table is deep (Abrol et al. 1988, Section 3.2.1). Therefore the process can fail in three ways. First, excessive evaporation can result in salts in the soil increasing faster than they can be leached away. Second, there may not be sufficient water to carry the dissolved salts away. Finally, even if there is sufficient water, poor drainage will lead to a re-contamination of the soil. If the salt-laden water table pools within two or three meters of the surface then the salts will return to the surface through capillary action.

Excessive irrigation only exacerbates the salt poisoning of the soil. As excess irrigation water evaporates it not only contributes additional salts to the soil but also raises the water table in areas of poor drainage. If the irrigation water was heavy in salts to begin with then the rate of contamination is more rapid. Fields that are further above the water table not only require pump-irrigation but also tend to have better drainage. As a result, such fields tend to have less salt poisoning than flow-irrigated land (Mahdi 2000, p. 118). The salinization problem is not new. There are regions of Iraq that in ancient times supported a large agricultural population but are now barren due to salt poisoning (Agnew and Anderson 1992, pp. 158–9).

Once salt contamination has occurred, the most practical means of restoring soil fertility is by leaching. This requires flooding the contaminated fields and then removing the salt-laden water through artificial or natural drainage. The amount of relatively salt-free water required is large. A useful rule of thumb is that it requires enough water to flood a field a meter deep in order to remove 80 percent of the salts in the top meter of soil. A more sophisticated estimate would depend on the initial amount of salt contamination and the type of soil. A study of leaching in three areas of Iraq shows that the higher amount of clay in the soil means that more water will be required (Abrol et al. 1988, Section 3.2.1.i). Preserving the fertility of soil requires a long-term perspective that Iraqi government policy towards land ownership discourages.

LAND OWNERSHIP

Iraqi agriculture policy over the last sixty years reflects a tug of war between the statist DNA of the Arab Ba'athist Socialist Party and the country's need for domestic food production. When government revenues were high, the GoI pushed cultivators into collective farms or state farms and heavily regulated any remaining private farmers. These government policies not only weakened the influence of large landowners but also there was a widespread belief, at least in the 1950s, that government-guided agriculture would be more productive than private cultivation. Of course, the latter belief turned out to be false, as developing countries around the world have discovered. Government control of farming tends to lead to reduced quantity and quality.

This truth was periodically recognized in Iraq whenever government revenues fell or access to foreign food markets was reduced. At such times, the government would create a window for a more private sector, entrepreneurial approach to farming. As a result, cultivators experienced an irregular cycle of policy initiatives and reversals in land rights, subsidies, water and equipment availability, and market access. Policy uncertainty has added to the severe impact that the years of conflict have had on Iraqi agriculture by stalling improvements in farm productivity and motivating a large rural to urban migration. With respect to land ownership, this policy tug of war has resulted in a transition from dominance by large landowners to dominance by government bureaucrats.

Current land ownership in Iraq defies easy categorization. Ownership is a bundle of rights. Ownership of farm land includes: the right to decide on what crops will be cultivated; the means of cultivation; the right to benefit from the sale of the farm's production; the right to benefit from any improvements in the farm; the right to use the land as collateral for loans; and the right to sell or otherwise alienate the land. While in some countries, the same individual or entity will have all of these rights, in Iraq the rights tend to be controlled by a variety of persons and agencies. Cultivators, tribal and other traditional groups, absentee landlords, and a variety of government agencies may all influence or control one and more of Iraqi land ownership rights. Only some of these land ownership rights are recorded in writing, many are matters of tradition or political influence. Many of these rights overlap and when they conflict, there is often no accepted adjudication process. It should also be noted that procedures in the KRG differ from those in the rest of Iraq.

Keeping in mind the complexities and ambiguities of agricultural land ownership in Iraq, there are four general types:

1. *Private ownership.* About 10 million donums (2.5 million hectares) or 32 percent of all non-KRG agricultural land is privately owned. Iraqi law governing privately owned land reflects somewhat contradictory Ottoman, British, and Islamic influences. Subject to legal limits on the maximum size of individual land holdings, privately owned land can be sold or otherwise alienated.
2. *Free distribution.* Beginning in 1958 and continuing through 1987, there were a series of land reform laws and modifications whose varied impacts are discussed below. Under these laws, the GoI confiscated large private land holdings and then, usually after a substantial delay, redistributed the land to individuals or groups of cultivators. While such free distribution land reached around 12 million donums at its peak, it is currently believed to be about 5.9 million donums (1.5 million hectares) or about 19 percent of non-KRG agricultural land. Cultivators can generally pass this land on to their heirs but otherwise it escheats to the GoI.
3. *Rented.* The Ministry of Agriculture rents to farmers around 15.3

million donums (3.8 million hectares) equivalent to roughly 48 percent of all non-KRG agricultural land. The cultivator has the right to use the land (usufruct) but the farmer is unlikely to be reimbursed for any improvements if he or she leaves the land.

4. *Other.* Religious endowments – waqfs – control 0.2 million donums, which is about 1 percent of all non-KRG agricultural land (COSIT 2012, Table 3/24).

Iraq has experienced a series of land reform initiatives. In general, these initiatives have had two substantial effects. There have been significant changes in the distribution of land ownership and the compensation of cultivators. Also, the series of often-contradictory land reform initiatives over the last six decades have created great uncertainty over the future of land ownership rights in Iraq. Cultivators and others respond to this uncertainty by adopting a more short-term outlook for agricultural investment.

The stated motivation for the first substantial Iraqi land reform in modern times, the Agrarian Reform Law Number 30 of 1958, was the severe concentration of Iraqi agricultural holdings. Almost two-thirds of holdings were small and accounted for less than 3 percent of the country's total agricultural land. At the other extreme, less than 3 percent of the holdings were very large and accounted for about two-thirds of Iraq's agricultural land. In fact, some of the landholdings were huge with about 0.1 percent of all holdings accounting for 28 percent of Iraq's total agricultural land. There were less than 300 of these very large holdings with an average size of 26 000 donums (exactly 6500 hectares or approximately 16 100 acres).

At the other end of the scale, there were very small farms with an average size of 1.4 donums (one-third of a hectare or 0.9 acres). Even with intensive agriculture, it was almost impossible to make a living on such small farms. These small farmers carried the burden of short and precarious leases, high rents, and high debts (Issawi 1982, p. 138). Most of the farmers of this scale were forced to supplement their farm earnings with other sources of income. Over three-quarters of the rural population were landless.

There was also a strong political motivation for land reform. Large rural landowners, often tribal sheikhs, had been supported by the British and, later, by the Hashemite Monarchy (1921–1958) as a counterweight to more nationalist urban elites. Therefore, urban elites saw land reform as a means to weaken their political opposition (Richards and Waterbury 2008, pp. 158–9).

After rebellious Iraqi army officers overthrew the monarchy in 1958, they took advantage of outrage over the wide disparity in land ownership to pass the dramatic changes of the 1958 Land Reform Law. Promulgated less than three months after the revolution, this law set an upper limit of 1000 donums (250 hectares or 620 acres) for irrigated land and 2000 donums for un-irrigated land. The landowners who owned more than the legally allowed amounts of land were asked to choose which land to keep, and the rest of the land was turned over to the authorities for later distribution to landless cultivators. Compensation was to be paid for the expropriated land. Government sponsored co-operatives were to be established to provide services to the newly independent cultivators especially seed, fertilizer, access to equipment, and marketing services. Because of the wide variance discussed above, the redistribution of land affected relatively few landowners, less than 3000 – but it did affect a great deal of land, almost two-thirds of all agricultural land.

The intention of the 1958 Law was to provide land to all cultivators. The authorities were to distribute 30–60 donums of irrigated land or 60–120 donums of un-irrigated land to each cultivator. With reasonably fertile soil, sufficient water, and equipment, this was an adequate sized piece of land for cultivators to make a living even if they were growing grain.

Severe opposition to this law meant that the initial wave of land reforms was not imposed on the Kurdish areas or in Maysan Province on the Iranian border. Even where the law was imposed, progress was very slow. After five years, only 6 percent of the confiscated land had actually been distributed to 29 000 cultivators and only 25 co-operatives had been formed so new small landowners lacked financial and technical support (Owen and Pamuk 1999, pp. 164–5). Since Iraqi agriculture still reflects the multiple impacts of the 1958 Law, it would be valuable to discuss five of the unexpected consequences of this law.

First, the division between irrigated, un-irrigated, and non-farm land was often difficult to establish. If annual rains are early and heavy then some fields that are usually irrigated might be rain fed. On the other hand, during a drought, irrigated areas will increase. Since large landowners were generally educated, politically influential, and had access to financial assets, they were often able to get favorable rulings on the nature of land in order to maximize the amount that they were allowed to retain.

Second, the large landowners tended to choose their 1000 or 2000 donums portions so that they controlled access to water and transportation. The cultivators on the remaining land often had difficulty in obtaining access to water and markets on a timely basis. As a result, many recipients of land were unable to support their families by farming and were forced to abandon the land and seek better living conditions in urban areas. The total amount of land under cultivation therefore declined.

Third, the 1958 Law was silent on tractors and other equipment. As a result, many large landowners took all or the best equipment to work their remaining holdings. The 1958 Law called for the establishment of farmers' co-operatives to provide equipment to small cultivators but these co-operatives generally failed to meet cultivators' requirements.

Fourth, on large land holdings, fields were previously allowed to remain fallow every other year in order to restore their fertility. Small cultivators could not afford to do without earnings during a fallow year and the resulting constant cropping led to a rapid loss in fertility or required increasing amounts of costly chemical fertilizer.

Fifth, the government was unable to rapidly distribute the expropriated land to cultivators. As a result, the government became the largest landowner. Also the government-sponsored co-operatives lacked both the knowledge and equipment to support the small cultivators that had received redistributed land. Over time, cultivator support for these co-operatives decreased and they became part of the government's efforts to control farmers (Mahdi 2000, Chapter 7; Owen and Pamuk 1999, pp. 169–71; Rivlin 2009, pp. 139–40).

Attempts to deal with these unintended consequences of the 1958 Land Reform Law as well as the impact of the Iran–Iraq War, Invasion of Kuwait, sanctions, and the 2003 invasion by US-led coalition forces led to a complicated series of often-reversed often-contradictory agricultural policies. (For a detailed discussion of the twists and turns of land reform, two works by Kamil Mahdi stand out: *State and Agriculture in Iraq* (2000) and *Iraq's Economic Predicament* (2002).) The most substantial impact of the extreme uncertainty concerning land ownership rights has been to create a short-term perspective among farmers.

Despite the drive for food independence over the last two decades, Iraq remains dependent on imports for most of its grain consumption while the Iraqi people obtain a great deal of their daily calorie intake, not from a market, but from a government run food distribution system – the PDS.

PUBLIC DISTRIBUTION SYSTEM

The PDS is a monthly distribution or "basket" of 11 food and household items. It is estimated that almost one million Iraqis are food-insecure while an additional 6.4 million Iraqi's are on the edge of food-insecurity. In the absence of the PDS, these 6.4 million would join the ranks of the food-insecure (WFP 2010, p. 2). The PDS is less than 15 years old and is one of the most popular government programs in Iraq.

The international sanctions imposed on Iraq after its 1990 invasion of Kuwait led to severe food shortages. To maintain political support, the GoI began to distribute certain foods. This program expanded after the 1995 establishment of the incredibly corrupt United Nations Oil for Food program, which allowed Saddam's Iraq to export oil in exchange for imported food. Under the PDS, every Iraqi is supposed to receive a monthly "basket" of basic food items in return for minimal payments. In early 2010, the per-person amounts were: wheat flour (9 kg), rice (3 kg), sugar (2 kg), milk for adults (250 g), children's milk (1.8 kg), tea (200 g), beans (250 g), tomato paste (500 g), cooking oil (1 liter), soap (250 g), and detergents (500 g) (IRIN 2010b). According to surveys, PDS items account for a large proportion of food consumed by Iraqis. For example, the average family received 90 percent of their total consumption of wheat flour and 74 percent of their rice consumption from their PDS basket (COSIT 2008, Table 7-00, p. 396).

Most of the PDS food is imported and then delivered to over 400 warehouses. Then thousands of local grain merchants obtain the food from the warehouses and distribute it once a month to each family's representative. The PDS, although managed by the Ministry of Trade, is actually executed by a combination of private firms and SOE. While the SOE handle food imports, warehouse operation, and rice processing; under contract with the Ministry of Trade, private firms handle transportation within Iraq, wheat processing, and retail operations (World Bank 2006a, p. 51).

The PDS baskets are not free and many Iraqis report paying amounts for their PDS baskets that are in excess of the official fees. According to one survey, in addition to the average ration fee of 489 ID ($0.42), Iraqis pay an average "bagging" fee of 37 ID ($0.03), and the average cost of transporting the PDS baskets to residences is approximately 236 ID ($0.20) making a total of 762 ID ($0.65) per PDS basket. While ration and bagging fees are about the same across Iraq, the delivery cost is approximately 20 percent greater in rural areas (COSIT 2008, Table 7-00, p. 384).

As a result of corruption on the part of the Ministry of Trade and the entities that operate the PDS, much of the better quality food imports intended for the PDS are diverted into the Iraqi or foreign markets and either lower quality items were substituted or the items were not provided that month. One survey showed that over 80 percent of the baskets nationwide were missing one or more items. The Ministry of Trade is considered to be one of the most corrupt ministries in Iraq and, in 2009, the former Minister of Trade, Abdul Falah al-Sdani, was arrested and charged with corruption in relation to imports for the PDS baskets (IRIN 2010a).

How much is each PDS basket worth? A 2007 survey put the value per monthly basket at approximately 36900 ID (about $31) (COSIT 2008, Table 7-10, p. 420). In other words, if the average Iraqi were to receive $31 then he or she should be able to purchase all of the items in the PDS basket in local markets.

If the value of a basket is $31 then how much does each PDS basket cost? This is a difficult question. Published data on the PDS by the Ministry of Trade is incomplete and is generally considered unreliable. According to the national budget, in 2009 social safety net expenditures, of which PDS is the major component, amounted to 6.2 trillion ID (about $5.3 billion or roughly 10 percent of total GoI current expenditures) (IMF 2010b, Table 2, p. 28). There was almost universal participation in the PDS in 2009 therefore per person per month cost of the national social safety net was about 17 200 ID ($14.65). However, this figure fails to include the salaries, pension costs, and so on of the Ministry of Trade employees. Even if employee compensation were included, this would still be an underestimate since it fails to include subsidies received by the Ministry of Trade for electricity, water, and fuel.

Iraqi households purchase many food items that are not available in the food baskets especially fresh fruit and meat. As a result, despite receiving heavily subsidized food, most Iraqis still spend a significant portion of their household income on food. While there is a wide divergence across provinces, the average Iraqi household spent almost 36 percent of its total expenditures on foodstuffs and non-alcoholic beverages. For comparison, the next highest categories of expenditures were dwellings (including water, gas, electricity, and fuel) that accounted for 29 percent, and transport at 10 percent (COSIT 2008, Table 8-3, p. 448). As expected, supplementary food purchases beyond the PDS food basket were greatest for higher income households.

What is Wrong with PDS?

The PDS, as currently structured, is an expensive program that distorts incentives for both domestic food production and consumption. However, modifications of the PDS run the risk of increasing the food vulnerability of the poor and will be resisted by the bureaucracy.

The impact of the PDS on GoI budget expenditures can be viewed from two contradictory perspectives. First, the PDS represents a transfer of oil export earnings to, until the recent exclusion of higher income government workers, almost every household in Iraq. It is possible to defend this transfer as favoring more diversified economic development. One might think of the monthly PDS basket as being the Iraqi equivalent of the annual check that each Alaskan resident receives from that state's oil production.

A second perspective on the impact of the PDS on the GoI budget is that the PDS funds could be better used for other government expenditures.

The PDS is an inefficient welfare program in that the cost per basket is high compared to the market value of the food provided, and the baskets go to many high-income individuals. The GoI with the assistance of the UN World Food Program, has begun a multi-year program to decrease the cost of each basket while excluding high-income individuals as recipients. But even if these cost reductions are achieved and the number of recipients reduced, the adverse impact of the PDS on both consumption and agricultural production will continue.

Most of the cereal distributed as part of the PDS is imported by the Ministry of Trade, which has resulted in lower domestic food prices. There are regulations that forbid the export of grains. As a result, Iraqi grain farmers find it difficult to sell their production in Iraqi markets at a price that covers their true costs of production. In order to prevent the complete collapse of domestic grain production, the Ministry of Agriculture not only provides water, fertilizer, and seed free or at heavily subsidized prices but also purchases the output at non-market prices. With the GoI determining input and output prices for grain producers, these farmers are really government employees – one step removed.

The PDS also distorts consumers' incentives. Since the items in the basket are available at a fraction of market prices, these increase the relative prices of items such as fresh fruit and meat. As expected, this has led the poor to consume a diet deficient in these relatively expensive items (World Bank 2006a, p. 52).

Of course, the PDS also represents a substantial increase in family income, in that families do not have to purchase PDS items which frees up income for other purchases. Such transfers almost double the effective household income of poor households. If instead of a PDS basket, the head of a family received its cash equivalent of approximately 36 900 ID ($31) per person then he or she might prefer to purchase non-food items such as medical care, education, and so on. While recipients have the option of trading or selling items from their basket, the local markets for these items are so inefficient that there is a strong incentive for Iraqi families to consume the basket items rather than sell or trade them. Therefore, the PDS probably increases the proportion of income that is spent on food.

AGRICULTURAL POLICY

Government's Role in Agriculture

The recent history of agricultural policy among developing countries is riddled with market and government failures. Programs introduced with great enthusiasm are quietly abandoned years or decades later after their unexpected consequences become too serious to ignore (Stiglitz 1987, pp. 400–403). Economic development theory identifies three possible government roles in agriculture that have been popular sequentially over the last six decades (Timmer 2005, pp. 394–6). First, there is benign neglect. This approach is usually accompanied by the belief that industry is the key driver of economic development and trust that open market economies will outperform economies closed to international trade and finance. This policy of benign neglect roughly describes the situation in Iraq through the 1950s.

The second possible role for agriculture is as part of an integrated development plan. The government develops, coordinates, and executes a detailed plan that incorporates all sectors of the economy including agriculture. Agriculture product and input prices are managed along with quantitative restrictions especially with respect to foreign trade and sometimes with respect to regional trade within a country. To the extent that the Arab Ba'athist Socialist Party had an explicit agricultural policy, it was one of state control primarily to achieve food security (GoI 2010, Section 5.1, p. 62). However, as was discussed above, this policy was subject to many contradictions and reversals based on the state of government finance and access to imported food. It gradually became apparent that government planners lacked both the necessary information to efficiently manage agriculture as well as effective tools to force farmers to act precisely according to the plan.

The third possible role is an awkward combination of the first two. Having recognized that direct government intervention to correct market failures in agriculture frequently leads to a further deterioration while the free market approach miscarries due to "missing" markets especially with respect to risk contingencies, a combined approach is attempted. The government reserves the right to intervene but limits its intervention to influencing key agricultural prices rather than direct quantitative intervention.

At this high level of abstraction, Iraq might be viewed as gradually moving from the direct quantitative intervention of the second approach to the "market policy" third approach. However, if the *National Development Plan: 2010–2014* is an accurate guide to GoI agricultural policy then the government reserves the right to continue to intervene in agricultural markets especially in the areas of irrigation infrastructure (GoI 2010, pp. 73–5). Progress should be expected to be uneven not only because the third approach is very demanding with respect to data and analysis, but also because there is a large sector of the bureaucracy that sees the abandonment of the direct intervention approach as reducing their authority.

As in previous chapters, there is a strong temptation to provide a long list of difficulties along with possible methods of ameliorating them. However, in view of the limited capability of the GoI for making rapid extensive structural changes, if might be more useful to focus on a few initiatives that aim at relaxing the more serious binding constraints.

Water Reform

The increased water usage in Turkey, Syria and, to a lesser extent, Iran combined with the increased Iraqi household and industrial use and widespread irrigation waste are expected to lead to a growing water shortage over the foreseeable future. The sheer complexity of these water-related challenges facing Iraq would probably defeat any attempt to resolve them by better planning and coordination at the ministerial level. Even disregarding the continuing problem of corruption at the Ministries of Trade, Agriculture, and Water, there is a shortage of personnel with the appropriate skills set to accurately estimate the costs and benefits of water usage throughout Iraq or to manage this complex system even if the cost-benefit analysis is completed in a timely manner.

The alternative of establishing a formal market price for water would be extremely controversial. Of course, water is already bought and sold informally under several guises. In urban areas, families often buy potable water from tanker trucks rather than risk the possibility of disease from the low-quality free water available from the public system. Entities including tribes that control the distribution of irrigation water expect financial, physical, or political support in return. Government officials are widely believed to be open to bribes to divert water. Finally, access to cheap (or free) irrigation water has become capitalized into the value of land. In fact, cultivators can be expected to resist creating a positive water price or raising existing water prices since this will lead to a drop in the rental value – a partial expropriation – of their land (Richards and Waterbury 2008, p. 173). In addition, at least one ministerial spokesperson stated publicly, without collaborating details, that selling water violates the Qur'an.

However, a formal pricing of water would provide the proper incentives for not only the efficient division of the scarce resource among alternative uses but also the efficient use by end users. Water charges should reflect not only the volume of water but its quality and timeliness as well.

One option is to divide the provision of water into a merit good amount that should be provided to everyone at low or zero price with any demand above this merit good amount priced at least at its marginal cost. For example, every Iraqi would receive his or her minimum water right of, say, 125 m^3/yr but any use of water above this amount must be purchased

(Richards and Waterbury 2008, pp. 165–6). Since the primary determinates of water supply: the dams, barrages, major irrigation canals, and urban water systems, will remain under public control, it will be necessary for the authorities to set an official price for all water above the minimum water right. The most efficient price would equal the long-run marginal cost of water – the cost of supplying an additional liter of water. Currently, among Middle Eastern countries, only Syria charges such a price (Richards and Waterbury 2008, p. 178, endnote 21). However, as is discussed in Chapter 11, in view of the large-scale corruption, Iraq may be better off charging its average cost – including capital costs – than the theoretically more appealing marginal cost.

If water is sold then it is likely that Iraqi agriculture will become the residual claimant. Surveys show that household demand is more inelastic than that of industry, which is more inelastic than agriculture (Richards and Waterbury 2008, p. 167). Facing a substantially higher cost of water will have both an income and price effect on farmers. Paying for water will not only reduce farmers' net income but also reduce the value of their land (by eliminating the land's capitalized water value). If this income effect is not offset then one can expect many farmers to abandon agriculture and migrate to urban areas. One method of dealing with this income effect would be to grant water rights to farmers and allow them to either use the associated water or sell the rights to others.

With a positive water price, strong incentives would be created to reduce water waste possibly by covering canals to reduce evaporation, repairing leaks, utilizing sprinkler or drip irrigation, and selecting crops that are less water intensive. Among grains, rice is extremely water intensive and would not be as popular a crop in Iraq in the absence of large water subsidies. In view of the estimates that over half of current irrigation water is wasted, increases in efficiency should allow more land to be brought under cultivation.

However, fighting water scarcity through improved irrigation efficiency is not a cure-all. Unintended consequences may include a reduction in the quality of water especially if there is an accelerated expansion of urban and industrial water use (Richards and Waterbury 2008, p. 170). In addition, while more efficient water use can be expected to reduce salt poisoning of the soil by lowering the water table, it will make it more expensive to flood fields in order to leach out existing salts.

The restoration and maintenance of the dams, barrages, and irrigation canals will be a major burden on both the budget and the administrative competence of the appropriate ministries. Since this subject is covered in Chapter 11, only a single example will be mentioned here. Due to poor site selection and inappropriate construction, the major dam on the Tigris river northwest of Mosul has been in a process of slow-motion collapse since before it was completed. Daily reinforcement of the dam's foundation has so far prevented disaster but a permanent repair may require temporarily draining the huge lake behind the dam with implications for irrigation and other downstream users.

Land Reform

The series of contradictory land reform initiatives since 1958 have resulted in a great deal of uncertainty about agricultural land ownership. This uncertainty has encouraged a focus on short-term gains since cultivators and others (who uncomfortably share land ownership rights in Iraq) lack the confidence that current legal relationships will not be overturned. The GoI proposals to further reform the legal environment of the agricultural sector (see GoI 2010, p. 75) further exacerbate this uncertainty.

The most needed land reform in Iraq is a long-term commitment to cease land reform. This would gradually lead to a longer-term perspective on the part of the cultivators and others, which would increase their willingness to invest in the land. Since the GoI lacks credibility, any announcement that no further land reform initiatives are planned will probably have little effect on incentives. However, if the central government can avoid making any land reform proposals for an extended period of time then gradually farmer behavior will change.

PDS

The PDS situation is complex. It provides essential nutrition to many poor families in Iraq – without the PDS the rate of malnutrition would be much greater. However, as currently structured, it combines strong incentives for corruption with disincentives for domestic agriculture. Two overlapping recommendations have received attention. One option would be to exclude high-income families from receiving the PDS baskets. In addition to reducing the cost of the PDS subsidy, this would force higher income families to increase their purchases in the local food markets providing more opportunity for local producers.

In fact, the GoI is currently engaged in an effort to reduce the expense of the PDS program by reducing its coverage. Ministerial employees who earn more than 1.5 million ID per month (about $1300) are being excluded from the PDS distribution lists. About 70 000 government employees exceed this limit; which, since their family members would be excluded as well should lead to an eventual reduction of 300 000 to 500 000 persons on the PDS rolls. In 2010, the GoI began the difficult process of attempting to identify high earners in the private sector so their families can also be excluded from receiving PDS baskets (IRIN 2010b). By restricting this pruning effort to high-income families only, the GoI is seeking to reduce the burden of the PDS on the national budget and provide a significant increase in domestic food demand while avoiding any increase the probability of malnutrition.

A second option would be to gradually replace the PDS baskets with their cash equivalent (GoI 2007, p. 17). For example, the head of the family would have the option each month of accepting the PDS basket or the value in ID of the basket. If the choice, quality, and prices of food in the local market were acceptable, many families would choose the cash equivalent. This would not only increase demand for domestic agricultural products but also make corruption in the PDS system more difficult. It is easier for local grain distributors to pass a counterfeit food product (for example substitute lower quality cooking oil) then to pass counterfeit money. As was discussed above, it will be difficult to determine the cost of replacing each PDS item in the local markets. Offering each family head the choice of taking either the food basket or the estimated cash equivalent would provide a mechanism to ensure that the cash offered was sufficient. If most heads of families chose to take the food basket then this will make it clear to the government that the cash alternative is insufficient.

Agribusiness

While farming in Iraq is unlikely to provide employment growth, there is potential for substantial growth from agribusiness involving the processing, packaging, transporting, and selling of agricultural products. A large amount of Iraq's food imports are such items as frozen chickens and canned tomatoes that could potentially be produced domestically. However, it is important to distinguish between the potential for grain and non-grain agribusiness development.

Because of the complex web of subsidies, non-market prices and detailed regulations, it is extremely difficult to determine the true cost – the market cost – of wheat and rice production in Iraq. Complicating any analysis is the fact that average productivity of cereal growers in Iraq is poor even by Middle Eastern standards. It can be argued that if the web of regulations, subsidies, and price controls were rationalized then this would lead to a substantial increase in the productivity of cereal production.

However, it is unlikely, after all costs are considered and adjusting for quality, that Iraq will be able to produce cereals for the domestic market cheaper than imported wheat (from, say, Argentina, Australia, Brazil, Canada, and the USA) or imported rice (from Thailand and the USA).

Even if the policy-imposed inefficiencies are disregarded, the barriers to efficient grain production are still high. Water is scarce and expected to become scarcer in the future. This is especially true for rice which uses about three times more water per hectare than vegetables and six times more water than wheat. In addition, Iraq lacks the large farms with advanced machinery that exemplifies high-quality, low-cost, large-scale wheat production. Finally, oil dominance of exports has contributed to a severe case of the "Dutch disease" appreciation of the ID that has resulted in lower prices for imported products.

One strategy for dealing with this long-term lack of competitiveness in Iraqi grain production is to accept the necessity of continuing large-scale subsidies in order to preserve domestic production, rural life, and employment. Of course, this is a political decision. But there are at least two economic issues that should be considered. First, as is discussed throughout this book, Iraq faces many expensive claims on its national budget. Unless there is a sharp increase in petroleum export volumes combined with higher world oil prices – a somewhat contradictory combination of events – the government and people of Iraq will have to choose. Funds spent on subsidizing grain production will not be available for other needs. Second, the subsidies and regulations necessary to preserve large Iraqi grain production have severely distorted the incentives facing cultivators.

While the trend is adverse, Iraq still possesses a generous water supply – compared to other countries in the region – and large skilled agricultural labor force. Therefore, Iraq has the potential of becoming a large food source in the Middle East. But rather than focus on grain production for the domestic market, it is probably more beneficial for the country to follow its comparative advantage in labor-intensive fruits, vegetables, and non-cattle meat such as goats and chickens. This will not only provide for domestic consumption and, if the challenges of processing and transportation can be solved, substantial exports. Especially since Iraq is surrounded by relatively prosperous nations that, with the exception of Turkey, are major food importers.

Iraq's crude oil exports supplemented by agribusiness exports based on fruit, vegetables, and meat will allow the importation of grain and grain products at lower opportunity costs than if these items were produced domestically. In one sense, Iraq is in an enviable situation with respect to international commodity trade because the relative price of its major export, crude oil, has increased substantially relative to that of its major import, wheat. In 1970, a barrel of crude oil sold for only about one-third more than a bushel of wheat ($1.33 per bushel and $1.80 per barrel). However, by 2009, a barrel of oil sold for almost ten times more than a bushel of wheat ($6.78 per bushel and $67.10 per barrel).

Farmers' own-price elasticity is low for example a rise in grain prices will not lead to a significant increase in grain production. But, at the same time, farmers' cross-price elasticity of supply is high for example a fall in grain prices relative to fruit prices will lead to a significant shift from grain production to fruit production. In other words, farmers tend to be highly responsive to price signals among crops (Richards and Waterbury 2008, pp. 161, 163). Therefore, in order to motivate cultivators to shift from grain production to products where Iraq has comparative advantage will require changing relative prices.

Changing the relative prices of grain and other crops can be done either: (1) by reducing or eliminating the subsidies for grain production; or (2) by imposing or increasing subsidies for non-grain agricultural production. The first option should result in greater efficiency over time. The *National Development Strategy 2007–2010* (GoI 2007, p. 36) noted that initial steps had been made towards enabling markets in agricultural inputs but progress has been uneven. Unfortunately, the GoI is also using the second option. In early 2010, the GoI imposed an import ban on tomatoes with the expected results. This reflects in part the inertia of statist economies that find it much more acceptable to impose a new distortion in an economy then remove an existing distortion. The import ban has resulted in a rise in tomato prices and farmers seem to be working towards increasing future production. However, the rise in prices has reduced tomato consumption among low-income families and it is expected that corruption will increase as a result of increased smuggling.

Of course, increasing reliance on market prices in Iraq's food economy will not guarantee that the country will experience higher quality, lower prices, and increased agribusiness employment. But without a rationalization of the prices of agriculture inputs and products, it is unlikely that substantial progress towards national agricultural goals will be met. Agricultural price reform is not a sufficient condition for economic growth but it is necessary.

8. Financial intermediation

> In the eighteenth century BCE: Grain and other valuables in Uruk and
> other Sumerian cities were stored in temples. Some argue that these
> temples, reposing on the safest shores of the Tigris and Euphrates,
> became the first institutions to issue inscribed tablets, or tokens, as
> 'receipts' for valuable deposits or trade purposes. It has been said
> that those secure and trusted institutions of safekeeping in ancient
> Mesopotamia were in fact the precursors of modern depository 'banks'.
> (Edwin Black 2004, p. 17)

Along with corruption and a hostile regulatory environment (Chapters 4
and 10), Iraq's dysfunctional banking system completes a trifecta of bad
policy that both impedes improvement in the average Iraqi's quality of
life and severely complicates the GoIs attempts to diversify the economy.
Checking accounts, credit cards, and simple electronic transfers are generally unavailable; as a result, most transactions are in cash, and with this
brings all of the associated security problems and inefficiencies. There are
few ATMs and mortgage loans are rare. For a private business to borrow
is a complex and drawn out process. Even if a loan is eventually approved,
private businesses can only borrow small amounts at a high interest rate
and only after pledging substantial collateral. Even the use of banks as a
safe place to keep funds is limited. With only about 900 bank branches in
a country of 31 million people, Iraq is the most "under-banked" country
among the MENA countries (Kami and Bayoumy 2012). Only about 10
percent of all Small and Medium Enterprises (SME) in Iraq have a bank
account.

Efficient financial intermediation serves several important purposes. It
facilitates the conversion of private savings into much needed investment.
Also, by providing bill paying and other services, financial intermediaries reduce the transaction costs of business. Finally, it aids the monetary
authorities in their difficult balancing act of providing sufficient liquidity to maximize real activity in the economy without fueling inflation.
Providing the appropriate regulatory framework to allow financial intermediaries to achieve these ends is difficult and especially so in countries
like Iraq that are attempting to make the transition from socialism to a
more market-oriented economy.

As a measure of the long path ahead in achieving reasonable efficiency in financial intermediation, it should be noted that the contribution of the banking and insurance sector to Iraq's GDP is very small even by MENA country standards. In 2010, it was estimated that Iraqi banks extended $8.1 billion of credit to the economy or less than 10 percent of GDP. The average for MENA countries was about 55 percent (Kami and Bayoumy 2012).

As a result of its socialist past, financial intermediation in Iraq is dominated by banking and the banking system is moribund. The two state-owned banks, Rafidain and Rasheed Banks, were once the leading financial institutions of the Middle East. Despite their relative deterioration, they still overshadow their private sector competition in Iraq. At the end of 2010, the Rafidain and Rasheed Banks, along with one large and four smaller state-owned banks, possessed estimated total assets of about 61.3 trillion ID – about $52 billion. This is equal to roughly 86 percent of all bank assets in Iraq. The state-owned banks have a nationwide system of branches that include most cities and large towns but generally exclude smaller towns and villages. With possibly one exception, these public banks are believed to be insolvent and grossly mismanaged. They generally suffer from large-scale over-employment and are extremely bureaucratic.

As of the end of 2011, there were also 42 private banks in operation. These private banks account for the remaining 14 percent of total banking assets. While these private banks have an estimated 383 branches, their branches are generally only located in major cities and provincial capitals. There are many large towns without any private bank branches. While it is difficult to obtain timely audited accounting statements, it is thought that about half of the private banks are insolvent. Most of the private bank's management personnel are former employees of Rafidain Bank and the quality of management varies widely.

Although it is technologically advanced, the Iraqi Stock Exchange (ISX) has a relatively low-market capitalization, only about 85 listed firms, very light daily trading, and almost all trading is in private bank shares. Future expansion of the ISX is dependent more on a substantial reduction in the GoIs regulatory hostility towards private business rather than any technical fixes of the exchange's operations.

Like banking, the nation's insurance business and pension funds are dominated by state-owned entities and these entities focus on providing insurance and pension services to other state-owned entities. Private sector insurance and pension services are in their infancy.

IRAQ'S UNBALANCED BANKING INDUSTRY

Public Banks

In 1965, the GoI nationalized all Iraqi private banks and all branches of foreign commercial banks. The government then gave Rafidain Bank, which had been established as a private bank in 1941, a monopoly of all banking in the country. In addition to providing banking services, Rafidain also acts as an executive fiscal agent for the GoI responsible for making government disbursements, transferring tax receipts, borrowing on the government's behalf, and making policy loans to SOE. Due to its fiscal responsibilities, Rafidain administratively fell under the Ministry of Finance rather than the CBI. Over the last two decades, Rafidain's net worth has deteriorated.

Public banks were forced to make loans to politically favored individuals and institutions and then roll over these loans in lieu of repayment. As a result, Rafidain's "bad loan" portfolio boomed during the economic turmoil of the 1980–1988 Iraq–Iran War. In addition, Saddam and his family used the banks' deposits as personal sources of ready cash. Also, in a problem that continues until today, there was an absence of reliable timely audited accounting information. In 1988, the GoI attempted to deal with Rafidain's devastated balance sheet by establishing a new bank, Rasheed Bank, and transferring the bulk of Rafidain's bad loans to the new institution. Although, Rasheed Bank's total assets are only about 5 percent of those of Rafidain, it is currently the third largest bank in Iraq with the second largest number of branches (World Bank 2011a, p. 15, Annex 11, p. 175, Annex 17, p. 187).

In addition to the Rafidain and the Rasheed Banks, there are five other state-owned banks that specialize in various sectors: the Trade, Agricultural Cooperative, Real Estate, Industrial, and Iraq Banks. The Trade Bank, established in 2004, is the second largest bank in Iraq by assets and focuses on supporting foreign trade and investment. It was created in response to Saddam-era lawsuits in several nations that made the assets of the existing financial intermediaries vulnerable to attachment. The Trade Bank is one of the few state-owned banks that not only has audited accounts but also publishes them online. Since it was originally intended to be a temporary fix pending a resolution of the foreign lawsuit problem, the Trade Bank of Iraq was not integrated into the existing financial regulatory system. As a result, the Trade Bank, until 2011, was perceived to have a degree of independence exceeding that of other state-owned or even private banks. However, in that year, the GoI replaced the Chairman of the Trade Bank with a former Rafidain Bank manager in an effort to reduce its independence (Gutman 2011, p. 3).

Private Banks

As of the end of 2011, there were 42 private banks in Iraq composed of 23 conventional banks, 11 Islamic banks, and eight banks with partial foreign ownership (CBI 2012a). However, firm specific data is not available for the six banks that were established in 2011: three conventional banks, two Islamic banks, and one foreign bank. Therefore, the following discussion focuses on the 36 private banks that were established prior to 2011. At the end of 2010, these banks had 383 branches and collectively reported total assets of 9.7 trillion ID ($8.3 billion). There is a wide divergence among private banks in age, asset size, number of branches, organizational structure, and business strategy.

The oldest private bank and the second largest private bank by total assets, the Bank of Baghdad, was established in 1992 but almost two-thirds of the nation's banks are less than a decade old, established after the 2003 overthrow of Saddam's regime. Private banks range widely in size. There are six banks with more than 500 billion ID ($427 million) in assets: Warka Bank for Investment and Finance – the largest private bank, Bank of Baghdad, Iraqi Middle East Bank for Investment, North Bank for Finance and Investment, United Bank for Investment, and Credit Bank of Iraq. At the other extreme, there are two banks with less than 10 billion ID ($9 million) each in assets. It is expected that the smaller banks will merge with their larger competitors since the CBI has announced that all private banks must meet minimum capital standards by mid-2013.

Most private banks have their headquarters in Baghdad although ten have their headquarters in Arbil in the KRG and one bank headquarters is located in Mosul in Ninawa province. Private banks have relatively few branches with the exceptions of Warka Bank's 61 branches and Bank of Baghdad's 31 branches. None of the private banks has branches in all 18 provinces of Iraq.

With respect to organizational structure, private banks can be divided into three types. There are 20 conventional banks with 194 branches that are neither Islamic nor have more than 10 percent foreign ownership. These conventional banks collectively possess total assets of 4.9 trillion ID ($4.2 billion) equivalent to about half of all private bank assets and about 7 percent of the nation's total bank assets including state-owned banks. The largest conventional bank is the North Bank for Finance and Investment (total assets of 0.8 trillion ID/$700 million) established in 2004.

At the end of 2010, seven private banks with partial foreign ownership had licenses to operate in Iraq. Foreign ownership ranged from 49 percent to 85 percent with three banks having majority foreign ownership: Credit

Bank of Iraq (75 percent owned by National Bank of Kuwait and 10 percent owned by World Bank International Finance Corporation), Dar Alsalam Investment Bank (70 percent owned by HSBC), and Mansour Bank for Investment (60 percent owned by National Bank of Qatar). Of the banks with partial foreign ownership, Dar Alsalam-HSBC is generally considered to have the most advanced operations. Banks with foreign ownership have 137 branches and total assets of 2.7 trillion ID ($2.3 billion) which is equivalent to about 28 percent of private bank assets and about 4 percent of the nation's total bank assets. Aside from security issues – much improved since 2007 – the binding constraint to a more rapid expansion of foreign banking in Iraq is the difficulty in hiring skilled local personnel especially for management positions.

Research has shown that when foreign ownership of a bank exceeds roughly 70 percent, there are measurable increases in banking efficiency. Of course, this increase in efficiency tends to promote economic development. However, in some former socialist countries, the expansion of foreign-owned banks has tended to increase banking concentration as less-efficient domestically owned banks lose market share (Haiss et al. 2005, p. 4).

Finally, there are nine Islamic banks that are dedicated to Sharia compliant operations. These Islamic banks have 52 branches and total assets of 2.0 trillion ID ($1.7 billion) which is equivalent to 21 percent of private bank assets and about 2 percent of the nation's total bank assets.

There are no Islamic banking regulations or even a consensus among Islamic legal authorities on the exact necessary characteristics of Islamic financial institutions. However, such institutions generally seek to avoid "riba" (usually translated as interest), "gharar" (risk or uncertainty), and "maysir" (gambling). In addition, Islamic financial institutions seek to avoid supporting activities that are "haram" (forbidden activities or products such as alcohol consumption, pork, or pornography). These restrictions are interpreted within the Sharia framework that good Muslims should practice brotherhood, ensure the fair remuneration of labor, and provide alms to the poor – "zakat". Islamic banks have a Sharia committee to ensure that the banks' activities are compliant.

Restrictions on interest and some other financial activities should not be interpreted to mean a generalized religious hostility to capitalism. Visser (2009, p. 48) quotes Mahmud Ahmad on the differences between capitalist, socialist, and Islamic economics: "Capitalism accepts both profit and interest, socialism rejects both, and Islam accepts the profit motive but rejects interest". As discussed in Chapter 10, far from being hostile to business, many historically prominent Islamic religious leaders were successful businessmen.

The prohibition of "riba" or interest is the most prominent characteristic of Islamic finance. But interpreting this prohibition is complex
and permitted interest-related activities can vary not only among Islamic
countries but also among different institutions in the same country. (For
detailed discussions of the various Islamic views of economic activity,
see Kuran 2004, Chapter 5, pp. 103–20; Visser 2009, Chapter 3, pp.
25–51.)

For example, in Iraq, some Islamic banks permit interest to be paid on
deposits since this benefits an individual depositor rather than an institution. Restrictions on interest on loans are more common. But even on loan
transactions, some institutions distinguish between consumption and production loans. These institutions may allow interest on consumption loans
providing the loan terms are clear to the borrower, the loan only carries
simple – not compound – interest, and the rates are not unacceptably high.
With respect to loans for productive purposes, almost all Islamic financial
institutions in Iraq seek to avoid the prohibition on riba by structuring
transactions so that the lender shares the risk of loss from each loan transaction. One of the most widely used Sharia compliant means of structuring
such a transaction is "murabaha". An example of a murabaha transaction
would be where a manufacturer wants to purchase raw material for his
plant. Rather than a bank simply making a loan that would have to be
repaid regardless of whether the manufacturer made a profit, an Islamic
bank might purchase the raw material and provide it to the manufacturer
in return for a portion of the profits. If the manufacturer's initiative fails
then the bank also suffers a loss.

Islamic banking is a relatively recent innovation in Iraq, only two
institutions predate the fall of Saddam. So far, the general public's interest in doing business exclusively with Islamic banks appears to be limited
to some residents of the sacred cities of Shi'a and conservative Sunni in
Anbar province. Surveys show that most Iraqis consider Islamic banking
to be one of several options – they will borrow from wherever they can
obtain the best terms.

BANKING ASSETS AND LIABILITIES

State-Owned Banks

With respect to state-owned banks, Tables 8.1 and 8.2 reveal a straightforward pattern: state-owned banks obtain deposits from both government
and non-government entities and then lend these funds to government
entities. Over 80 percent of the liabilities of these banks are government or

Table 8.1   Bank assets (2010)

	Foreign assets	Deposits with CBI	Claims on govt	Credit to economy	Other assets	Total
7 State banks	19%	48%	13%	11%	9%	100% 60.3 T ID ($51.5 billion)
36 Private banks	14%	31%	7%	30%	18%	100% 9.7 T ID ($8.3 billion)
Of which: 20 Conventional	13%	30%	2%	37%	18%	100% 4.9 T ID ($4.2 billion)
Of which: 9 Islamic	15%	25%	0%	30%	30%	100% 2.0 T ID ($1.7 billion)
Of which: 7 Foreign owners	16%	36%	19%	18%	11%	100% 2.7 T ID ($2.3 billion)
43 Total banks	18%	46%	12%	13%	11%	100% 70.0 T ID ($59.8 billion)

Source: Table 8.1 is a modified version of World Bank (2011a), Table 4.2a, p. 20.

Table 8.2   Bank liabilities (2010)

	Foreign liabilities	Capital, reserves	Govt deposits	Non-govt deposits	Other liabilities	Total
7 State banks	3%	5%	32%	50%	10%	100% 60.3 T ID ($51.5 billion)
36 Private banks	0%	30%	0%	64%	6%	100% 9.7 T ID ($8.3 billion)
Of which: 20 Conventional	0%	32%	0%	60%	8%	100% 4.9 T ID ($4.2 billion)
Of which: 9 Islamic	0%	35%	0%	45%	20%	100% 2.0 T ID ($1.7 billion)
Of which: 7 Foreign owners	0%	27%	0%	71%	2%	100% 2.7 T ID ($2.3 billion)
43 Total banks	2%	9%	27%	51%	11%	100% 70.0 T ID ($59.8 billion)

Source: Table 8.2 is a modified version of World Bank (2011a), Table 4.2b, p. 20.

non-government deposits while over almost 60 percent of the assets are either deposits at the CBI, loans to government agencies, or loans to SOE. According to the official statistics, due to the high rate paid by the CBI on reserves, all of the state-owned banks are profitable; and, of course, due to their large holdings of reserves, they are very liquid (World Bank 2011a, p. 19).

In addition to the legal reserve requirement of 15 percent, the state-owned banks had almost 33 percent in excess reserves equivalent to almost 20.0 trillion ID ($17.0 billion). These excess reserves are almost three times the amount of credit provided to the non-government economy. Despite their inefficiencies, state-owned banks receive a large inflow of deposits for which the banks pay zero or low interest. Not only do government entities and state-owned enterprises deal almost exclusively with state-owned banks but also the Rafidain and the Rasheed Banks receive a large amount of deposits from private firms and individuals. The primary motivation for these deposits is the lack of other secure savings instruments and the almost universal belief that deposits at state-owned banks, unlike their private sector competitors, are guaranteed by the GoI.

Interest rates are not yet market determined in Iraq. Following a 2004 agreement between the CBI and Ministry of Finance, the CBI announced that, pending the development of a liquid secondary market in short-term GoI debt, the CBI will announce a Policy Rate that will signal its target not only for interbank overnight transactions but also provide a benchmark rate from which the overnight deposit as well as the rates at which the CBI will lend to banks will be determined (CBI 2004, p. 6). This policy rate was initially 6 percent, rose to 20 percent for 12 months in 2007/2008 as part of the anti-inflation campaign, before declining back to 6 percent in April 2010 where it remained through at least the end of May 2012.

Prior to 2009, the CBI paid an interest rate on reserves substantially above alternative possibilities. This encouraged banks to hold excess reserves which reduced the rate of monetary expansion. During this period, taking deposits and holding them as excess reserves was not only low risk but also very profitable for state-owned banks. Beginning in 2009, the CBI has attempted to reduce the amount of bank reserves through both a reduction in the policy rate – and therefore the rate paid on excess reserves – as well as reducing the legal reserve requirement. A complex system of five reserve requirements was simplified to a single 25 percent requirement in March 2009. This reserve requirement was reduced to 20 percent in April 2010 and then to 15 percent in September 2010 (CBI 2012b).

Private Banks

The pattern of assets and liabilities of Iraq's 36 private sector banks is very different from those of state-owned banks. As can be seen in Table 8.1, private banks have much greater relative exposure to the non-governmental economy than state-owned banks – 30 percent compared to 11 percent. However, because the total assets of state-owned banks are over six times larger, their total credit to the non-governmental economy is actually also larger than that of private banks – 6.5 trillion ID ($5.5 billion) compared to 2.9 trillion ID ($2.5 billion). It should also be noted that private banks have a lower proportion of their total assets on deposit with the CBI.

Another distinction between the assets of the state-owned and private banks is the breakdown of their loans. The three greatest recipients of the loans of state-owned banks are: social services that is, government (30 percent of all loans); wholesale, retail trade, and hotels (23 percent); and finance, insurance, real estate, and business services (6 percent). In contrast, almost two-thirds of private bank loans are to wholesale, retail trade, and hotels (67 percent); with the next most important sectors building and construction (11 percent); and finance, insurance, real estate, and business services (8 percent). Private bank loans for social services only accounted for 6 percent of all loans. While private banks are more willing to make small commercial loans, most of their loans are to larger entities. In fact, less than 5 percent of SME in Iraq's formal economy have ever received a bank loan (World Bank 2011a, p. xviii and Table 4.3, p. 22).

On the liabilities side, Table 8.2 shows three sharp differences between state-owned and private banks. First, private banks report zero deposits from government agencies since such agencies are legally forbidden to make deposits in private banks. Second, private banks have zero exposure to foreign entities. This is caused in part by legal limits on providing services to foreign entities. For example, the state-owned Trade Bank of Iraq has a monopoly on issuing letters of credit to finance trade although it may delegate low-value letter of credit authority to private banks. Finally, private banks have a greater percentage of bank capital, reserves, and loan-loss provisions than state-owned banks – 30 percent compared to 5 percent. Although in the absence of quality auditing, these estimates of bank capital, reserves, and loan-loss provisions should be taken with more than a few grains of salt.

As shown on Table 8.1, the asset distributions of conventional, Islamic, and foreign-owned banks are fairly similar with the possible exception of the fact that Islamic banks do not make loans to government agencies while foreign-owned banks actually lend more to government agencies than to non-government entities. This asset pattern of foreign-owned banks in Iraq differs from that in most post-socialist states where foreign banks tend to lend more to the private sector (Haiss et al. 2005, p. 5). When the two types of claims – loans to government and non-government entities – are added together, the range is small: conventional 39 percent, foreign owned 37 percent, and Islamic 30 percent. Table 8.2 tells a similar story on the liability side. The distribution of liabilities is fairly similar among the three types of private banks and very different from that of state-owned banks.

The loan process at both state-owned and private banks tends to be long drawn out and bureaucratic in part because a large percentage of all loans must be approved by the banks' Board of Directors (USAID 2007a, p. 23). There is a widespread belief that to obtain a bank loan requires connections or a bribe. For all of these reasons, state-owned or private banks rarely lend to smaller firms in the formal economy and entities of any size in the informal economy are excluded entirely.

CHALLENGES FACING IRAQI BANKING

Need for Recapitalization

With the possible exception of the Trade Bank, the state-owned banks suffer from opaque accounting systems. The banks generally either fail to release the standard banking data in a timely manner or use entirely unrealistic assumptions that severely distort the bank's situation. The most extreme cases of unrealistic data involve the foreign exchange transactions of the Rafidain and the Rasheed Banks. Acting as agents of the GoI, these banks borrowed large amounts denominated in foreign currencies and transferred the funds to the Ministry of Finance. However, as a result of the sharp depreciation of the ID in the decade prior to 2003, the foreign liabilities of these banks – in terms of ID – exploded. Despite a detailed plan developed by the GoI in 2006, the necessary recapitalization of these banks by the GoI has not begun nor have the discrepancies among state-owned banks' assets and liabilities been completely reconciled.

A 2008 study estimated that despite portfolios containing almost 60 percent of non-performing loans, the recapitalization requirements of Rafidain and Rasheed Banks although large were lower than expected since both banks loan portfolio was quite small. To bring both banks into compliance with Basel II (an international standard of safe levels of bank capital) would require 15.7 trillion ID ($13.4 billion) (IMF 2008b, Box 3, p. 16). This was equivalent to 18 percent of 2008 total budget expenditures or 14 percent of 2008 GDP. In addition to loan losses, there are also large discrepancies in the recorded assets and liabilities.

The Rafidain Bank situation is especially worrisome. Although this bank reported total assets of 302 trillion ID ($258 billion) at the end of 2010, possibly 85 percent of these assets reflected unrealized exchange rate losses. There is wide disagreement between the state-owned banks and the CBI on the scale of the unrealized losses but the World Bank has provided its own estimates on the actual total assets/liabilities of the state-owned banks and these estimates will be used throughout this chapter (World Bank 2011a, pp. 13–14). According to these estimates, the total assets of all state-owned banks were approximately 61.3 trillion ID ($52.4 billion) – about one-fifth of the unadjusted assets of the Rafidain Bank alone.

Rent-Seeking

It is believed that much of the exposure of state-owned banks to non-government entities is composed of loans to either bank employees or politically connected persons. These loans facilitate corruption since, in many cases, neither the borrowers nor the bank actually expect the loans to be paid back.

Lack of Deposit Insurance

Although non-government entities and persons account for almost two-thirds of private banks' total liabilities, further growth of such accounts is constrained by two factors. There is no program of deposit guarantees in Iraq so many depositors choose to keep their funds in state-owned institutions with their implicit government guarantee. Also, the Minister of Finance has decided that checks drawn on private banks would not be accepted for tax payments. This decision was based on the difficulty that the Ministry of Finance had with cashing the checks of two small private banks. As a result, all private bank checks are excluded for an undetermined length of time from being used for tax and other payments to the GoI, which further reduces the attractiveness of having a deposit account at a private bank.

Communication Issues

Among the complications of dealing with Iraqi banks is that not all banks have adopted "core banking". Core banking focuses on facilitating banking transactions by small businesses such as being able to make a deposit in one branch of a bank and withdraw the funds in another branch of the same bank with little delay. In Iraq, some banks have a substantial delay before deposits are recognized and any withdrawals must be from the same bank branch where the deposit was made (Kami and Bayoumy 2012). These delays and limited core banking help to support the dominance of cash in private and business transactions (*Reuters* 2011a).

Survey results show that private Iraqi businesses use cash for 87 percent of their purchases compared to only 13 percent of payments made with bank transfers (CIPE 2011, Chart A6, p. 47). Not only are loans to private businesses rare, it is very difficult for private businesses to arrange electronic fund transfers to pay their suppliers or employees, to establish a checking account, or to obtain a credit card (Gutman 2011, p. 1). Most banks do not offer ATM or credit card services nor can they arrange for international payments (Kami and Chaudhry 2011).

Lending to Private Entities

Loans to individuals or non-SOE firms are generally only made for short-term trade financing. Generally, collateral – at a multiple of the value of the loan – is required. There is little cash-flow lending. As a result, a survey of Iraqi businesses revealed that bank loans were only the fourth most important source of financing for private firms: business saving was the most important accounting for 43 percent of total financing; operating profits (33 percent); private savings (8 percent); and bank loans (7 percent). Difficulty of obtaining loans was cited by almost 50 percent of Iraqi private businesses as negatively affecting growth of their companies. As a related note, issuing equity accounted for almost none of private firm financing (CIPE 2008b, pp. 14, 26).

The Iraqi Company for Bank Guarantees (ICBG) was established by 11 Iraqi private banks in August 2007. The ICBG is intended to reduce the risk to banks of making Micro Small Medium Enterprises (MSME) loans. The ICBG now provides partial guarantees of both principal and interest for loans to MSME by member banks. Member banks can obtain a guarantee for up to 75 percent of the loan principle in return for a 2 percent loan guarantee fee. The allowable loans are extensive with loans to manufacturing, services, tourism, trade, and agriculture entities allowed. The major exclusion is loans to purchase other financial instruments. Loans are permitted for either cash-flow or collateral lending. Maturity is limited to one year for working capital and five years for loans for fixed assets (USAID 2007a, pp. 21–2).

MICROFINANCE INSTITUTIONS

Since 2003, 12 microfinance institutions (MFI) have been established in Iraq specializing in small loans to individuals and entities that lack access to state-owned or private banks either because of lack of collateral or because small loans tend to be unprofitable because of higher costs. Iraqi MFI have grown rapidly although their loans tend to be outliers compared to those of other MENA country MFI. Iraqi MFI tend to make larger loans with an average loan size of $1400 compared to $360 average in the rest of the MENA countries. Also, Iraqi MFI make fewer loans to women, 16 percent compared to almost 68 percent. In addition, Iraq MFI have a higher on-schedule repayment rate, almost 99 percent through the end of 2010 (USAID 2011, p. 10). Finally, Iraqi MFI loans are dominated by individual loans – 85 percent of the total – rather than solidarity group or Islamic loans that are more prevalent in the rest of the MENA countries (USAID 2011, p. 44).

The different pattern of Iraqi MFI lending compared to that of the rest of MENA is primarily a result of counterinsurgency operations. The US Government sought to use MFI loans as a way of reducing support for the insurgency by reducing unemployment among young men. As a result, MFI favored larger loans intended for production purposes to individual males rather than the smaller poverty-reduction loans to groups of women that are more common in the rest of the MENA countries. With the substantial improvement in security that began in approximately 2008, Iraqi MFI have gradually begun to shift their loan procedures in the direction of smaller solidarity group and Islamic loans to women. (For an extended discussion, see Gunter 2009b.)

At the end of 2010, as a result of rapid growth, these MFI had 75 200 loans outstanding for a total of 124 billion ID ($106 million). To provide a sense of scale, loans by public and private banks to non-government entities on the same date totaled about 9.4 trillion ID ($8 billion) (USAID 2011, p. 5).

Organizationally, ten of the MFI were established as domestic non-governmental organizations (NGO) while two were established as international NGO. Initially, the legal framework for Iraqi MFI was ambiguous and, in fact, some commentators argued that at least 11 of the MFI were illegal. However, in March 2010, MFI legality was clarified. There is a wide divergence in the size of MFI in Iraq with two – CHF International and Al Thiqa – accounting for almost 60 percent of MFI loan volume (USAID 2011, p. 19). Like banks, MFI face the challenge of making loans in the absence of reliable credit information as well as the difficulty in training and retaining management personnel. But MFI also face two unique challenges.

First, the Ministry of Labor and Social Affairs, the Ministry of Industry and Minerals, and the Ministry of Agriculture are making loans to the same types of borrowers as MFI. The Ministry of Labor and Social Affairs was established to assist workers seeking employment and protect Iraq's most vulnerable citizens through a network of social services. In October 2006, its responsibilities were expanded to create jobs by making low (or zero) interest loans (USAID 2007a, p. 2) on a very large scale. In fact, the first budget for this purpose was 600 billion ID ($510 million). This one-year budgeted amount is equal to roughly five times the total loans of all MFI. In the last several years, the Ministry of Industry and Minerals and Ministry of Agriculture have adopted or expanded similar programs. These loans are expected to injure MFI in several ways.

One concern is that as government bureaucracies, the Ministry of Labor and Social Affairs, the Ministry of Industry and Minerals, and the Ministry of Agriculture will be more concerned with the volume – not the quality – of loans. Officials will see their primary responsibility in lending out the full amount as soon as possible rather than ensuring that the borrowers will be able to pay it back. Also, interest rates on these loans are substantially below those charged by either private banks or MFI. A further concern is that the after a period of time the elected officials of the GoI will come under a great deal of political pressure to declare a debt holiday suspending or canceling loan repayments to government entitles (USAID 2011, pp. 16, 23).

It has been argued that the need for loans to micro and small enterprises is so great that there is plenty of room for both ministerial lending as well as MFI. However, the ministerial programs further weaken the culture of credit in Iraq. Individuals and businesses that have heard about low/zero interest government loans that allow repayment schedules to be continuously extended are confused when MFI officials explain that not only will interest be charged but also it is expected that loans will be repaid according to the contracted terms. Some potential borrowers are suspicious – and maybe rightfully so – that they are being stuck with less advantageous terms on their loans because they lack the proper connections.

Second, the long-term sustainability of MFI depends upon being able to charge a high enough interest rate to cover both the cost of funds as well as the costs of operation. Since they were established, Iraqi MFI obtained their loan capital mostly through grants supplemented by retained earnings. Since substantial expansion of lending is dependent on winning new grants, this has slowed the rate of growth of MFI lending. In many MENA countries, MFI also obtain loan capital by borrowing. However, if Iraqi MFI seek to expand their loan activities by borrowing then they run the risk of reduced competitiveness. For example, in 2010, MFI charged 12 percent to 15 percent interest (USAID 2011, p. 23). While sufficient to cover costs of operation, this interest rate did not include any cost of funds. If MFI begin to borrow funds to relend then the necessary interest rate will be 20 percent to 30 percent. This is almost twice the rate charged by state-owned and private banks and at least five times greater than the loan interest/fees charged on loans from the Ministry of Labor and Social Affairs, the Ministry of Industry and Minerals, and the Ministry of Agriculture . The limited access to loans from banks or MFI would not be as severe a challenge to the private sector if it had access to equity finance. However, such finance is in its infancy in Iraq.

IRAQI STOCK EXCHANGE

The ISX is relatively new and its trading is dominated by private bank shares. While the structure of the ISX is well designed for facilitating equity finance of Iraqi businesses, the regulatory hostility towards private businesses in Iraq – discussed at length in Chapter 10 – severely limits the usefulness of the ISX. In the absence of a radical change in private business regulations, attempts to further improve the operation of the ISX can be expected to have limited impact. Government securities with a maturity of one year are traded on a separate system operated by the CBI. Only banks currently have access to this system. There is no trading in government bonds with a maturity of greater than one year since the GoI has issued few such bonds. This partially explains the absence of a market in private sector bonds since there is no information on the "risk free" return on government bonds to allow realistic pricing of private bonds (World Bank 2011a, p. 54).

Founded in 2004, the ISX has a monopoly on securities trading in Iraq. In April 2012, there were 47 brokers and 85 listed companies. The total market capitalization of listed companies is approximately \$4 billion or 3.5 percent of GDP. Compared to the other stock exchanges in MENA countries, this ratio of market capitalization to GDP is extraordinarily low (World Bank 2011a, Table 6.1, p. 46).

Relatively few shares are traded. As can be seen in Table 8.3, the shares of only 66 out of the 87 listed companies traded on even a single day during April 2012; and bank shares accounted for most of this thin trading. The 22 private banks, while only one-quarter of companies listed, accounted for 39 percent of all trades and 81 percent of all shares traded.

Severe security concerns had an adverse impact on firms' profitability and even likelihood of firms' survival through the end of 2007. However,

The political economy of Iraq

Table 8.3   Overview of Iraqi Stock Exchange (April 2012)

	Companies listed	Companies traded	Number of trades	Traded shares
Banks	22 (25%)	17	39%	81%
Insurance	5 (6%)	4	2%	~0%
Investment	9 (10%)	3	~0%	1%
Services	10 (11%)	8	14%	2%
Industry	25 (29%)	19	26%	13%
Tourism and hotels	10 (11%)	9	13%	1%
Agriculture	6 (7%)	6	6%	2%
Total	87 (100%)	66	100%	100%

Source: ISX (2012).

despite the dramatic improvement in the security environment discussed in Chapter 1, stock market prices have been almost flat since early 2008 although with much month-to-month variance. More recently, the ISX stock index increased 35 percent in 2011 but fell by 15 percent in the first five months of 2012 (ISX 2012). Stock market optimists point to the fact that the non-Iraqis are free to purchase stock through the ISX except for restrictions on the percentage of bank shares that can be in foreign hands. There is also evidence that foreigners became strong buyers beginning in 2011. Since the ISX is well organized, the potential for increased foreign buying would seem to be substantial except for the general regulatory hostility towards private businesses, opaque firm balance sheets and income statements, and the absence of credit rating agencies.

The rules of the ISX are conservative. A buyer must have 100 percent of the necessary funds in his or her account before making a bid to buy a stock. A seller must have 100 percent of the necessary shares in his or her account before making an offer to sell a stock. All trades are electronic and settled through the Iraq Deposit Center (IDC) on a same-day basis (T+0). Neither short selling (borrowing a stock and selling it with the hope of buying back the same stock at a lower price in the future) nor derivatives (such as stock options) are currently allowed. However, some brokers have expressed interest in increasing the settlement period to one or two days (T+1 or T+2) as well as allowing trade in stock options (puts and calls). These changes would allow buyers to effectively purchase stock before accumulating the necessary funds or sellers to sell stock that they do not own on the date of the sale. The argument is that these changes would increase the activity and liquidity of the ISX by encouraging buyers to enter the market. However, it is unlikely that either of these changes will have a substantial impact on ISX activity in the absence of dealing with the binding constraint on investing in Iraqi equities – severe information asymmetry that strongly favors firm insiders. In addition, the conservative rules including T+0 settlements limit systematic risk (World Bank 2011a, p. 51). In view of the undermanned ISX staff assigned to monitor trades and the absence of clear relevant regulations, liberalization of the current trading rules would probably be destabilizing.

This information asymmetry in the ISX is caused both by the lack of reliable corporate data and an uncertain legal environment. As a result, corporate insiders – especially those who are politically connected – have access to more accurate information about corporate prospects that is not available at reasonable cost to outsiders. Company income statements and balance sheets are either unreliable or missing critical pieces of information. The asymmetry is partly a function of archaic Iraqi accounting standards. While the country is on the path to adopting the International Financial Accounting Standards, this adoption process will take several years at least.

Compounding the problem of obtaining accurate up-to-date business information from corporate balance sheets and income statements is weak auditing. There is a severe shortage of trained accountants. In addition, there is little acceptance of the notion that auditors should provide an independent evaluation. Especially in the case of state-owned enterprises, balance sheets and incomes statements are more policy statements than attempts to accurately evaluate the status of the firms. The regulatory authority, the Iraq Securities Commission, is severely understaffed and apparently focuses its attention on receiving and filing the unaudited annual and quarterly company reports.

The Iraqi legal system provides weak protection for shareholders. The relevant laws are incomplete and contain numerous uncertainties. For example, there are no anti-trust laws and the World Bank ranks Iraq's bankruptcy system as the worst among 183 countries evaluated in 2011. Apparently, firms do not go bankrupt in Iraq rather their former managers loot them. In addition, the court system's backlog of cases is large and resolution can take years (World Bank 2011a, p. 30).

The situation is exacerbated by the fact that members of the judiciary generally lack even a basic knowledge of commercial law. At a Baghdad conference, attendees heard a senior Iraqi legal advisor to the GoI on commercial issues deny that a bank issuing a letter of credit substituted the bank's credit for that of the Iraqi importer that purchased the letter of credit. The final investor concern about judicial resolution of stock market disputes is the perception of widespread corruption. Judges and other court officials have been suspected of favoring more powerful or influential individuals or organizations.

The conclusion is grim. Until there is a substantial improvement in access to quality audited corporate income statements and balance sheets, a rewritten commercial code that sharply reduces uncertainties especially with respect to bankruptcy, and a substantial improvement in the quality and perceived integrity of the judicial system; investing in equities in the ISX is a game that only insiders – those with connections – can win.

INSURANCE

The exact size of the Iraqi insurance industry is unknown although, like banking, it is dominated by state-owned entities. One way of measuring the scale of the Iraqi insurance industry is by looking at gross written premiums. Gross written premiums are an estimate of the revenues (premiums) expected over the life of an insurance contract. The three state-owned insurance companies are believed to have a total of 280–470 billion ID ($240–$400 million) in gross written premiums. The 18 private insurance companies are thought to do less than one-quarter as much business as the state-owned firms – between 70 and 95 billion ID ($60–$80 million) in gross written premiums. An estimated, 15 percent–25 percent of gross written premiums are paid out for reinsurance (World Bank 2011a, pp. 59–66).

The primary reason for the dominance of the state-owned insurance firms is their near monopoly on providing insurance for government entities. This monopoly exists despite the requirement of Article 18 of the Insurance Business Regulation Act that government entities make a public tender, or call for bids, whenever they seek to purchase insurance. In the rare cases where a public tender is actually made, few private firms win the contract to provide insurance.

The size and organization of private insurance companies varies greatly. At one extreme, there are five private insurance firms listed on the ISX with a combined market capitalization of 18 billion ID ($16 million). However, only three of these firms are actively traded. At the other extreme, some of the private insurance companies are very small acting only as brokers (100 percent reinsurance) or maybe not operational. With respect to organization, there are five types currently in operation, three of which have unlimited liability that is not an accepted international practice in insurance.

There are two reasons given for the low level of insurance business in Iraq. First, no insurance is required either for operating an automobile or to cover employee workplace injuries. If both of these common requirements were put into effect then the demand for insurance would increase substantially. However, in the absence of more effective enforcement of Article 18 requiring public tenders, much of the increase will probably be captured by the state-owned insurance companies.

Second, there is the challenge of dealing with religious objections to insurance. A common view of Islamic scholars is that: "Conventional insurance is tainted with riba [interest] and ghara [gambling] and is therefore to be rejected" (Visser 2009, p. 102). Specifically, there are three objections: (1) insurance companies often invest premiums in interest bearing assets that, as discussed above, are probably not consistent with Sharia law; (2) life insurance is a form of gambling, a person makes periodic payments with only a possibility of receiving a payoff; and (3) as discussed in Chapter 10, since there are strict rules in Islam on the division of an inheritance, Islamic scholars think that a policy purchaser should not be allowed to avoid these rules by designating a beneficiary for his or her life insurance.

Throughout the Islamic world, there have been attempts to create "takaful" or Sharia compliant insurance organizations. There is not yet a widely accepted pattern for takaful. Some are cooperative forms of insurance that focus on mutual assistance, which is justified by the Islamic call for brotherhood. Essentially, members of a community each contribute to a common fund that is used to help any members of the community that suffer unexpected difficulties. These cooperative insurance organizations may have professional management and often hold little or zero year-to-year reserves. If premiums are insufficient in any year to meet commitments then the organization deals with the shortfall through some combination of reducing promised payments to those members in difficulty and requesting additional voluntary contributions from its other members. One of the biggest problems facing takaful is the absence of Sharia compliant reinsurance.

One troubling development for those interested in reducing GoI influence in the economy is the substantial investment by state-owned insurance companies in the stock exchange. While data is difficult to obtain, it appears that state-owned insurance companies are major holders of equity in the manufacturing materials and services sectors of the private economy. This large – possibly majority – ownership of private firms by state-owned entities can be expected to lead to contradictory incentives. On the one hand, the state-owned insurance companies want the private firms to be as profitable as possible in order to enable the insurance companies to meet its claims but, on the other hand, GoI policy objectives might require state-owned entities to pressure private firms to engage in socially desirable actions that will reduce their profitability (World Bank 2011a, p. 56).

PENSIONS

Pensions in Iraq are in a state of flux. There are two separate funds, which annually require the equivalent of 4–5 percent of GDP with pay-as-you-go financing. This is one of the highest pension burdens in the region. The State Pension System (SPS) covers civil servants, the military, and employees of SOE while the Social Security System (SSS) is responsible for pensions in the private sector. Civil servants tend to receive much more generous benefits (World Bank 2005, pp. iv–v).

Both pension systems seek to replace 100 percent of the last salary received for all persons who earned less than twice the average income. An employee is eligible for a full pension at age 60 (age 50 for women in the private sector) after only 15 years of covered employment in the public sector or 20 years in the private sector. This very generous program mostly benefits government employees. Although public information on pensions is severely limited, it is thought that, as of December 2004, only about 2 percent of the non-governmental (including SOE) labor force – approximately 80 000 persons – were enrolled in private sector pensions compared to over one million civil servants and one-third of a million persons in the military. The opportunity open to government employees to boost their last months' salary – and therefore their pension – allowed some to earn annual pensions that exceeded 100 percent of their last year's wage.

The disparity between the large number of government employees eligible for generous public sector system pensions and the relatively few private sector employees eligible for less generous pensions from the SSS frames the major challenge facing Iraqi pension reform. There are three options – all of which are considered unacceptable by important constituencies. First, the status quo – the current system – is viewed as fundamentally unfair to private sector employees. Not only do they receive less generous pensions, if they receive a pension at all, but they are forced to contribute to the public sector pensions. This contribution is disguised by the fact that GoI revenues are primarily from oil exports rather than from the extremely low tax rate in Iraq. However, private sector employees indirectly bear part of the burden of public sector pensions since oil revenues diverted to pay for these pensions could have been spent on infrastructure, education, health, security, or other public/merit goods.

The second option, expanding the coverage and retirement payments of private sector pensions to rough parity with those offered by the SPS has widespread support. However, such an expansion will be very expensive – possibly 15–20 percent of GDP even with $100 per barrel oil – with further increases as the population ages. This cost would grow rapidly if there were a decline in oil prices that more than offset the planned increase in oil export volumes discussed in Chapter 6. As mentioned in Chapter 13, if oil prices fell below roughly $55 pb then even the current SPS/SSS pension commitments would be unsupportable. In addition, if private pensions, which are only an option in the formal sector, were substantially increased then this would also have an adverse impact on entrepreneurial activity. It would increase administrative costs of running a private business. As discussed in Chapter 10, generous public sector pensions contribute to the problem of potential entrepreneurs being diverted into government service rather than establishing and operating private firms.

The third option of increasing pension coverage of the private sector while reducing the generosity of public sector pensions is the one that has been adopted by the GoI. A 2006 Pension Law sought to combine the SPS and the SSS but even optimistic estimates found it to be fiscally unsustainable; some estimated that pension costs under the 2006 Law would reach 60 percent of GDP. In 2007, a short (15 pages) revised Unified Pension Law was ratified. In general terms, this law sets more reasonable limits on the payments into the pension system, eligibility standards, and expected pension payments (World Bank 2011b, p. 66). The GoI, with support from the World Bank and other international organizations, has been making slow progress in developing recommendations for revisions to the Unified Pension Law as well as writing the specific regulations necessary to make the law operational.

The delays are in part a function of missing data. For example, the GoI does not know how many people it actually currently employs either in the ministries or state-owned enterprises. The GoI knows how many people it pays but the failure to complete the 2006 census of government employees makes it difficult to separate real government workers from "ghost" employees. The six-year delay of the completion of the government employee census exemplifies the ability of the bureaucracy to delay any change that is expected to have an adverse impact on bureaucrat welfare. In fact, there is no modern precedent in Iraq for the Baghdad bureaucracy to accept even a minor reduction in its compensation even during a national financial crisis. Primarily as a result of this bureaucratic obduracy, little real progress had been made on pension reform in the six years since the World Bank's first detailed analysis of the problem.

Pensions do not face the same problems of Sharia compliance as insurance. The only serious restriction is that the investments in the pension fund must be "halal" – acceptable or good. There are definitional complications with determining which investments are halal. It is haram (that is, not halal) to invest in liquor stores but what about investments in a trucking company that delivers liquor to stores?

OTHER FINANCIAL INTERMEDIARIES

While data on total assets is not available, the following five financial intermediaries are thought to be relatively small: (1) the Postal Savings Fund accepts deposits in its 640 branches and invests them in a variety of sectors; (2) Exchange Companies are engaged in buying and selling foreign currency inside Iraq, most of the 308 Exchange Companies are located in Baghdad; (3) the 32 Financial Transfer Companies are non-banks that specialize in transferring funds inside and outside Iraq using accounts they have established in Iraqi banks; (4) there are nine Financial Investment Companies listed on the ISX who funnel savings into equity, debt, and deposits; and (5) there are relatively new institutions that specialize in making small and medium loans. Currently, only one such firm has been established – the Iraq Company for Short-Term Loans (World Bank 2011b, pp. 10–11).

INFORMAL FINANCE

There are informal alternatives to the banking system and other formal sources of finance. Informal finance, including loans from traditional moneylenders, family, friends, tribal leaders, and suppliers, has always served as an important source of finance. As in most trading cultures, larger merchants often give credit to smaller ones not as a distinct transaction but as part of a complex (especially to outsiders) business relationship. The fact that such credit transactions are part of more extensive relationships may explain why some borrowers prefer more expensive credit from their business partners than cheaper credit banks, MFI, or even government-subsidized sources. However, financing from these various sources cannot fulfill all credit requirements because they tend to be small scale, require intense family, social, or business connections and are often expensive. There is also a concern that informal finance may involve criminal or insurgent groups.

THREATS TO THE CULTURE OF CREDIT

Prior to Saddam's attempt to establish a socialist economy in Iraq, the country's merchants were renowned for their business savvy and their acceptance of the culture of credit. The culture of credit is the concept that loans should be used to expand productive capacity – not for consumption – and that loans should be paid back on schedule. Persons who live according to this culture can expect to not only be able to borrow larger sums in the future but also, as their reputation for using credit wisely spreads, have increased business opportunities. On the other hand, failure to repay loans on schedule leads both to inability to borrow in the future and sanctions.

During the 25 years of Saddam's rule, the culture of credit was undermined in two ways. First, loans were generally made not on the basis of credit worthiness and a solid business plan but because of friendship, political imperatives, or corruption. Second, it was understood, even when not explicitly stated, that these loans would not have to be repaid. The banks would periodically simply mark interest as paid and add the value of the formerly overdue interest to the principle of the loan. On paper, the banks were profitable while in reality they were drowning in defaulted debt.

These activities substantially weakened the culture of credit in Iraq. Fortunately, there was only one generation between Saddam's attempt to establish a statist economy and its subsequent collapse. As a result, there still exists an older generation that understands the market. Also, financial institutions such as MFI have served a valuable role over the last five years in reviving the credit culture.

SEQUENCING OF FINANCIAL SECTOR REFORM

Both the GoI and the IMF have a long list of reforms for Iraq's financial sector. Although there is general agreement that the most important reforms are regulatory reform, recapitalization of the state-owned banks, and the liberalization of international capital flows; the sequencing of these reforms is critical. If state-owned banks are recapitalized before regulatory reform is achieved then, the experience of other post-socialist nations shows that the newly recapitalized banks will rapidly accumulate massive losses. Also, one of the lessons of the 1997 Asian financial crisis is that if the door to international capital movements is opened before there is a vigorous well-regulated domestic banking system then there is a tendency towards financial instability including large-scale capital flight.

Based on these lessons, the GoI should sequence policy changes as follows. First, rationalize the regulatory environment of financial intermediation. Second, the management of the state-owned banks should be restructured followed by recapitalization. And, finally, when both of these goals have been achieved, only then should the GoI seek to liberalize international capital flows.

First, Regulatory Change

Despite the long recognized inefficiencies, reforms of financial interme-diation in Iraq have been continually delayed. Many in the bureaucracy are happy with the current state of financial intermediation. State-owned banks, insurance companies, pensions funds, and so on provide a variety of valuable services to the Baghdad bureaucracy. These range from provid-ing individual loans to government officials with no expectation of repay-ment to financing major SOE projects that lack any reasonable chance of return. In addition, the state-owned financial intermediaries provide a large number of jobs that can be distributed to favored individuals or members of favored groups.

But as much as members of the bureaucracy favor the current regula-tory environment, the ability of Iraq's banking, equity, insurance, and pension intermediaries to facilitate strong long-term economic growth and development is severely constrained. Iraq's regulations are not just consid-ered relatively hostile towards private business by OECD standards, Iraq was last among the Arab countries according to "Doing Business in the Arab World 2011" (World Bank 2011e, Table 1.1, p. 2). Table 8.4 summa-ries five indicators of the impact of regulations on financial intermediation in Iraq. The country with the most favorable business regulatory environ-ment is ranked 1st while the most hostile environment is ranked 183rd.

The first indicator, registering property, refers to the procedures required to legally transfer title on immobile property. Unregistered prop-erty is very unlikely to be accepted as collateral for loans. The "getting credit" indicator includes the existence and efficient operation of credit information systems as well as protection of the rights of borrowers and lenders. Regulations to protect investors should clearly define the responsibilities of investors and firms, promote clear disclosure, require shareholder participation in major company decisions, and set rules for company insiders. Finally, an effective and quick system for resolving insolvencies – bankruptcies – should both ensure the survival of economi-cally efficient companies and provide for the reallocation of the assets of inefficient ones. There have been no cases of a legal resolution of a bankrupt company in Iraq for the last eight years.

Table 8.4   Regulation of financial intermediation

	Iraq ranking 2012	Iraq ranking 2011	Average MENA ranking 2012
Registering property	98th	95th	82nd
Getting credit	174th	170th	119th
Protecting investors	122nd	120th	95th
Enforcing contracts	140th	140th	113th
Resolving insolvency	183rd	183rd	98th

Source: World Bank (2012a), Table 1.1, pp. 10–13.

In 2012, Iraq not only ranked in the bottom half of the 183 countries evaluated for these five indicators but Iraq's relative position deteriorated with respect to three out of the five indicators and failed to improve in the other two. In addition, Iraq ranked below the MENA country average – a region not known for quality financial regulation – for all five indicators. In fact, Iraq is the worst in the world when it comes to resolving business insolvencies.

Since financial intermediation in Iraq is dominated by the banking industry, the "getting credit" indicator is probably deserving of the most immediate attention. Fundamental to making loans is a reliable source of detailed credit information, that is, a credit registry. Currently, Iraq has neither a private nor public credit registry for firms or individuals (World Bank 2012a, pp. 55–6). This absence of credit history or even a reliable listing of current credit use by firms or individuals makes it very risky to make loans unless borrowers leave movable assets at the bank as collateral. Creditors' legal rights are also very limited. Out of the ten items in the legal rights index, Iraq only achieves three. Combined with the regulatory hostility reflected in the other four indicators, it is difficult for banks to evaluate the risk of loans, for potential shareholders to judge companies, for insurance companies to estimate premiums, or for pension funds to safely invest. A longer discussion of the other costs of this regulatory hostility towards private business is included in Chapter 10.

With respect to creating a vibrant private financial sector, there are also technological gaps. The country lacks a secure modern communication system to support: electronic funds transfers between different banks; core banking to connect checking accounts across multiple branches of the same bank; as well as debit and credit cards. Such a system, by increasing the usefulness of private banks, should gradually reduce the dominance of cash transactions.

Regulatory reform in Iraq is more than a matter of having smart bureaucrats in Baghdad writing good regulations that are then approved by elected representatives. Actual execution of regulations is equally important. In many cases, current regulations appear adequate to address the problems of financial intermediation but these regulations are ignored.

Second, Management Restructuring and Recapitalization of State-Owned Banks

Prior to recapitalization, it is important to reform the management of the state-owned banking system by adjusting managerial incentives. Otherwise, recapitalization will simply lead to further losses. The state-owned banks, especially Rafidain Bank, have acted more as fiscal agents of the GoI rather than traditional banks. In addition to making salary and pension payments for the GoI, the state-owned banks are involved with substantial policy lending to SOE and other entities. As a result, managers of the state-owned banks have been evaluated and promoted more on their political and bureaucratic abilities than their ability to make good loans.

Changing the incentives for the management of state-owned banks will be difficult. It will require ceasing to use these banks as fiscal agents while, at the same time, encouraging them to making loans on commercial terms. Evidence from other post-socialist countries shows that a growing private banking sector tends to be associated with improved operation at state-owned banks in the same country. This is in part because improvements in the private banking sector put competitive pressure on state-owned banks forcing them to become more efficient. Further complicating changing the managerial culture of the state-owned banks is ambiguous guidance from the CBI.

In general, the CBI must move away from directing policy lending and focus instead on exercising supervisory responsibilities to enforce sound banking practices and common regulations for all banks, state owned or private. Progress has been made but at a very slow rate.

While recapitalization of the state-owned banks should be delayed until the restructuring of managerial incentives is completed, the ongoing delay in recapitalization seems to have little to do with waiting for managerial changes. In 2006, the CBI and Ministry of Finance agreed to a plan to recapitalize these banks using GoI Treasury Bonds. However, the GoI has regularly announced delays in this recapitalization that is currently scheduled for 2013, seven years after. The announced reasons for this continuing delay is the necessity of gathering detailed information on the banks' government accounts as well as the need for the CBI to prepare to effectively regulate the newly recapitalized institutions. However, there might also be bureaucratic pressure to delay the recapitalization process for fear that the banks will no longer be so willing to fund projects supported by the various ministries. The delays in managerial reform and recapitalization are not costless since every year that Iraq stumbles along with extremely inefficient financial intermediation results in slower economic development.

Third, Liberalization of International Capital Movements

Other post-socialist societies have benefitted by allowing domestic banks to borrow internationally and encouraging foreign banks to purchase substantial ownership rights in domestic banks. In addition, to providing new capital, foreign ownership tends to lead to greater efficiency and increased availability of new financial products. This increase in efficiency occurs not only in the banks with foreign ownership but also by motivating greater efficiency in non-foreign-owned banks through increased competition.

There is concern that increased foreign ownership will exacerbate financial and economic instability possibly by facilitating capital flight. Also there is doubt that the CBI will either have the necessary knowledge or cooperation of foreign regulatory authorities to effectively regulate foreign banks. Regardless of the motivation, the CBI has made is difficult for foreign banks to either establish new wholly owned subsidiaries or to buy substantial shares of existing Iraqi private banks.

In addition, the GoI is encouraging large-scale foreign investment and loans in order to finance a rapid expansion of the nation's infrastructure especially in the petroleum sector. In many developing countries, increased international capital flows when the financial markets are both fragile and inflexible has led to acute financial instability. However, since this risk of financial instability is strongly influenced by the GoIs exchange rate policies, it is more appropriately discussed in Chapter 13, which focuses on fiscal, monetary, and exchange rate policy.

9. State-owned enterprises

> The previous ban on non-Arab foreign direct investment and the
> effects of three wars and a decade of international economic sanctions
> have meant that something like 90% of Iraq's industrial capacity – the
> SOE share – is seriously decapitalized, asset-starved, obsolescent,
> inefficient, saddled with high production costs, over-staffed, and
> – as a result of looting – in a state of physical degradation.
> (World Bank 2004, p. i)

An estimated 192 SOE and 43 mixed ownership firms continue to dominate the economy of Iraq despite the fact that they tend to be high-cost, low-quality producers. Not only are they are the leading providers of essential services such as electricity and water but also SOE account for a large proportion of all consumer goods and industrial inputs. Further reflecting their major impact on the country, SOE are, collectively, the largest employers after the national government. An estimated 580000 persons work for SOE accounting for almost all of Iraq industrial employment.

The products and services produced by Iraqi SOE include almost all of those consumed by a modern economy. In addition to producing construction materials, petroleum production, weapons, and electricity generation; state-run entities also rent limousines, operate dairies, manufacture household furniture and cigarettes, weave carpets, and operate automobile dealerships and gas stations.

Although the quality of data is poor, it is estimated that roughly 20 percent of existing SOE factories are currently profitable or potentially profitable with a reasonable amount of investment. Most of these profitable SOE factories are in the petroleum or construction industries. Another quarter of the SOE factories are empty shells – destroyed during the conflict, severely mismanaged, or looted to bare walls. However, employees of these wrecked SOE continue to be paid for showing up. The remaining 55 percent of SOE are either considered essential to national security, for example weapons repair, or would require large-scale investment, managerial restructuring, or a sharp workforce reduction in order to have any chance of achieving profitability (USAID 2006a).

ORIGIN OF SOE

SOE dominance of the Iraq economy is less than thirty years old. Saddam had at least three motivations for establishing SOE after he took over the Iraqi government in 1979. First, consistent with the economic philosophy of the Arab Ba'athist Socialist Party, SOE were seen as a way of accelerating economic development by forcing the adoption of what were then considered modern management techniques by firms large enough to internalize economies of scale. Existing private firms were combined into government run organizations while other SOE were newly established in industries that the leadership of the Arab Ba'athist Socialist Party thought exemplified a modern industrial state. This "cargo cultism" led to the creation of industries such as truck and bus assembly where Iraq was at a severe competitive disadvantage.

The second motivation for establishing SOE was political. In common with other socialist leaders, Saddam found that SOE provide the government with both a means of rewarding supporters and of punishing opposition. Directing a SOE provided a member of Saddam's family or other supporter with a well-remunerated position of status and political influence. The director of each SOE ensured that, whenever possible, jobs in their SOE were reserved for persons loyal to Saddam, the regime, and themselves. At the same time, SOE dominance of the economy made it more difficult both financially and personally for persons to oppose the regime. Any incipient opposition found it difficult to raise financial support since most of the non-agricultural economy was controlled by the regime. In addition, individuals realized that if they were too vocal in their opposition to Saddam's regime then they and their families would be excluded from employment.

Finally, it was believed that SOE would allow the state to capture the profits that would otherwise have accrued to the private sector. Saddam wanted to ensure that a substantial portion of these funds would be diverted into the pockets of himself, his family, and closest supporters. In other words, SOE provided a means of facilitating large-scale corruption.

CURRENT STATUS OF SOE

It is challenging to get a clear understanding of the current status of Iraq's SOE for several reasons. First, while each SOE falls under the control of one of the Baghdad ministries, periodically a SOE or one of its factories will be shifted to another ministry or merged with/split from another SOE.

In fact, while the number of SOE is usually given as 192, actual counts have ranged from 188 to 195.

Second, each SOE is comprised of between one and 15 enterprises or factories, often of very different sizes. Some are quite small, with less than 100 employees, while others are huge. The enterprises under the Ministry of Trade employ on average 4000 people; those of the Ministry of Oil, 3500 people; while those of the Ministry of Industry and Minerals, 3000 people (Ministry of Industry and Minerals 2009; World Bank 2004, pp. 5–6). These enterprises are often located at a distance from their SOE headquarters and often act as separate entities with respect to technical issues. However, the enterprises are not registered as legal entities, cannot sign contracts with customers, nor can they sign for bank loans.

Finally, the balance sheets and income statements of SOE are either non-existent, works of fiction, or presented in a non-standard format. Even fundamental information is lacking. For example, most SOE firms cannot accurately report their number of employees. While SOE have a rough estimate of the amount paid in salaries and benefits, the actual number of workers is generally unknown. This is in part explained by the fact that many SOE have an unknown number of "ghost workers" who are collecting pay from the SOE but not showing up for work. For some SOE, it is estimated that up to 25 percent of all employees are "ghosts" while two-thirds of the workers in some individual factories are ghost workers. Iraq's Special Borrowing Agreement with the IMF required a detailed census of all government employees to be completed by the end of 2006. However, six years later, the census is still incomplete due to the lack of cooperation and, in some cases, the open hostility of the SOE. Large-scale over-employment in SOE provides opportunities for enterprise managers to gain influence or, by auctioning off jobs, accumulate substantial wealth.

Since their beginnings under Saddam, SOE have received financial support from the GoI in four ways. First, SOE receive direct subsidies in the form of cash transfers from the national budget. These subsidies continued after the 2003 fall of Saddam's regime and by 2010 amounted to approximately $2.5 billion or roughly 3 percent of total GoI budget expenditures (IMF 2011a, Table 3, p. 18). As a matter of scale, $2.5 billion is equal to almost 90 percent of GoI annual expenditures for all elementary and secondary education. Second, there are large indirect subsidies. SOE receive free or inexpensive electricity, water, fuel, credit, and capital equipment. Third, transfer pricing aids non-oil SOE. Since oil-related enterprises represent the only sector that has large annual cash surpluses, transfer pricing generally involves oil-related enterprises paying too much to SOE that provide supplies to the oil industry while receiving too little

Table 9.1   Ministry of Industry and Minerals SOE

	Companies	Factories	Products	Employees	2009 Profit
Engineering	21	90	200	57000	−$250 mn
Petrochemical	15	61	37	34000	−$110 mn
Foodstuffs and drugs	6	35	535	24000	−$50 mn
Construction	8	21	20	33000	+$5 mn
Textiles	8	38	14	35000	−$130 mn
Industrial services	9			6000	−$20 mn
Ministry overhead				900	−$20 mn
Total	67	245	806	190000	−$600 mn

Source: 2009 Master Strategic Plan of Ministry of Industry and Minerals, pp. 27–31.

payment from SOE that purchase fuel products. Finally, there are regulatory subsidies. As will be discussed in detail in the next chapter, Iraq has a regulatory environment that is extremely hostile to private business. This ensures that any private sector competition is limited and creates captive markets for the high-cost, low-quality products and services produced by SOE.

While the absence of audited accounts combined with the organizational changes makes it difficult to provide a detailed analysis of the financial health of SOE or their component enterprises, the little information that is available points to one conclusion. Despite large indirect subsidies, favorable transfer pricing, and regulatory hostility that limits private sector competition, most Iraqi SOE have lost money every year since the mid-1980s.

For example, Table 9.1 illustrates the situation of the 67 SOE associated with the Ministry of Industry and Minerals. The Ministry of Industry and Minerals has the reputation of being one of the better managed of the 34 Iraqi government ministries. Only the construction category of the Ministry of Industry and Minerals's SOE was barely profitable in 2009. As a group, the Ministry of Industry and Minerals's SOE lost – required net budget transfers of – $0.6 billion in 2009.

In addition to excessive employment, the distances between factories further complicate the difficulty of profitably managing SOE. Factory locations were often determined more by political considerations than those of economic efficiency. In view of the degraded transportation and communication infrastructure that will be discussed in Chapter 11, physical distance not only increases costs of production but also inhibits coordination. The primary argument that is made to preserve a system of geographically distributed SOE is to provide industrial employment outside of the large metropolitan areas of Baghdad, Basrah, and Mosul. However, in some cases, the impact on local employment is minimal. SOE employees are bused in from the major metropolitan areas to work at the outlying SOE plants or, at least to collect their paychecks.

There was little international interest in investing in Iraqi SOE during the widespread inter-communal violence of 2004 through 2007. However, with the improvement in the security situation, foreign interest in SOE increased. Initially, foreign investment interest was limited to only a few sectors. For example, in 2008, there was substantial private investment in only seven SOE factories; five of these factories produced cement while the other two were in the electricity and fertilizer industries. While the total committed by international investors to these seven firms was an estimated $910 million, it is unknown how much was actually disbursed in Iraq (SIGIR 2009a, Appendix A, p. 24).

As security stabilized, there was an increase in both the number of SOE sectors that received foreign direct investment (FDI) as well as the countries that were sources of this investment. Chinese interest was particularly strong. For example, in the cement industry in 2010, there were Chinese contracts for one upgrade of an existing plant and two green field investments. Merchantbridge (UK) and Lafarge (France) contracted to upgrade a large cement factory in Karbala under a 15-year lease. Sinoma International Engineering (China) and China National Building Material and their Iraqi partners contracted to build plants in Sulaymaniyah province (Kurdish region) and in the city of Samawah in Muthanna province. Upon completion, the Iraqi partners will operate the plants. Other examples are French Telecom and Agility (Kuwait) that purchased a 44 percent stake in Iraqi telecommunications operator Korek Telecom. Korek Telecom mainly operates in the three Kurdish provinces but also has coverage in Kirkuk and Baghdad (National Iraqi News Agency 2011). The Ministry of Industry and Minerals also reached an agreement with a Chinese producer to assemble 10 000 cars in Iraq. These will compete with the large number (estimated 31 000 in 2010) of cars imported (smuggled?) from Iran (*Aswat al-Iraq* 2010).

While over 100 foreign firms have announced investments in Iraq through the end of 2010 (TFBSO 2011, Summary), it is difficult to determine the exact amounts invested. Cases of double counting and wishful thinking probably mean that actual investment will be a fraction of the amounts announced in press releases. Many of the medium and small investments originate from Iraq's neighbors and may include substantial "false foreigner" participation. False foreigners are Iraqi refugees that are investing in Iraq. Investors in neighboring countries and especially former residents, who have stayed current with business and economic changes, probably have a more accurate idea of which investments have the best risk to reward ratio. Also, it is believed that the GoI will be more transparent and less arbitrary with international investors then with its own nationals.

SHOULD IRAQ REFORM ITS SOE?

The establishment of SOE in oil-exporting and other natural resource "rentier" states, like Iraq, is not rare. In three – Saudi Arabia, Qatar, and UAE – SOE appear to be relatively well-managed SOE (Hertog 2010, pp. 262–3). In Iraq, the results are mixed. On the favorable side, Iraq's SOE are the primary providers of most domestic producer and consumer goods and services. In addition, since SOE provide large number of reasonably well-paying jobs, maintaining SOE are considered a practical means of reducing political instability in post-conflict Iraq. There is also a privatization-related fear that the elimination of the favored status of SOE will lead – not to a shift to private sector production in Iraq – but rather to a sharp increase in imports and, therefore, increased dependency on foreign suppliers.

The arguments against continuing to heavily subsidize SOE extend beyond the substantial budget burden. First, since SOE in Iraq tend to be low-quality high-cost monopoly or oligopoly producers, they reduce the efficiency of both upstream and downstream business entities. It is not just a matter of the quality of the products and services provided, suppliers to SOE and consumers of their products realize that the SOE are, by their very nature, politically powerful. Any commercial disputes will most likely be resolved in favor of the SOE. As a result, private suppliers to SOE and private purchasers of their goods and services must suffer not only from quality issues but also acute uncertainty about whether any agreement with a SOE will be executed as contracted.

Second, heavily subsidized SOE tend to crowd out private sector competitors and stall market development both directly and indirectly. Directly, private producers find it difficult to compete with heavily sub-sidized SOE products and services. Indirectly, each SOE is associated with a ministry which, in order to minimize its subsidy costs, often uses available regulatory authority to prevent private sectors from successfully competing with its SOE.

Third, SOE dominance in Iraq reduces the country's ability to compete in global markets. Foreign purchasers do not have to tolerate the quality issues and unpredictability associated with trading with an Iraqi SOE. Iraqi consumers have shown a willingness to pay a premium for the predictable quality of imported goods ranging from automobiles to halal frozen chickens. Whether state ownership acts as a barrier to FDI is more ambiguous. Having the GoI as a partner can both ensure political support for the enterprise and also reduce profit opportunities if one's government partner is corrupt.

Fourth, proponents argue that excessive SOE employment reduces political instability by providing jobs for unskilled young men. However, expanded SOE employment may actually be destabilizing. It is not uncommon for the SOE of a ministry to be "captured" by a religious sect, party, sect, or tribe as a means of providing funding for the organization as well as jobs for its members. Thus SOE employment can be destabilizing by supporting, with government funds, members of political parties or other groups that may be in opposition to the rule of law.

Fifth, SOE tend to be less concerned with the environment. World Bank reports on studies in Bangladesh, India, Indonesia, Thailand, and Brazil point to a direct relationship between SOE dominance and pollution levels (World Bank 1995, pp. 38–41). The report concludes that: "SOE are better placed to evade pollution regulators than their private counterparts" (World Bank 1995, p. 40). This is not just a function of the fact that SOE tend to have outdated infrastructure or that SOE are concentrated in industries that tend to be more polluting. Even after adjusting for infrastructure age, SOE tend to pollute more than private firms in the same industries.

Finally, there is an increasing consensus that, in addition to the effects of microeconomic inefficiencies discussed above, a large dependency on SOE has an adverse impact on a country's long-term macroeconomic growth. In part, this results from divergence of scarce government spending from education or infrastructure investment to SOE subsidies. In addition, government ministers face contradictory demands when making ministerial decisions that could help the economy but also injure their associated SOE. Galal et al. (1994) estimated that for nations such as Iraq where SOE accounted for 10 percent or more of GDP, cutting the SOE percentage of GDP in half would raise real GDP growth by 1 percent per year for the foreseeable future.

HOW CAN IRAQ REFORM ITS SOE?

All too often the debate over SOE reform in Iraq treated as a choice between two extremes. One must choose either the status quo or the radical

Table 9.2   SOE reform options

Type of reform		Ownership	Management
1	Status quo	State	State
2	Improved state management	State	State
3	Managerial contracts	State	State/private
4	Private-public partnership	State/private	State/private
5	Regulated privatization of natural monopolies	Private	State/private
6	Complete privatization	Private	Private

reform of privatizing all SOE. But this is a simplistic view since there are at least six options for Iraq SOE reform. The options are: status quo; better state management of SOE; managerial contracts to allow private management of SOE; public-private partnerships; the privatization of natural monopolies but with detailed state regulation; and complete privatization. As can be seen from Table 9.2; three of these options assume continued state ownership, one proposes joint private-state ownership, and the remaining two options are forms of privatization.

One issue that requires careful consideration is the precise standard for successful SOE reform. There are four standards commonly discussed in Iraq. First, maintenance of employment levels is often cited as an important goal. In fact, this is probably the most important criterion in Iraq – any SOE reform program that is expected to result in an increase in unemployment is probably a non-starter. Second, successful reform would result in the recovery of a stagnant industry. In this case, reform would lead to the production of better quality goods and services at lower real costs. Third, successful reform should contribute to the country's economic development. This could result from setting free resources including labor that are "trapped" by moribund SOE. Finally, since most SOE are a burden on the national budget, successful reform would be one that reduces or eliminates this burden. The reduction in the SOE-related budget burden would occur through some combination of the reduction or elimination of the substantial direct and indirect subsidies that most SOE receive and the transition of some SOE firms into profitable enterprises that could transfer funds to the GoI. Unfortunately, the first two definitions of success – preservation of traditional industries and associated employment – are often inconsistent with the latter two definitions – acceleration of economic growth and reduced burden on government budgets.

But there are also political limitations on SOE reform even if it has desirable impact on economic development. Government ministers and SOE directors seem willing to accept SOE reform as long as there is no change in the geographical distribution of factories, and the authority of the ministries. Of course, these restrictions make substantial reform very difficult to achieve.

The situation is similar to that of the People's Republic of China in the 1980s in that the motivation for SOE preservation is both political and economic. Within Iraq's current coalition government, the 34 ministries are divided up among the various political parties reflecting election results and party leadership's ability at political negotiation. Some of the ministries are important because of their critical roles in the nation. These would include the Finance, Foreign Affairs, and Oil Ministries as well as those of Defense and Interior (police). However, some of the other important ministries are only valued because they control SOE. These SOE provide the ministers with large budgets and status as well as the capability to distribute government jobs to loyal supporters. If a ministry loses its SOE to privatization then there will be fewer prizes – desirable ministries – to divide among coalition members and important members of the opposition. This would complicate government coalition formation in Iraq since there would be fewer desirable ministries to be divided as political spoils. SOE privatization could be politically destabilizing. In fact, only the first four options in Table 9.2 – status quo through private-public partnership – are seen as viable alternatives for Iraqi SOE reform in the foreseeable future.

Among the SOE that have the strongest political support to continue under state ownership are defense-related firms; firms engaged in petroleum exploration, production, exports, and sales; and firms that are empty shells. Among the 192 SOE, 19 produce defense products such as missile propellant, guns, electronic warfare systems, or provide various types of security services. While some low-income countries have experimented with private production of defense items and services, most maintain these as a state monopoly.

The argument against even a partial privatization of production, export, and sales of petroleum and natural gas is primarily political. As was discussed in Chapter 6, oil is generally viewed as a national legacy of all of the people of Iraq. It would be political suicide for a leader to propose the privatization of an Iraqi oil-related firm. As a result, the 15 oil-related SOE will probably remain under state ownership and management for the foreseeable future.

The third group of SOE that is most likely exempt from substantial reform is – strangely enough – the 25 percent of SOE that were either destroyed in the multiple conflicts of the last twenty years or are uncompetitive at any possible set of input and output prices. Reform is unlikely for these empty-shell firms because any reform short of liquidation will be unlikely to provide any benefit. These firms should be viewed as a form of welfare, the employees continue to receive their paychecks despite the lack of any need for their labor. Even if these empty shell SOE factories were reopened, actual direct job creation might be small. Most of the direct spending on equipment and spare parts (60 percent) for revitalized SOE factories went for imports – not domestically produced items.

But there is a danger of overstating the arguments in favor of the status quo. There are factories where the advantages of substantial reform are clear. The ISX estimated that as many as 296 factories could be at least partially privatized in order to sell stock on the ISX (World Bank 2011a, pp. 52–3). Some ministries appear to be willing to experiment with either substantial change in SOE operation or even privatization. But how can the management of existing SOE be improved to either prepare them for partial privatization or, at least, to reduce the burden on both the national economy and the national budget? The answers to these questions might be best discussed under three headings: increased transparency, management reform, and joint venture versus privatization.

Increase Transparency

Increased transparency combined with reduced ambiguity of SOE managerial incentives is not only a necessary precursor to privatization but also should lead to increased efficiency in SOE that will not be privatized. The most important component of increased SOE transparency is to replace indirect subsidies by direct ones in order to allow the more accurate targeting of GoI assistance.

Unraveling the knot of indirect subsidies is difficult especially since many SOE are either customers of or suppliers to other SOE. The "prices" of goods and services involved in these inter-SOE transactions diverge greatly from those that would balance demand and supply. This non-market transfer pricing enables Iraq's oil and financial sectors to subsidize the rest of the SOE. In addition, it is even difficult to obtain accurate information on the volumes of electricity, water, other utilities, and credit utilized by individual SOE factories. In many cases, metering or other measurement methods are not even attempted. Even when estimates of the volume of these utilities and credits are collected, this information is treated as confidential within each SOE factory and generally not shared with the parent SOE, the national government, elected officials, or – least of all – the public.

In addition, even when reasonably accurate estimates of the volume of subsidized utilities are available, there is the question of the proper prices. Official prices are based more on politics than market clearing. These official prices are often below the average costs of production and sometimes they are less than marginal costs.

If SOE were a relatively small part of the Iraqi economy then determining the correct transfer prices would not be as difficult. Officials could observe the input and output prices received and paid by firms in the private sector and use these observations to estimate the correct relative prices for transactions involving SOE. However, since SOE dominate the Iraqi economy, there is a shortage of domestic private sector price observations for officials to extrapolate from. In addition, there is a simultaneity problem. For example, for the electrical industry to estimate its real shadow price of electricity generation, it requires information on fuel costs. However, for the fuel refineries to estimate their costs of fuel production, they require knowledge of the price of electricity.

The pricing problem is exacerbated by, as will be discussed in Chapter 10, Iraq's extremely hostile regulatory environment for private businesses. This hostility towards private businesses has two effects. It reduces the scope of the private sector and forces most of the private businesses that do exist in Iraq into the underground economy to avoid the hostile regulations and bribe demands from officials. This not only reinforces SOE dominance of most Iraqi markets but also limits information on relative market prices for SOE planning.

Therefore, to increase the transparency of indirect SOE subsidies, it is necessary to not only do a better job of estimating the volume of utilities and credit received but also attempt to value these subsidized inputs either by attempting to estimate real shadow prices or using relative prices from a revived private sector market. It is expected that increased transparency will lead to a deterioration of the income statements of most SOE factories with the exception of those in the energy field.

Improved SOE transparency will probably face ministerial opposition because it will reveal a more realistic estimate of the true budget impact of SOE inefficiencies. However, by converting hidden subsidies into explicit budget expenditures, this reform may strengthen the public's desire for further reform. The next step would be to improve SOE management.

Management Reform of SOE

Current management of firms in Iraqi SOE suffers from ambiguous incentives. The managers are assigned multiple – often contradictory – goals that are evaluated according to bureaucratic not market standards. For example, loyalty will probably be more valued than efficiency. Incentive ambiguity can be reduced in several ways. Large firms can be unbundled so that managers are not required either to manage very diverse products lines or to manage product lines that compete with each other. Rationalization of private sector regulation and the resulting growth of private sector competition will not only motivate SOE managers to do a better job but also enable state-owned firms to sell their output and buy their inputs in larger markets. SOE could also be restructured so as to provide factory directors with greater autonomy, to reduce the number of decisions that must be referred to the SOE headquarters or the ministry in Baghdad (see the detailed discussion in World Bank 1995, Chapter 5).

Another approach that is often advocated is that the SOE sign a formal agreement or contract with an individual manager explicitly laying out the SOE firm's goals and means, and providing financial or other incentives for successfully achieving these goals. When the individual contracted to lead a firm is a government official it is a performance contract and when a SOE contracts with a private sector firm or individual to administer a state-owned firm then it is referred to as a management contract. Both are widely utilized. In 1995, the World Bank found over 550 performance contracts in 32 countries and 202 management contracts in 49 countries being utilized (World Bank 1995, pp. 107–8). While the research is difficult to interpret, it appears that performance contracts generally fail to achieve the desired results while management contracts are generally successful.

The failures of performance contracts – contracts between a government and a manager who is a public employee – to result in a substantial improvement in SOE management are caused by asymmetrical information, the lack of meaningful rewards for success, and lack of trust in government's commitment to its agreement. Public sector managers of a SOE factory know much more about their firm's activities than an outsider. They can use this information asymmetry to negotiate a performance contract that provides them with complex but easily achievable – soft – targets. These complex soft targets ensure that the manager will be evaluated as a success even if little real progress is made.

In addition, one would expect that a contract would have the greatest motivational impact on the residual claimant; the claimant who is allowed to keep whatever is left after other contractual parties have been paid. But most performance contracts state that the government, not the manager, is the residual claimant. The additional reward to the public official who successfully manages a SOE may be zero or a very small fraction of the gains from his or her managerial success. Maybe the manager will receive an earlier promotion to the next level of the bureaucracy. But, if honest, the manager is unlikely to become rich from success or devastated by failure.

Finally, since in a performance contract one element of the government is contracting with another, it is difficult for the manager to have confidence that any commitments that the government make will be executed as contracted. Typically, the government will make a wide range of promises to the manager concerning everything from managerial autonomy to delivery dates for required inputs as well as commit to specific prices for expected outputs. However, both parties realize that these promises are likely to be modified in response to political or bureaucratic changes (World Bank 1995, pp. 120–133).

Management contracts – contracts between a government and a private party to operate the SOE firm for a fee – have been more successful. In a study of 158 management contracts in 50 countries, a World Bank study found that two-thirds of the firms experienced improvements in both profitability and productivity (World Bank 1995, pp. 137–8). Unlike performance contracts for government managers, management contracts for private sector managers appear to have a better chance of overcoming the problems of asymmetrical information, adequate risk and rewards, and trust in government's commitments.

Management contracts tend to have fewer and more transparent performance standards. The private managers are granted greater autonomy and their financial rewards are more closely connected to firm success. Finally, management contracts provide options for the government to improve the credibility of its commitments. The government can offer long-term contracts with the possibility of renewal. These contracts motivate the manager to take a long-term view of investment and training since the manager expects to be able to benefit from any resulting improvements. In addition, the government signals its serious commitment by engaging in the expensive search for the right manager, by making announcements that are perceived as politically costly for example allowing layoffs or price increases, or by making substantial investments (World Bank 1995, pp. 140–148).

It should be noted that, in addition to the exact terms of the management contracts, Iraq's economic environment would probably have a substantial impact on whether there is a measurable improvement in SOE firm performance. Management contracts tend to be more successful when the SOE firm that has implemented a management contract is in a competitive industry – when there are other SOE firms or private sector firms competing for the same customers. In Iraq, this would argue that management contracts will be more successful if they follow a reduction in the country's regulatory hostility to private businesses.

Management contracts tend to be more successful when the managers have broad authority to hire, train, and fire workers without government interference. This will result in some of these SOE firms experiencing a drop in the firm's wage bill – the total amount paid to employees. However, most reformed SOE firms actually expand their wage bill. Either they have fewer workers but pay them more or the increase in labor productivity, as a result of improved management, leads to increases in both production and employment. Despite these optimistic results for the wage bill, it is expected that allowing SOE private sector managers the necessary authority to prune unnecessary employment, especially "ghost" workers, would be extremely difficult in Iraq. Even in joint ventures, the GoI has made it very clear that not only are workers not to be fired regardless of performance but also, in some joint-venture agreements, if a worker quits or retires, he or she is to be replaced with the selection of the new employee which is handled by the Iraq partner.

Research also shows that management contracts tend to have more favorable results when foreign finance is involved. This is most likely because the presence of such finance reflects a more serious commitment to the contract on the part of the domestic government. In other words, it is believed that the government of a low-income country would be less willing to break an agreement with a foreign financial institution, government, or international organization than one with its own people. If the foreign interests have an equity agreement in an Iraqi firm then it is a joint venture, which is a form of privatization in that the government, while still the dominate partner, gives up some control over a SOE firm.

Joint Ventures or Privatization

In Iraq in early 2006, T.W. Curran developed five "success" factors and five "failure" factors that could be used to determine whether a SOE joint venture or privatization would succeed. Curran then evaluated each of the almost 200 SOE according to each of these factors with a ranking of one to four with a "four" most likely associated with joint-venture or privatization success. The results are shown in Table 9.3.

Success factors

A joint venture or privatization of an Iraqi SOE is more likely to be successful if it possesses one or more of the following characteristics. First, natural resource-based firms that utilize petroleum, phosphate, or other inputs that Iraq possesses in generous amounts.

Second, SOE that produce products that have high transportation costs relative to its value. Due to their high transportation costs, such products tend to face reduced competition from imports. A prime example would be cement for construction.

Third, SOE that produce goods or services that are in demand from

Table 9.3   Successful joint-venture/privatization scores

Score	Likelihood of joint-venture/ privatization success	Number of SOE	Examples
35–40	Excellent	6	Cement, oil production
31–34	Good	58	Refining, fertilizer, electrical generation
21–30	Fair	126	Textiles, software
10–20	Poor	5	Missiles, PDS food imports

Source: Curran (2006).

Iraqi consumers will have a greater likelihood of success than firms that sell most of their output to other SOE or the government. This is somewhat controversial since some argue that another SOE or the government would provide a guaranteed market for the output of a new joint-venture or privatized SOE, which would make it unnecessary for the firm to engage in cutthroat market competition. However, as discussed above, SOE tend to be untrustworthy business partners.

The fourth favorable characteristic is the degree to which a SOEs good or service is used in construction. Iraq will experience large construction expenditures over the next decades for three overlapping reasons. As a result of three decades of conflict and mismanagement, reconstruction requirements are great. Also, a large proportion of the population is ill housed. Finally, the GoI plans for a dramatic expansion of oil and gas production, refining, and exports will require substantial downstream and upstream infrastructure construction.

The fifth favorable characteristic is whether a SOE is actually operating – currently producing a product even in an inefficient manner. If a SOE factory is just an empty shell then a successful joint venture or privatization is unlikely.

Failure factors
First, any firm that relies on a complex supply-chain will find it very difficult to survive in Iraq's current environment. As will be discussed in the transportation section of Chapter 11, Iraq currently lacks reliable reasonably inexpensive transportation. For example, Iraq's substantial promise as a producer of fresh and frozen agricultural products is severely constrained by the lack of a reliable cold-chain.

Second, similar reasoning supports a pessimistic view concerning the eventual profitability of firms engaged in complex or time-sensitive manufacturing. Unexpected disruptions in the quantity or quality of electricity and other common inputs, in transportation, and unpredictable application of government regulations generally results in production delays and halts, inventory losses, and sometimes damaged manufacturing equipment.

A third factor is associated with Iraq's relatively small population of about 30 million persons. As a result, products with strong economies of scale such as automobiles will require access to an export market in order to make a profit. However, as will be discussed in Chapter 12, Iraq suffers from a severe case of the Dutch Disease. The dominance of oil exports has resulted in a strong ID that increases the foreign price of Iraqi exports.

Fourth, since one of the purposes of establishing a joint venture or privatization is to reduce the budget burden, production of a good or service that is largely dependent on highly subsidized inputs such as fuel, electricity, and water will find it difficult to survive privatization.

The final joint-venture or privatization failure factor is that it is unlikely that Iraq will be able to successfully achieve a sustainable market share in any market that is already dominated by low-cost high-quality international suppliers. For example, in view of the dominance of South Asian producers, it is very unlikely that an Iraqi firm will succeed in profitably making cotton clothing.

Likelihood of successful joint venture/privatization

Each success factor was scored one to four with one representing a poor showing. Failure factors were evaluated inversely, that is, scored one to four but with a four showing an almost complete absence of the failure factor. Using this scoring system, a score of 40 represented an ideal candidate for a successful joint venture or privatization while a score of ten represented a very poor candidate (Table 9.3).

The validity of this joint-venture/privatization metric shown in Table 9.3 is supported by the initial seven joint ventures. Five were cement plants (Sinjar, Fallujah, Kubaysa, Kirkuk, and Al Qaim) and one each of fertilizer (Baiji) and electrical equipment (Diyala) (SIGIR 2009a, Appendix A, p. 24). At the time of writing this book, there have been no privatizations. However, if this metric is correct then the likelihood is low that the GoI can successfully dispose of all of its non-oil/non-defense SOE through joint ventures or privatization. Almost two-thirds have only a "fair" or "poor" chance of being part of a successful joint venture or privatization although some SOE firms might be attractive as "shells" for foreign investors – providing an Iraqi partner who is already authorized to do business in Iraq. If the GoI decides to actually privatize one or more SOE factories then there is a growing body of research on privatization that might guide the GoI to a successful privatization.

SOE privatization: lessons learned

Of course, there have been many attempts to privatize SOE in other countries that might provide useful lessons for Iraq. Since the conclusions of this growing field of research are wide ranging, only a few of the most important will be mentioned here. (For more extensive discussions, see Galal et al. 1994; Megginson and Netter 2001; World Bank 1995.) Probably most relevant to Iraq's situation are the experiences of other post-socialist states in Eastern Europe and Asia. The primary conclusion is somewhat cynical. The likelihood of successful privatization is very low unless government leaders benefit either professionally or personally: that a SOE privatization will benefit the entire economy is insufficient. For example, much has been made of the regulatory and other changes that led to a rapid acceleration of Chinese economic growth. However, it should be noted that the People's Republic of China did not reform its SOE; it outgrew them (Qian 2003).

The specific form of privatization is critical: privatization alone does not guarantee more efficient performance because some SOE are harder to successfully privatize than others. Even with "successful" privatizations, improvements in efficiency tend to occur slowly (Stallings and Peres 2000). Also, successful privatizations impact the quality of life in a country as well as the quantity of goods and services. For example, privatization of water services tends to lead to reduced child mortality as water quality improves (Galiani et al. 2006). Finally, as discussed above, SOE privatization tends to have a favorable impact on the environment since the state has difficulty policing itself. (Hettige et al. 1996). The challenges facing privatization are many and best method of privatization is industry specific.

As noted in Table 9.1, there is an option where the state gives up all ownership rights but continues to substantially influence the management of a former SOE firm. If the former SOE firm is a natural monopoly then the most common transition is to a heavily regulated private firm. Whether this transition is successful or not is dependent on the economic and political environment. To the extent that there is a vibrant private sector economy and the government's commitments are credible then a regulated private natural monopoly tends to be more efficient than a SOE. However, if either of these requirements are missing then there is little evidence that a transition to a regulated private sector firm is beneficial. The potential for resuscitating Iraq's private sector is the subject of the next chapter. But believing that a transition to managerial contracts, joint ventures, regulated natural monopolies, or privatization is more efficient than the status quo is a necessary but not a sufficient condition for successful SOE reform. There must also be a will to reform.

WILL IRAQ REFORM ITS SOE?

According to a World Bank study (1995, pp. 233–6), there are two indicators that government leaders will support substantial SOE reform: a recent change in a country governing regime or coalition, and an economic crisis. A regime change or economic crisis will tend to decrease – at least for a period – political and economic dependency on SOE. In addition, if the SOE, their leadership, or their workers are associated with the former regime or coalition then it is easier for the new regime or coalition to reform or even eliminate them. A crisis has a similar impact in that, during a crisis situation, the government may be more willing to try a dramatic restructuring of the economy.

Of course, there have been two fairly dramatic regime changes in Iraq in the last decade. In 2003, Saddam's regime fell to the US-led coalition and Iraq entered a period of occupation. This continued until the constitutional referendum of December 2005 and the succeeding national and regional elections established a new Iraqi government. Periods of occupation by US-led coalitions were accompanied by radical SOE reform in Japan and Germany after World War II. In fact, the initial reconstruction program in Iraq proposed widespread privatization of SOE (Gunter 2007). However, an internal US Government debate on the merits of radical SOE reform combined with an upsurge in violence prevented substantial SOE reform prior to the referendum on the new constitution.

The new Iraqi government has publicly taken a measured approach of examining the benefits of various types of SOE reform on a factory-by-factory basis. In private conversations, Iraqi officials, with the possible exceptions of those of the Ministry of Industry and Minerals and the Ministry of Finance, have little interest in any substantial changes in the country's SOE. In the absence of another political or economic crisis, this attitude is unlikely to change.

For at least the next decade, the health of the Iraqi economy and budget will be determined primarily by the value of petroleum exports. When oil prices were low in 2006 (about $70 per barrel at 2010 prices), it was recognized that direct and indirect subsidies to SOE were a large drain on the shrunken government revenues. This recognition led to increased interest in SOE reform. However, a drop in official interest in SOE reform accompanied the sharp increase in oil prices to almost $100 per barrel in

2008. The moral is that only an extended period of lower than expected oil prices will fuel an Iraqi political consensus in favor of radical SOE reform.

The shift in GoI attitudes towards privatization is evident from the difference in the treatment of SOE in the periodic documents on development strategy. In the National Development Strategies for the years 2005–2007 and 2007–2010, the restructuring and privatization of SOE was a major component of the GoI strategy for "revitalizing the private sector" (GoI 2005b, pp. 25–6; 2007, pp. 51–2). However, the *National Development Plan: 2010–2014* is more pessimistic. It notes that the "economic, financial, legal, and administrative measures necessary to restructure public institutions" are lacking. As a result, it counsels delay until the proper foundation in all of these areas can be prepared (GoI 2010, p. 172).

If this planning document accurately reflects the beliefs of the GoI then it appears that future privatization will be restricted both to a small proportion of factories and any reform will be structured so as to maintain a degree of state control, that is, excluding options 4 and 5 in Table 9.2. In this situation, Iraq's best long-term SOE strategy would be a modified version of the Chinese model. Such a policy would have four major components. First, where possible, engage Iraqi SOE factories in joint ventures with foreign investors. Second, increase the efficiency of remaining SOE by implementing managerial contracts (option 3 of Table 9.2). Third, as discussed in the Chapter 10, liberalize the regulatory environment that impedes growth of Iraq's private sector. Finally, allow the private sector to gradually become Iraq's major source of national income and employment by outgrowing SOE.

10. Entrepreneurship in post-conflict Iraq

Economic attitudes and mentalities of the propertied urban classes in Babylonia [sixth century BC] can be described in terms of two basic (although necessarily idealized) models: a rentier type and an entrepreneur type. Rentiers seek to obtain a reliable income from mostly inherited positions and resources with little risk, by exploiting prebends [temple benefices] and landed property. Entrepreneurs tend to engage in highly profitable but also risky venture businesses in a competitive environment.
(Cornelia Wunsch 2010, p. 45)

Iraq faces a severe unemployment problem because of its rapidly growing population. Any year in which the economy creates less than 250 000 new jobs will lead to further growth in the pool of unemployed young men with associated political instability. As discussed in previous chapters, the public sector is limited in its capacity to absorb each year's addition to the labor force since government services are already severely overmanned. Almost 50 percent of Iraq's labor force is currently directly or indirectly on the public payroll.

Prior to 2003, with the exception of non-grain agriculture, the private sector was suppressed as part of the Arab Ba'athist Socialist Party's philosophy. Since then, private sector growth has occurred mostly in the informal sectors of the economy. The quality of employment data is very low but an estimated 20 percent of the labor force was employed in the informal economy in 2009. As expected, most firms in the informal economy are very small and in the service sectors.

In economic terms, Iraq is well inside its production possibility frontier and – due to innovations and technological change in the rest of the world – that frontier is moving out at a rapid rate. To reduce unemployment and achieve higher living standards for its people, Iraq needs to expand its non-oil dependent economy. The creation and growth of MSME has the best potential to create the jobs needed. While the situation is complex, it appears that the binding constraints on the expansion of private sector MSME is a mismatch between the demand for and supply of entrepreneurs in Iraq combined with very high transaction costs for entrepreneurial acts.

While there has been relatively little empirical research on entrepreneurship in Iraq, the CIPE surveys (2008a; 2008b; 2011) and the high-quality analysis of Desai (2009) have laid a strong foundation for future work.

WHAT DO ENTREPRENEURS DO?

"Entrepreneurs are individuals who, in an uncertain environment, recognize opportunities that most fail to see, and create ventures to profit by exploiting these opportunities" (Gunter 2012, p. 387).

It is widely accepted that entrepreneurs specialize in business-related "judgmental decisions" where there is no obviously correct answer *and* information is costly (Casson 1987, p. 151; see also Casson et al. 2006, pp. 3–4). In other words, entrepreneurs make business decisions based on insights in an uncertain environment. Uncertainty is different from risk. Risk occurs when there are well-defined possible outcomes, a sufficient sample size, and an accepted statistical procedure (Knight [1921] 1971). If one or more of these characteristics is missing then a possible outcome is uncertain.

The entrepreneur faces a challenge when he or she seeks to profit from his or her judgmental decision or insight. Usually, the entrepreneur's ability to immediately sell the insight is severely limited because the insight is either too simple or it is too complex. If too simple then the mere description or demonstration of the insight to a prospective purchaser will allow its theft. At the other extreme, it is difficult to convince another that the insight will eventually lead to a substantial return on investment. As a result, the most common method for an entrepreneur to benefit from an entrepreneurial insight is to establish a new firm.

Especially in a developing, transitional economy like Iraq, it is useful to distinguish between Kirznerian and Schumpeterian entrepreneurship. The former primarily involves arbitrage or speculation. Error, conflict, natural disaster, or unexpected regulatory changes create disequilibria in one or more markets. The Kirznerian entrepreneur – motivated by profit – creates new ways of buying in one existing market and selling in another market. These entrepreneurial acts of arbitrage or speculation resolve market disequilibria as well as reduce profit opportunities for others who later perform the same arbitrage or speculative act (Kirzner 1979, p. 92). In other words, a successful Kirznerian entrepreneur moves an economy from inside its existing production possibility frontier towards its efficient limit.

The Schumpeterian entrepreneur is also motivated by profit. However, this entrepreneur seeks to earn a profit through innovation even in markets that are initially in equilibria. He or she perceives new possibilities for products, markets, manufacturing processes, and so on that are not apparent to others. If the Schumpeterian entrepreneur is successful then creative-destruction will occur. As new processes, products, or markets are created, old products rapidly lose market share, former manufacturing processes are unexpectedly rendered obsolete, and so on (Schumpeter 1911, pp. 214, 228). A successful Schumpeterian entrepreneur shifts an economy's production possibility frontier outwards.

Figure 10.1 illustrates the interrelationship of innovative Schumpeterian and arbitrage/speculative Kirznerian entrepreneurs. The demand for entrepreneurial acts, from which the demand for entrepreneurs is derived, is a function of change. A state that is experiencing no change (no change in consumer preferences, production methods, trade patterns, demographics, and so on) will have little demand for entrepreneurs since uncertainty is low and any profits for filling gaps in this stationary state economy have long since been competed away (Kuran 2010, p. 64).

Of course, such a stationary state is hypothetical. Shocks or advances in human knowledge constantly disturb real economies. The former causes disequilibria in multiple markets that provide arbitrage/speculative profit opportunities for Kirznerian entrepreneurs. Advances in knowledge create innovative profit opportunities for Schumpeterian entrepreneurs that lead to the disruption of existing markets as new markets, new products, or new processes rendering existing practices obsolete. Thus Schumpeterian entrepreneurship also creates disequilibria and, therefore, opportunities for arbitrage/speculation on the part of Kirznerian entrepreneurs.

Currently, Iraq has a desperate need for Kirznerian entrepreneurs to fill the gaps – disequilibria – in its economy. However, at the country's current stage of economic development, the need for Schumpeterian entrepreneurs is not so great.

Aside from their effects on market equilibria, Kirznerian and Schumpeterian entrepreneurs also differ in their characteristics. Successful Schumpeterian entrepreneurs tend to have more formal education, create larger entities, and require more finance. Kirznerian entrepreneurs are more likely to establish small – possibly single person – firms, tend to have limited education, and their need for finance can often be met from informal sources such as family.

There has been some progress in determining the characteristics of entrepreneurship in developing countries. Most relevant to a discussion of entrepreneurship in Iraq are:

1. At a low level of economic development, much entrepreneurial activity is invisible to an outsider or an official. Among the reasons for this

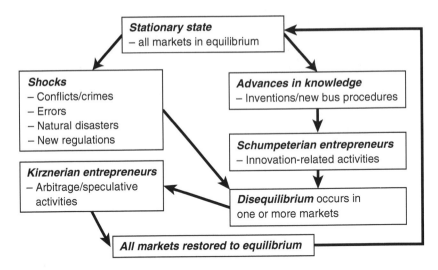

Source: Gunter (2012), Figure 1.

Figure 10.1   Entrepreneurship

invisibility is that entrepreneurs seek to avoid taxation, demands for bribes, or hostile regulations by establishing themselves in the informal economy.

2.   Entrepreneurial activity can be either "opportunity driven" or "necessity driven". In the former case, someone becomes an entrepreneur as a matter of choice while, in the latter case, a person becomes an entrepreneur because he or she has no other options. Acs (2006; and also see Estrin et al. 2006, pp. 712–14) notes that opportunity driven entrepreneurial activity has a greater impact on economic development. It should be noted that most entrepreneurship in Arab countries – including Iraq – is thought to be necessity driven (Noland and Pack 2007, p. 245).

3.   Entrepreneurs in developing countries tend to spread their attention over several related businesses as a form of diversification (Lingelbach et al. 2005, p. 3; Stevenson 2010, p. 174). It is almost a cliché that when an Iraqi entrepreneur decides to give you a business card that he has to shuffle through the cards of his multiple businesses in order to give you the correct one.

4.   In many developing countries, the personal and professional rewards to unproductive rent-seeking are greater than those of productive entrepreneurship. There may be higher profits from persuading the

government to put your competition out of business then to attempt to produce and sell a better product.

DEMAND FOR ENTREPRENEURS

Iraq is experiencing a series of strong shocks. The major causes are oil-funded economic growth, the transition from a socialist to a market economy, and the recovery from severe domestic and international conflict. These shocks create market disequilibria and opportunities for Kirznerian – arbitrage – entrepreneurs.

Natural Resource Dominance

As shown in Table 6.1, the GoI is planning to increase petroleum output and exports by more than 400 percent over the next decade. This will require massive foreign and domestic investment in the discovery, exploitation, refining, and transportation of oil and the accompanying natural gas. The rapid expansion of the country's energy sector is expected to severely disrupt the non-oil economy with respect to consumer goods and services as well as employment.

Transitional Economy

Iraq is also engaged in a transition from centrally planned economic development – which long predates the Arab Ba'athist Socialist Party regime – to a more market-oriented or capitalistic economy. This transition will require changes in both the macroeconomic environment – exchange rate, inflation, budget expenditures – and the microeconomic environments in Iraq. Based on the Eastern European experience, one would expect a shift: from industry to services, from domestic to international markets, and from intermediate to final goods (Estrin et al. 2006, p. 698). International organizations such as the IMF as well as the US Government tend to focus on macroeconomic stabilization, not improving microeconomic efficiency, as the most important policy initiatives.

Unlike most Eastern European transitions, macroeconomic stability was achieved relatively quickly in Iraq (Estrin et al. 2006, p. 699). The currency is stable, the central bank has been willing to act aggressively to contain inflation, and the ratio of national debt to GDP is fairly low as a result of debt forgiveness and GDP growth. However, the microeconomic transition has barely begun. Both Iraqi SOE and the few large private trading firms are products of the statist period and are expending a great deal of managerial energy to avoid substantial change. Therefore, existing firms are more likely to be part of the problem than the solution when it comes to economic liberalization and employment creation (Estrin et al. 2006, p. 693).

Post-Conflict Society

A third source of shocks that contributes to the demand for entrepreneurship in Iraq is the rebuilding of a war-and-sanctions devastated economy. The GoI, the USA and the many international organizations that are involved in the post-conflict rebuilding of Iraq have focused on an intellectually simple effort to return the economy to its antebellum state. In other words, these organizations have concentrated on returning infrastructure, SOE, and the general economic environment of Iraq to its condition in some previous, more favorable, period.

But much of this rebuilding ignores the dramatic social, political, and economic changes in Iraq and the world since Saddam first imposed a socialist template on the country. During the long war with Iran, the UN sanctions period following Saddam's invasion of Kuwait, and the long-drawn out insurgency following the US-led coalition invasion of Iraq in 2003; there have been substantial changes not only in the product and employment preferences of the Iraqi people but also in the people themselves. They have different skills and knowledge, social circumstances have changed, and people have different aspirations. The world outside Iraq has changed as well since began its 45-year experiment with socialism. As a result, Iraqi attempts to return to some halcyon antebellum world are likely to lead to a lower quality of life. Iraq's businesses along with the rest of its society must adapt to a new labor force, new demands, new sources of supply, and new technologies. This requires entrepreneurship.

Furthermore, markets in Iraq are fragmented both geographically and economically. Products that are usually sold together elsewhere in the world, in Iraq are sold separately or on different schedules. Prices and supplies of many food products and utilities are controlled by various government agencies. The SOE contribute to the uncertainty in many markets. Some SOE continue to produce high-cost/low-quality goods and services. Others are not currently producing any products but are attempting to obtain government loans or grants to restart production. This increases the uncertainty facing private firms. Demand for a good or service might be currently strong but if SOE reenter the markets with heavily subsidized products then private firms may find it difficult to compete. All of these structural and institutional changes have greatly enhanced the demand for entrepreneurs. But given that there is a large demand for entrepreneurs in Iraq, will there be a sufficient supply?

SUPPLY OF ENTREPRENEURS

Baumol (1990, p. 894), Schumpeter (1911), and others see the supply of entrepreneurs as determined primarily by culture and history and, therefore, exogenously determined. Although, it is important to note that entrepreneurs are not homogeneous. As Desai et al. (2010, p. 3) point out, entrepreneurs possess differing amounts of skills, discount factors, access to markets and networks. Therefore, the discussion of the supply of entrepreneurs in Iraq will consider not only the impact of history and culture but also the impact of rent-seeking and of two other characteristics that tend to be associated with successful entrepreneurship – appropriate human capital and the capacity to make credible financial commitments (Harris 1970, pp. 348–9).

Are the Iraqis an entrepreneurial people? Since entrepreneurship tends to be associated with self-employment, a Gallup Organization survey on preference for self-employment provides some depressing results. Iraq, along with Egypt, Yemen, and Syria, has the lowest self-employment preference among young people in MENA countries (Stevenson 2010, p. 185). Why do not more young people in Iraq seek to be entrepreneurs? Countries that have recent experience with a market economy tend to have a more favorable entrepreneurial environment (Stevenson 2010, p. 174). This is partly caused by the fact that entrepreneurs tend to come from families with previous entrepreneurial traditions (Estrin et al. 2006, p. 714). One might contrast the strong reaction to economic liberalization of the People's Republic of China with its roughly 35 years (1949–1982) of exclusive socialism to the more troubled reaction of the USSR/Russia which banished market activities for about 75 years (1914–1989). Iraq had about 45 years of socialism (1958–2003), which means that only the oldest family members remember relatively free markets. Another determinate of the supply of entrepreneurship and entrepreneurs is the general attitudes in a society.

Cultural Environment for Entrepreneurship

While there is a continuing debate on which cultural characteristics are actually essential for entrepreneurship to flourish, the following characteristics receive a great deal of attention. Entrepreneurs tend to be young and youthful societies tend to be more willing to try innovations (Estrin et al. 2006, p. 707). Therefore, Iraq's low average age should contribute favorably to its entrepreneurship environment. Entrepreneurship friendly societies or cultures tend to focus more on the individual than the community, have less respect for authority or age, are more focused on financial rewards rather than position and status, and accept that any rewards from accomplishment should accrue primarily to the individual and not be mostly diverted to the members of an extended family, tribe, or the state.

About 97 percent of the Iraqi people are Muslim and most Iraqis state that their religion is an important influence on their lives. Therefore the supply of entrepreneurs in Iraq is, in part, a function of whether Islam provides a favorable environment for entrepreneurship. Some researchers look for evidence in religious writings but these are difficult to interpret or contradictory (Kuran 2010, Chapter 3; Lewis 2002; Patai 2002). A more productive approach would be to examine how Islam and other cultural factors have shaped the institutions that affect present day entrepreneurship.

Since the prophet Mohammed was a merchant, it is no surprise that Islam was initially very entrepreneurial. In fact, as late as the tenth century, almost three-quarters of all Islamic religious scholars earned a living from business (Kuran 2010, p. 66). In outstanding examples of successful entrepreneurship, Muslim traders crossed the world and founded trading posts in Africa, India, and China. Baghdad became a major world-trading center where merchants bought and sold hundreds of products from the far reaches of the three continents. The city was also renowned for manufacturing especially in textiles and metal products. Cross-national economic comparisons are always challenging but the limited data available shows that Baghdad may have been the richest, most populous, most economically dynamic city in the world in the first centuries of the second millennium. Supported by an extensive system of irrigation, what is now Iraq supported a population estimated at more than two million persons, approximately the same population as the UK during the same period.

Baghdad's golden age of business, along with its scientific and artistic creativity, came to an end in 1258 AD when the Mongols sacked Baghdad. Most of the population was slaughtered – including the last Caliph of the Abbasid Caliphate – and the city was devastated (Previté-Orton 1952, p. 754). Attempts to rebuild the city were frustrated over the next forty years by further vicious raids that not only smashed the urban areas in the Tigris and Euphrates valleys but also destroyed large parts of the ancient irrigation systems that had fed a large and growing population. It was not until over six hundred years later, in the late nineteenth century, that Iraq finally returned to the population and per capita real income levels that the land had achieved before 1258 AD (Ansary 2009, pp. 87–8; Maddison 2007, p. 192).

Whether the destruction of Baghdad combined with later military setbacks in Western Europe (the final "reconquista" of Spain in 1492, the failed Siege of Vienna in 1529, and the defeat at the Battle of Lepanto in 1571) shook the confidence of the Islamic leadership is difficult to determine. After all, the three major Islamic states continued to win battles on their periphery and dominate the social and political life at the core of the Islamic world. However, in retrospect, Islam's period of geographic expansion came to an end, to be replaced by a period of growing European influence in Islamic states (Ansary 2009, pp. 217–46).

According to Bernard Lewis (2002, pp. 151–60), there was a gradual acceptance that the Islamic states were losing power and influence compared to the growing and innovative states in the West. This led to a search for the reason behind this reversal of power. One response was that believers had fallen away from the pure Islam of the first half-millennium after Mohammed. Therefore, the remedy was to throw out any innovations that were not firmly grounded in the Qur'an or Sunnah (the words and practices of Mohammed), the sources of Sharia law – Islamic law (see also Ansary 2009, Chapter 13, pp. 247–68).

This centuries long movement towards a more conservative, less creative perspective on a variety of issues had an adverse impact on attitudes towards business in general and entrepreneurs in particular. It was necessary to ground business innovations in Islamic precedents. This had two consequences that still influence attitudes towards entrepreneurship in Islamic countries such as Iraq. Business institutions were developed that favored personal over impersonal exchange. In addition, the practice of justifying innovations in centuries' old writings concealed the significant innovations of the period.

Douglass C. North (1990, pp. 34–5) developed a framework for the study of exchange that might be useful. The most restrictive type of exchange has characterized trade through most of history. Such trade is limited to the "personalized exchange involving small-scale production and local trade". In the absence of what most would recognize as established norms, rules, or laws, trade-related agreements are "enforced" by repetitive transactions and shared cultural values among persons who know each other well.

Over time, there arose a second form of exchange that allowed transactions with persons who were not members of the same family, tribe, or village. These transactions permit more complex agreements over greater time and distance. However, such exchanges are subject to demanding conditions. They required that the parties to such an exchange have "kinship ties, bonding, exchanging hostages or merchant codes of contract. Frequently, the exchange is set within a context of elaborate rituals and religious precepts to constrain the participants" (North 1990, pp. 34–5). An individual or firm who fails to live up to such an agreement can not only expect exclusion from future trade opportunities but also this trader will run the risk of being shunned or spurned by his community. These non-formal methods of enforcing exchange agreements are a complicated but effective entrepreneurial response to the lack of formal third party enforcement. (See Estrin et al. 2006, pp. 716–19 for a further discussion of "coping strategies".) However, the transaction costs of negotiating such non-formal agreements are high.

North's (1990) third form of exchange is impersonal exchange with third-party enforcement. This third party, usually a government, enforces agreements with reasonable predictability, fairness, and cost. This allows the possibility of mutually beneficial transactions among domestic or even international strangers. The expenditure of effort to build and maintain the elaborate relationships required by the second form of exchange is unnecessary with effective third-party enforcement.

Islamic business culture is consistent with North's first and second forms of exchange but is generally inconsistent with the third. The national governments of Islamic states have tended to avoid creating the institutions that are intended to directly support private business activity with the possible exception of building grand bazaars in major cities. The motivation for such bazaars might have been more to facilitate the regulation and taxation of commerce than to encourage it (Kuran 2010, p. 77).

However, as long as most non-Islamic trading peoples also primarily dealt in North's (1990) first two forms of exchange, Islamic traders were not at a disadvantage. But when institutions with reasonably efficient third-party enforcement of contracts appeared in the West, Islamic businessmen started losing the competitive race (Kuran 2010, pp. 63, 71). It is not that any Middle Eastern country lacks laws to govern sophisticated transactions among strangers. These institutions of a modern economy are almost universal. However, they are not as a natural outgrowth of pre-existing domestic business institutions. Rather they were either imposed by colonial powers or adopted in an attempt to prevent the dominance of foreign traders and firms. This reduced both their effectiveness and perceived legitimacy.

Modern commercial laws in Islamic states operate somewhat in an institutional vacuum that makes contracting and enforcing transactions both more difficult and more expensive than in other cultures. This not only reduces the incentives to engage in many entrepreneurial efforts but also allows foreign entrepreneurs to compete more effectively. Examples of institutions that complicate the contracting and enforcement of agreements with strangers are seen in the laws of inheritance and corporation.

In the West, a successful businessperson could will his or her business to one or more of his or her children either directly or by establishing a corporation and ensuring that his or her preferred heir or heirs have a controlling interest. Sharia compliant inheritance laws restrict the ability of a wealth holder to distribute his assets by a will since these inheritance laws set out specific shares for each family member. The impact on entrepreneurial activity is significant. Under Islamic inheritance laws, it was very difficult to pass on a family business. If there were multiple children then it is likely that a family business will be dismantled upon the death of the founder (Kuran 2010, p. 69).

Nor can this problem be avoided by establishing a corporation, a legal person, to continue the entrepreneur's business. Islamic law only respects flesh and blood persons, corporations (as understood in the West) cannot be established (Kuran 2010, p. 69). Since Islamic law only recognizes flesh and blood persons and yet enforces strict inheritance laws, most business entities, however successful, rarely last longer than a single generation.

The adverse impact on entrepreneurship of Sharia laws such as those of concerning inheritance and corporations should not be exaggerated. It is possible to develop Sharia compliant alternatives for incorporating innovations or "bid'ahs". A bid'ah is any type of innovation in Islam. If the Qur'an and Sunnah outline a way of life that cannot be improved upon then any bid'ah is suspicious and should be examined carefully before it is considered acceptable. Since the Qur'an provides guidance for an extensive range of government and business activities, judging the acceptability of a business innovation can be both complex and controversial. Among the products whose adoption was delayed because of concerns that the innovations were unacceptable were coffee, the printing press, and, in 1960s Saudi Arabia, television (Kuran 2010, pp. 72–3).

As a result, entrepreneurs are often forced to spend extensive amounts of time and influence to negotiate an acceptable religious decision on a business-related bid'ah. Or complex procedures may be necessary in order to construct a relatively simple business transaction in a manner that is religiously acceptable. For example, the prohibition against interest may be overcome by the use of "murabaha" where one party (a bank perhaps) who has at least constructive ownership of an item, announces the actual cost and any mark-up to the buyer (see Chapter 8; and Schoon 2008, pp. 32–3). Developing, coordinating, and executing such acceptable alternatives to otherwise forbidden activities may substantially increase the difficulty of bringing an innovation to market. Kuran (2010, p. 81) compared dealing with bid'ah to the difficulties of dealing with environmental regulations in the USA. Such regulations rarely explicitly forbid an activity but however worthy their purpose, they tend to make it more complex and expensive to produce a new product or adopt a new way of doing business.

This adverse impact of Islam on entrepreneurship is strengthened by the tendency to see new business products and procedures as "discoveries" rather than "innovations". Only those changes that can be traced back to religious writings, the more ancient the better, are considered legitimate. Successful entrepreneurs are careful to deny the existence of genuine innovations in what they do. As a result, the discussion of business in much of society, especially in schools, downplays the role and importance of entrepreneurship. An analogy might be if Bill Gates, the co-founder of Microsoft, or Sam Walton of Walmart, felt that it was necessary to not only credit the Federalist Papers as the source of all of their business success but also encourage young potential entrepreneurs to concentrate on intensive study of the Papers if they also wished to become successful.

While Islam dominates the religious environment of Iraq, the participation of other religious sects is not insignificant. When over 1600 small businessmen were asked for their religious affiliation, 6 percent of those that responded stated that they were either Christian or another non-Shi'a, non-Sunni religious affiliation. This 6 percent response is twice their estimated representation in the population at large. It should be noted, however, that almost 22 percent of those surveyed refused to answer the question about religious affiliation (CIPE 2008a, Table 30). Jews are not represented in the sample. As late as 1947, there were an estimated 117 000 Jews in Iraq, 2.6 percent of the total population, almost half of which lived in Baghdad. In fact, contemporary records from 1908 estimate that almost one-third of the population of Baghdad was Jewish (Issawi 1988, p. 124). This Jewish community of Baghdad was formerly considered to be a fruitful source of entrepreneurs in Iraq and was responsible for a variety of business initiatives. However, growing hostility towards Iraqi Jews since the late 1940s drove almost all of them into exile (Tripp 2000, pp. 123–6, 196).

Socialism and Entrepreneurship

The changes in Iraq's entrepreneurial environment brought about by the rise to power of the Arab Ba'athist Socialist Party in 1968 are more a matter of degree than kind. Since at least the Hashemite Monarchy (1941–1958), non-agricultural economic activities were dominated by a relatively small number of Iraqis who gained economic power through familial and friendship relations with the national political leadership. These patron-client relationships ensured political power by providing a mechanism to reward loyalty to the regime with status and economic rewards (Tripp 2000, p. 197).

Creating and maintaining patron-client relations were one of the motivations for the establishment of SOE. SOE in Iraq are widely criticized for being high-cost producers of low-quality products but, to an extent, this criticism is irrelevant since the primary purpose of SOE was not to produce quality goods and services but rather to provide power, status, and economic returns to supporters of the regime and to exclude the opposition from such benefits. Therefore SOE generally oppose the creation of new firms in their industries especially since new firms may support further economic reform (McMillan and Woodruff 2002, p. 153).

In Iraq, this opposition takes the form of: harsh regulation of private business (discussed below); harassing private businesses where SOE are important suppliers to or buyers from private firms; and, as was discussed in Chapter 4, through massive corruption. As a result, many small firms choose to stay in the informal (underground) economy with all of its associated inefficiencies. In a 2011 survey, only 44 percent of all businesses met the legal requirement to register with the GoI. There was a wide divergence among industries, with the highest rate of registration in the construction industry (51 percent) since registration is necessary to bid on government contracts (CIPE 2011, pp. 18–19). These percentages may exaggerate the actual level of compliance since unregistered entities are probably less likely to participate in surveys.

Unregistered or informal firms account for an estimated 20 percent of Iraq's employment. Since informal firms are unable to access the legal system, they tend to engage in North's (1990) first two forms of exchange. Surviving in the informal economy with its lack of formal regulation is inherently an entrepreneurial act. However, small firms in the informal economy often survive more by their agility at navigating the various layers of governmental authority rather than their ability to recognize purely economic opportunities (Estrin et al. 2006, p. 699). If this pool of active entrepreneurs could be freed from the high transaction costs associated with the informal economy then the potential for real economic growth and employment are significant.

The fact that both Islam and socialism tend to discourage entrepreneurship should not be taken to mean that they support similar economic policies. For example, Muhammad Baqir al-Sadr, a renowned twentieth-century Iraqi cleric, wrote a major economic work where he spent eight times more space attacking socialism than capitalism (Kuran 2004, pp. 98–9). His view – which is widely held among Iraqi religious leaders – is that there are three alternative economic structures: socialism, capitalism, and Islamic economics.

Wage Takers, Entrepreneurs, and Rent-Seekers

As Baumol (1990, p. 894) pointed out, if the supply of entrepreneurs is almost entirely a function of culture and history then it is a "counsel of despair" since nothing can be done to increase the supply of entrepreneurs. However, he states that it is possible that a potential entrepreneur will engage in unproductive or even destructive entrepreneurship as opposed to the productive type that leads to economic development. Therefore, it might be possible by creating the proper incentives and institutions to persuade potential entrepreneurs to engage in welfare increasing initiatives (Baumol 1990, pp. 897–8).

It is useful in the case of Iraq to divide career opportunities into three categories: wage takers, entrepreneurs, and rent-seekers. Wage takers are satisfied with jobs with minimum compensation uncertainty. While such employment can exist in both the private and public sectors, in Iraq public sector employment provides the most favorable environment for wage takers. On average, employment with a government ministry or SOE provides 40–60 percent higher wages than equivalent jobs in the small formal private sector. In addition, public sector jobs in Iraq provide stronger job security, better benefits, a pension, and a more relaxed pace of work. Thus any improvement in the number or relative compensation of public sector employment in Iraq can be expected to reduce the pool of potential entrepreneurs. Even for those potential entrepreneurs who avoid the temptation of a government job, there is still the problem of diversion from entrepreneurship to rent-seeking.

Rent-seekers are persons who seek to make a living by capturing economic rents rather than by engaging in voluntary trade (Krueger 1974; Tullock 1967, pp. 224–32) For example, a rent-seeker could bribe a government official to restrict auto imports to a single port controlled by the rent-seeker. This monopoly misallocates resources, reduces aggregate welfare, and redistributes income away from consumers in favor of the monopolist (see Tullock 2005a, p. 9). Rent-seeking can also take the form of legal activities such as lobbying the government to award a contract to a company that is not objectively the high-quality/low-cost producer.

Rent-seeking impacts the pool of Iraqi potential entrepreneurs in two ways. First, if potential entrepreneurs were attempting to maximize their wealth or status then one would expect them to choose to be either entrepreneurs or rent-seekers based on whichever one had the greatest potential return. Second, some rent-seekers could work at diverting entrepreneurial profits into their own pockets. This would discourage potential entrepreneurs by reducing possible entrepreneurship profits. The implications for public policy are clear although difficult to execute. If incentives and institutions can be created that discourage rent-seeking without placing a burden on productive entrepreneurship then an economy would gain in two ways: reduced damage to the economy from unproductive or destructive entrepreneurship; and an acceleration of economic development from more persons engaged in productive entrepreneurship. Changing these incentives and institutions will be a much more rapid process than waiting for cultural change (Baumol 1990, pp. 916–19).

Incentives in Iraq may be shifted in the direction of productive entrepreneurship by increasing the supplies of complementary inputs in the entrepreneurship process. These would include providing the potential entrepreneur with the necessary knowledge or skills, and ensuring that he or she is able to provide adequate financial guarantees. Without appropriate education and ability to provide financial guarantees, the likelihood of entrepreneurial success is low.

Education of Entrepreneurs

The smaller businesses of Iraqi entrepreneurs are often referred to as MSME. At the micro end, enterprises can be expected to have few (or one) employees, negative economies of scale, and require only low-skilled labor in production and management (El-Gamal et al. 2000, p. 10). At the medium enterprise level, one could expect up to 500 employees, economies of scale, and the need for skilled and educated workers and management.

The *Iraq Household Socio-Economic Survey: 2007* (COSIT 2008, Table 6-22, p. 330) provided data on firm size based on a survey of employed persons in over 127 000 Iraqi households. Including all forms of employment, this survey showed that about 55 percent of all Iraqi workers were in firms with less than 50 employees.

But the COSIT (2008) survey included government employment at both the ministries and SOE. One would expect that employment in the private sector to be in smaller entities. In fact, this expectation is supported by a 2011 CIPE survey of about 900 Iraqi businessmen. This survey shows that private business in Iraq is primarily composed of micro and small firms. According to the survey:

Four employees or less: 65%
Between five and ten employees: 20%
More than ten employees: 11%
Refused to answer question: 4%

Of these businesses, about 83 percent were sole proprietorships, 13 percent family owned, and 2 percent non-family partnerships or domestic corporations (CIPE 2011, Charts A1 and A3, pp. 43–5).

With respect to education, a study of entrepreneurs in Egypt found a wide distribution of educated workers among MSME. For example, while 20 percent of the entrepreneurs in micro enterprises possessed a university degree, 13 percent were barely literate or illiterate (El-Gamal et al. 2000, p. 13). Harris (1970, pp. 352, 354) found similar results in Nigeria where many successful entrepreneurs were illiterate or not very educated. Using the distinction discussed above, while Schumpeterian entrepreneurship in the OECD countries tends to require substantial formal education, this is not true for Kirznerian entrepreneurs in countries at Iraq's stage of economic development. Successful Kirznerian entrepreneurship at the MSME level requires relatively low levels of formal schooling.

However, without being able to read, write, and calculate; the odds are strongly against becoming a successful entrepreneur. Unfortunately, as discussed in Chapter 3, the proportion of the Iraqi population that is either illiterate or failed to complete elementary education is high. Aside from the social and political benefits, it can be expected that more universal elementary education will lead to more persons attempting entrepreneurship and a greater likelihood of success for those who make the attempt.

Aside from basic general education, research has shown that the best education for potential entrepreneurs is working for or being associated with an independent businessman (Stevenson 2010, p. 178). As Lingelbach et al. (2005, p. 7) states: "Entrepreneurship is a lonely profession rendered more difficult without the benefit of mentorship and apprenticeship". Of course, there may be a self-selection bias; potential entrepreneurs may seek out current entrepreneurs to work for. However, the tendency for family members of independent businessmen to become businessmen themselves points to a learning process in addition to self-selection. It is not clear whether the learning involves specific business skills (for example how to keep accurate records), the inculcation of a business attitude or both. In contrast, having worked for a government agency or SOE appears to reduce the likelihood of becoming a successful businessman. Since an estimated 50 percent of the Iraqi labor force work directly or indirectly for the government, this reduces the learning-by-doing opportunities for potential entrepreneurs.

Ability to give Financial Guarantees.

If a potential entrepreneur is unable to provide financial guarantees then his or her likelihood of success is low (Harris 1970, p. 351). Without finance, the entrepreneur must try to convince others to advance resources without a reasonable assurance of payment based on limited information. In other words, he or she must try to convince others to become entrepreneurs like himself or herself without providing so much information that his or her prospective partners will steal his or her innovation. The adverse impact on in the Iraqi economy of the serious problems in the banking, bond and stock markets were discussed in Chapter 8. However, the difficulty of obtaining finance is a special burden to potential entrepreneurs.

"Getting Credit" and "Protecting Investors" are two of the nine subcategories that are used to estimate the World Bank's (2012a) "Ease of Doing Business". In 2012, Iraq ranked 174th in getting credit (out of the 183 countries in the sample) while it ranked 122nd in protecting investors. Not only is the regulatory environment bad in Iraq but also it is deteriorating. In 2010, Iraq's "getting credit" and "protecting investors" rankings were 168th and 120th. The low ranking with respect to getting credit was caused by weak legal rights for creditors and an almost complete absence of either private or public credit information on firms or individuals. The relatively small number of non-SOE bank loans are primarily to government workers, bank employees, and influential politicians, not entrepreneurs. The poor "protecting investors" ranking is based on low rankings in three metrics; the extent of disclosure of significant firm transactions, the extent of director liability, and the ease of shareholder lawsuits.

Of course, bank loans and equity sales are not the only sources of finance for an Iraqi entrepreneur. Many entrepreneurs raise needed finance by borrowing from family members or obtaining credit from suppliers or buyers. A nationwide survey of all Iraqi households showed that the primary source of loans was family members in Iraq or abroad. These family loans accounted for over 81 percent of all loans. Trade credit from merchants was the second most popular source at about 11 percent. State-owned or private banks supplied about 6 percent of total loans with moneylenders, employers, and NGO accounting for the rest (COSIT 2008, Table 10-2, p. 756; see also CIPE 2011, Chart A6, p. 47).

The dominance of family savings and retained earnings as financing sources has an adverse impact on potential Iraqi entrepreneurs. Not only is finance for future operations limited by previous business profitability but achieving any significant scale of production will probably be a gradual process as each stage of production must finance succeeding stages. Gradual growth makes an entrepreneur more vulnerable to rent-seeking by regulatory authorities.

Just like new born animals in the wild, a firm is most vulnerable to regulatory predators when it is small. But as noted by Parkinson (1957) in one of the more controversial chapters of his classic work, since bureaucracies tend to operate at a very slow pace, rapid growth will reduce the period of vulnerability to regulatory exploitation. Once a firm becomes large enough, its vulnerability to regulatory predation falls since a large firm can demand (or pay for) political protection from the grasping bureaucracy (Parkinson 1957, pp. 92–4). On the other hand, a slow growing private firm gives regulators an extended opportunity to perceive, evaluate, plan, and execute the successful exploitation of the firm.

External Sources of Entrepreneurs

There are external sources of entrepreneurs that could also help meet the demand. Since the rise of Saddam, large numbers of Iraqis have fled the country. The UN estimated that almost two million persons (7 percent of the population) have fled including 40 percent of the country's middle class. While most are living lives of poverty in neighboring countries, a substantial number reached the West.

Over the last thirty years, many of these former Iraqis have either become entrepreneurs by choice or necessity in their new home countries, or have obtained the skills and access to financing essential for successful entrepreneurship. The return of this Iraqi diaspora would be especially valuable since they can be expected to have a realistic view of the Iraqi business environment.

TRANSACTION COSTS FACING ENTREPRENEURS

Transaction costs are the costs involved in negotiating, executing, and enforcing an agreement to trade, a good, or service other than the costs to the seller of producing the product and to the buyer to consume it.

Rule of Law

The scope for entrepreneurship is a function of the size of the market since a larger market allows for increased specialization. Since the days of Adam Smith (1776, p. 9) it has been recognized that increased specialization facilitates invention and innovation and therefore entrepreneurship. However, the size of a market is determined not only by geography, culture, and technology but also by the rule of law.

As discussed above, private sector trade in Iraq is comes in three types: the first two are local personalized exchange and impersonal exchange enforced by non-formal means. The third type of exchange, trade between strangers with third-party enforcement, is limited. The primary cause of

Table 10.1   Ease of doing business in Iraq

Best business environment in world has ranking of 1 Worst business environment in world has ranking of 183	Iraq ranking	Range of MENA rankings
Overall ranking (out of 183 nations)	164	12 to 170
1. Starting a business	176	10 to 179
2. Dealing with construction permits	120	4 to 164
3. Getting electricity	46	10 to 164
4. Registering property	98	1 to 167
5. Getting credit	174	48 to 177
6. Protecting investors	122	17 to 179
7. Paying taxes	49	2 to 164
8. Trading across borders	180	5 to 180
9. Enforcing contracts	140	38 to 177
10. Closing a business	183	25 to 183

Source: World Bank (2012a), "Ease of Doing Business" Index.

this limitation is the lack of a commercial code that provides for predictable, fair, and inexpensive resolution of commercial disputes. This has severely constrained the size of the market for many goods and services. Smaller markets tend to mean lower entrepreneurial profits and, therefore, fewer entrepreneurs.

The current Iraq commercial code severely limits transactions among private strangers as a complex ubiquitous bureaucracy attempts to manage most economic activity. This is a common situation in transition economies. Business regulations were developed during a previous planned-economy regime and are inappropriate to a more market-oriented economy (Stevenson 2010, pp. 190–191). Relatively simple business activities require substantial paperwork and the approval of multiple levels of the Iraqi government. Like all sophisticated bureaucracies, these agencies take a great deal of time to approve routine requests but tend to stall completely when faced with any kind of innovation. If under common law "All is allowed except what is specifically forbidden" then in Iraq "All is forbidden except what is specifically allowed" .

These complex business regulations also tend to provide large rewards for rent-seekers. As was discussed in the corruption chapter, the Iraqi economy is structured so as to discourage private business and facilitate very profitable rent-seeking. Table 10.1 shows the results from the World Bank's 2012 "Ease of Doing Business" survey (2012a) for Iraq and, for comparison, the other nations in MENA.

Of the 183 nations in the 2012 survey, Iraq ranked 164th overall, which not only showed it to have one of the most hostile regulatory environments for business in the MENA countries but also in the world. Of the ten subcategories evaluated by the World Bank, Iraq scored particularly poorly in starting a business (176th out of the 183 countries evaluated), getting credit (174th), trading across borders (180th), and closing a business (183rd, tied with the West Bank and Gaza as the worst in the world). Iraq not only ranks in the bottom quintile in most subcategories, its relative standing has deteriorated over the last four years – its overall ranking was 153 in 2008. The Iraqi regulatory environment for private business is bad and getting worse.

Particularly damaging to any attempt to encourage entrepreneurship in Iraq are the regulatory barriers to starting a new business, getting credit, and closing a business. The required procedures are complex, difficult, and expensive. As a result, these regulations act as a severe "tax" on entrepreneurship that either discourage entrepreneurs from attempting to create a new business or encourage him or her to operate in the informal or underground economy with all of the associated inefficiencies that were so vividly described by De Soto (1989; 2000).

As an illustration, consider starting a new business in Iraq. The World Bank "starting a new business" ranking is based on a survey to determine the procedures needed to start a small or medium size business legally – without paying bribes. In Iraq, there are 11 separate procedures involving multiple government offices. If the potential entrepreneur knows exactly what to do and is unwilling to pay bribes then it will take 77 days and about 116 percent of the average Iraqi annual income (about $3500) to register a new business. Contrast this to registering a similar business in the state of Delaware in the USA which can be accomplished online in about half an hour and costs $139.

Getting credit is made difficult because of the absence of most standard legal protections for creditors. On a ranking of 0–10, Iraq's legal rights index is 3. Also, there is neither a public nor private registry of collateral or credit ratings.

Trading across international borders is also very difficult for an Iraqi entrepreneur. Iraq ranked 180th out of the 183 nations surveyed when it came to the difficulty of importing or exporting a dry container of ordinary legally manufactured goods to or from a business located on the periphery of the country's largest business city. For example, what are the costs of shipping a container from dockside in Basrah to the suburbs of Baghdad? Not only does it take 83 days to complete the paperwork and obtain the necessary approvals but also the cost per container is an estimated $3700. Exporting is equally complex and expensive: 80 days and $3600 per container. These costs include fees, document preparation charges, terminal handling charges, and inland transport. The fees do *not* include tariffs, duties, or bribes. For comparison purposes, a similar shipment to or from Saudi Arabia would take only 13 days to process and cost about $620. Only high-value goods that can be ordered with a long-lead time will be legally traded. Other products will either not be traded or, more likely, smuggled.

Finally, Iraq has the worst ranking in the world with respect to "closing a business" which, considering the competition from some other extremely dysfunctional countries is an impressive achievement. For example, in a country in the top-third of surveyed nations such as Kuwait (ranked 48th), closing a business takes about four years and stakeholders recover an average of 44 percent. In Iraq, the average recovery is zero since no firm has successfully completed a legal bankruptcy. The impact of this dysfunctional bankruptcy law on entrepreneurs is twofold. Since there is little chance that a creditor will be able to recover even a fraction of his or her investment if a business fails, they will hesitate to lend. Also, without a bankruptcy law, it is difficult for an entrepreneur to recover from a failed endeavor. If an entrepreneur attempts to establish a new business then the unsatisfied creditors from previous endeavors will seek to attach the assets of the new firm.

Not only are Iraqi business regulations generally hostile to private business but also they are difficult for even an educated businessman to understand. Across the six cities in a CIPE survey, only 16 percent of businessmen thought that the regulations were understandable while 31 percent responded in the negative. The remainder thought that parts of the commercial code were clear and others obscure (CIPE 2008b, Table 18, p. 7). This creates unnecessary uncertainty that further discourages potential entrepreneurs.

A related issue is whether Iraqi businessmen are confident that, after expending substantial time and money complying with incredibly complex laws and regulations, the authorities will carry out their end of the "bargain" (Estrin et al. 2006, p. 705). This confidence is apparently low in Iraq. Security aside, when Iraqi businessmen were asked to name their top three items that had the most adverse impact on the growth of Iraqi business, the results were surprising. The top two factors cited nationwide were, as expected, corruption (volunteered by 61 percent of all businesses surveyed) and the weakness of Iraqi infrastructure weakness (cited by 48 percent). However, in third place was "not applying laws and regulations" that was cited by 41 percent. This law and regulation factor has been interpreted as revealing a lack of confidence that even if correct procedures are followed, the authorities will do what they said they would do. According to the survey, this has a greater adverse impact on businesses then difficulties in obtaining finance, high fees, or the problems of obsolete equipment (CIPE 2011, Table 1.1, p. 17).

The complexity and obscurity of business regulations in Iraq are not unloved artifacts of the Saddam regime. Rather the expense and time required for a businessman to comply with the regulations increases the incentives to pay bribes to avoid the regulations.

Corruption

Whether corruption (the abuse of public power for private benefit) amounts to a significant transaction cost in Iraq is sometimes debated. As an Iraqi businessman told me: "In the West, firms pay lawyers to ensure that transactions are executed in the intended manner while, in the Middle East, firms pay bribes for the same purpose". If, as in Iraq, the legal system is opaque, inefficient, and unpredictable then paying bribes may be not only more efficient but also cheaper.

This argument that, in view of the ineffectiveness of the Iraqi legal system, businessmen should use a "second best" corruption solution has at least two weaknesses. First, corruption is a very expensive way of facilitating business transactions. In a 2011 survey of business owners in nine Iraqi provinces, the CIPE reported that over half of the businesses stated that corruption accounted for more than 20 percent of their total costs of doing business (CIPE 2011, Chart 5.1, p. 29). This is consistent with an earlier survey that revealed that between 12 percent (Kirkuk city) and 26 percent (Basrah city) of firms reported that corruption accounted for 40 percent or more of total costs (CIPE 2008a, Table 27).

In addition, the costs of corruption tend to worsen over time. There are strong incentives for government officials to continually increase the complexity and expense of complying with regulations in order to encourage businessmen to pay more substantial bribes. Thus widespread corruption not only increases the cost of doing business but, as discussed above, it discourages potential entrepreneurs.

Transportation Costs

Especially in developing countries, transportation costs can be a substantial contributor to overall transaction costs. Just as the absence of various institutions can reduce expected entrepreneurial profits by restricting the size of the market in which the entrepreneur can trade; absent or low-quality infrastructure can have the same effect. For example, an Iraqi agribusiness entrepreneur saw an opportunity in producing high-quality chickens using modern feed and veterinarian care but was unable to bring his product to market because of the lack of rapid road transport. Much of his stock was dying before it reached the urban market.

Of course, this problem could be seen as another entrepreneurial opportunity – to provide secure cold-chain truck transportation so that a quality product can be provided to the market despite bad roads. However, much infrastructure is non-excludable and, therefore, requires government or charitable provision. This topic is discussed at greater length in Chapter 11. The take-away is that poor or non-existence infrastructure increases transportation costs and therefore reduces potential entrepreneurial profits.

In summary, there is currently a great need for an increase in private sector employment in Iraq in an environment of rapid change and entrepreneurs can play an important role in creating this employment. This leads to the critical question of which policy initiatives should be adopted to increase the likelihood of successful entrepreneurship?

WHAT CAN BE DONE?

There is a strong temptation to provide a laundry list of the many initiatives that individually or collectively have facilitated entrepreneurship in other countries (see, for example, Stevenson 2010, pp. 197–201). In fact, the US Embassy in Baghdad and the Multi-National Force-Iraq, in the economic annex to their 2009 joint campaign plan were unable to resist this temptation. However, such a laundry list may do more damage than good unless the points are carefully crafted to the specific conditions of Iraq. First, as discussed in Chapter 4, Iraq suffers from corruption at every level of the government. Any policy recommendation intended to facilitate entrepreneurship that can possibly be distorted to elicit bribes will be so distorted. For example, it is believed that the 2009 GoI program to provide microloans to potential entrepreneurs had very little impact since most of the funds were diverted to ministerial clients.

Second, ministerial capacity is limited not only by a general lack of managerial experience but also because of the strict hierarchy in ministerial decisionmaking. Even relatively minor decisions must proceed up the bureaucracy step-by-step with each layer attaching carefully crafted comments until it arrives at the top. As a result, the minister and his few trusted aides struggle to deal with a flood of requests for decisions. Routine decisions are long delayed; innovative requests involving new programs often cause the bureaucratic decision process to seize up entirely.

Finally, cooperation among ministries is more the exception than the rule. As was discussed in Chapters 6 and Chapter 11 the Ministries of Oil and Electricity are often unable to coordinate either the supply of fuel to the major big city electrical generation plants or the supply of electricity to the three largest refineries. As a result, Iraq continues to suffer from shortages of both electricity and refined fuels. The moral is that any pro-entrepreneurship policy that requires inter-ministerial cooperation or even cuts across different ministries areas of responsibilities will be difficult to execute with any efficiency.

Because of corruption, limited managerial capacity, and the difficulties of inter-ministerial coordination, it is best to focus on a few initiatives with a reasonable chance of success rather than spread limited legislative and managerial resources over a large number of policies. I think that strong arguments can be made that corruption, regulatory hostility, and low levels of education are the most serious problems. The possible causes and cures of corruption were analyzed in Chapter 4 so I will focus on the other two constraints.

Regulatory Hostility

Along with corruption, the greatest barrier to Iraqi entrepreneurship is regulatory hostility towards private business especially with respect to: starting a new business, getting credit, trading across borders, and closing a business. Since 2004, the World Bank and the US Government have strongly encouraged the GoI to rationalize its Saddam-era business regulations. However, little progress has been made. One reason is that in Iraq, as in the rest of the MENA countries, the government has focused more on encouraging large-scale foreign investment than on efforts to encourage the creation of domestic small businesses (Stevenson 2010, p. 173).

However, re-writing Iraq's commercial code would provide massive corruption opportunities, task ministerial managerial capacity to the limit, and require extensive inter-ministerial cooperation; the odds are poor that such a re-write could be completed and implemented in less than a decade even with strong support from the Prime Minister's office. But Iraq cannot afford to wait a decade for the increased employment and market efficiency that greater entrepreneurship is expected to produce (Gunter 2009a). Aside from the economic impact, a substantial rise in the pool of unemployed young men may threaten the nation's new born democracy. A more radical approach should be considered – the wholesale adoption of an existing set of business regulations of another country.

Adoption of the existing regulations of OECD countries would require difficult and controversial translations into Arabic and Kurdish and are thought to be too non-sectarian for Iraq with its constitution that emphasizes the role of Islam. Kuwait's World Bank (2012a) "Ease of

Table 10.2   Starting a new business in Iraq, Saudi Arabia, and the UAE

Starting a business	Iraq	Saudi Arabia	UAE
World ranking (out of 183)	176th	10th	42nd
Procedures	11	3	8
Time	77 days	5 days	13 days
Cost (% of income per capita)	116%	6%	6%
Minimum capital required (% of income per capita)	36%	0%	0%

Source: World Bank (2012a), "Ease of Doing Business" Index.

Doing Business" ranking is 67th (out of 183) compared to Iraq's ranking of 164th. However, recent history between these two countries makes the Iraqi adoption of Kuwait's code extremely unlikely. Possibly the best choice for adoption are the business regulations of either Saudi Arabia or the UAE. In fact, the GoI has sent delegations to Dubai, one of the seven Emirates that compose the UAE, to discuss methods of facilitating business (*Khaleej Times*, 2012). Saudi Arabia or the UAE do not have the language or religious issues of the Western nations. Saudi Arabia's "business friendly regulatory environment" ranks 12th internationally in the World Bank's (2012a) "Ease of Doing Business" classification while the UAE ranks 33rd.

In the critical category of starting a new business, both Saudi Arabia and the UAE provide a much better environment for entrepreneurs than Iraq's current regulatory morass. As shown in Table 10.2, there are fewer procedures that require much less time to complete, less than a week in Saudi Arabia or 13 days in the UAE, compared to over two months in Iraq. Despite the fact that average per capita income adjusted for cost of living (PPP) is almost seven times greater in Saudi Arabia and 15 times greater in the UAE than in Iraq; the actual out-of-pocket cost of starting a business is greatest in Iraq.

Similar improvements would be made in the areas of getting credit (Saudi Arabia is ranked 48th and the UAE is 78th in the world compared to Iraq at 174th), trading across borders (18th and 5th compared to 180th), and resolving insolvency (73rd and 151st compared to 183rd). Obviously, the Saudi Arabian or UAE commercial codes are not perfect and the argument is made that, rather than adopt a flawed commercial code from another country, Iraq should instead perfect its own code. But as Voltaire (2010) reminds us: "The best is the enemy of the good". A reasonably good commercial code for Iraq in the near future would have a much more favorable impact on economic development in Iraq then a perfect code that will not be implemented for a decade.

Primary, Intermediate, and Secondary Education

Education increases the likelihood that an entrepreneur will be successful (Baumol et al. 2007, p. 153). Most Kirznerian entrepreneurship does not require high levels of formal education or training. In most cases, a solid primary and intermediate education generally provides an adequate foundation. Unfortunately, in 2008, 14 percent of Iraqi children were not receiving primary education while almost one-third of children aged 12–14 years were not attending intermediate schools. For secondary education (15–17 years), the rate of non-attendance rose to 45 percent of males and 62 percent of females or 54 percent overall (COSIT 2008, Table 3.4, p. 228). As recommended in Chapter 3, the GoI should focus on achieving 100 percent attendance at elementary school for boys and girls aged 6–11 years as well as eradicating illiteracy among older Iraqis. This should increase the potential pool of entrepreneurs.

Reducing corruption, regulatory reform, and extending education in the direction discussed above face several challenges. First, asking the ministries to "do less" with respect to regulating private businesses will be difficult since a reduction in ministerial responsibilities will be seen as leading to reduced power and status as well as reduced opportunities to extract bribes. Second, easing the entry of new firms is necessary but the degree of its success in bringing about a substantial entrepreneurial-led expansion of private sector employment will depend on whether the GoI intentionally or unintentionally offsets improvements in the regulatory environment with adverse budget changes (Stevenson 2010, p. 172). Finally, if oil prices are "too low" or "too high" over the next decade then regulatory reform will most likely stall. If oil prices are "too low" then – in a repeat of 2006 – the GoI will probably respond to the resulting severe budget constraint by defunding all new initiatives in order to reserve spending on oil production and the compensation of current and former government employees. However, if oil prices are "too high" then there will be little sense of urgency in encouraging entrepreneurship and the expansion of Iraq's private sector. The GoI can respond to demands for employment by further increasing the already bloated government payrolls.

What is needed is the political will to push change through a bureaucracy distinguished by its inertia. Elected and appointed officials may discover this political will through necessity. In view of the rapidly growing labor force in Iraq, entrepreneurship creating private sector jobs might be the only viable alternative to political instability.

11. Infrastructure and essential services

> This is an enterprise which at first sight appears gigantic, but its
> accomplishment, in the opinion of those who are acquainted with
> the localities, and have examined its capabilities, is considered
> comparatively easy. An Imperial firman has lately been granted
> to an English Company . . . for the construction of a railway
> to cross Turkey in Asia, by the Valley of the Euphrates.
> (Count Edward de Warren 1966, p. 138)

Almost every history of modern Iraq states or implies that Iraq is an artificial construction (see, for example, Catherwood 2004). Much is made of
the fact that the British constructed the country from three separately gov-
erned Ottoman provinces: Basrah, Baghdad, and Mosul. However, these
"artificial construction" arguments generally focus on ethnic and political
differences among the regions and ignore the trade and routes that have
tied the country together for millennia.

Traditional trade routes in Iraq reflect geography, which favors North–
South movement. The riverbeds of the Euphrates and the Tigris not only
provided water and power but also were the home of most of the population throughout history. Between the cities of Baghdad and Basrah and
the port of Al Faw on the Persian Gulf, these rivers were navigable for
fairly large vessels while roads and railroads ran parallel to the Euphrates
to middle Syria and along the Tigris through Mosul to northern Syria near
the Syrian–Turkish border.

In fact, before the completion of the Suez Canal in 1869, the Basrah–
Baghdad–Mosul route was a critical route for world trade. The products
of the East converged on Basrah and proceeded up the Tigris and the
Euphrates in large boats to Baghdad. There they traded for the products
of the West brought overland from Antioch on the Mediterranean or from
what is now Turkey through Mosul (Rousseau 1966, pp. 135–6). Steam
navigation on the Tigris and the Euphrates and railroads connected the
major cities and carried large amounts of goods and passengers that tied
the three cities together in complex trade transactions (Issawi 1966, pp.
137–53, 179–85). Therefore transportation – like the power and communication infrastructure of Iraq – is more than a means for providing goods
and essential services to the population, it is also a means of strengthening
the bonds among the Iraqi people.

Since the complete destruction of Baghdad by the Mongols in 1258 CE, a succession of governments in what is now Iraq have gradually created and maintained an extensive infrastructure to provide essential services such as water, power, and transportation. But in the last three decades, civil conflict, the long Iraq–Iran War (1980–1988), the wars with US-led coalitions in 1990–1991 and 2003, the associated UN sanctions, and the more recent fight with the insurgency have resulted in a sharp deterioration of national infrastructure both from direct damage and foregone maintenance. While the engineering problems are challenging enough, the incentives issues are even more difficult. Saddam bought loyalty by providing most public goods and services for free or at very low cost. These subsidies were massive and were financed by crude oil exports and large-scale foreign borrowing. Since these fees were generally insufficient to cover maintenance costs, much less the capital costs required for any expansion, infrastructure improvements and expansions were driven not by demand but rather by the willingness of the Baghdad bureaucracy to expend funds. Both during Saddam's regime and in the immediate period following his fall from power, these expenditure decisions appear to be made more for political than economic reasons.

In this chapter the focus will be on electricity generation, potable water, airports, water transportation, railroads and roads, and communication. The equally important infrastructure associated with exploration, production, and transportation of Iraq's large oil and gas resources was discussed in Chapter 6; and dams and the extensive irrigation system were treated in Chapter 7.

ELECTRICITY GENERATION

Providing reliable quality round-the-clock electricity is the most critical infrastructure challenge facing Iraq. Despite billions of dollars in maintenance and investment as well as the hard work of many Iraqis, the gap between the demand and supply of electricity is greater than ever. This has resulted in outages that not only have stalled economic development but also have worked a genuine hardship on the population. Without air-conditioning, summer temperatures in Central Iraq of 43°C (110°F) are almost unbearable and constitute a public health hazard for the very young, the very old, and the sick.

Electricity in Iraq faces problems of both quantity and quality. There are scheduled and unscheduled blackouts in almost all Iraqi cities. In 2010, it was estimated that the quantity demanded of electricity was about 9500 kWh while the actual quantity supplied was about one-third less – 6400 kWh. Despite its huge energy resources, Iraq had to import about 14 percent of its electricity. In 2010, total electrical consumption was 55.7 billion kWh while only 49.0 billion kWh was produced domestically (US CIA 2012); the rest was imported from Turkey and Iran. With respect to quality, for the reasons discussed below, electricity from the grid is often substantially below the 50 hertz frequency promised. This can damage consumers' electrical devices.

In 2009, there were over 180 electricity generation units in Iraq. Seven large thermal power plants produced more than 54 percent of the country's electricity. These thermal plants use HFO. HFO is in excess supply because Iraqi refineries are inefficient and, as a result, produce a lower proportion of valuable lighter fuels and a higher proportion of sludge-like HFO than refineries in other countries. In fact, some refineries in Jordan and Turkey sometimes use Iraqi HFO instead of crude oil as feedstock. However, exporting HFO is difficult since it must be heated before it can be pumped and it tends to contaminate the pipelines, railroad tanker cars, or trucks in which it is carried. In fact, inability to dispose of HFO has led to shutdowns of some Iraqi refineries. Therefore, the use of HFO for electricity generation in Iraq is a good second-best solution. The remaining electrical generation in Iraq was almost evenly divided between two hydroelectric facilities (24 percent of total electricity generated) and nine gas-turbine power plants (21 percent) (SIGIR 2009b, pp. 146, 148).

There is a close relationship between electricity generation and refineries. Unexpected electrical blackouts shutdown refineries while failure to produce and deliver the proper quality and quantity of fuel leads to either a reduction in electricity generation or increases in maintenance costs as inappropriate fuel use increases wear on the generation equipment. This symbiotic relationship requires close coordination between the Ministries of Electricity and Oil that unfortunately does not exist.

By 2009, Iraq's electricity supply finally exceeded pre-2003 levels. However, the estimated gap between demand and supply continued to grow. This gap was taken as a clarion call for increased investment in electrical infrastructure. However, such statements ignore the challenges of estimating true electricity demand as well as the difficulty of increasing productivity in power generation.

Prices and Physics

The first problem is that until October 2010, the official price for electricity, 2.5 ID/kWh (or about 0.2 cents/kWh), was not only less than the estimated cost of electrical production, roughly 17 ID/kWh (about 1.2 cents), but also was substantially below estimates of the market-clearing price. As a result, the demand for electricity was not constrained by the cost of the electricity as much as by incomes and the availability of goods and services that use electricity.

When there was an increase in incomes, especially of civil servants with their strong job security, this led to an increase in the purchases of air conditioners and other electricity-using appliances resulting in an increased demand for electricity (Allawi 2007, p. 257). By the same reasoning, a drop in the price of air conditioners or other electrical appliances also leads to an increase in demand for electricity. While there are several estimates of the demand for electricity, in the absence of a realistic market price for electricity, these estimates – including the 9500 kWh estimate referenced above – are almost meaningless. Since the marginal cost to the user of additional electricity consumption is near zero, any increase in the supply of electricity leads to the purchase of more electricity-using goods and services. As a result, the gap between amount demanded and supplied never closes. This problem with artificially low electrical prices was recognized fairly early in the reconstruction process by both military and civilian authorities (see, for example, Robinson 2008, p. 173). But inertia and leadership overload prevented any serious attempt to charge reasonable electrical charges until late 2010.

In October 2010, the Ministry of Electricity introduced, for the first time, a tiered system of charges for electricity. However, in response to widespread protests, the pricing system was modified in February 2011. According to the new system, the first 1000 kWh each month will be free, between 1000 and 2000 kWh per month will cost the consumer 50 ID/kWh (4.3 cents/kWh), between 2000 and 3000 will cost 80 ID/kWh (6.8 cents/kWh), and higher charges for larger usage (*Reuters* 2011c). While a small step in the direction of rationalizing electricity demand, there are at least two unresolved issues.

First, metering is not available in many areas and is considered unreliable. Second, and more importantly, the 2011 decision to make the first 1000 kWh free, while popular and politically astute, eliminates most of the efficiency benefit that the pricing was intended to achieve in the first place. The GoI stated that the purpose of the change was to help the poorest 8 million Iraqis obtain the electricity they need. But a 1000 kWh is a lot of electricity, the average US household only uses between 900 and 1400 kWh per month depending on the season. By allowing free electricity up to 1000 kWh, the GoI has committed itself to providing free power to more than half the population. It will not take very long for many higher income Iraqis to figure out how to consume much more than 1000 kWh at no charge, for example a home will become two "households" with two connections to the grid – each drawing less than a 1000 kWh. There will also be perverse impact on the incentives facing the Ministry of Electricity. There is little incentive for the Ministry of Electricity to connect and maintain electrical connections to low-income districts since each new customer will impose a cost on the Ministry of Electricity but no revenue. Since the new price system will have little effect on restraining demand, the Ministry of Electricity will be forced to continue an unending effort to increase supply. Some of the methods used to increase the short-term supply of electricity have adverse long-term implications.

Like most of Europe and the Middle East, Iraq operates on a frequency of 50 hertz (hz) standard. (The USA operates on a 60 hz standard which means that most electrical equipment is incompatible.) Part of the difficulty of supplying reliable electricity is the physics involved. Because there is no reasonably economical way of storing electricity, a continuous flow of electricity must be maintained between where it is generated – the power plant – and where it is consumed – the load. Since electricity travels at almost the speed of light, it must be simultaneously generated, transmitted, and consumed. In other words, at every instant of time, the amount of electricity generated must equal the amount consumed within a fairly small margin of error.

If the amount generated exceeds that consumed then the excess must be immediately shed. This shedding is accomplished by rapidly bringing additional loads onto line (Jurewitz 1987, pp. 10–11). On the other hand, if the quantity of electricity consumed exceeds that generated then there are really only two possibilities. If the differential is small then a temporary decrease in frequency will allow continued operation while additional generation capacity is added to the grid. However, an excessive drop in the electrical frequency will damage equipment. If additional generation capacity cannot be immediately added then, to avoid a large frequency drop, there must be a rapid reduction in load by dropping consumers – unexpected power outages. Of course, there are patterns to electricity usage in Iraq that allow some scheduling of generation. For example, in the summer, the demand for power hits a maximum in late afternoon while, on Fridays, industrial demand is down. Ideally, system operators can adjust capacity to prevent a drop in frequency or a power outage.

Unfortunately, the power grid is dysfunctional in Iraq. There are almost daily power outages as a result of both mismanagement and criminal/insurgent acts. With respect to management of the electric grid, grid operators have sought to increase the available power by normally operating at between 49.0 and 49.5 hz instead of the 50 hz standard. However, operating at lower than standard frequencies reduces the system's capability to deal with unexpected spikes in electrical demand. For example, if the system was running at 50 hz then, in response to an unexpected increase in

demand, the grid could temporarily drop to 49.7 hz until additional generation capacity was brought online. However, if the grid is already running
at 49.0 hz then a further cut in frequency runs the risk of damaging electrical equipment. As a result, grid operators have no choice but to drop load
– cease supplying electricity – to as many consumers as necessary to reduce
demand until it equals the available supply. Therefore, while operating at
lower than standard frequency does allow a small increase in power, it also
degrades system stability and increases the likelihood of unannounced
outages (Meese 2007, p. 1).

Electricity cannot be directed to take a particular path. Rather, it travels
over all available paths between generators and loads with the power flow
on each path being in inverse proportion to the impedance of each line
(Ohm's Law). As the output of different generators changes to match
consumption and there are changes in the location of new loads, flows
on transmission lines are constantly changing. Therefore the electrical
grid must not only maintain sufficient generation capability to meet the
maximum load at any time but also there must be sufficient capacity on
transmission lines so that each can safely accept rapid increases in electrical flows. Due in part to the destruction of 2003–2007, several of the major
electrical lines in Iraq lack this necessary reserve transmission capacity.

Politics of Power

Electrical generation and distribution during the Ba'athist regime were
dominated by two political considerations. First, central control over
electricity was maintained through the use of a few large power gener-
ating units. Second, electricity was directed to favor particular regions
and cities. For example, in the summer of 2002, Baghdad had electricity
24 hours per day, seven days per week while other parts of the country
received no electricity even though there were electrical generation units or
transmission lines within their boundaries (Allawi 2007, p. 257).

Despite efforts by the US-led coalition to minimize damage to the electrical grid following the 2003 invasion, widespread looting crippled the
system. In addition, de-Ba'athification and "brain drain" to surrounding
countries combined with the adverse effect of years of isolation during
the sanctions period, had resulted in a severe shortage of trained Iraqis
to maintain and operate the electrical system. The situation was exacerbated by not only a shortage of the refined fuels but also an inability to
deliver the correct fuels to the power generation plants in a timely manner.
Finally, the insurgency targeted the electrical grid in 2005–2007. Attacking
the grid was a powerful tactic because there had been a widespread expectation that the 2003 US-led invasion would be followed by an increase in

both the supply and reliability of electricity. Therefore, the insurgency found attacks on the electrical grid a relatively risk-free way of undermining confidence in the GoI and coalition forces (SIGIR 2009b, pp. 144–5).

Also, regions and cities that had received little or no electricity in the final days of Saddam's regime demanded a more equitable distribution. Attempts to achieve such a distribution resulted in energy outages in Baghdad and other major cities even as national electrical generation slowly climbed back to pre-invasion levels. These shortages are exacerbated by illegal diversion of electricity. At the local level, these diversions of electricity lead to "rats nests" of illegal wire taps on almost every city block as individuals and small entities attempt to obtain electricity without payment. In addition to the impact on electrical supply, these connections by non-professionals lead to fires and periodic accidental electrocutions. However, the more serious diversions occur at the regional or provincial level.

Throughout Iraq there are relays that are built to "trip" when the frequency drops to dangerous levels, producing a local or regional blackout in order to protect the national grid. To protect their local consumers, grid operators in some regions of Iraq disabled the relays. As a result, if there is an excessive drop in frequency, blackouts will occur in other regions where the relays are not disabled. As expected, this motivates the operators in other regions to also disable their relays. Of course, if enough relays are disabled nationwide then there is the increased potential for either a drop in frequency sufficient to cause severe equipment damage or unexpected nationwide blackouts.

For the reasons given above, it is difficult to determine exactly who is receiving electricity that is either generated in Iraq or imported. Excluding the Kurdish region, an estimated 20 percent of Iraq's generated electricity in 2009 was lost; dumped because there was no demand or transmission lines had temporarily reached capacity. Of the remainder, the largest user was residences (received 51 percent of electricity) followed by industrial users – mostly SOE (21 percent), government offices (19 percent), commercial establishments (6 percent), and pumps and other agricultural equipment (4 percent) (COSIT 2012, Tables 17/17 and 17/18). Even within each general category of user there are favored consumers. For example, Baghdad has an emergency grid intended for essential services such as hospitals, police stations, and so on. During periods of shortage, the regular grid may go black but the emergency grid will probably still have power. However, a variety of individuals and entities have used their influence to obtain a connection to the emergency grid for their residences or businesses. There is even a tractor factory in Iskandariyah – a town south of Baghdad – that was connected to the emergency grid. In addition to fairness, the addition of many non-emergency establishments increases the likelihood that the emergency grid itself will go black. Of course, as long as there is a gap between the demand and supply of electricity, its distribution will be controversial. So how can Iraq increase its supply of electricity?

Factors Limiting Electricity Generation

By mid-2010, the nameplate capacity of national electrical generation, the maximum output under ideal conditions, was almost 15600 megawatts (MW). This is substantially above the estimated demand of 9500 MW. But conditions are never ideal in Iraq! A better standard is feasible capacity defined as the estimated maximum output in view of actual conditions at power plants. In other words, if: (1) no power plants were offline for scheduled or unscheduled maintenance; and (2) sufficient fuel (for combustion turbine, thermal power, and diesel plants) or water (for hydroelectric plants) were available then Iraq should have the feasible capacity to produce enough power to meet peak demand without electrical imports. However, actual peak production is only about 61 percent of feasible capacity for a variety of reasons. Planned outages for maintenance accounted for 5 percent of the reduced capacity while unplanned maintenance outages accounted for another 13 percent. Shortages of fuel or attempts to use substandard fuel combined with low water at the hydroelectric dam amounts to an additional 10 percent. Finally, there are a variety of miscellaneous factors that cost another 11 percent of feasible capacity (SIGIR 2010, Figure 2.29). As a result, even with an additional 6.7 billion kWh of imports, there is a severe shortage of electricity.

In its simplest form, Iraq has five possible ways of reducing the gap between the demand and supply of electricity.

1. Increase the price of electricity.
2. Increase nameplate generation capacity.
3. Increase efficiency of existing power plants.
4. Increase imports of electricity from Turkey and Iran.
5. Increase private (non-grid) generation of electricity.

The October 2010 increase in the price of electricity to cover the average cost of electrical generation (estimated 17 ID/kWh) combined with an effort to ensure accurate metering of electrical usage should have substantially increased the efficiency of power generation and use. However, the cancelation of all tariffs for usage less than 1000 kWh per month in early 2011 eliminated expected efficiency gains. One option would be to restore the electrical tariff for the first 1000 kWh combined with a new transfer payment to low-income families to allow them to purchase electricity. While this would increase efficiency and reduce wasted electricity without burdening low-income families; this proposal is probably a political non-starter. The 2010 increase in electrical prices was extremely unpopular and politicians may consider it political suicide to revisit this issue for at least several years.

Increasing nameplate generation capacity is by far the most popular option among politicians and bureaucrats. Massive construction projects especially with a large imported component provide much greater opportunities for graft and favoritism than efforts to improve efficiency of existing capacity. However, adding substantial capacity is often fraught with engineering challenges. For example, delivering new generators from the Syrian border to a Baghdad power plant required the reinforcement of bridges along the route (Robinson 2008, p. 327). The cost of increasing nameplate capacity is substantial. The Ministry of Electricity has proposed spending \$77 billion over the next twenty years (*Reuters* 2011c).

Unfortunately, despite the great cost and effort, the actual increase in electrical generation from new capacity is much less than expected. For example, the GoI has shown a bias towards purchasing and installing gas turbines because they can quickly be brought online. In addition, such turbines can be fueled with processed natural gas that is in generous supply in Iraq. In 2009, almost 1.48 billion cubic meters of Iraq natural gas waste was wasted – it was flared off for safety reasons.

Yet, in addition to the large burden on the national budget, this imported power requires highly skilled labor and management. Unlike the existing system of generators that burn HFO, gas turbines require fuel that meets specific tolerances and trained maintenance personnel. Iraq has neither. For example, in 2007, almost half of the new turbines designed for burning natural gas were being fueled with diesel or heavy fuels. This resulted in both an efficiency loss and an increased maintenance burden (SIGIR 2009b, p. 312).

The most controversial option is to accept that Iraq does not have a shortage of capacity but rather is incredibly inefficient in its use of existing capacity. If Iraq were able to increase the efficiency of existing power generation then a substantial increase in electrical supply would be possible without the massive investment under consideration. For example, if the grid operators were able to minimize unscheduled maintenance outages and – with the cooperation of the Ministry of Oil – ensure that the correct standard fuel was available in sufficient quantities for existing generators then the existing electrical infrastructure could produce an additional 2800 MW raising total production to over 10 000 MW.

Generally, increasing the efficiency of electrical generation is almost

Table 11.1   Electrical supply in Baghdad and other provinces (%)

Source of electricity	Public generator (the grid)	Community generator	Private generator	No source
Baghdad primary	55	33	12	0
Baghdad secondary	28	18	37	17
Other provinces primary	87	10	4	0
Other provinces secondary	11	35	26	29

Source: COSIT (2008), Table 2-28, pp. 124–5.

always treated as an engineering challenge. But a more productive approach might be to focus on incentives. Currently, managers and workers at electrical generation plants are not rewarded for long-term increases in efficiency nor financially punished for unnecessary drops in the quality or quantity of electricity. In the absence of such incentives, politically motivated efficiency drives can be expected to have only a short-term impact on electrical production often paid for with a long-term degradation of equipment.

The fourth option is to increase electrical imports from Turkey and Iran. In 2010, Iraq imported almost 12 percent (6.7 billion kWh) of its total electrical consumption (US CIA 2012, Economy Summary Table). There are complex political and economic issues associated with these imports. Exporting electricity allows Iran to earn additional foreign exchange in the face of the sanctions related to its nuclear program. At the same time, Iraq is engaged in complex negotiations with both Turkey and Iran concerning support for rebel groups and, in the case of Turkey, water flows in the Euphrates and the Tigris. Iraq's increasing dependency on imported electricity weakens its negotiating position. Also, importing electricity seems to conflict with Iraq's comparative advantage. As discussed in Chapter 6, Iraq's currently flares off large quantities of natural gas. Using this currently wasted gas for electrical production should enable Iraq to become a regional low-cost electricity exporter.

Finally, due to the uncertainty of electrical supply from the grid, many Iraqis have turned to private electrical generation often using black market fuel for the generators. As can be seen in Table 11.1, this is especially true in Baghdad where about 45 percent use either community or private generators as their primary electrical source. In the rest of Iraq, only 14 percent rely on community or private generators as their primary source of electricity but more than half use community or private generators when the grid is down.

WATER AND AIR TRANSPORTATION

Ports

There has been substantial river transport in Iraq for millennia. Beginning in 1839, the use of steamers led to not only a sharp decrease in the cost of shipping from Basrah to Baghdad cities by both the Euphrates and the Tigris rivers but also reduced transportation times dramatically. By the 1860s, shipping times had fallen to two to three days from Baghdad to Basrah and four to five days on the more difficult upstream voyage from Basrah to Baghdad (Issawi 1966, pp. 146–7). Until the railroad construction boom after World War I, river transport dominated Iraq's domestic and international trade.

Currently pipelines, railroads, roads, and air transport carry most of Iraq's current trade and the future for river transport is limited due to falling water levels in both rivers but especially in the Euphrates. However, the ports of Iraq will continue to be the major routes of imports and exports especially for imported commodities such as wheat and exports such as petroleum products and fertilizer that have a low value to weight ratio. But to restore substantial port throughput will require at least four expensive initiatives: clearing wrecked vessels from the navigation channels, restoration of bridges that were destroyed during conflict and "temporarily" replaced by floating or low-clearance bridges, dredging the channels, and a substantial upgrade of the port facilities.

Iraq's access to the Persian Gulf is severely constrained by geography and politics. The Euphrates and the Tigris rivers join north of Basrah city to form the Shatt al-Arab waterway, which then flows into the Gulf. From Abu al Khasib to the city of Al Faw on the Gulf, a distance of about 100 km (60 miles), the Shatt al-Arab waterway forms the border between Iraq and Iran. This border was heavily fought over during the Iran–Iraq War in the 1980s and still suffers from periodic cross-border military raids and the traffic of well-armed smugglers in consumer goods and antiquities. The distance from where the Shatt al-Arab waterway enters the Gulf to the border with Kuwait is only about 60 km (37 miles).

Iraq has five major ports crammed into this relatively small area of Basrah province.

The anchorages for large oil tankers to take on cargoes of Iraqi oil are just off Al Faw on the Shatt al-Arab waterway. The largest cargo ports are Umm Qasr (7.5 million tons annual capacity) and Khor Al Zubair (6.4 million tons). Umm Qasr is near the border with Kuwait on the Khawr Az Zubayr river, which flows north and is connected by a canal to Basrah city and the Shatt al-Arab waterway. The port of Khor Al Zubair is on the same river about half way between Basrah city and the Gulf. The much smaller ports of Magal (1.5 million tons) and Abou Flous (0.5 million tons) are near Basrah city on the Shatt al-Arab waterway. The current depth of the channels and alongside the port docks is at most 10 meters – too shallow for the largest container and cargo ships. As a result, many shippers are bypassing Iraqi ports to offload in Kuwait, Saudi Arabia, or Iran.

As a result of almost thirty years of conflict, there are over 200 vessels sunk in or near the port of Umm Qasr and hundreds more in the channels from Umm Qasr north to Basrah city. Not only do these vessels limit access to the port but also the sunken ships are believed to be leaking hazardous chemicals from munitions, pesticides, refined fuels, and unknown toxins. Although the GoI with the support of the Government of Japan and the UN have begun to remove some of these wrecks, it will be a long process. As a matter of priorities, the GoI is focusing its initial efforts on removing those wrecks that block the main channels rather than those believed to be leaking dangerous chemicals. This priority has international implications since chemicals from wrecks in Iraqi waters may contaminate the water drawn into desalinization plants in Kuwait with a possible adverse impact on that nation's drinking water.

With channels cleared of wrecks and dredged deep enough to allow large container vessels to dock, the North and South Railroad Lines upgraded, and customs officials corruption controlled; Iraq has a good chance of returning to its century-old role as the preferred route for shipments from Asia to Turkey, Syria, and Jordan. The *National Development Plan: 2010–2014* contains a detailed strategy for achieving this long-term goal (GoI 2010, pp. 88–100). However, the 2005–2007 and 2007–2010 National Development Strategies also contained plans, although less-detailed, for port and rail restorations and upgrades but these plans were not executed primarily due to a lack of funding (GoI 2005b, p. 25; 2007, pp. 49–50). It remains to be seen whether the newest plan will also fail from lack of investment.

Airports

Since 2008, Iraq has experienced a dramatic increase in international air travel. While the total number of airports with paved runways has remained almost unchanged; the number of airports with runways longer than 3 km, that can accommodate the largest civilian aircraft, has increased from two to 20. There are six major international airports in Baghdad, Mosul, Basrah, Najaf, Arbil, and Sulaymaniyah cities. Baghdad International Airport (BIAP) has gone from two regularly scheduled non-governmental civilian international flights per day in 2007 to over a dozen daily departures and arrivals in mid-2012. In addition, there is a growing volume of airfreight shipments. The Najaf International Airport (NJF), converted from a military airbase in 2008, continues to expand in order to accommodate large numbers of religious tourists. International businessmen and women, many in the energy industry, account for many of the passengers flying into Basrah and Mosul. Arbil and Sulaymaniyah are located, of course, in the KRG and receive a growing business trade and tourist traffic.

One of the most serious challenges facing Iraq's air industry is the requirement to develop and maintain an up-to-date air traffic control system with the necessary radar, communication, and coordination systems. The difficulty is not obtaining the necessary equipment but rather in training the personnel to perform these critical jobs. Of course, air travel while quick, is expensive especially for bulky products. For intra-Iraq shipments of such goods, reliance must be placed on railroads and motor traffic.

GROUND TRANSPORTATION

Railroads

After water transport, rail is by far the most efficient means of transporting bulk goods such as agricultural products or fertilizer. It is estimated that compared to truck transport, railroads can reduce transport costs by up to 90 percent (Easterly 2006, p. 280). Iraq's almost 2300 km (1400 miles) of rail lines generally follow the routes of the Euphrates and the Tigris rivers. The nation's railroads are almost a century old beginning with the Baghdad North Line, from Rabiya on the Syrian border to Mosul to Baghdad that was completed by a German construction firm in 1918. This was followed by the Baghdad South Line, from Baghdad to Basrah that was completed by the British in 1920. The newest lines are

Table 11.2   Major rail lines

	Major cities	Length	Status
Baghdad North Line	Baghdad, Mosul, Rabiya (Syrian border)	524 km (325 miles)	Substandard rail
Baghdad South Line	Baghdad, Basrah, Umm Qasr (port on Persian Gulf)	609 km (380 miles)	Some sections with substandard rail
Baghdad West Line	Baghdad, Fallujah, Al Qaim, Akashat (Syrian border)	520 km (320 miles)	Excellent
Traverse Line	Haqlaniya (near Haditha in Anbar), Bayji, Kirkuk	252 km (160 miles)	Damaged bridge on Bayji–Kirkuk section

Source: US Department of State (2006), pp. 10–13.

the Baghdad West and Traverse Lines that were completed in 1987. The former line was originally built to carry phosphate from its sources in the Western Iraq to Baghdad and then to Basrah for export. In addition to poor maintenance and the effects of conflict, rails that are too light for modern railroad operations limit the two older lines' capacities. Table 11.2 lists the four major rail routes, distances, and a summary of their current state of repair.

In addition to the problems discussed above, the Iraq railroad system also suffers from outdated and poorly maintained engines and other rolling stock as well as an outdated communication system. The wide mix of engines and other equipment reflects a long history of politically driven railroad investment. For example, immediately after the invasion in 2003, the Iraqi Republic Railroads (IRR) listed engines from Japan, China, Turkey, Czech Republic, Russia, and France. Most of these engines were not operational as a result of the inability to obtain parts, the lack of maintenance, or the post-invasion looting. As a result, the number of usable locomotives decreased by almost 60 percent from 157 in 2004 to only 62 in 2010 (COSIT 2012, Table 6/13).

Ridership ceased during the worst of the insurgency and has just begun to recover. Passenger-kilometers (number of passengers multiplied by the average trip length) grew from almost zero in 2007 to about 100 million in 2010 although this is still one-third less than before the 2003 invasion. Almost 99 percent of all passengers were riding the Baghdad South Line between Baghdad and Basrah. Cargo ton-kilometers have also increased dramatically over the last several years from 49 million in 2007 to 249 million in 2010. Again the Baghdad South Line was the busiest carrying 46 percent of the total railroad tonnage. The Baghdad West Line between Baghdad and Al Qaim on the Iraq–Syria border was second with 41 percent of all freight tonnage. The Baghdad North Line between Baghdad and Mosul accounted for the remaining 13 percent of freight tonnage (COSIT 2012, Table 6/14).

Among the engineering challenges facing the IRR is completing the construction of a microwave communication system that will allow the centralized dispatch, control, and tracking of trains throughout Iraq. Next most important is upgrading track on existing lines to world standards including parallel tracks, which will allow faster, longer, and heavier trains. Priority should be given to: first, upgrading the Baghdad South Line from the Persian Gulf port of Umm Qasr to Baghdad and, second, upgrading the Baghdad North Line from Baghdad to Mosul to the Syrian border at Rabiya. Integrated with port improvements, the upgrading of the Baghdad North and South Lines to world standards would have several advantages for Iraq. The railroad would provide lower cost transport of bulk imports (grain) and exports (phosphate-based fertilizer). If substantial container capacity could be developed then there is potential for substantial carrying trade from the Persian Gulf to Turkey, Syria, and Jordan. Another advantage is political. An efficient north–south rail system would further tie together the residents of Iraq's three largest cities with trade and travel.

However, lack of physical investment in communication, and rails are not the binding constraints on IRR productivity. Like most of the other SOE, IRR suffers from excessive employment – over 10 000 employees – inefficiently running a system that in other countries would require from one-fourth to one-tenth as many employees. As is true with the other SOE, the employees cannot be fired for failure to perform their assigned tasks to expected standards or even have their pay docked for failure to show up for work.

Despite or, possibly, because of the massive over-manning of the IRR, it is extremely bureaucratic. There were 11 operating divisions each with its own division head for a 2300 km (1400 mile) system. Based on the experience of other developing countries, at most four operating divisions would be more than adequate. Combined with over twenty non-operating departments, the large number of operating divisions means that there are over thirty division and department chiefs reporting directly to the Director General of the IRR. Modern management theory recommends that the number of reporting subordinates be six or less. In addition, many of the employees lack the necessary skill set for their jobs. Rather than provide the necessary training or education, it appears that the IRR compensates for unskilled employees by requiring a series of checks to be performed by upper level management before even relatively minor decisions are made. For example, despite the improved national rail communication system, dispatchers in Baghdad still hesitate to actually dispatch trains. Rather, stationmasters generally authorize each train to proceed to the next station where it must wait for permission of the next stationmaster to continue.

In addition, cargoes are often transported based on ministerial level decisions driven by relationships and mutual favors rather than on the impact on railroad revenues or costs. As a result, many trains are severely delayed, carry products that are not those of the highest net-revenue, or have empty cars. The Ministries of Trade and Oil have a strong bias in favor of using truck transport for transporting bulk goods rather than rail despite the greater expense. This preference is partially motivated by the fact that they do not want to be dependent on the IRR. The expensive investment in railroad infrastructure can be expected to have little long-term impact on railroad efficiency if there is no rationalization of managerial organization and incentives.

Roads

Like its railroads, much of Iraq's 41 700 km (26 000 miles) of paved roads follow the Tigris and the Euphrates rivers. There has been little expansion of the road network over the last several decades with only about 30 percent (11 300 km or 7000 miles) of the roads designed for high-volume traffic (COSIT 2012, Table 6/1). Road usage has increased sharply since 2003 for two reasons. The suspension of rail passenger and freight services forced shippers to put their cargoes on trucks. Also, there has been a large increase in the number of passenger cars in Iraq – many smuggled into the country from Iran. Since there is neither a legal requirement for automobile insurance nor drivers' permits, the roads are increasingly filled with bad drivers. Compounding the problem of increased traffic, the existing road network is badly located and suffering from much deferred maintenance.

Driven by Saddam's military strategy, the road network reflects military necessity rather than economic needs. The major roads run from Baghdad west to the Syrian and Jordanian borders and from Baghdad south to Basrah. While there is a divided highway from Baghdad to Mosul, there are no first class roads running either north to the three Kurdish provinces (or Turkey) or east to Iran. Again, reflecting military needs, one of the two first class roads from Baghdad to Basrah runs east of the Tigris through the cities of Al Kut and Al Amarah. This road runs roughly parallel to the Iraq–Iran border about 40 km (25 miles) away and was designed to allow the rapid transfer of military forces along the border.

As in many developing countries, the critical road transportation constraint in Iraq is not building roads but maintaining them (Easterly 2006, p. 165; Szirmai 2005, p. 622). Road maintenance would seem to be relatively inexpensive in Iraq. In the lower two-thirds of the nation, temperatures rarely, if ever, fall below freezing which excludes a major cause of road deterioration. Also, in the lower two-thirds of the nation, the land is relatively flat which simplifies roadway engineering although there are almost 1300 bridges required not only for the two rivers but also for the large number of irrigation canals. However, failure to limit overweight trucks has led to rapid deterioration of major trucking routes.

Bad roads impede economic development in nations like Iraq with substantial agricultural sectors (Easterly 2006, p. 22). Bad roads increase the cost of transporting agricultural products by an estimated five-times and the increased time required to bring crops to market tends to reduce their quality. Since there is no cold-chain truck transportation network in Iraq, a substantial portion of agricultural products are bruised or spoiled before they reach urban markets. In fact, in Baghdad, Basrah, and other urban areas, foreign imported vegetables and meats are often cheaper and of higher quality than those produced in the same or neighboring provinces.

Of course, the inadequate road network in Iraq has broader implications. Bad roads isolate villages from medical care. Teachers, especially female teachers, are reluctant to accept teaching positions in inaccessible villages. In addition, almost all railroad crossings of roads are at ground level that can result in long delays and rail–car accidents. As expected, poor quality roads tend to be more dangerous and have contributed to the doubling of road traffic fatalities in only three years (COSIT 2012, Table 6/11).

While it is widely accepted that Iraq would greatly benefit from better maintenance or upgrades of existing roads, incentives make this difficult to achieve. Most roads are public goods – neither rival in consumption nor excludable at reasonable cost. Therefore, most roads in Iraq are financed by the national government but built and maintained by contractors chosen by provincial or local governments.

Unfortunately, in Iraq, the road construction and maintenance business is riddled with corruption. A large proportion of the money committed to road maintenance or construction is diverted into other uses or private accounts. The construction firms are generally chosen on the basis of political or family connections as well as a willingness to pay bribes. This leads to a bias in favor of building new roads instead of maintaining old ones since building new roads provide more corruption opportunities as well as photo opportunities for governmental officials. The quality of road construction and maintenance is low because of the substitution of lower quality materials for those specified in contracts. This results in more rapid roadway deterioration and additional contracts for restoration.

There are no easy answers to the problems associated with upgrading Iraq's road system. The continuing security challenges in the border areas of the country combined with the division of responsibility and, therefore, accountability among national, provincial, and local entities makes progress difficult. The lesson from the rest of the developing world is that the effectiveness of local democracy determines the quality and quantity of roads. If decisions about road construction and maintenance are made in the capital city and funding comes from the national treasury then quality tends to be low. However, when residents not only pay taxes to care for roads but also play a major role in selecting local government officials then roads tend to be of better quality. In view of the dominance of the Iraqi central government in planning and funding the country's road network; Iraq can expect to suffer from a poor road network for the foreseeable future.

COMMUNICATION

The rapid growth of telephone access was one of the very few unambiguous successes of the early reconstruction period. Access to a phone service increased from approximately one million (one per 27 Iraqis) pre-invasion to approximately 26 million (equivalent to 80 percent of the population) in 2009. Almost 95 percent of this 2009 phone access was by cell phones (US CIA 2012). In 2012, in some urban areas, cell phone ownership now exceeds 100 percent. In developing countries, cell phone ownership tends to be a very productive investment. This is especially true in countries like Iraq that still lack widespread Internet access, reliable mail, or package delivery services. Cell phones are not only used by Iraq's private sector to coordinate their businesses but also they are also important to government agencies, SOE, and even the Ministries of Interior and Defense (USAID 2009). Internet access is still limited although there are over 450 Internet cafes in urban areas.

There has also been a sharp increase in the general public's access to media. Within one year of the US-led invasion, the number of television stations increased to 21 while the number of radio stations rose to over 80. Both in urban and rural areas, satellite dishes have sprouted on almost every roof. It is estimated that about half of all families have access to television while radio reception is almost universal. While these TV and radio stations are not government stations, almost all are associated with one of the religious, political, or tribal groups. There is a wide range of programming from Iraqi soap operas, to foreign films and shows, to religious services.

Whether the transition from the government-controlled media of the Saddam-era to the current media "free-for-all" has been entirely favorable is widely debated. It may provide unifying themes across tribal, political, and religious divides. For example, some soap operas seem to have wide national viewership. Other analysts think that the association of media outlets with various groups will tend to divide the population and encourage instability. Another connection between increased access to diverse media and political instability is found in Huntington's (1968) hypothesis that was discussed in Chapter 5 of this book. According to this hypothesis, increased media access leads to the creation of new aspirations or desires for a better life as Iraqis learn how people in the developed world live. Unless these new aspirations are at least partially matched by economic development then social frustration will increase. Political instability is not inevitable as a result of this frustration; increased geographic or professional mobility combined with flexible political institutions may ameliorate social frustration.

ENGINEERING EFFICIENCY VERSUS ECONOMIC EFFICIENCY

While the various types of infrastructure all suffer from specific problems, there are some common themes. There is a tendency among both Iraqis and foreigners to see solutions to infrastructure problems primarily in terms of engineering proposals and budget expenditures. This is only partially true; without improved incentives, progress will be expensive, difficult, and temporary.

For example, in Baghdad in 2006, I sat in on a presentation concerning a relatively new water purification plant that was suffering from deterioration in water quality combined with a decrease in throughput. Apparently, the plant was suffering from poor maintenance that resulted in clogged pipes and pump damage. The presentation focused, first, on the most efficient way of clearing the pipes and replacing the pumps and, second, on how this repair could be financed. I raised the issue of incentives. The Iraqi supervisors and workers at the purification plant were very knowledgeable about the plant's operation. They knew what maintenance had to be performed in order to keep the plant operating at acceptable levels of efficiency. Therefore, the fact that this maintenance had not been performed probably meant that they lacked incentives to do it. Without changing incentives, the same problem would reoccur in a few years. I was informed that any discussion of incentives would have to wait since there was a long list of similar problems with deferred maintenance throughout the province that had to be resolved first.

When expanding or maintaining Iraq's infrastructure is under consideration, questions of incentives should not be an afterthought. Iraq is not Sweden. The Baghdad bureaucracy is less professional, less well trained, and – to be blunt – less honest than that of any of the OECD countries.

In Iraq, almost all of the infrastructure construction and maintenance costs throughout the 15 non-KRG provinces are paid for by the national government. For example, with respect to the provision of clean drinking water in urban areas, the national government builds the reservoirs, purification plants, and the system of pumps and pipes that will bring adequate quantities of clean drinking water to each consumer. Then an agency takes responsibility for operation and maintenance of the system possibly charging a small fee – less than the average cost – for the water. This causes several problems.

First, there is a tendency for a significant portion of the funds dedicated for any area of infrastructure to be spent by the ministerial bureaucracy in Baghdad on salaries and benefits for the ministerial employees. When the national ministry makes the decisions on which water system to build and who shall build it, the primary motivation is often not the welfare of the ultimate water consumer but rather how building the necessary infrastructure can increase the influence or wealth of the ministry and its officials. When construction material is purchased, it will often be from entities that have relationships with ministerial officials. Hiring is driven more by connections than competency. Promotions are based on the ability to successfully navigate a complex web of political relationships rather than on engineering or other competency. Maintaining well-paid employment of ministerial employees is generally more important than consumers receiving adequate clean water.

Second, since the consumer pays little or nothing for the water, his or her needs can safely be ignored. The only exceptions are if the consumer has political connections or is willing to offer a bribe. The bureaucracy has little incentive to provide services to anyone who lacks political or other connections since they will not receive increased funds for providing the service to a particular customer. As a result, consumers must pay bribes to receive basic essential services.

Thus the national financing of both the fixed and variable cost of Iraqi infrastructure leads to perverse incentives on the part of both the bureaucracy and the consumer. Since Baghdad ministries pay the agencies responsible for providing the "last mile" of public goods from the earnings from crude oil exports (and not from the payments by the customers), they have little incentive to meet customer needs. At the same time, since customers pay little or nothing for the services provided by the infrastructure, they have little incentive to either avoid waste or make rational decisions among several inputs. When there is electricity available from the grid, there is no reason not to use all electrical appliances at maximum capacity. The air conditioner in a family shop will be running at maximum cooling with the shop door open.

What is the alternative to the traditional means of providing public infrastructure in Iraq? A second-best solution would be to charge the consumer a price equal to the average cost of providing essential services. This system rationalizes incentives. Since consumers will be able to withhold payment unless the promised goods or services are provided, agencies managing infrastructure will focus less on the Baghdad ministries and more on actually providing the goods or services demanded. The adverse impact on the living standards of low-income Iraqis could be offset by a GoI transfer payment to poor families to offset the cost of utilities. Then if the government is unable to provide reliable potable water or electricity then the consumer can purchase them from a water truck or community generator.

This is a very unpopular option in Iraq where surveys have shown that consumers of essential services are not interested in paying anything for these services but, as expected, they want the government to efficiently provide almost unlimited essential services for free. Politicians across Iraq feed this desire for efficient free essential services arguing that if they are elected or appointed to ministerial positions then things will work the way they are supposed to. Of course, once in power, these politicians face the same perverse incentives as their predecessors. And without innovation that provides rational incentives, it is unlikely provision of essential services will improve without a great deal of wasteful expenditures.

12. International trade and finance

> From Basra dates, rice, and sometimes wheat and barley are shipped
> to Musqat, Surat, and the Gulf of Cambay. The writing pens used
> by Persians and Turks are made out of reeds that grow east of the
> Shatt al-Arab; a large amount is also sent to India. Horses bred by
> the Arab tribes living west of Basra and Baghdad are highly valued in
> India. A large number is shipped each year to Surat and Gujarat.
> (G.A. Olivier 1988, p. 179)

Iraq's international trade and capital flows exhibit four salient characteristics. First, reflecting its long history as a major trading route between
Europe and Asia; the Iraqi economy is dominated by international merchandise trade. Combined with its $53.9 billion in merchandise imports,
Iraq's $73.4 billion in merchandise exports produced an estimated 2011
foreign trade to GDP ratio of 117 percent. There are few countries in
the world at any level of economic development whose economies are so
dominated by international merchandise trade. Since they exclude smuggling, the official statistics understate the actual value of trade.

Second, Iraq is more dependent on the export of a single natural
resource than any other country in the world. Oil accounted for almost
99 percent of the country's 2011 estimated $78.4 billion in merchandise
exports.

Third, Iraq's balance of payments experiences large year-to-year
changes. When oil prices are high, as in 2008 and 2011, the country
reports a large surplus in its balance of trade but when the price of oil
is low such as in 2009 then the country runs a trade deficit. In addition,
its capital balance also changes sharply year to year most likely because
of changed perceptions of political instability. For example, in 2007 and
2008, its capital balance was negative – more capital left Iraq then arrived.
However, despite the sharp changes in trade and capital balances since
2003, Iraq has accumulated a large holding of international reserves, an
estimated $54 billion by the end of 2011.

Finally, there is evidence of large-scale capital flight from Iraq possibly
as much as $33 billion in the last five years.

MERCHANDISE TRADE

Data Quality

The quality of data on both the volume and value of Iraq's merchandise trade is very low. Massive smuggling across the borders with Iran, Syria, and Turkey mean that the official statistics capture only a fraction of all cross-border transactions. In fact, international organizations generally disregard the trade data reported by GoI preferring to rely instead on adjusted counterpart data.

Counterpart data is used as follows. In theory, Iraq's reported exports to, say, the UK should equal that country's reported imports from Iraq adjusted for the difference between the price of exports that are usually listed as fob (free on board – insurance and freight costs are not included) while imports are usually recorded as cif (including cost, insurance, and freight). If the adjustment for the difference between fob and cif is made then one can use counterpart data to estimate Iraq's exports and imports. However, in Iraq's case, counterpart data is of limited value since several of its major regional trading partners – Turkey, Syria, and Iran – also have difficulty with accurately reporting their exports and imports.

However, the counterpart data of individual countries with respect to Iraq may provide some insight into changing trade patterns that are not apparent in the official data. For example, the USA reported that exports to Iraq grew 63 percent in 2011 to $5.4 billion (NUSACC 2011). This puts Iraq in fourth place behind Egypt, Saudi Arabia, and the UAE as a destination of US exports to the Arab World. Apparently the bulk of these exports are intended for construction in Iraq's oilfields. The rapid growth of such exports reflects both the aggressive plans of the GoI to expand oil exploration, exploitation, and export (see Chapter 6) as well as to the improvement in the security environment that began in 2008.

With respect to unreported merchandise trade, probably the most disturbing is the extensive trade in stolen or looted historical artifacts. Some of these objects of both artistic and historical interest are obtained from Iraqi museums or government storage facilities either by theft or, more commonly, by bribing the guards. However, many of the items are obtained directly from the many archeological sites in southern Iraq that lack security. As a result, not only do artifacts that illustrate the incredible history of Iraq disappear into the international black market in art but also tomb raiders, in their eagerness to quickly find items of value, often damage the sites. The most used smuggling routes are between Iraq and Iran in the south where looted Iraqi artifacts are sent east using the same routes that are used for black market consumer goods from Iran moving west.

Exports

According to official estimates, in addition to oil, current Iraqi exports include some trade in crude materials such as phosphate, food, and live goats. The major recipients of its exports are the USA that received an estimated 24 percent of Iraq's 2010 exports, India (17 percent), China (12 percent), South Korea (8 percent), and Italy (7 percent). However, because of the usual difficulty of determining the true destination country of any product, the importance of these countries as destinations for Iraqi exports is probably exaggerated. Some of these exports including oil are only initially shipped to these countries before being transshipped elsewhere.

As can be seen in Table 12.1, oil exports accounted for almost 99 percent of total dollar value of exports. Almost 80 percent of petroleum exports are loaded in tankers near the port of Umm Qasr at the head of the Persian Gulf while the bulk of the remainder goes through the pipeline through Turkey. Relatively small volumes are exported by tanker trucks.

In addition to smuggling, the low value of non-oil exports has several causes. First, as discussed in Chapter 10, Iraq has an extremely hostile regulatory environment towards private business. In particular, regulations make it very difficult to legally export any item from Iraq. According to the World Bank's 2012 report on "Doing Business" (2012a), to legally export a standard container of goods requires the completion of ten documents, 80 days of administrative processing, and costs $3550. For comparison, exporting from the average MENA country requires only six documents, 20 days, and costs $1057. The complexity, delay, and expense of exporting make Iraq's products uncompetitive on the basis of price.

Second, Iraq's long conflict with Iran and almost a decade of UN-imposed economic sanctions have disturbed traditional trade flows and allowed competitors to capture foreign markets that were formerly Iraq's. For example, as discussed in Chapter 7, Iraq's dates were formerly renowned for their quality and Iraq was the world's largest exporter of dates. However, conflict-related destruction of many Iraqi date orchards combined with Iraq's long absence from the market have allowed other nations to greatly increase both the quality and quantity of their dates. It will be very difficult for Iraq to recover this market.

Third, Iraq suffers from the Dutch disease as large oil export earnings caused an appreciation of the ID that reduced the competiveness of non-oil exports.

Table 12.1   Balance of payments ($ billions)

	2006	2007	2008	2009	2010	2011ᴾ
Merchandise exports (fob)	$30.5	$39.6	$63.7	$39.4	$51.8	$78.4
Oil	($29.2)	($37.1)	($61.9)	($39.0)	($51.5)	($77.6)
Oil price ($ per barrel)	$55.60	$63.00	$91.50	$55.60	$74.20	$85.50
Merchandise imports (cif)	−$19.6	−$24.4	−$35.0	−$41.5	−$43.9	−$63.4
Balance of trade	$20.1	$15.2	$28.7	−$2.1	$7.9	$15.0
Current account balance	$1.3	$20.1	$28.4	−$1.1	$6.4	$9.1
Capital balance	$5.9	−$4.7	−$1.3	$1.4	$8.6	−$6.2*
Errors and omissions	$0.1	−$4.1	−$8.4	−$6.1	−$8.7	
Change in reserves	$7.3	$11.3	$18.7	−$5.8	$6.3	$2.9
Reserves (December 31)	$20.0	$31.5	$50.2	$44.3	$50.6	$53.5

Notes:
ᴾ Projected
* Net capital balance plus errors and omissions.

Sources: 2006–2010, CBI (2012b) and IMF (2011a), Table 7, p. 22; 2011, US CIA (2012) and author's estimates.

Imports

The country's imports are primarily food, medicine, and manufactures although, as discussed in the chapters on petroleum (Chapter 6) and essential services (Chapter 11), Iraq also imports a significant amount of energy in the form of fuel and electricity. The country's major import partners are Turkey that was the source of an estimated 24 percent of Iraq's imports, Syria (19 percent), China (14 percent) and the USA (7 percent) (US CIA 2012). The absence of Iran from a list of Iraq's major trade partners reflects the fact that most of this trade is smuggled and therefore unreported or under-reported. Again, because of transshipment, these countries may not be the actual country of origin of Iraq's imports. In particular, there is large-scale transport by trucks across the Turkish–Iraq border into the Kurdish provinces. This is a source of much of Iraq's imported consumer goods from Europe.

There is also a wide gap between the perception and reality of the ease of legally importing products into Iraq. On the surface, Iraq is open to foreign imports. With the exception of weapons and drugs, all goods may be imported. There is a flat tariff ("reconstruction levy") of only 5 percent on all imports except food, medicine and medical equipment, clothing, books, and items of humanitarian assistance (IMF 2010c, p. 1208). However, in reality it is extremely difficult and expensive to legally import items into Iraq.

According to official data, government ministries and SOE account for the bulk of Iraq's imports. In 2010, various government agencies were responsible for $24 billion of reported imports, over half of the total. These government imports were dominated by non-oil-related machinery and other capital goods of $10.4 billion or 43 percent of total government imports, consumption goods including food products for the PDS totaled $8.3 billion or 34 percent, oil-related machinery and other capital goods of $3.5 billion or 14 percent, and refined fuel products of $1.9 billion or 8 percent. As the GoI pursues its aggressive strategy over the next decade (discussed in Chapter 6) of expanding petroleum production, refining, and exports, it is expected that government imports will shift towards oil-related machinery and other capital goods partially offset by a reduction in imports of refined petroleum products.

Balance of Trade

Since merchandise exports are determined by the price of oil while merchandise imports steadily increase because of aggressive expansion of GoI purchases of equipment and supplies in order to expand the oil industry, Iraq's balance of trade has shown a great deal of year-to-year variance. For example, as shown in Table 12.1, the 2009 collapse in oil prices led to an almost 40 percent drop in exports and yet imports increased by almost 20 percent. The result was an almost $30 billion change in the balance of trade from a large surplus in 2008 to a small deficit in 2009. Fortunately, Iraq has not recently suffered from an extended period of low prices such as the two decades of less than $40 pb oil prior to 2005. However, to the extent that Iraq's access to the international capital market remains limited then a period of extended low oil prices will require either a scaling back of oil sector expansion or use of the country's international reserves. As discussed in the next chapter, this can put pressure on the exchange rate.

INTERNATIONAL TOURISM

Millions of international tourists visit Iraq every year and there is great potential for a further increase. There is a wide disagreement among the number of tourists reported by the GoI – approximately 2.5 million per year – and the numbers referenced by local governments and organizations which tend to be much larger (COSIT 2012, Table 16/4). Tourists to Iraq can be roughly divided into three groups: religious, historical, and geographic. Of these, religious tourism, primarily the Shi'a from Iran, currently accounts for the greatest volume of visitors.

Several of the most sacred places for Shi'a Muslims are in Iraq. One of the most important is the city of Najaf, about 155 km (95 miles) south of Baghdad on the Euphrates river. There, the Imam Ali Mosque contains the tomb of the First Shi'a Imam, Ali, the cousin and son-in-law of the Prophet Mohammed. While estimates are unreliable, it is safe to say that, since the border with Iraq was reopened after the fall of Saddam, at least five million Shi'a tourists and possibly as many as ten million have visited Najaf. Anecdotal evidence supports the claim that Iranian firms capture much of the financial benefit from such tourism since they control the travel firms, hotels, and even restaurants used by visitors to Najaf.

Karbala, about 90 km (55 miles) south of Baghdad situated just west of the Euphrates river, is also sacred to Shi'a Muslims since both the Imam Husayn Shrine and the Al Abbas Mosque are located there. It is estimated that several million religious tourists have visited Karbala.

The Al-Askari Mosque, also known as the Golden Mosque after its large dome covered in gold, is the major religious site in Samarra, about 115 km (70 miles) north of Baghdad on the Tigris river. This mosque contains the tombs of the seventh and ninth Shi'a Imams and is considered by many to be the third holiest site in Shi'a Islam. The Golden Mosque is probably best known to non-Muslims because of the explosion that destroyed the dome on February 22, 2006. Best evidence is that an extreme Sunni-insurgent group associated with the terrorist group Al-Qaida detonated the explosives. I was in Baghdad on February 22, 2006 and realized the seriousness of the bombing from the stunned reaction of all Iraqis – Shi'a, Sunni, and Christian – that I spoke to on that day. To them, the bombing of the Golden Mosque was an unthinkable outrage that had torn apart the fabric of their culture. As Al-Qaida had hoped, the bombing of the Golden Mosque lit the fuse to an explosion of savage inter-sectarian violence that continued for almost two years. It was not until April 2009 that security had finally improved to the point where the Golden Mosque with its newly restored dome was reopened to pilgrims.

While there is no reliable data on the expenditures of religious tourists in Iraq, even with most of their travel expenses captured by Iranian firms, spending totaled at least $1 billion and possibly as much as $2.5 billion. While religious tourism is strong, historical and geographic tourism is far from reaching its potential.

As is well known, Iraq – Mesopotamia – has been the home of many great ancient civilizations. Since 6000 BC, these include the Sumerian, Akkadian, Gutian, Amorite, and Elamite civilizations before one of the greatest of the ancient civilizations – the Babylonian – rose to prominence in about 1800 BC. The land of the two rivers contains the ruins of some of the greatest cities of human literature and history: Ur, Lagash, Uruk, Babylon, Ashur, and Nineveh. There are few nations in the world that can boast of so much history within a relatively small area (GoI 2010, pp. 128–31). The potential for historical tourism with the accompanying expenditures and employment opportunities is great. The major constraints are continuing concerns about security, the lack of appropriate infrastructure, and the necessity of preparing the sites so as to protect them from further damage. Some recent desecration of ancient sites was deliberate. In the mid-1980s, Saddam embarked on an extensive rebuilding of several ancient cities mixing – to the horror of archeologists – ancient structures with modern construction. As in Egypt, there is the possibility of fairly large ships carrying foreign tourists up the rivers to stop at various sites.

Geographic tourism is also in its infancy but the Kurdish region provides a cool green mountainous terrain that offers a welcome contrast to the hot brown flat terrain in much of the region. So far, most tourism in the Kurdish region has been from other parts of Iraq but the number of foreign tourists is growing rapidly albeit from a very low starting point.

The major barriers to increased tourism are security especially at the historical sites, the difficulty in obtaining valid tourist visas, and the shortage of hotels. In 2010, the number of hotels outside of the KRG was only 590, less than half the number of a decade before. Of these hotels, only seven were considered "Five Star" hotels (COSIT 2012, Table 16/6). However, there is currently a rapid expansion of hotels, many financed by foreign investors, restaurants, and other services for tourists.

While the potential for increasing the number of foreign tourists in Iraq is great; currently the outflow of tourism dollars is greater than the inflow. Many well off and even middle-class Iraqis have traveled extensively in both the Middle East and Europe seemingly unconstrained by the $10 000 legal limit on the amount of currency that can be taken out of the country. Although there are fewer tourists leaving Iraq each year than enter it, Iraqi's spend a greater amount per person on their foreign trips. Combined with other service transactions, the large amount spent by Iraqi tourists results in a services deficit of an estimated $7 billion in 2010.

REMITTANCES AND TRANSFER PAYMENTS

Iraq also runs a deficit on transfer payments. Primarily because of official transfers, the deficit reached about $2.6 billion in 2010. It is believed that the actual deficit might be larger since individuals and non-government entities may avoid processing transfer transactions through the banking system that would report them to the Iraqi authorities. Therefore to avoid bureaucratic delays, excessive administrative fees, and possible demands for bribes or other illegal charges; many cross-border transactions are made using "hawalas" rather than legal financial intermediaries.

Hawala, which have a long history in Islamic states, is a method of transferring money without actually moving it across borders. For example, assume that you want to send funds to your brother who is in another country. You give funds to a hawala broker in your own country and he authorizes a hawala broker in the other country to pay the same amount, minus a commission, to your brother. There is no contract between the brokers for this transfer; it is based on trust. The increasing prevalence of high-speed Internet connections has recently led to high-tech competition for traditional hawalas. Assume that you are in Detroit, Michigan, which has a large population of recent immigrants from Iraq and you want to send $5000 to your brother in Baghdad. A search of the web might find someone in Baghdad who wants to send $5000 to a relative in Detroit. Connected by the Internet, possibly live on Skype, the Detroit and Baghdad transaction are performed simultaneously (Desai 2011). Of course, such a transaction would not be reported in the current account statistics of either country. While it is difficult to estimate the value of these unreported transfers, they are believed to be a large and growing component of the capital flight discussed below.

CAPITAL FLOWS

Foreign Direct Investment

FDI and official borrowing account for the bulk of Iraq's international capital inflows. Foreign purchasing in the Iraq's stock exchange is increasing rapidly but from a very low level and, as a result, is not yet a major source of foreign finance. From less than an estimated $0.1 billion in 2006, FDI increased to $1.9 billion in 2010 before almost doubling to an estimated $3.9 billion in 2011 (IMF 2008b, Table 7, p. 25; 2011a, Table 7, p. 22). The GoI has announced over $100 billion in new investment projects not only for petroleum infrastructure but also for expanding access to

electricity, water, and housing. While it is unlikely that all of these investment plans will actually be executed, it is expected that FDI will double
again to almost $8.0 billion by 2015.

It is difficult to obtain accurate data on the sources and uses of FDI
especially since announced investments are rarely executed as described.
However, a 2009 study of FDI by Dunia Frontier Consultants provides
some insights. With respect to sources of FDI, over two-thirds comes
from five countries: UAE (24 percent of total 2009 FDI), South Korea
(16 percent), USA (14 percent), the UK (7 percent), and Lebanon (6
percent). The presence of the USA, UK, and South Korea among the
top five sources reflects their roles in repairing and expanding oil and gas
infrastructure. In fact, the largest single project announced in 2009 was
$25 billion to improve production of the West Qurna 1 Oilfield by an
ExxonMobil–Dutch Shell consortium. When oil and other government
investments are excluded then the US portion of total FDI drops to less
than 1 percent and Iraq's regional neighbors take the lead in FDI (Dunia
Frontier Consultants 2009, Tables 1, 4, 7, pp. 8, 11, 16).

Iraqi oil and gas industries were the recipients of about 47 percent
of all FDI in 2009 followed by "Mixed" Investments (35 percent) and
Real Estate (18 percent). All of the other major sectors, transportation,
tourism, non-governmental infrastructure, and manufacturing received
less than 0.3 percent each. "Mixed" investments refer to large-scale
projects intended to create industrial zones with residential and commercial activities. An example would be the proposed South Korean financed
new industrial city in Anbar province (Dunia Frontier Consultants 2009,
Table 2, p. 9).

The dominance of energy and "mixed" FDI determines which provinces received the bulk of FDI. In 2009, three provinces received about
70 percent of FDI: Basrah province (recipient of 39 percent of all FDI),
Anbar province (18 percent), and Baghdad province (13 percent). The
three provinces of the KRG received less than 7 percent of total FDI in
2009 compared to over 90 percent in 2006 (Dunia Frontier Consultants
2009, Table 3, p. 10). This severe drop in FDI to the KRG was not related
to any adverse occurrences in the KRG. Rather the reversal was a result
of the drop in violence in the rest of Iraq beginning in 2007–2008 as well
as the ongoing dispute between the GoI and the KRG over the validity of
KRG contracts for oil exploration, exploitation, and shipment.

That FDI is expected to account for the bulk of Iraq's foreign capital
inflows over the next decade is good for Iraq. Unlike portfolio and debt
flows, transfers of managerial and technical skills usually accompany
FDI. By working for or with foreign firms, Iraqi managers, engineers, and
so on will be exposed to world standard techniques and procedures. In

order to increase the amount of FDI, the 2006 Investment Law (#13) provided for a ten-year tax holiday for new FDI and established a National Investment Commission (NIC) as well as Investment Commissions for individual regions (RIC) or provinces (PIC). In addition to providing information on regulations and possible investments, the NIC provides a "one stop shop" intended to provide a streamlined process for obtaining an investment license. After a completed application is submitted then an investment license should be obtained within 45 days. The usefulness of the RIC and PICs varies greatly. One-third of the PIC websites could not be accessed in mid-2012 while some of the other websites contain outdated information.

One of the more complicated issues facing FDI in Iraq is obtaining a land allocation. In some provinces, over 90 percent of all land is controlled by one or more of the ministries under land laws that date from the Saddam regime. Therefore even when a foreign investor has obtained the necessary investment licenses and other approvals from the appropriate national and provincial authorities, it is necessary to petition the appropriate Baghdad ministry to obtain a land allocation.

Foreign Borrowing and Equity Purchases

Iraqi entities have little debt exposure to foreign banks. At mid-year 2011, loans to Iraqi entities from banks in the almost thirty nations that report bank exposure to the Bank for International Settlements (BIS) was less than $1.6 billion. This is an extraordinarily low exposure to foreign banks for a developing country with the GDP and volume of international trade of Iraq. In fact, Iraq's net situation with respect to those banks that report to the BIS was actually positive since Iraqi entities had $4.4 billion in deposits at BIS banks. Loans from multilateral institutions such as the IMF are also relatively low. At mid-year 2011, this exposure was about $2.1 billion (BIS 2012, Table 1, Lines 01, 06 and 29).

Equity investment in the ISX is open to foreigners with the exception of limits on foreign ownership of bank stock. However, as discussed in Chapter 8, foreign investors face several difficulties in buying stock on the ISX. First, it is difficult to obtain reliable balance sheet and income statement information on the 87 firms currently trading on the ISX. Second, trading on the ISX is shallow. In April 2012, about one-quarter of the firms on the ISX did not trade a single share (see Chapter 8, Table 8.3). Finally, there is little protection for shareholders in the event of corporate mismanagement or bankruptcy. In fact, there is evidence that the net flow of capital whether equity and debt is not in but out – capital flight.

CAPITAL FLIGHT

"Capital flight is a large outflow of capital from a low-income less developed country" (Gunter 2008a, p. 434). Some analysts favor a more restrictive definition that capital flight represents a situation where funds are fleeing or propelled illegally across national borders in search of sanctuary. This definition emphasizes that capital flight is often a response to high (or increasing) political or economic risks. Such flight can be seen as a quantifiable measure of how much confidence people have in the political and economic future of their country. On the other hand, some portfolio holders may attempt to secretly move funds out of their country because these funds represent ill-gotten gains of crime or corruption. An alternative view is that capital flight simply represents an attempt to create a diversified international portfolio in the face of unreasonable government restrictions on cross-border financial transactions. If one accepts this view then one might say that using the term capital flight is more of a judgment than a definition – when Americans transfer funds to London, it is international diversification, but when Iraqis transfer funds to London, it is capital flight (Gunter 2004, pp. 63–4).

Regardless of the appropriateness of the definition, is there evidence of large-scale capital flight from Iraq? During the upsurge in violence in 2005–2007, many Iraqis left the country as refugees and took, whenever possible, their financial and other assets with them. But even with the more recent sharp decrease in violence and the recent return of many refugees, there are signs that Iraqi portfolio holders are still moving large amounts of funds out of the country. Estimating capital flight is difficult since there are a large variety of creative options that can be used to avoid any government controls. These include manipulating legitimate financial or trade transactions as well as the simple although often dangerous expedient of taking a briefcase full of cash across a border. More sophisticated methods of estimating capital flight involve comparing financial and trade transactions reported by a country to the counterpart data reported by the countries that are its financial and trade partners. (See Gunter 2004, pp. 65–9; 2008a, p. 435.) Although Almounsor (2005, p. 249) found evidence of over $108 million in mis-invoicing consistent with capital flight during the period 1980–2002, the detailed counterpart data needed for this type of estimate is not yet available for the post-2003 Iraq economy.

In the absence of better data, a crude measure of capital flight is possible using the balance of payments numbers reported by the CBI. Because of double-entry bookkeeping, the current account balance of a country plus its capital balance must equal any change in its international reserves. For example, if a country exports more goods and services than it imports (positive current account balance) then either it must lend some of its current account earnings to entities in other countries (negative capital balance) or Iraq's international reserves must increase. If these numbers do not balance then it might represent capital flight.

The current account balance is the sum of a country's net goods and services trade plus net income and transfers. According to the 2010 data – the most recent available – Iraq's current account balance was in surplus, $6.4 billion (CBI 2012b). If the country's net capital balance – investment, equity, and debt flows – was zero in 2010, then one would have expected that the country's holdings of international reserves would increase by the same $6.4 billion. However, according to the CBI, the 2010 net capital position was a *positive* $8.6 billion. Since Iraq experienced a surplus in both its current and capital accounts then one would have expected – in the absence of capital flight – a $15.0 billion ($6.4 billion plus $8.6 billion) increase in Iraq's international reserves. However, the actual increase was only $6.3 billion.

This $8.7 billion gap between expected and actual changes in international reserves might be simply a statistical artifact, accumulated errors and omissions that would disappear with more accurate data gathering. In fact, this is how the CBI classifies this discrepancy. However, in many developing countries such large negative "errors and omissions" is associated with capital flight, that is, that an estimated $8.7 billion in capital was transferred out of country without being reported in 2010 (Cuddington 1987, pp. 85–9). As a matter of scale, $8.7 billion was equal to 17 percent of Iraq's oil export earnings in 2010. The 2010 estimate appears to be part of a trend of large balance of payments discrepancies consistent with capital flight. In 2009, errors and omissions were a negative $6.1 billion; in 2008, they were −$8.4 billion; and in 2007, they were −$4.1 billion (COSIT 2012, Table 8/10). Pessimistically, Iraq may have experienced total capital flight of over $27 billion from 2007–2010. This trend is apparently continuing. While 2011 balance of payments data is still being revised, there appears to be at least $6 billion in errors and omissions and maybe much more. These results are consistent with a study of capital flight from the MENA countries that found a positive relationship between capital flight and crude oil prices (Almounsor 2005, p. 246).

One response to this estimate of capital flight is surprise that it is so low. In view of the combination of large oil revenues, ubiquitous corruption, and great political uncertainty; one might expect much larger volumes of capital leaving the country. There seem to be at least two explanations for the lower than expected capital flight. First, surveys show that the average Iraqi is fairly optimistic about the future of the country. This optimism may translate into a willingness to suffer the current inefficiencies and inequalities since they are thought to be temporary rather than send their wealth, their children, and themselves to another country. Second, the sheer complexity and inefficiency of Iraq's financial system makes it difficult, risky, and expensive for most Iraqis to move their assets abroad.

In view of Iraq's great need for capital to expand oil production while at the same time develop infrastructure so as to improve the quality of life of the average Iraqi, the possible diversion of more than $33 billion into foreign accounts should be a matter of concern since this estimated capital flight is equal to over 40 percent of the GoI total 2007–2011 investment expenditures. There are two possible solutions. One option is that Iraq can impose draconian rules in an attempt to stop (or slow) capital flight. This option is probably doomed since other countries with governments that have lower levels of corruption and a greater willingness to use harsh measures to enforce rules have been unable to make more than a temporary dent in capital flight. (For an example of the successful avoidance of capital controls in the case of the People's Republic of China, see Gunter 2004, pp. 81–2.) The other option is to make Iraq a more attractive place to invest so as to not only catch the attention of foreign investors but also encourage domestic portfolio holders to keep their funds at home. But creating a more favorable investment environment in Iraq will require the careful phasing of substantial changes in financial regulations and monetary policies which is discussed in Chapter 13.

FOREIGN DEBT

By the collapse of Saddam's regime in 2003, Iraq's foreign debt had become grossly unsustainable. Not only was Iraq's estimated foreign debt of $133.0 billion equivalent to almost five times (517 percent) of the war-ravaged country's GDP but also it was very difficult to determine precisely how much was owed to each creditor. Further complicating the analysis of Iraq's foreign debt burden was the widely varying estimates of the compensation that must be paid for the damage done during Saddam's wars.

One estimate is that servicing that $133 billion of foreign debt would have required almost two-thirds of the GoI total revenues for the foreseeable future. However, as is well known, the major creditor nations not only suspended debt service but also agreed to large-scale debt forgiveness. Since 2003, Iraq's foreign debt to GDP ratio has fallen sharply to about 107 percent in 2011 and 46 percent in 2012. However, the attention paid to debt forgiveness should not distract from the major cause of the drop in the country's debt to GDP ratio, which was the surprisingly strong growth in GDP. Because of the US-led invasion, the GDP data for 2003 is a crude estimate. But since 2004, Iraq has grown rapidly from an estimated 37.5 trillion ID ($25.8 billion at 2004 exchange rate) to 114.7 trillion ID ($98 billion) in 2011. This is equivalent to a nominal growth rate in the country's GDP (in dollars) of 21 percent per year for seven years. Even if there had been zero debt forgiveness then the debt to GDP ratio would still have declined from over 500 percent in 2004 to 136 percent at the end of 2011.

Debt forgiveness proceeded in stages. Of Iraq's 2003 external public debt – excluding war reparations – of approximately $133 billion, only a very small amount – $0.9 billion (1 percent of the total) – was owed to the World Bank, the IMF, or other multi-lateral organizations. The bulk of the debt was to foreign governments, about $111.4 billion (84 percent), with commercial creditors accounting for the remaining $20.7 billion (16 percent) (IMF 2005, Table 1, p. 71; Weiss 2009, p. 1. Of the total owed to foreign governments, $42.6 billion was owed to Paris Club members and $68.8 billion to foreign countries who are not permanent members of the Club. The Paris Club is a meeting of 19 major creditor nations where disputes concerning government-to-government debt are resolved.

In addition to foreign debt, Iraq was also considered liable for war reparations; these reparations were estimated at over $200 billion mostly from the 1990 invasion and subsequent devastation of Kuwait.

After the collapse of Saddam's regime, it was argued that most of the country's debt should be canceled. Both ethical and practical reasons were given for debt relief (*The Economist* 2003, p. 68). The legal theory of "odious debt" says a nation should not be held ethically responsible for debts incurred for purposes that are not beneficial to the state. In a sense, these debts were incurred under coercion since a free public would not have borrowed the funds for this purpose. The theory of odious debt has a long history extending, at least, to the eighteenth-century Condorcet–Jefferson theory that, under certain conditions, every generation had the right to repudiate the excessive debts of previous generations (see Gunter 1991). Since Saddam was clearly a tyrant who ruled by terror and instigated multiple internal and externals conflicts that caused incredible hardships for the Iraqi people, the odious debt argument was a strong one. However, the practical reasons were probably more persuasive.

The scale of Iraq's foreign debt was so large at the end of 2003 that most of the GoI revenue would have to be diverted to debt service. This would prevent using oil export earnings to fund the nation's reconstruction and possibly spread fuel on the smoldering fires of ethnic and religious animosities. On the other hand, Iraq does possess huge oil reserves and, after a decade of the large oil-related infrastructure investments discussed in Chapter 6, it should be able to service its foreign debts. This would seem to support a temporary suspension of debt service rather than debt cancelation. However, in a historically rare case of victors disregarding their own self-interests; the USA and its Paris Club coalition partners canceled most of their Iraqi debt.

The 19 permanent members of the Paris Club approved a total 80 percent reduction in three phases, with the first 30 percent in 2004, the second 30 percent in 2005 when Iraq accepted an agreement with the IMF, and the final 20 percent upon successful completion of the IMF program. To obtain the complete reduction, the GoI and specifically the CBI agreed to make substantial procedural and structural changes intended to improve efficiency and transparency of governmental operations (IMF 2005, Table 2, p. 21, Table 3, p. 22). In retrospect, the GoI acceptance of the IMF recommendations may have had a stronger favorable impact on Iraq's long-term economic development than the debt decrease itself.

Over half of Iraq's debt is owed to non-Paris Club states although no authoritative breakdown of this debt exists. However, it is believed that of the approximately $68.8 billion owed to non-Paris Club states, about 85 percent was owed to only two nations: Saudi Arabia and Kuwait. While some non-Paris Club countries reduced their Iraqi debt right after the Paris Club negotiations, negotiations to reduce the rest of the non-Paris Club debt dragged on until 2011 when most of the remaining countries finally accepted – in principle – an 80 percent reduction. However, the signing of legal documents related to this debt reduction continues to be delayed over a variety of technical and political issues. Some commentators believe that the Persian Gulf creditors will continue to delay until they are able to negotiate favorable terms with the GoI on other issues.

Iraq's approximately $20 billion in commercial debt involved many relatively small creditors with almost two-thirds of the unpaid loans amounting to less than $10 million. Iraq successfully negotiated to buy back with cash the debt of small creditors at 10.25 cents on the dollar while issuing new bonds to the larger creditors of $200 per $1000 of existing debt (Weiss 2009, p. 9).

The issue of war reparations to Kuwait was also resolved although both parties felt ill-treated. Under the extremely corrupt UN "Oil for Food" program, 25 percent of Iraq's oil export earnings were to go to a pay for reparations. With the end of the "Oil for Food" program, a UN resolution stated that 5 percent of Iraq's future gross oil export earnings would go to Kuwait until the reparations – plus interest – were completely paid. Kuwait sees this transfer as inadequate to compensate the nation for the terrible damage done by the Iraqi invasion. On the other hand, many Iraqis feel that it was the dictator Saddam who invaded Kuwait and, since he is dead, it is wrong to demand that the Iraqi people pay for his crimes.

Until the debt reduction by the remaining non-Paris Club states is finalized, some sources are listing two debt figures. With the reductions, Iraq's 2011 foreign debt was about $52.6 billion or 64 percent of GDP (US CIA 2012). However, until all of the documentation has been completed, the debt is technically about $35 billion more. Despite some lumpiness in debt service payments over the next decade, Iraq should be able to service its remaining debt without substantially adversely affecting the GoI economic development plans. In 2011, interest on the national debt was about 1.4 trillion ID ($1.2 billion) or 1.4 percent of total expenditures.

INTERNATIONAL RESERVES

A country's current account balance plus its capital balance should sum to the change in official reserves. Iraq's international reserves, mostly held in US treasury securities, amounted to about $53.5 billion at the end of 2011 (US CIA 2012), equal to about ten months-worth of the country's total imports. One motivation for holding international reserves is to provide an emergency fund that will allow a country to purchase necessary imports even if its ability to export was temporarily blocked. This is an important motivation for Iraq for at least two reasons. First, in view of the fact that petroleum shipments through the Persian Gulf account for most of its exports and Iran periodically boasts of its capability and intention to close the Gulf. Second, as discussed in Chapter 6, Iraq's export earnings are primarily determined by the extremely variable price of oil. If oil prices fall during a period of low reserves, such as occurred in 2006, then Iraq finds itself essentially living "hand to mouth" – unable to import food each month for the PDS baskets until the payment is received for the previous month's oil exports.

The second motivation for Iraq's large holdings of international reserves is to maintain stability of the ID. Since January 2009, one of the great successes of the CBI has been the stabilization of the ID at a value of approximately 1170 ID per dollar. Previously, the CBI had managed a gradual appreciation of the ID of almost 20 percent from 1467 ID per dollar in 2006 to 1170 in January 2009. Since then the CBI has operated daily auctions for commercial banks. For example, in mid-2012, the CBI stood ready to sell US dollars at 1166 ID per dollar and buy dollars at 1164 ID per dollar (CBI 2012a). Despite substantial violence, political turmoil, and the sharp year-to-year earnings from petroleum exports; the country's large reserves have ensured the credibility of what is now described by the CBI as having transitioned from a "crawling peg" to a "stabilized arrangement against the dollar". This stabilized dinar/dollar value has done much to enhance the credibility of the CBI and, to a lesser extent, the rest of the GoI.

But is this period of a stable exchange rate coming to an end? Political instability in Syria and the adverse impact of sanctions on the economy of Iran have led to a severe shortage of dollars in both countries. This has increased the demand for dollars in Iraq as intermediaries seek hard currency that can be sold to Syrians and Iranians. This has put severe downward pressure on the ID at the same time, as the CBIs options to prevent depreciation of the ID are increasingly limited. Since this challenge will affect fiscal, monetary, and exchange rate policy; it is appropriate to treat it in the next chapter.

13. Fiscal, monetary, and exchange rate policy

> The chief limiting factor to the success of development in Iraq
> may prove to be neither the amount of money for investment,
> nor even the limits of skilled labour and materials available,
> but the efficiency of the administrative machine.
> (Lord Salter 1955, p. 96)

Compared to the governments of most developing countries in 2012, the GoI was in an enviable position. With high world oil prices and steadily increasing crude oil exports, the government expected a 26 percent increase in total revenues. In fact, one of the problems facing the GoI was that it literally could not spend money fast enough. With respect to monetary and exchange rate policies, the country had maintained a steady exchange rate for almost three years. This greatly contributed to the CBIs reputation for professional management.

But the future may not be as bright. As discussed in Chapter 8, Iraq's financial markets are moribund as a result of state bank dominance and inadequate regulation on financial intermediation. The equity market is in its infancy and extremely shallow. Also, Iraq is still a two-currency economy – ID and US dollar. Both the inefficient financial markets and dollarization substantially limit Iraqi monetary and exchange rate policies especially when faced with substantial hard currency loss. In addition, there is increasing evidence of large-scale capital flight although not yet large enough to be destabilizing.

Finally, a dysfunctional system of financial intermediation combined with the need for large amounts of foreign infrastructure investment puts the GoI on the horns of a dilemma. By impeding the liberalization of financial markets, the GoI limits destabilizing "hot money" capital flows that could, in the worst-case scenario, force a devaluation of the ID. However, the primitive level of financial intermediation in the country acts as a drag on the non-oil economy hindering economic growth and preventing needed employment growth.

FISCAL POLICY

The demands on the GoI national budget are great. The salaries of about half of the labor force are dependent on government expenditures. Security expenditures – both policy and military – continue to grow while poverty alleviation in the form of the PDS food baskets and other social safety net expenditures are large. With respect to investment expenditures, the GoI must not only pay for the restoration of a national infrastructure severely degraded by sanctions and war (as discussed in Chapter 11) but also the nation's long-term development strategy calls for massive investment in oil exploration, production, and shipment (see Chapter 6). Finally, in coordination with monetary and exchange rate policy, fiscal policy must be crafted so as to further the country's macroeconomic goals of real growth, price stability, low unemployment, and external balance.

GoI Revenues

As shown in Table 13.1, Iraq's fiscal policy is hostage to the value of the country's oil exports. Although Iraq's oil export volume tends to change gradually, there have been dramatic year-to-year changes in oil prices. Oil prices averaged $91.50 pb in 2008 before collapsing to $55.60 pb in 2009. It was only in early 2012 that oil prices returned to 2008 levels before falling again in mid-2012. In 2011, oil export earnings accounted for almost 88 percent of the national government's 81.3 trillion ID (approximately $69.5 billion) total revenues. The 22 percent increase in the GoI total revenues between 2010 and 2011 was caused by a $2.30 increase in the price of a barrel of oil world oil prices to $76.50 combined with a 320 000 bpd increase in the volume of oil exports to 2.17 mbpd.

From 2007 through 2011, GoI budget assumptions concerning world oil prices and export volumes have been subject to offsetting errors. Each year, the GoI budget has overestimated the volume of oil exports while underestimating the world price of oil. For example, the 2011 budget assumed daily exports of 2.25 mbpd while the actual export volume was 2.17 mbpd. In the same budget, it was assumed that the world price of oil would be $68.00 pb while the actual price was closer to $76.50 pb (IMF 2011a, p. 8). However, this five-year pattern may be broken in 2012. The 2012 budget assumed a substantial increase in oil exports to 2.625 mbpd and by April, exports had already reached 2.5 mbpd (UPI 2012). Barring delays in the expansion of the petroleum infrastructure discussed in Chapter 6, Iraq may be able to meet its volume targets for the first time since 2004. The 2012 budget assumed an average oil price of $85.00 pb.

Table 13.1   Iraq's fiscal accounts (trillions of ID)

	2008[E]	2009[E]	2010[E]	2011[E]	2012[P]
Total revenues	82.0	54.7	66.4	81.3	102.3
Oil export revenues	73.9	45.6	58.6	71.9	94.4
(Oil prices per barrel)*	($91.50)	($55.60)	($74.20)	($76.50)	($85)**
(Oil exports mbpd)	(1.82)	(1.88)	(1.85)	(2.17)	(2.63)**
Total expenditures	83.2	71.4	76.6	97.0	117.0
Current expenditures	55.9	57.5	57.2	64.0	79.9
Investment expenditures	27.3	16.7	19.5	33.1	37.1
Budget balance	−1.2	−16.7	−10.2	−15.7	−14.70

Notes:
[E] Expected.
[P] Projected.
* Indicative price – not the actual price received by GoI.
** 2012 oil price and oil export volumes are budget-planning assumptions, not actual values as in previous years.

Sources: IMF (2011a), Table 2, p. 17; *Reuters* (2012), February 23.

Not only are the earnings from crude oil exports the major source of GoI revenues but also they have grown in importance since 2004. The other major source of revenue, grants from other nations and international organizations, is falling. These grants accounted for almost 26 percent of total GoI revenues in the immediate post-war period but are expected to fall to less than 2 percent in 2012 (IMF 2011a, Table 2, p. 17).

Revenues from Iraq's oil exports are not immediately deposited in GoI accounts. In 2003, the GoI faced many lawsuits from foreign governments, entities, and individuals who were injured as a result of the 1990 invasion of Kuwait or other activities of Saddam's regime. When oil sales resumed after the US-led coalition invasion of Iraq in 2003, it was feared that foreign courts would seize earnings from Iraq's oil exports in order to compensate these injured parties. Therefore, in 2003, United Nations Security Council Resolution 1483 sanctioned the establishment of the Development Fund for Iraq (DFI). Various moneys from the UN "Oil for Food" and other programs as well as the earnings of the Iraqi oil sales were deposited into the DFI account that is managed by the New York Federal Reserve. The DFI receives these funds, ensures that Kuwait receives 5 percent of these revenues as reparations for the 1990 invasion, and holds the remainder until the GoI requests a fund transfer. There have been several extensions of the DFI authority with the most recent expiring in May 2012.

What occurs after the expiration of the DFI depends on the legal status of the many court attachments, liens, garnishments, and so on that have been filed against the GoI. If they are all successfully resolved then revenues from Iraqi oil exports will be deposited directly into GoI accounts. However, it is possible that a court somewhere in the world might unexpectedly seize some of Iraq's oil export earnings.

Current Expenditures

About two-thirds – 64.0 trillion ID ($54.7 billion) – of the GoI 2011 expenditures are for current activities. The major components of current expenditures are: salaries and pensions that account for about 50 percent of current expenditures, and transfer payments (social security, PDS food baskets, SOE subsidies) that account for about 25 percent. The remaining quarter of current expenditures was spent on purchases of goods and services, interest, war reparations, and so on. Regardless of the changes in total revenues of the GoI, the amount spent on government salaries and pensions has increased every year since 2003. As GoI expenditures on salaries and pensions increased faster than the other components of current expenditures, its proportion of current expenditures has almost quadrupled from about 13 percent in 2004 to about 50 percent in 2011 when spending on salaries and pensions reached 32.2 trillion ID ($27.5 billion).

As salaries and pensions increased, GoI spending on goods and services fell. Annual spending on goods and services has decreased almost one-third from 18.2 trillion ID ($12.4 billion) in 2005 to 12.3 trillion ($10.5 billion) in 2011. In 2011, such purchases accounted for less than 13 percent of total expenditures. While a deceleration in spending for goods and services was foreseen as the GoI recovered from the damage done by the 2003 US-led invasion, the actual reduction is much greater than expected. Apparently, freeing up funds for government salaries was a higher priority than ensuring that those workers have the equipment and consumables necessary to do their jobs.

The other major components of current expenditures have changed little. Transfer payments accounted for about the same proportion of total expenditures in 2011 – 14.6 percent – as in 2005. War reparations are a function of the value of oil exports with Kuwait receiving 5 percent of

Iraq's oil export earnings. These reparations reached 3.6 trillion ID (about $3.1 billion) or about 3.7 percent of total expenditures in 2011 about the same proportion as in 2005. As a result of Iraq's major creditors canceling substantial amounts of debt and suspending or, at least, reducing interest on the remainder; interest accounts remain a fairly small proportion of GoI expenditures. In 2011, interest was 1.4 trillion ID ($1.2 billion) or about 1.4 percent of total expenditures.

Investment Expenditures

These expenditures change substantially year to year. After falling almost 40 percent in 2009 to 16.7 trillion ID ($14.3 billion), investment expenditures grew 17 percent in 2010 to 19.5 trillion ID ($16.7 billion), which was then followed by a further 70 percent increase in 2011 to 33.1 trillion ID ($28.3 billion).

These unforeseen changes in government investment not only have a substantial impact on capital accumulation but also lead to great inefficiency and encourage corruption. Public investment accounted for almost 93 percent of all fixed capital formation in 2009 (COSIT 2012, Table 14.10). Therefore, when the GoI rapidly cuts investment expenditures; most infrastructure and other investment in roads, electricity, schools, clinics, water supply, and so on slows or grinds to a stop. Partially completed multi-year building projects are abandoned for months or years until investment spending is restored in a future budget. When projects are restarted, it is often discovered that previous work must be redone due to looting, vandalism, environmental damage, or planned revisions. What drives this pattern of on-again, off-again investment? Investment expenditures are the primary shock absorbers of the GoI budget. Adverse oil price shocks translate into large unexpected revenue drops and, since Iraq's ability to borrow is limited, the GoI cuts investment expenditures.

The drop in oil prices in 2009 and the delays in fund receipts in 2006 illustrate how the GoI dealt with unexpected drops in revenues. As shown in Table 13.1, salaries and pensions, which in "normal" times accounted for almost one-third of total expenditures, continued to increase during a revenues crisis while the burden of adjustment fell on non-salary current expenditures and investment expenditures. For example, in 2009, in the face of a 33 percent *decrease* in total revenues to about 55 trillion ID ($46.8 billion), salaries and pensions expenditures *increased* by about the same percentage to 28 trillion ID ($23.8 billion). The rise in salary and pension expenditures exacerbated the impact of the downturn on social safety net transfers (down 33 percent) and investment expenditures (down 39 percent). The remaining deficit was financed through the sale of GoI treasury bills and by transferring about 9 trillion ID ($7.7 billion) from state-owned banks.

Crisis Price of Oil

Assuming that GoI access to world capital markets continues to be severely constrained except for foreign investment in the oil sector; how low will oil prices have to fall before the GoI adjustment process fails? In other words, what is the lowest world oil price that will allow the GoI to pay salaries and pensions, purchase the supplies necessary for the army and police, maintain a minimum social safety net, pay interest and war reparations, and continue the minimum necessary infrastructure maintenance and construction to allow a steady increase in the volume of oil exports? With all the necessary assumptions, this number will be no more than an educated guess but, adjusting for inflation, the crisis price of oil is about $55 pb. If the world price of oil falls to or below this level, then the GoI will be forced to make spending cuts that were politically unacceptable even during the worst periods of the insurgency. It should be noted that although world oil prices fell to $55.60 pb in 2009, the level of GoI "essential" spending was much lower that year, for example spending on salaries and pensions was 30 percent less.

Budget Balance

Table 13.1 provides estimates of Iraq's budget balance but one should probably have little confidence in the accuracy of this data. The actual results are probably better than reported. In other words, the true budget balance is either a smaller deficit or larger surplus than reported in the official summary. There are at least two sources of uncertainty on the revenue side. The GoI tends to underestimate world oil prices. These underestimates result in increases in actual oil export earnings over the budgeted amounts. In addition, several accounts have been discovered with hundreds of billions of ID (hundreds of millions of dollars) of what is apparently revenues from oil sales that, for some reason, has not been officially reported to the Ministry of Finance. However, the biggest failures to execute the budget are on the expenditure side.

The problem begins with delays by Iraq's coalition government in developing a consistent budget and submitting it in a timely manner to the 325 member Council of Representatives (CoR). In addition to the usual political disputes that surround any country's budget, the GoI is a new organization primarily composed, to a great extent, of officials and elected members who are new to government. The written and unwritten practices and procedures necessary (but not sufficient!) for passing the budget in a timely manner and ensuring that it is executed as planned are only gradually being developed. For example, the GoI presented the 2012 budget to the CoR in early December, which did not allow enough time for CoR evaluation, discussion, and approval before the beginning of the fiscal year on January 1. As it turned out, the CoR did not approve the 2012 budget until February 23 – about seven weeks into the fiscal year. Even when budget funds are released to the various ministries, there is a wide variance in the ability of ministries to actually spend these funds before the end of the fiscal year. There were unpublished reports that one major ministry was only able to actually spend about 2 percent of its investment budget during a recent fiscal year.

Along with administrative delays and mismanagement, corruption tends to delay expenditures in two somewhat contradictory ways. Corrupt officials will often use bureaucratic methods to delay expenditures until they can divert some of the funds into their own pockets or those of their supporters. At the same time, attempts to reduce corruption may also lead to delays. Some ministries severely constrain the authority of the lower levels of the bureaucracy to make any decisions that could conceivably facilitate corruption. As a result, relatively minor expenditure decisions must be approved at a very senior level, sometimes by the minister himself.

Although the most recent five budgets were supposed to result in deficits, higher than expected revenues combined with failures to spend mean that the final budget balance was in surplus for at least three and possibly four of these budgets. Even when the fiscal year has ended, it is difficult to determine actual expenditures although the Ministry of Finance has adopted new systems that should allow it to more accurately monitor spending in the future.

If more accurate revenue estimates combined with better budget execution actually lead to a budget deficit then Iraq has several options to finance it. It can draw upon its funds in the DFI although it is difficult to determine the exact amount in the DFI. It is believed to be at least $10 billion and may be a great deal more. The New York Federal Reserve prefers not to release information on the status of the DFI without the permission of the GoI and the GoI is hesitant to give this permission because of the impact on budget negotiations in Baghdad. In addition to taking funds from the DFI, there are several trillions of ID (billions of dollars) in various GoI accounts at state-owned banks. A portion of these funds are "float" and therefore not available to finance a budget deficit. However, some of these funds represent payments made for discontinued projects that could be transferred back to the Ministry of Finance.

Domestic borrowing is limited due to lack of a formal government bond secondary market. Regulatory change would allow the ISX to trade GoI bonds in a secondary market. However, there is currently a shortage of both bonds and bond buyers. The few GoI bond sales have been more as a proof of principle rather than as a means of raising funds. In mid-2012, the CBI website lists only a single GoI long-term bond issue. In 2006, the GoI issued $2.7 billion in dollar-denominated bonds at 5.8 percent with a maturity date of 2028. Another possible barrier to an increase in non-bank public holdings of GoI bonds is concern about the confidentiality of bond purchases. Because of widespread official corruption, many Iraqis think that to openly purchase a government bond will expose them to official harassment and demands for bribes. One proposal is for the GoI to issue bearer bonds at a discount and redeem them – no questions asked – at par when they mature. Since bearer bonds are unregistered and no information is kept concerning the purchaser, they reduce the vulnerability of the purchaser to official interference. However, until there is a substantial expansion of the domestic appetite for GoI debt, the country must continue to depend on foreign borrowing.

Iraq's Fiscal Multiplier

The fiscal multiplier attempts to estimate the total impact on an economy of changes in government spending or taxes. Since taxes are an insignificant source of funds in Iraq, we can concentrate on the fiscal multiplier for increased spending by the GoI. There are no published estimates of Iraq's fiscal multiplier. However due to the high proportion of imports in the average Iraqi's market basket combined with the high rate of saving, the multiplier is probably very small – maybe between 1.0 and 1.3. This means that when the GoI increases expenditures, the effect dies out quickly as funds either leave the country to purchase imports or are held as savings. This severely limits the use of fiscal policy to smooth the Iraqi business cycle.

MONETARY AND EXCHANGE RATE POLICY

Since Iraq adopted a fixed exchange rate, it does not have an independent monetary policy. Or, to be more precise, its monetary and exchange rate policy are the same. Any attempt to adopt an expansionary monetary policy, by reducing interest rates or expanding the monetary base, will encourage Iraqi portfolio holders to reduce their holdings of ID, that is, exchanging ID for dollars at the CBI foreign exchange auctions. But as the CBI buys these ID – to maintain the fixed exchange rate – this will

Table 13.2   Monetary and exchange rate variables

	2008	2009	2010	2011	2012
Inflation rate	6.8%	−4.4%	2.2%	5.5%	5.0% (1Q)
Exchange rate					
CBI auction (ID/$)	1193	1170	1170	1170	1166 (1H)
Market (ID/$)	1203	1182	1186	1198	1236 (1H)
Rate "gap"	10 ID	12 ID	16 ID	28 ID	70 ID
Interest rate					
policy	16.75%	8.83%	6.25%	6.00%	6.00% (1H)
Monetary base growth	49%	6%	19%	9%	2% (1Q)
Reserve requirement	Multiple	25%	20%/15%	15%	15%

Sources: Exchange rates and policy rates, COSIT (2012) Annual Abstract, Table 8/5 and 8/7; other data, CBI (2012a).

offset the attempted monetary expansion. The reverse happens if there is an attempt to adopt a contractionary monetary policy, possibly to fight inflation. (In terms of the standard IS/LM/FE macroeconomic model, a fixed exchange rate results in a horizontal FE curve.)

There are similar difficulties with CBI attempts to encourage growth by lowering interest rates. While decreasing the policy rate from 16.75 percent in 2008 to 6 percent in 2011 probably had limited effect on real growth because of the banking issues discussed at length in Chapter 8; the lower rate decreased the willingness of Iraqi non-bank entities and individuals to hold ID instead of dollars (see Table 13.2). If they start to sell ID for dollars then the CBI may be forced to raise the policy rate back to its former level.

The exchange rate system is straightforward. The CBI announces daily – except Friday and Saturday – the rates at which it will sell and buy dollars from approved dealers. From January 2009 until mid-January 2012, the CBI stood ready to sell dollars for ID at a rate of 1170 ID/$. However, beginning on January 17 2012, the CBI announced a slight appreciation to 1166 ID/$. This means that the CBI stands ready to sell dollars at 1166 ID/$ or buy them at 1164 ID/$ from approved dealers.

Of course, there is a fundamental difference between the CBI selling ID, thereby accumulating dollars, and the CBI buying ID, experiencing a dollar outflow. There is no practical limit to the amount of ID that the CBI could create through its purchases of foreign exchange. However, its ability to buy ID at the fixed exchange rate is limited by its foreign exchange holdings plus those that it is willing and able to borrow.

Like all countries that have adopted fixed exchange rates, Iraq faces the danger of becoming a target for almost riskless speculation. If speculators with a billion ID thought that the GoI would depreciate the ID in the near future then they could buy dollars from the CBI at a rate of 1166 ID/$ (CBI 2012a, May 31 exchange rate). This would give the speculators about $857 600. If the GoI did allow the ID to depreciate to say 1280 ID/$ then the speculators could convert their dollars back into ID at the new higher rate and make almost a 10 percent profit. However, if the speculators are wrong and the GoI does not allow a depreciation then they could convert their dollar holdings back into ID at the rate of 1164 ID/$ with a loss of only 0.02 percent. This riskless speculation makes the CBI vulnerable to a speculative attack on the ID. If speculators are able to sell large amounts of ID for dollars at the daily auction then the decrease in CBI dollar reserves will be perceived as increasingly the likelihood of a future devaluation of the ID. This perception will motivate speculators to buy even more dollars in the next auction until the devaluation becomes a self-fulfilling prophecy.

The official CBI auctions are not the only source of dollars for non-public entities and individuals. There is also a currency market that operates in parallel to the CBI auctions and is used by those who are not approved to participate directly in the CBI currency auction. Until November 2010, there was a predictable relationship between the CBI auction and market with dollars selling for about 11 ID more in the market than at the auction. This gap is consistent with the market acting as a more open secondary market for those who were unwilling or unable to purchase dollars at the CBI auction. The 11 ID was a small (about 1 percent) return to those entities that purchased dollars at auction in order to resell them in the parallel market.

But this pattern came to an end in December 2010 with evidence of a sharp increase in the demand for dollars. Not only did the gap between auction and market rates increase from 11 ID to an average of 28 ID in 2011 but also the volume of dollars sold at auction increased. From a daily average of $170 million in December 2010, the daily average auction reached $197 million in December 2011. During the first two weeks of January 2012, volumes continued to rise to a daily average of $237 million or a total of $2.1 billion in the first nine trading days of the year.

This rate of dollar sales would eventually lead to exhaustion of the CBI international reserves and, therefore, in February 2012, the CBI reduced access to the daily dollar auctions. Auction participants must be members of the Chamber of Commerce, to ensure that they are part of the formal economy, and they must provide documentation on the purpose of the transaction. The effect of this regulatory change was strong but temporary. Dollar sales at auction fell from $201 million on January 31, 2012 to just $2 million on February 1, 2012. However, by the end of February 2012, $200 million auction days were once again a common occurrence (CBI 2012a).

As expected, reducing access to the CBI auction led to a growing gap between auction and market exchange rates. Iraq became a two exchange rate economy with a better rate – the CBI auction rate – only available to a favored minority while most buyers and sellers had to be satisfied with the less advantageous market rate. On April 10, 2012, the auction rate was 1166 ID/$ while the market rate rose to 1285 ID/$ – a gap of 119 ID. While the gap narrowed to 62 ID by the end of May, it appears that Iraq has entered a period of not only larger gaps between the auction and market rates but also more day-to-day variation than during the first two years of the 1170 ID/$ exchange rate (2009–2010). Also, most countries that allow multiple exchange rates have experienced an increase in government interference in the currency markets as some groups use their political influence to obtain access to the best rates, that is, corruption worsens. These changes tend to result in a deceleration in economic growth and an acceleration of capital flight. If this occurs then the GoI may be forced eventually to change its exchange rate policy.

Why was the ID under such pressure in 2011–2012 when the performance of the Iraqi economy had improved substantially compared to the previous four years? This exchange rate divergence is probably a function of the continuing dollarization of the Iraqi economy combined with severe dollar shortages in Iraq's neighbors Syria and Iran. Dollarization is the common use of US dollars as both a means of exchange and a store of value in a country where dollars are not the official currency. Iraqis make widespread use of dollars both to make purchases as well as a form of savings.

For two currencies to simultaneously circulate in the same country, they must have different characteristics. US dollars are widely accepted in international transactions, the dollar inflation rate is relatively low, and the dollar is available in more valuable denominations than the ID. The largest ID note in circulation is only 25000 ID, which is worth about $21. Since many transactions in Iraq are for cash, using dollars can sharply cut the number of bills to be transported and counted. However, the interest rate paid for banks on dollar deposits is less than that for ID deposits. In the first quarter of 2012, banks paid about 3.6 percent on dollar accounts but 6.9 percent on ID accounts (CBI 2012a). Another advantage of ID is that they are legal tender and can be used to pay taxes and other transactions involving the government. Although, I was told several times that officials prefer to be bribed with dollars.

Dollarization makes it more difficult for the CBI to develop effective monetary/exchange rate policy. Dollarized economies tend to experience more rapid pass-through of exchange rate changes to domestic inflation. In most countries, there is a lag between depreciation (or appreciation) of its currency and the resulting acceleration (or deceleration) of inflation. However, in dollarized economies the lag is much shorter, reducing the time available for the authorities to adjust policy during a crisis. Also, dollarization breaks the connection between growth in the supply of ID and the inflation rate. For example, there has been increasing concern that the acceleration in the growth of Iraq's monetary base (currency plus bank reserves) – an average of 19.6 percent per year growth from 2008–2011 – will lead to increased inflation. But, as discussed below, the large-scale smuggling of dollars from Iraq to both Syria and Iran has greatly reduced the dollar component of Iraq's money supply. As a result, a portion of the increase in the ID monetary base simply offsets the ongoing dollar loses and is not inflationary. However, as the CBI expands the ID supply to replace the dollars that are lost to Syria and Iran, this will increase pressure for a devaluation of the ID. But if the CBI reduces the growth rate of the monetary base in order to protect the exchange rate then this will lead to a money shortage, higher real interest rates, and slowdown of the economic growth. Apparently, the CBI has chosen the latter option; the monetary base only grew about 2 percent in the first quarter of 2012.

But dollarization by itself does not explain the growing gap between auction and market exchange rates. The primary cause is the difficulties engulfing Iraq's neighbor to the west, Syria, and to the east, Iran. Since 2011, the Government of Syria has used military force in an attempt to crush a widespread popular protest. The resulting violence combined with international sanctions has resulted in an economic downturn in Syria and a shortage of hard currency. Iran is also experiencing economic difficulties and a shortage of hard currency as a result of tightening international sanctions intended to discourage the country from pursuing its nuclear program. As both residents and non-residents lose confidence in the Syrian and Iranian currencies, both countries have experienced sharp depreciations. By the end of May 2012, the Syrian pound had fallen from a pre-crisis rate of 47 Syrian pounds/$ to 64 Syrian pounds/$ – a loss of about 27 percent of its pervious value. The Iranian rial which traded at 10 500 rials/$ in December 2011 fell to 12 300 rials/$ by late May 2012 – a 14 percent depreciation. The black market depreciations for both currencies were even greater.

The effects on Iraq's real economy are mixed. As a result of these depreciations, Iraqi consumers are able to obtain imported goods from Syria and Iran at lower prices, reducing inflation. However, Iraqi producers of goods and services are losing the market share at home and abroad due to increased competition. For example, large numbers of religious tourists from Iran are important to the economies of the four cities in Iraq sacred to the Shi'a. But the depreciation of the Iranian rial has made these pilgrimages more expensive and, according to some sources, the number of such tourists is decreasing.

The large depreciations of the Syrian pound and the Iranian rial are also putting severe pressure on the CBI. Entities and individuals in Iraq buy dollars with ID either at the CBI auction or from the market and use these dollars to buy low-cost goods or services from Syria or Iran. These transactions are draining Iraqi dollar reserves at an unsustainable rate. In addition, as discussed in Chapter 12, capital flight may have reached $6.3 billion in 2011 and a total of $33 billion in 2007–2011. This flight poses another challenge to maintaining a sustainable exchange rate policy during difficult times.

One option to reduce the impact of these currency outflows is to make Iraq a more attractive place to invest so as to encourage foreigners as well as domestic portfolio holders to invest in Iraq. But creating a more favorable investment environment in Iraq in an increasingly globalized environment will require the careful phasing of substantial changes in financial regulations and monetary policies.

HORNS OF A POLICY DILEMMA

In the second decade of the twenty-first century, the GoI will be forced to make fundamental policy choices. The moribund financial system slows economic growth (see Chapter 8) but the complexity and expense of performing even the simplest financial transactions raises the costs of, and therefore discourages, capital flight. If the GoI liberalizes the financial system in order to achieve greater efficiency and economic growth then it will also make it easier for capital to flee. In addition, inadequately regulated and capitalized private financial intermediaries provide incentives for their management to engage in excessive risk taking using offshore funding (Eichengreen 2000, p. 1108). On the other hand, failure to liberalize will burden the non-oil sector and maintain the dominance of oil exports in GDP and the government as the chief employer.

The status quo is not an option. Growing international capital mobility is unavoidable especially for a country like Iraq that seeks large amounts of foreign direct and portfolio investment to pay for the modernization of its infrastructure. The challenge is to order the changes in the liberalization of both internal and external financial activities so as to maximize the likelihood of accelerating economic development without increasing the economy's vulnerability to destabilizing capital flows. Eichengreen

Table 13.3   Eichengreen on phasing financial liberalization

Phase 1: Liberalize and decontrol domestic financial markets
          Rationalize regulations
          Recapitalize state-owned banks
Phase 2: Liberalize foreign direct investment
Phase 3: Liberalize stock and bond markets next
Phase 4: Liberalize offshore bank borrowing last

Source: Eichengreen (2000), pp. 1107–10.

(2000, pp. 1105–16) argues that there is a phasing of financial liberalization that historically has had the best chance of simultaneously achieving economic development and financial stability. His recommended phasing is summarized in Table 13.3.

Liberalize and Decontrol Domestic Financial Markets

As discussed at great length in Chapters 8 and 10, there are steps that could be taken to substantially improve access of individuals and entities to the Iraqi debt and equity markets. Probably the most important is the creation of a credit registry. In addition, the CBI and other regulatory authorities should act to increase the competitiveness of private banks. This would include providing some reasonable amount of deposit and savings account insurance as well as allowing checks or electronic funds transfer from private banks to be used to make tax and other payments to the GoI. Accounting and auditing standards should require the timely release of accurate information especially with respect to loan losses and loan loss reserves. At the same time, it is important to ensure that private bank capitalization is adequate otherwise management will have strong incentives to engage in risky loans and investments (Eichengreen 2000, p. 1108). Only after regulations have been rationalized to support a vibrant banking system, should the GoI recapitalize the state-owned banks. If they are recapitalized before the CBI and other regulatory authorities are ready to closely monitor their activities then one could expect to see a return to large-scale loan losses.

Liberalize Foreign Direct Investment

Failure to complete the rationalization of financial regulation and the recapitalization of state-owned banks before opening an economy to

FDI led to severe financial difficulties in South Korea and Thailand (Eichengreen 2000, p. 1108). However, once the domestic financial system is prepared, Iraq should seek to further increase FDI since it provides two advantages over foreign portfolio investment or foreign bank loans. First, FDI tends to be accompanied by managerial and technological expertise that will be needed to achieve the GoIs goals of rapid improvement of both oil and non-oil infrastructure. Second, FDI tends to be more stable than either portfolio or bank finance.

Liberalize Stock and Bond Markets Next

The second most beneficial capital inflow is foreign purchases in the Iraq equity and bond markets. Equity and bond purchases are more stable than bank debt, less likely to reflect volatile "hot money". As discussed in Chapter 8, the ISX has the potential of being a major financial intermediary between Iraqi companies and foreign investors. However, for this to occur the GoI must adopt a more rational commercial code that provides potential investors with timely audited income statements and balance sheets of non-bank companies listed on the ISX. Until this happens, the ISX will continue to be a shallow market dominated by insiders. With respect to bond markets, if the Ministry of Finance would authorize the sale of short, medium, and long-term government bonds then this would not only lead to a more robust secondary market in government debt but also, by providing a "base rate", facilitate bond issuance by other entities.

Liberalize Offshore Bank Borrowing Last

Although it can provide substantial benefits, the international transaction with the greatest potential for destabilizing Iraq's current system of financial intermediation is offshore bank borrowing. There are often strong short-term incentives to engage in financial transactions that result in severely mismatched maturities or currency exposures. The 1997 Asian financial crisis and the post-2008 European financial crisis should be warnings on the risks and uncertainties involved in allowing Iraqi financial and non-financial institutions to engage in offshore – cross border – transactions. In addition, without increased transparency and improved regulation, increased access to offshore borrowing can lead to rapid distortion of the Iraqi economy including large-scale capital flight (Eichengreen 2000, pp. 1106–7). But regardless of the careful phasing of integration into the global economy, Iraq's current exchange rate system will continue to be vulnerable to external shocks.

SHOULD IRAQ ABANDON ITS FIXED EXCHANGE RATE POLICY?

Iraq's fixed exchange rate facilitates foreign trade and investment. This is especially true since almost all of Iraq's exports, most of its imports, and a large proportion of its FDI are already denominated in US dollars. But a fixed exchange rate negates monetarist policy. To protect its fixed exchange rate, the CBI must maintain a domestic ID interest rate above the dollar rate and this higher real ID interest rate is a further burden on the non-oil sector. In addition, a fixed rate is vulnerable to the riskless speculation discussed above. For the last several years, the GoI has been free to ignore the adverse effect of higher real interest rates, relying on oil-funded expansionary fiscal policy to grow the country's GDP. But this policy has maintained the dominance of the state sector.

However, in 2012, the ID came under attack by speculators due to dollar shortages in Syria and Iran. In the short run, the CBI responded restricting access to dollars at the official exchange rate. While necessary, this reaction reduced the credibility of the GoI commitment to ensuring access to dollars at a fixed rate. It is expected that if the dollar outflow continues then the CBI will increase the policy interest rate in order to make it more valuable to hold ID. However, restricting access to dollars and raising interest rates not only injures the credibility of the country's fixed exchange rate regime but also tends to slow economic growth. The longer such restrictions are maintained, the more damage they do to the efficiency of banks and other financial intermediaries. Almost all countries whose fixed exchange rate comes under widespread speculative attack are forced to eventually abandon their fixed exchange rate regimes, often after large-scale losses of reserves. Should Iraq adopt a more credible exchange rate regime before the situation reaches a crisis? If Iraq decides to abandon its current fixed rate regime then what are its options?

Floating Exchange Rate

In theory, a country should adopt a floating – market determined – exchange rate if most of its trade and financial activities are domestic, the international trade and financial transactions that do occur are widely diversified among multiple currencies, and the government can credibly adopt a domestic nominal anchor such as inflation, or nominal income growth. Iraq has none of these characteristics.

With imports equivalent to almost two-thirds of the country's GDP as well as the large amount of foreign investment, Iraq must be considered a very open economy. In addition, not only are 99 percent of its exports denominated in dollars but also much of its import trade is in homogeneous products like grain that also tend to be dollar denominated. Especially in the oil sector, much of the investment is dollar denominated. Since there is no world demand for substantial amounts of ID denominated debt, if public or private Iraqi entities wish to borrow internationally then they will have to borrow in a hard currency – probably dollars. A floating or managed exchange rate would make it more complicated and expensive for Iraq to engage in these international trade or capital transactions.

Also, a country with a floating rate must target another nominal variable – a nominal anchor – such as the inflation rate or nominal GDP in order to maintain price stability. For reasons discussed in Chapter 2, there is a shortage of reliable data on variables such as the inflation rate or nominal GDP that could serve as a nominal anchor for the Iraqi economy. But even if reliable data on a nominal anchor was available to the GoI, neither the average Iraqi nor the average foreign investor trusts the GoI to accurately report these nominal targets. The public can easily observe changes in the exchange rate whereas changes in the calculation of inflation or nominal GDP are difficult to evaluate even by experts. For all of these reasons, adopting a floating or managed exchange rate is probably a mistake.

Return to a Currency Board

While a fixed exchange rate is a better option than a floating one for Iraq, maintaining credibility is the chief challenge facing a fixed exchange rate regime. Regardless of the political or financial surprises that the future may hold, the market must be confident that the CBI will continue to buy or sell ID at the fixed rate. With the current structure, this commitment is not credible which is why interest rates on ID denominated deposits and loans are higher than those for dollar denominated transactions. There is a fear in the market that the GoI will choose in some future crisis – whether a deep and sustained drop in oil prices or, possibly, a civil war in Iran – to depreciate the ID. There are two options that can increase the credibility of a fixed exchange rate: official dollarization or establishing an orthodox currency board.

While there are nine non-US countries that have adopted the dollar as their official currency, including Ecuador in 2000, this is probably an unacceptable option for Iraq. In addition to being perceived as an affront to Iraqi sovereignty, official adoption of the dollar would eliminate seigniorage – the revenue that a country obtains from printing its own currency. Printing a 25 000 ID note costs less than 60 ID, the difference is revenue to the GoI.

Table 13.4   Hanke on currency boards

Necessary characteristics
  Supplies notes and coins only
  Full convertibility
  Foreign reserves of 100–115 percent
  Not a lender of last resort
  Does not regulate commercial banks
  Cannot finance spending by domestic government
Other characteristics to further increase credibility
  Director of another nationality
  Conversion office in world capital center, e.g. Switzerland

---

Source: Hanke (2002), Table 1, p. 205.

An alternative is for Iraq to return to using a currency board. Iraq had a currency board based on the British pound from 1930 until 1949. This board provided a stable currency for Iraq through a period of both severe internal conflict and World War II. The National Bank of Iraq, that in 1956 became the CBI, succeeded the currency board. The National Bank of Iraq continued some of the conservative actions of its currency board predecessor including maintaining 100 percent reserves behind its currency issuance (CBI 2012a, "History of the CBI", p. 1). But the golden age of conservative monetary policy and a fixed exchange rate came to an end in 1964 with the nationalization of all banks.

How does a currency board differ from a central bank? Steve Hanke, who has advised multiple governments and international organizations on establishing currency boards, states that there are six characteristics of an "orthodox" currency board. These necessary characteristics along with two desirable characteristics are listed in Table 13.4 (Hanke 2002, Table 1, p. 205; see also Hanke and Schuler 1994, Chapters 4 and 5; Walters and Hanke 1992, pp. 558–61). Most central banks with fixed exchange rates stand ready to convert a variety of financial instruments including deposit accounts. But currency boards guarantee convertibility at the fixed rate for physical notes and coins only. A board is able to make this guarantee since it maintains 100 percent reserves for all of the currency and coins in circulation. This is an important distinction because it eliminates risk-less speculation.

In a classic speculative raid, a speculator takes out a loan denominated in the local currency and then goes to the central bank to convert his local currency deposits into a hard currency such as dollars. The amount that the speculator could present for conversion is limited only by his or her ability to borrow deposits. When the central bank has exhausted its hard currency reserves, it is forced to depreciate its currency producing a profit for the speculator. But a currency board cannot be overwhelmed in this fashion since its maximum liability for conversion is both fixed and known because it is limited to the amount of currency and coins placed in circulation by the board. Currency boards tend to be profitable because they earn the equivalent of seigniorage from the earnings on short-term liquid hard currency bonds in their portfolios. These profits – in excess of required reserves – would be paid to the establishing government.

To further reinforce the credibility of a currency board, it does not engage in typical central bank activities of regulating commercial banks, lending to the government, or acting as a lender of last resort in a crisis. Upon the establishment of a currency board, these activities would become fiscal responsibilities, for example if a lender of last resort was required then the GoI would make the loans as part of its budget.

In addition, if it chooses to establish a currency board, Iraq can further increase the credibility of its currency board by having a director of another nationality and establishing a conversion office in another country. These were both components of Iraq's previous currency board with an English director and the ability of any ID holder to exchange ID for English pounds at the fixed exchange rate in the London office. A foreign director (a Swiss banker?) and conversion office (in New York?) improves the credibility of the fixed exchange rate since it prevents or, at least, complicates any future Iraqi government's attempt to confiscate the assets of the currency board as occurred in 1964.

It appears that the CBI currently has more than enough reserves, even with full conversion of bank reserves, to establish a currency board with a fixed exchange rate of 1166 ID/$. At the end of April 2012, the monetary base was composed of about 29 141 trillion ID in currency and about 28 404 trillion ID in bank reserves – cash equivalent – for a total of 57 545 trillion ID. To provide the 100 percent reserves necessary for a currency board at an exchange rate of 1166 ID/$ would require about $49.4 billion. In mid-2012, the CBI reported net foreign international reserves, mostly dollars, of about $63.0 billion. Based on these numbers, the GoI could establish a currency board with almost $14 billion to spare. It should be noted that both the IMF and US Government generally oppose the establishment of currency boards. (For a discussion of their hostility to an Indonesian currency board, see Hanke 2002, pp. 215–18.)

Status quo is not a viable option for the Iraqi exchange rate. As the dollar smuggling brought about by the 2012 economic troubles in Iran and Syria demonstrates, sooner or later the ID will come under attack. When it does then the CBI will have to decide whether to devalue immediately or run the risk of an eventual devaluation after a substantial loss of reserves. It really comes down to a choice of making a major change in exchange rate policy during reasonably good times or making the change when the system and the government is under a great deal of stress.

14. Iraq in 2025

> The loss of the strategic compass in the arena of the Iraqi economy
> has cost us dearly and led us to waste time and money. The country
> has not prospered and has left the Iraqi people to suffer despite the
> affluence they could have due to Iraq's wealth and illustrious history.
> (Ali Ghalib Baban, Minister of Planning 2010, in GoI 2010, p. 3)

> We drive through this village every week. And we see nothing. But
> today, there is an open-air market. Who told them to hold a market?
> (Anonymous email from patrol in rural Iraq 2006)

What will the political economy of Iraq look like in 2025? That will
depend, of course, on both external surprises and the policy decisions
made by the GoI. At the same time, the Iraqi people are not pawns or
simply numbers in a survey. They will not only respond to unexpected
exogenous shocks or policy initiatives in unexpected ways but also create
new realities that will probably defy prediction. Does this make attempts
to predict the future a waste of resources? That depends on its purpose. If
it is an attempt to lay out in detail the characteristics of Iraq in 2025, then
it is a waste of time. However, it can be a valuable exercise if it forces one
to think about trends, priorities, and resources. In this way, it can help
private and public Iraqi entities make choices.

EXOGENOUS DRIVERS OF 2025: OIL PRICES

Oil will remain an important part of the Iraqi economy for the foreseeable
future. Oil prices have been on a rollercoaster for almost four decades
and there is no reason to think that the future will be any different. In
their June 2012 *Annual Energy Outlook*, the US Energy Information
Administration (EIA) estimated three oil price scenarios for 2025. The
low oil price scenario posits that the 2025 price of internationally traded
oil similar to that exported by Iraq will be about $50 pb (in 2010 dollars).
The 2025 reference oil price – the most likely price – is about $120 pb
while the high oil price is $180 pb (EIA 2012, Table C1, p. 183). Both the
low price and high price will probably have an adverse impact on Iraq's
political economy.

Low Oil Price Scenario

How likely is $50 pb oil? After adjusting for inflation, average annual oil prices were below this level for almost twenty years, from 1986 through 2005 (see Chapter 6, Figure 6.2). Such a price could result from lower demand combined with increased supply. With respect to demand, it is possible that not only will the economic recovery of the OECD nations after the 2008 financial crisis require more than a decade but also there will be a slowdown in the real growth of the BRIC countries (Brazil, Russia, India, and China). Combined with continuing improvements in energy conservation, the reduction in oil demand growth from these economic slowdowns will be substantial. This reduction in the growth rate of energy demand could be accompanied by an increase in energy supply as a result of two trends.

First, technological innovations such as hydraulic fracturing or "fracking" have permitted relatively inexpensive access to natural gas in the USA and other nations. While some countries such as France have banned fracking, many nations are aggressively pursuing this and related technologies. There has already been a sharp decrease in natural gas imports into the USA and this country may become a large net natural gas exporter within a decade. In addition to the direct impact on the natural gas market, in which Iraq is a small producer, there is the potential for secondary effects that will seriously impact the oil market. The large gap between the energy equivalent prices of the two petroleum products is leading to an expensive but fairly rapid re-engineering of many electrical generation and plastic production plants from oil to cheaper natural gas.

A second trend that may contribute to lower future oil prices is the current GoI plan to rapidly increase the volume of oil exports. As discussed in Chapter 6, demand for oil is inelastic – a relatively small percentage increase in the world supply of oil tends to lead to a larger percentage decrease in oil prices. If the GoI were to succeed in increasing its export volume by the almost 7.5 mbpd by 2017 in the GoI plan then the impact on world prices would be significant even if other oil exporters maintain current levels of production. Whether caused by decreased demand or increased supply, low oil prices will have a severe adverse impact on both economic development and political stability in Iraq.

If Iraq's 2025 economy is still dominated by oil exports then an extended period of low oil prices could lead to a drop in the country's GDP. The accompanying decrease in GoI revenues will lead to a reduction in government investment and transfer payments followed by a rise in unemployment and underemployment. A growing pool of unemployed young men who have despaired of obtaining a good job and being able to start a family will be politically destabilizing. If Iraq still has a fixed exchange rate then the fall in oil export earnings will reduce foreigners' confidence that the ID will keep its value. Especially if the Iraq's international reserves are tapped to compensate for the drop in oil export earnings, the ID will come under increasing speculative pressure.

There will also be an adverse effect on government employees. As discussed in the previous chapter, if oil prices fall to $55 pb or less for an extended period of time, the GoI would have to make unprecedented budget cuts that would probably be politically destabilizing. Since the overthrow of the monarchy in 1958, Iraq has joined most modern states in that there is an unwritten understanding between the country's leadership and the bureaucracy that runs the government on a day-to-day basis. The bureaucracy support whoever is in power and, in return, the person in power ensures that the bureaucracy continues to receive high levels of compensation and status. This was exemplified in 2006, when in the face of a sharp unexpected drop in GoI revenues, almost all components of government expenditures were radically cut except for salaries and pensions of the already generously compensated current and former government employees.

However, a drop of oil prices below roughly $55 pb would force the GoI, in the absence of large-scale foreign borrowing, to cut compensation or employment of government employees. At best, this will lead to creative-non-compliance with the bureaucracy stalling government initiatives until compensation is restored. At worst, government employees will attempt to bring about a change in leadership by unconstitutional means. An angry and disloyal bureaucracy combined with a large number of unemployed young men will turn an economic downturn into a situation of acute political instability.

High Oil Price Scenario

In view of the technological innovations and the GoI plans for rapid expansion of oil exports discussed above, what argument can be made of substantially higher oil prices in the future? A rapid return to moderate growth in the OECD countries and rapid growth in the BRIC countries would increase energy demand while a failure of the natural gas revolution would reduce supply. A conflict that leads to the long-term loss of a major oil exporter such as Iran or Venezuela would have a more dramatic effect on world oil supply. Possibly by the time this book is published, Iran's dispute with the rest of the world over its nuclear ambitions will be resolved. However, if the dispute rises to conflict then the world faces the potential of a loss of some or all of Iraq's production for an extended period of time.

For a short period of time, world oil prices in 2008 exceeded $140 pb (in 2010 dollars) but oil prices have never reached $180 pb so the world would be breaking new ground. In 2025, if oil prices reach $180 pb and Iraq is able to raise its exports to 10.0 mbpd then Iraq's export earnings would reach $657 billion (in 2010 dollars) compared to $50 billion in 2010. With an expected 2025 population of 47 million, average per capita income would reach about $16 000 (in 2010 dollars) – seven times greater than in 2010. This is about the same level of per capita income as Saudi Arabia had in 2010. With this massive increase in oil export earnings, everything would be possible: increased government employment and higher wages for government workers, sharp rises in investment, generous provision of free essential services, agricultural restoration, accelerated construction of homes, factories, and government offices. The Al Rahman Mosque in Baghdad would finally be completed. New soccer stadiums would appear in every town. But there would be an explosion in corruption. Efforts to diversify the Iraqi economy away from its dependency on oil would probably grind to a stop. Without diversification, Iraqi nascent democracy would be threatened.

Concentration of economic power tends to lead to concentration of political power. If the party that controls the government also controls the economy and therefore access to education, employment, and income, then those in power begin to believe that elections are too important to entrust to the voters. There is also a psychological effect. In most long-lived democracies, the major source of government revenue is tax receipts. People in such countries feel that they are "buying" government services and if the government fails to provide, at reasonable cost, the services demanded by the taxpayer-citizens then they will attempt to "fire" the government through the ballot box. But in Iraq with $180 pb oil, the GoI will not need to tax citizens. Cynically, the primary role of Iraqi citizens will be to receive – and be grateful for – whatever level of service that the government decides is appropriate. In this sense, Iraqi citizens will not be independent entities that support the GoI. Rather they will become symbolically, and often in reality, clients of a "beneficent" government. As Huntington (1991, p. 65) stated: "'No taxation without representation' was a political demand; 'no representation without taxation' is a political reality" (see also Ayubi 1995, p. 400).

Reference Oil Price Scenario

If oil prices in 2025 reach $120 pb then the percentage increase in real oil prices over the next 13 years will be less than the expected increase in population. However, if the GoI is able to increase oil exports to 10.0 mbpd then average per capita 2025 income will rise to approximately $12 000 roughly five times greater than in 2010. As a matter of scale and adjusting for inflation, this would give Iraq a per capita income in 2025 roughly equivalent to that of Libya or Poland in 2010.

While this scenario is not as dire as those that predict low or high oil prices, it serves to emphasize two priorities for Iraq's development. First, higher oil prices alone are insufficient to provide rising real incomes for Iraq's rapidly growing population. Even though $120 pb is a higher average annual price then ever recorded for the international oil market, in the unlikely case that oil export volumes in 2025 are the same as in 2010, per capita income would only be about $3000 due to rapid population growth. Therefore even in the favorable scenario of $120 pb world price of oil, Iraq must increase in oil exports to provide a higher living standard for its people. Second, the expansion of the oil industry by itself will not provide sufficient employment opportunities for the large cohort of young people who will be joining the labor force between now and 2025. Note that the young men and women who will be seeking their first jobs in 2025 have already been born. There must be a rapid diversification of the Iraqi economy to provide employment opportunities for the coming cohorts of young Iraqis.

EXOGENOUS DRIVERS OF 2025: REGIONAL CONFLICT

Iran and Syria

By the time this book is published, it is possible that regional circumstances will be very different. However, in late 2012, both of Iraq's neighbors were in crisis. Iran was fighting against attempts by most of the world community to impose sanctions intended to get Iran to abandon its nuclear ambitions. The adverse impact on Iran's petroleum exports has led to a severe economic recession and loss of confidence. Real growth is slowing while unemployment – especially among the young – is increasing. Syria is racked by a harsh government crackdown on "Arab Spring" groups.

So far, the difficulties in both countries have had a mixed impact on Iraq. As discussed in the previous chapter, both countries' currencies are losing value. This has resulted in lower prices for goods imported by Iraq and, by draining dollars from the Iraq economy, put pressure on the GoI to devalue the ID. There is also smuggling of weapons and other supplies from western Iraq to Syrian rebels. In addition, some analysts think that the internal difficulties in both countries have forced their governments to focus on these issues, leaving less time to engage in trouble making in Iraq.

However, if violence increases in either or both countries then the impact on Iraq will be adverse. If the Syrian conflict continues to expand then it will probably spill over the border into the western provinces of Iraq. Iraq can expect both a wave of refugees and fighters seeking temporary sanctuary. On the eastern border, if Iran, the USA and the other parties involved in the sanctions dispute misjudge each other then there is the possibility of a shooting war. This will probably not only reduce production from the major oilfields on the Iraq–Iran border but also temporarily close the Persian Gulf stopping the bulk of Iraq's exports. Even after the US Navy reopens the Gulf to transit, it can be expected that Iraq oil will sell at a discount to world prices to compensate for the increased risk.

In addition, conflict in Syria or Iran will strengthen the perception that Iraq is in a "bad neighborhood" leading to a decline in the willingness of foreign companies to invest in Iraq. As the Latin American debt crisis of the 1980s and the Asian financial crisis of the late 1990s showed, foreign investors tend to think regionally – they are not always careful to distinguish between countries in a region that are in difficulty and their neighbors that might be well managed.

Water Conflict

Both the Euphrates and the Tigris rivers originate in Turkey. While the Tigris then flows directly into Iraq, the Euphrates detours through Syria. As discussed in Chapter 7, while there are informal agreements on water sharing among the three countries, there is no formal treaty with the force of international law. As a result, the extensive dam building programs by both Turkey and Syria has already substantially reduced the cross-border water flow into Iraq with the potential of even greater reductions over the next decade. If Iraq is unable to negotiate a water agreement with Syria and Turkey then a water shortage will lead to a decrease in agricultural production and increased migration into urban areas. In addition, it will be necessary to increase food imports. The GoI is aware of all of these external or exogenous challenges but, regrettably, its planning for the future is flawed.

GOI STRATEGIC PLANNING

Following its five-decade socialist tradition, the GoI continues to develop national development strategies or plans. In the post-2003 period, plans were published in 2005, 2007, and 2010. Over time, these documents have become increasingly comprehensive and detailed with growing participation. In addition, the GoI has received national development proposals from a variety of organizations including the IMF (2005; 2008a; 2008b; 2010b; 2011a), USAID (2009), Iraq Partners Forum (2010, a joint plan reflecting the contributions of multiple nations and organizations), and proposals not affiliated with a particular organization, for example White et al. (2003).

There is a large overlap among the proposed initiatives listed in these plans. The emphasis may change; for example the *National Development Strategy: 2005–2007* (GoI 2005b) was more private sector-oriented than the *National Development Plan: 2010–2014* (GoI 2010). However, the differences among the various plans are generally more of emphasis than kind. Therefore, it is curious that the later plans generally ignore the progress or lack thereof of the earlier ones. For example, the *National Development Strategy: 2007–2010* (GoI 2007) fails to even mention the 2005 development strategy possibly because of the belief that foreigners dominated the writing of the 2005 document.

Similarly, the *National Development Plan: 2010–2014* (GoI 2010), while it discusses the current state of Iraqi society and its political economy in detail, makes few attempts in its 185 pages to directly evaluate progress made in achieving the goals set out in either the 2005 or 2007 national strategy documents. In fact, the GoIs (2010) document does mention the previous efforts but only to disparage them. According to the Minister of Planning, Ali Ghalib Baban:

> The new plan [*National Development Plan: 2010–2014*] cannot be compared to previous development plans in Iraq because it is different from other plans developed in the past. This is an advanced and unique plan that includes modern methods and approaches to technical planning and related practices. Previous planning was based on listing projects and distributing them among the various economic sectors. In contrast, this plan is based on scientific methodology and analysis of data. (GoI 2010, p. 3)

However, this most recent plan suffers from three weaknesses. The GoIs (2010) plan fails to set priorities, provide quantifiable goals for all of its initiatives, and it does not recognize the unique role of the private sector.

First, although the GoIs (2010) plan lists many initiatives in different sectors of the Iraqi economy, there is unwillingness to set priorities. In Chapter 1 of the plan, there is a listing of nine "Strategic Objectives" but no statement of which is the most important, unless the ordering of the objectives is intended to be meaningful (GoI 2010, pp. 24–5). In fact, in the 12 chapters of the plan, dozens of objectives are listed but one looks in vain for a clear statement that this initiative is more important than that initiative. Preventing illegal well drilling and reducing corruption are both worthy goals (GoI 2010, pp. 74, 178). However, a future Iraq that severely reduces corruption but fails to stop illegal well drilling will be in much better shape than a future Iraq where the reverse is true.

Second, unlike the IMF under the Stand-by Arrangement, and the UN Millennium Challenge, the GoIs efforts to actually measure progress towards stated goals are very uneven. The IMF (2005) *Iraq – Request for Stand-By Arrangement* laid out both Quantitative Indicators (Table 2, p. 21) as well as Structural Benchmarks (Table 3, p. 22) with specific targets. Every succeeding IMF review then evaluates the progress towards each target and, after discussion with the GoI, explicitly modifies them if necessary. The UN Millennium Challenge also clearly delineates quantifiable goals for 36 initiatives. As discussed in Chapter 3, the GoI regularly documents its progress towards the 2015 Millennium Challenge goals (COSIT 2012, Table 19/1).

In contrast, the GoI (2010) plan in some sections provides detailed quantifiable goals and, yet, in other sections, it is satisfied with non-quantifiable exhortations to virtue. For example, the plan objectives for the energy sector are very specific, for example, Objective 6: "Increasing the current refining capacity ... to approximately 1.45 mbpd by 2016" (GoI 2010, pp. 81–2). But the plan objectives for the financial sector seem unnecessarily vague, for example, Objective 4: "Activating the role of specialized banks [by] 1. Supporting bank capital, 2. Encouraging interbank lending ..." (GoI 2010, pp. 59–60).

This is not to say that Iraq's development plans should not be flexible enough to adjust to unexpected changes in domestic or foreign political and economic environments. However, in those sections of the GoI (2010) plan where there is little effort to either announce specific goals or document progress towards achieving these goals, one is forced to conclude then the GoI is not engaged in a serious planning process. Rather, in these sections, its purpose seems to be to provide an overview of the current challenges facing Iraq and present broad objectives to meet those challenges along with general statements on the best means to achieve each objective by subordinate organizations. But if advising subordinate organizations was the primary purpose of the *National Development Plan: 2010–2014* then the failure to set priorities to guide subordinate organizations is an even greater failing.

The third difficulty with the most recent GoI economic planning exercise is that it simultaneously "proposes a new economic philosophy that is based on the market economy" (GoI 2010, p. 3), but seeks to maintain a "government knows best" top-down setting of very specific economic goals. In other words, the private sector is welcome to provide its investment and managerial skills but only to accomplish the goals delineated in detail by the GoI bureaucracy. This runs the risk of severely limiting private sector entrepreneurship, which is the primary source of economic development and growth (see Chapter 10 this book; Gunter 2012).

As one of many examples, the GoI (2010) plan discusses the severe housing shortage in Iraq and notes that home construction is within the capability of small and medium private firms. But, at the same time, the GoI proposes that certain customers receive priority (civil servants), certain construction materials are used, that homes be built in certain areas, and that a specific complex system of funding is utilized. All of which will require "an expansion of the housing legislative framework" (GoI 2010, pp. 124–7). This combination of complexity, uncertainty, and arbitrary bureaucratic decisionmaking seems specifically designed to discourage private sector home building. It is interesting to note that among the hundreds of persons involved in developing the *National Development Plan: 2010–2014*, all or almost all were government officials; representatives of Iraq's private sector were not at the table when the topic for discussion was increasing the role of the private sector.

SEVEN KEY POLICY DECISIONS

Long detailed lists of possible policy initiatives are given in the IMFs (2011a) *Iraq: Second Review Under the Stand-By Arrangement*, the GoIs (2010) *National Development Plan: 2010–2014*, the Iraq Partners Forum (2010) *Iraq Briefing Book*, and the USAIDs (2009) *Iraq: Economic Recovery Assessment*. But what are the most important policy recommendations? In other words, what are the few policies that, if successfully implemented by 2025, have a high probability of leading to a better quality of life for the average Iraqi even if little or no progress is made dealing with the many other challenges facing the country? I think there are seven: passing the Oil Laws: developing an effective anti-corruption policy: reducing the regulatory hostility towards private business; achieving 100 percent literacy of all Iraqis and 100 percent primary education of the young; restructuring the financial system; adopting a rational water pricing plan; and advancing federalism. Each is discussed below along with a proposed standard that will allow the measurement of progress towards achieving each goal.

1. *Oil Law.* Pass and implement the four major components of the Oil Law that have been awaiting approval since 2007. As discussed in

Chapter 6, this law is needed not only to efficiently expand oil production but also to clarify the distribution of oil revenues among the different provinces as well as between the current and future generations of Iraqis.

2. *Anti-corruption strategy.* Develop and execute a multi-pronged anti-corruption strategy until Iraq reaches the top third of Transparency International's "Corruption Perception Index". All of the planning documents note the devastating impact of Iraq's ubiquitous corruption on economic development and political stability. But then, with possibly one exception, they propose anti-corruption strategies that have failed in every country that has tried them. As discussed in Chapter 4, better governance, more arrests for corruption, and expensive publicity campaigns are necessary but not sufficient to achieve a long-term reduction in corruption. The few anti-corruption successes in the world have also included changing incentives to reduce the rents that reward corruption. It should be noted that the *National Development Strategy: 2005–2007* did not include reducing such rents in its discussion of corruption (GoI 2005b, p. 36) but many of the policy recommendations throughout this document should have that effect (for example, GoI 2005b, Chapters IV and V, pp. 12–27).

3. *Regulatory reform.* Reduce regulatory hostility towards private business until Iraq reaches the top third of the World Bank's "Ease of Doing Business" survey. When it comes to regulating the private sector; the GoI is simultaneously ubiquitous, weak, opaque, contradictory, arbitrary, and corrupt. As discussed in Chapter 10, Iraq not only provides the worst overall regulatory environment for private business in the MENA countries; in one subcategory, it actually provides the worst regulatory environment in the world (Subcategory 10, Table 10.1). Unless there is a serious effort to reduce regulatory hostility towards private business then the GoIs attempts to reduce dependence on oil by diversifying the economy will fail. Among the reasons for maintaining a hostile environment towards private businesses in Iraq is to prevent competition to SOE that tend to be low-quality, high-cost producers. Closing or privatizing the SOE might have been possible a decade ago but that ship has sailed. The best option might be the Chinese solution of neither closing – nor expanding – SOE but letting growth of the private sector gradually reduce SOE dominance of production and employment.

4. *Primary education and literacy.* Educational resources should be directed towards literacy training for all ages and primary education for those younger than 12 years of age until Iraq achieves 100 percent literacy among all Iraqis and 100 percent primary education among

the young. The high level of illiteracy, especially among older Iraqis, those in rural areas, and women, not only slows economic development and facilitates corruption but also weakens democracy. As discussed in Chapter 3, achieving 100 percent literacy and 100 percent primary education will require not only more local schools but also more female teachers.

5. *Financial liberalization.* Restructure exchange rate/monetary policy until the gap between the CBI auction rate and the parallel market rate is less than 1 percent (currently about 12 ID). Or, as an alternative, return to the kind of currency board that provided Iraq with decades of monetary stability. Then, revise the regulation of financial intermediation until Iraq is in the top-third worldwide with respect to the "Getting Credit" subcategory of the World Bank's "Ease of Doing Business" survey. Finally, recapitalize state-owned banks until they meet Basel III standards. As discussed in Chapter 13, reform of the financial sector requires deliberate phasing of initiatives to prevent an acceleration of capital flight or large loan losses among state-owned banks.

6. *Water pricing.* Above a certain minimum water right – say 125 m³/yr per person – the government should price water at its average cost. Currently, Iraq is one of the few countries in the region with enough water to support large-scale agribusiness. However, the country's access to water is becoming increasingly precarious. Turkey, Syria, and Iran are diverting water from the Euphrates and the Tigris rivers in order to generate electricity and provide irrigation water to their own farmers. At the same time, increased oil production and industrialization in Iraq will require increasing quantities of water while pollution in the Euphrates and the Tigris rivers continues to worsen especially south of Baghdad. Ensuring adequate quantity and quality of water is a complex issue involving not only many entities in Iraq but also involving difficult negotiations with its neighbors. But without pricing water at its average cost, not only is water planning almost impossible but such planning leads to corruption and huge amounts of waste because: if something is free then people act as if it has zero cost.

7. *Iraqi federalism.* Thirty percent of gross oil export earnings should be transferred to the provinces on the basis of population to be spent solely according to the priorities set by provincial governments. Also, administration of business regulations, with the exception of the regulation of financial intermediaries, should be delegated to the provinces. Attempting to manage a 32 million person economy from Baghdad has been an exercise in inefficiency and corruption. With the

geographic, economic, historical, and cultural differences across Iraq, a "one size fits all" strategy is not the best method for achieving rapid economic development. Because they are physically and emotionally closer to the average Iraqi, provincial and local governments are probably more responsive to their needs. Also, it can be expected that competition among provinces will lead to more creative solutions to the many challenges facing Iraq. Finally, provincial and local governments will provide training and experience for persons who might later enter the national government.

In most cases, the seven proposed policies reinforce each other. A reduction of the regulatory hostility towards the private sector tends to reduce corruption. Achieving 100 percent primary education will strengthen private business and should also reduce corruption. Passage of the Oil Laws, reduced corruption, reduced regulatory hostility, and improved banking regulation will encourage inward capital flows thereby reducing pressure on the exchange rate.

There will be opposition to some of these initiatives on the grounds that they weaken GoI control of the economy. There is a tendency in Iraq to think that if the GoI does not do something then it will not be done. To me this was exemplified by the anonymous email that is quoted at the beginning of this chapter. Among the GoI leadership, this attitude reflects a socialist mindset reinforced by a lack of experience with market operations. Anti-market attitudes among the Iraqi leadership are reinforced during discussions with advisors from foreign governments and international organizations who themselves generally favor detailed state control over the economy.

While this view of the primacy of the state in economic development was widely held among development specialists several decades ago, the collapse of the socialist states throughout the world combined with the rapid acceleration of real growth and resulting higher living standards in countries that pursued economic liberalization has led to its intellectual abandonment. Iraq should not try to build a twenty-first-century political economy guided by mid-twentieth-century knowledge.

My final thought is this. History has given Iraq a second chance to achieve better lives for its people. However, current conditions are less auspicious than when Lord Salter predicted the country's bright future in 1955. More than in previous periods, the future of Iraq is in the hands of the Iraqis. Over the next decade, Iraq will make – or fail to make – critical irrevocable decisions. Rich countries with long histories of stable government can afford to make stupid decisions. Iraq cannot.

Bibliography

Abrol, I.P., J.S.P. Yadav, and F.I. Massoud (1988). *Salt-Affected Soils and Their Management*. Rome. FAO Land and Water Development Division, Bulletin 39.

Acemoglu, Daron and James A. Robinson (2006). Paths of Economic and Political Development. In Barry R. Weingast and Donald A. Wittman (eds), *The Oxford Handbook of Political Economy*. Oxford: Oxford University Press, pp. 673–92.

Acemoglu, Daron, James A. Robinson, and Simon Johnson (2001). The Colonial Origins of Comparative Development: An Empirical Investigation. *American Economic Review*, 91: 1369–401.

Acs, Zoltan J. (2006). How is Entrepreneurship Good for Economic Growth? *Innovations*, Winter: 97–107.

Ades, A. and R. Di Tella (1999). Rents, Competition and Corruption. *American Economic Review*, 89: 982–94.

AFP (2010). Iraq Signs Electricity Deal With Alstom. August 1.

Agnew, Clive and Ewan Anderson (1992). *Water Resources in the Arid Realm*. New York: Routledge.

Ahmad, Mahmood (2002). Agricultural Policy Issues and Challenges in Iraq: Short- and Medium-term Options. In Kamil Mahdi (ed.), *Iraq's Economic Predicament*. Reading, UK: Ithaca, pp. 169–99.

Ajami, Fouad (2006). *The Foreigner's Gift: The Americans, The Arabs, and The Iraqis in Iraq*. New York: Free Press.

Ajrash, Kadhim and Dahlia Kholaif (2012). Iraq to Raise Crude Oil Production to 4 Million Barrels in 2013. *Bloomberg News*. February 23.

Ali, Abdullah Yusuf (1985). *The Holy Qur-an*. Medina, Saudi Arabia: King Fahd Holy Qur-an Printing Complex.

Allawi, Ali A. (2007). *The Occupation of Iraq: Winning the War, Losing the Peace*. New Haven, CT: Yale University Press.

Allawi, Ali A. (2009). *The Crisis of Islamic Civilization*. New Haven, CT: Yale University Press.

Almounsor, Abdullah (2005). A Development Comparative Approach to Capital Flight: the Case of the Middle East and North Africa. In Gerald A. Epstein (ed.), *Capital Flight and Capital Controls in Developing*

Countries. Cheltenham, UK and Northampton, MA, USA: Edward Elgar, pp. 234–61.

Alnasrawi, Abbas (1994). *The Economy of Iraq: Oil, Wars, Destruction of Development and Prospects, 1950–2010.* Westport, CT: Greenwood Press.

Alnasrawi, Abbas (2002). *Iraq's Burdens: Oil, Sanctions, and Underdevelopment. The Economy of Iraq: Oil, Wars, Destruction of Development and Prospects, 1950–2010.* Westport, CT: Greenwood Press.

Ansary, Khalid al- (2011). Iraqi Journalists Face Sacks of Gold, Fists of Fire. *Reuters.* January 26.

Ansary, Tamim (2009). *Destiny Disrupted.* New York: Public Affairs Books.

Arab News (2011). Iraq's Cabinet Approves $692 Million Cement Factory. June 16.

Arango, Tim and Clifford Krauss (2012). Oil Output Soars as Iraq Retools, Easing Shaky Markets. *New York Times.* June 2.

Arraf, Jane (2009). Iraqi Voters Show Preference for Can-do Over Creed. *Christian Science Monitor.* January 23.

Askari, Hossein (2010). *Corruption and its Manifestation in the Persian Gulf.* Cheltenham, UK and Northampton, MA: Edward Elgar.

Aswat al-Iraq (2010). China and France to Set Up Car and Truck Assembling Plants in Iraq. August 23. At: http://en.aswataliraq.info.

Ayubi, Nazih N. (1995). *Over-stating the Arab State.* New York: I.B. Tauris.

Baghdadiya, al- (2009). PM Suspends Article 136.

Banerjee, Abhijit V. (2000). Prospects and Strategies for Land Reform. In Boris Pleskovic and Joseph E. Stiglitz (eds), *Annual World Bank Conference on Development Economics.* Washington, DC: World Bank, pp. 253–72.

Bank for International Settlement (BIS) (2012). BIS Quarterly Review, June.

Bardhan, Pranab (1997). Corruption and Development: A Review of Issues. *Journal of Economic Literature*, 35(3): 1320–1346.

Barkey, Henri J., Scott B. Lasensky, and Phebe Marr (eds) (2011). *Iraq: Its Neighbors and the United States.* Washington, DC: United States Institute of Peace.

Bauer, Peter T. and Basil S. Yamey (1957). *The Economics of Under-Developed Countries.* Chicago: University of Chicago Press.

Baumol, William J. (1990). Entrepreneurship: Productive, Unproductive and Destructive. *Journal of Political Economy*, 98(5): 893–921.

Baumol, William J., Robert E. Litan, and Carl J. Schramm (2007). *Good Capitalism, Bad Capitalism, and the Economics of Growth and Prosperity.* New Haven: Yale University Press.

Bayati, Hamid al- (2011). *From Dictatorship to Democracy.* Philadelphia: University of Pennsylvania Press.

Bennathan, Esra and Alan A. Walters (1979). *Port Pricing and Investment Policy.* New York: Oxford University Press.

Black, Edwin (2004). *Banking in Baghdad.* Hoboken, NJ: John Wiley.

Black, Jeff (2009). Background: Key Provinces in Iraq Provincial Elections 2009. *Middle East News.* January 27.

Bliss, Christopher and Rafael Di Tella (1997). Does Competition Kill Corruption? *Journal of Political Economy,* 105(5): 1001–23.

Bobroff-Hajal, Anne (2006). Why Cousin Marriage Matters in Iraq. *Christian Science Monitor.* December 26.

Brookings Institution (2007, 2009, 2010, 2011, 2012). *Iraq Index.* At: http://www.brookings.edu/about/centers/saban/iraq-index.

Brunetti, Aymo and Beatrice Weder (2003). A Free Press is Bad News for Corruption. *Journal of Public Economics,* 87(7–8): 1801–24.

Casson, M.C. (1987). Entrepreneur. In John Eatwell, Murray Milgate, and Peter Newman (eds), *The New Palgrave Dictionary of Economics.* New York: Palgrave Macmillan, pp. 151–3.

Casson, M., B. Yeung, A. Basu, and N. Wadeson (eds) (2006). *The Oxford Handbook of Entrepreneurship.* Oxford and New York: Oxford University Press.

Catherwood, Christopher (2004). *Churchills' Folly: How Winston Churchill Created Modern Iraq.* New York: Carroll and Graf Publishers.

Center for International Private Enterprise (CIPE) (2008a). Business Attitudes Towards Political and Economic Reconstruction in Iraq. February 29, 1–38.

Center for International Private Enterprise (CIPE) (2008b). Iraq Business Owner Survey. Project 08081, February 29, 1–13.

Center for International Private Enterprise (CIPE) (2011). Iraqi Business Attitudes on the Economy, Government, and Business Organizations: 2011 Iraqi Business Survey, Final Report. 1–49.

Central Bank of Iraq (CBI) (2004). Press Communique. At: www.cbi.iq/index.php?pid=Thecbi.

Central Bank of Iraq (CBI) (2012a). Iraqi and Foreign Financial Institutions. At: www.cbi.iq/index.php?pid=IraqFinancialinst.

Central Bank of Iraq (CBI) (2012b). Balance of Payments. At: www.cbi.iq/documents/bop.pdf.

Central Organization for Statistics and Information Technology (COSIT) (2008). *Iraq Household Socio-Economic Survey: 2007.* Amman, Jordan: National Press.

Central Organization for Statistics and Information Technology (COSIT)

(2012). *Annual Abstract of Statistics: 2010–2011*. At: http://cosit.gov.iq/english/index.php.

Chalabi, Fadhil (2002). The Oil Capacity of Post-War Iraq: Present Situations and Future Prospects. In Kamil A. Mahdi (ed.), *Iraq's Economic Predicament*. Reading, UK: Ithaca Press, pp. 141–68.

Chattopadhyay, Raghabendra and Esther Duflo (2005). Women as Policy Makers: Evidence From a Randomized Experiment in India. In Gerald M. Meier and James E. Rauch (eds), *Leading Issues in Economic Development*. New York: Oxford University Press, pp. 284–91.

Cheung, S.N. (1996). Simplistic General Equilibrium Theory of Corruption. *Contemporary Economic Policy*, 14(3): 1–5.

Cooper, John C.B. (2003). Price Elasticity of Demand for Crude Oil: Estimates for 23 Countries. OPEC. March.

Cooprider, Zoë, Merriam Mashatt, and James Wasserstrom (2007). State-Owned Enterprises: Post-Conflict Political Economy Considerations. USI Peace Briefing. March.

Cordesman, Anthony H. and Khalid R. al-Rodhan (2006). *The Changing Dynamics of Energy in the Middle East*. Volume 2. Westport, CT: Praeger Security International.

Cordesman, Anthony H., Charles Loi, and Adam Mausner (2011). Iraq's Coming National Challenges: Economy, Demographics, Budget, and Trade. Center for Strategic and International Studies. Slides. January 5.

Cordesman, Anthony and Sam Khazai (2012). *Iraq After US Withdrawal: US Policy and the Iraqi Search for Security and Stability*. Washington, DC: Center for Strategic and International Studies.

Crisis Group (2009). *Iraq's Provincial Elections: The Stakes*. Crisis Group Middle East Report No. 82. January 27.

Cuddington, J.T. (1987). Macroeconomic Determinants of Capital Flight: An Econometric Investigation. In Donald R. Lessard and John Williamson (eds), *Capital Flight and Third World Debt*. Washington, DC: Institute for International Economics, pp. 85–96.

Curran, Timothy W. (2006), Success and Failure Factors for Iraq State Owned Enterprises. Mimeo.

De Soto, Hernando (1989). *The Other Path: The Invisible Revolution in the Third World*. New York: Harper and Row.

De Soto, Hernando (2000). *The Mystery of Capital: Why Capitalism Triumphs in the West and Fails Everywhere Else*. New York: Basic Books.

Del Castillo, Graciana (2008). *Rebuilding War-Torn States: The Challenges of Post-Conflict Economic Reconstruction*. Oxford: Oxford University Press.

Desai, Sameeksha (2009). Measuring Entrepreneurship in Developing

Countries. Research Paper No. 2009/10. United Nations University – World Institute for Development Economics Research. March, 1–12.

Desai, Sameeksha (2011). Remittances from Iraqis in the US (conversation with the author).

Desai, Sameeksha, Soltan J. Acs, and Utz Weitzel (2010). A Model of Destructive Entrepreneurship. Research Paper No. 2010/34. United Nations University – World Institute for Development Economics Research. April, 1–16.

Djankov, Simeon, Rafael La Porta, Florencio Lopez-di-Silanes, and Andrei Shleifer (2002). The Regulation of Entry. *Quarterly Journal of Economics*, 117(1): 1–34.

Dobbins, James, Seth G. Jones, Benjamin Runkle, and Siddharth Mohandas (2009). *Occupying Iraq: A History of the Coalition Provisional Authority.* Santa Monica, CA: Rand.

Dolatyar, Mostafa and Tim S. Gray (2000). *Water Politics in the Middle East: A Context for Conflict or Cooperation?* New York: St. Martin's Press.

Duflo, Esther (2001). Schooling and Labor Market Consequences of School Construction in Indonesia: Evidence from an Unusual Policy Experiment. *American Economic Review*, 91(4): 795–813.

Dunia Frontier Consultants (2009). Private Foreign Investment in Iraq. November.

Easterly, William (2001). The Middle Class Consensus and Economic Growth. *Journal of Economic Growth*, 6(4): 318–26.

Easterly, William (2006). *The White Man's Burden.* New York: Penguin Books.

Economist, The (2003). Paying for Saddam's Sins. May 17. 68.

Economist, The (2007). Islam vs. Science. September 10.

Economist, The (2009a). Global Heroes: A Special Report on Entrepreneurship. March 14.

Economist, The (2009b). Iraq's Elections: A Real Choice for the People. January 22.

Economist, The (2010). Hard to get Out. August 21. 38.

Economist Intelligence Unit (2012). Iraq. At: http://country.eiu.com/Iraq.

Efird, Neil (2010). The State Owned Enterprise as a Vehicle for Stability. US Army, Strategic Studies Institute.

Eichengreen, Barry (2000). Taming Capital Flows. *World Development*, 28(6): 1105–16.

El-Gamal, Mahmoud A., Nihal El-Megharbel, and Hulusi Inanoglu (2000). Beyond Credit: A Taxonomy of SMEs and Financing Methods for Arab Countries. Paper presented at ECES Workshop in Cairo. March 6–8.

Energy Information Administration (EIA) (2010). *Country Analysis Briefs: Iraq.* September.

Energy Information Administration (EIA) (2012). *Annual Energy Outlook: 2012.* June.

Estrin, Saul, Klaus E. Meyer, and Maria Bytchkova (2006). Entrepreneurship in Transition Economies. In Mark Casson, Bernard Young, Anuradha Basu, and Nigel Wadeson (eds), *The Oxford Handbook of Entrepreneurship.* Oxford: Oxford University Press, pp. 693–725.

Faruqi, Anwar (2011). Fuel Theft Hits Iraq Power Grid: Inspector. *Agence France-Presse.* June 23.

Finance, Minister of (2005). Joint letter with Director of Central Bank of Iraq to International Monetary Fund. December 6.

Finance, Ministry of and Ministry of Planning (2003). Iraq Budget 2003: State-Owned Enterprises, July–December.

Food and Agricultural Organization of the United Nations (FAO) (2012a). *Faostat: Iraq.* At: http://faostat3.fao.org/home/index. html#VISUALIZE_BY_AREA_IRAQ.

Food and Agricultural Organization of the United Nations (FAO) (2012b). *Aquastat: Iraq.* At: http://www.fao.org/nr/water/aquastat/ counties_regions/IRQ/Index.stm.

Frye, Timothy and Andrei Shleifer (1997). The Invisible Hand and the Grabbing Hand. *American Economic Review,* 87(2): 354–8.

Fukuyama, Francis (2011). *The Origins of Political Order: From Prehuman Times to the French Revolution.* New York: Farrar, Straus and Giroux.

Fund for Peace (2012). Failed States Index. At: www.fundforpeace.org/ global/library/cfsir1210-failedstatesindex2012-06p.pdf.

Galal, Ahmed, Leroy Jones, Pankaj Tandon, and Ingo Vogelsang (1994). *Welfare Consequences of Selling Public Enterprises: An Empirical Analysis.* New York: Oxford University Press.

Galiani, Sebastian, Paul Gertler, and Ernesto Schargrodsky (2006). Water for Life: The Impact of the Privatization of Water Services on Child Mortality. At: www.iadb.org/res/publications/pubfiles/pubS-233.pdf.

Gallup (2010). Religiosity Highest in World's Poorest Nations. August 31. At: www.gallup.com/poll/142727/Religiosity-Highest-World-Poorest-Nations.aspx.

Gimbel, Barney (2007). In Iraq, One Man's Mission Impossible. *Fortune.* September 4.

Glaeser, Edward, Rafael La Porta, Florencio Lopez-de-Silanes, and Adnrei Shleifer (2004). Do Institutions Cause Growth? *Journal of Economic Growth,* 9(3): 271–303.

Godolphin, Francis R.B. (1942). *The Greek Historians.* Vol. 1, Book VI. New York: Random House.

Goldman, David P. (2011). *How Civilizations Die.* Washington, DC: Regency Publishing.

Grigorian, David A. and Udo Kock (2010). Inflation and Conflict in Iraq: The Economics of Shortages Revisited. *IMF Working Paper WP/10/159.*

Gunter, Frank R. (1991). Thomas Jefferson on the Repudiation of Public Debt. *Constitutional Political Economy*, 2(3): 283–301.

Gunter, Frank R. (2004). Capital Flight from China: 1984–2001. *China Economic Review*, 15(1): 63–85.

Gunter, Frank R. (2007). Economic Development during Conflict: The Petraeus-Crocker Congressional Testimonies. *Strategic Insights*, VI(6): 1–15.

Gunter, Frank R. (2008a). Capital Flight. In William A. Darity, Jr (ed.), *International Encyclopedia of the Social Sciences.* Detroit: Macmillan Reference, pp. 434–6.

Gunter, Frank R. (2008b). Corruption. In Vincent N. Parrillo (ed.), *Encyclopedia of Social Problems.* New York City, NY: Sage Publications, pp. 173–6.

Gunter, Frank R. (2009a). Liberate Iraq's Economy. *New York Times.* November 16. A25.

Gunter, Frank R. (2009b). Microfinance During Conflict: Iraq, 2003–2007. In Todd A. Watkins and Karen Hicks (eds), *Moving Beyond Storytelling: Emerging Research in Microfinance.* Bingley, UK: Emerald Group Publishing, pp. 183–214.

Gunter, Frank R. (2012). A Simple Model of Entrepreneurship for Principles of Economics Courses. *Journal of Economic Education*, 43(4): 386–96.

Gutman, Roy (2011). Dysfunctional Banking Sector Helps Keep Iraq in Economic Shambles. *The Kansas City Star.* December 25.

Haddad, Fanar (2011). *Sectarianism in Iraq: Antagonistic Visions of Unity.* New York: University of Chicago.

Hafedh, Mehdi, Ibrahim Akoum, Imad Zbib, and Zafar Ahmed (2007). Iraq: Emergence of a New Nation from the Ashes. *International Journal of Emerging Markets*, 2(1): 7–21.

Hafidh, Hassan (2011). Iraq Tackles Its Next Oil Bottleneck. *Wall Street Journal.* April 25.

Haiss, Peter, Katharina Steiner, and Markus Eller (2005). How do Foreign Banks Contribute to Economic Development in Transition Economies – How Much do we Know about Challenges and Opportunities? IMDA. At: http://fgr.wu-wien.ac.at/institut/ef/nexus.html.

Hall, Peter A. and David Soskice (eds) (2001). *Varieties of Capitalism: the*

Institutional Foundations of Comparative Advantage. Oxford: Oxford University Press.

Hanke, Steve H. (2002). On Dollarization and Currency Boards: Error and Deception. *Policy Reform*, 5(4): 203–22.

Hanke, Steve H. and Kurt Schuler (1994). *Currency Boards for Developing Countries: A Handbook.* San Francisco, CA: ICS Press.

Hanushek, Eric A. (2005). Interpreting Recent Research on Schooling in Developing Countries. In Gerald M. Meier and James E. Rauch (eds), *Leading Issues in Economic Development* (8th edn). New York: Oxford University Press, pp. 201–5.

Harris, John R. (1970). Some Problems in Identifying the Role of Entrepreneurship in Economic Development: The Nigerian Case. *Explorations in Economic History*, VII(2): 347–69.

Hayes, Brian (2005). *Infrastructure: A Field Guide to the Industrial Landscape.* New York: W.W. Norton.

Hertog, Steffen (2010). Defying the Resource Curse: Explaining Successful State-Owned Enterprises in Rentier States. *World Politics*, 62(2): 261–301.

Hettige, Hemamala, Mainul Huq, Sheoli Pargal, and David Wheeler (1996). Determinates of Pollution Abatement in Developing Countries: Evidence from South and Southeast Asia. *World Development*, 24(12): 1891–904

Huntington, Samuel P. (1968). *Political Order in Changing Societies.* New Haven, CT: Yale University Press.

Huntington, Samuel P. (1991). *The Third Wave: Democratization in the Late Twentieth Century.* Norman, OK: University of Oklahoma Press.

Hussein, Aqeel and Colin Freeman (2007). U.S. to Reopen Iraq's Factories in $10 millionU-Turn. *Sunday Telegraph.* January 29.

Hyne, Norman J. (2001). *Nontechnical Guide to Petroleum Geology, Exploration, Drilling, and Production.* Tulsa, OK: Penn Well Corporation.

Ibn Khaldun ([1384] 1967). *The Muqaddimah: An Introduction to History.* Princeton, NJ: Princeton University Press.

Industry and Minerals, Ministry of (2009). Master Strategic Plan. Ministry of Industry and Minerals Study.

Integrated Regional Information Network (IRIN) (2009). Iraq: HIV-positive Persons Fear Reprisals. News Release of UN Office for the Coordination of Humanitarian Affairs. January 14. At: http://www.irinnews.org/Report/82357/IRAQ-HIV-POSITIVE-PERSONS-FEAR-REPRISALS.

Integrated Regional Information Network (IRIN) (2010a). Iraq: Iraqis

Welcome WFP Role in State Food Aid System. January 6. At: http://www.wfp.org/content/IRAQ-IRAQIS-WELCOME-WFP-ROLE-STATE-FOOD-AID-SYSTEM.

Integrated Regional Information Network (IRIN) (2010b). Iraq: Streamlining the State Food Aid System. February 9. At: http://www.irinnews.org/Report/88041/IRAQ-STREAMLING-THE-STATE-FOOD-AID-SYSTEM.

Integrated Regional Information Network (IRIN) (2010c). Iraq: Killing for Water. June 23. At: http://www.irinnews.org/Report/89586/IRAQ-KILLING-FOR-WATER.

International Monetary Fund (IMF) (2005). *Iraq – Request for Stand-By Arrangement*. Washington, DC: International Monetary Fund. December 8.

International Monetary Fund (IMF) (2008a). *Iraq: First Review Under the Stand-by Arrangement and Financing Assurances Review.* IMF Country Report No. 08/303. Washington, DC: International Monetary Fund.

International Monetary Fund (IMF) (2008b). *Iraq: Second Review Under the Stand-by Arrangement and Financing Assurances Review.* IMF Country Report No. 08/383. Washington, DC: International Monetary Fund.

International Monetary Fund (IMF) (2010a). *Regional Economic Outlook: Middle East and Central Asia.* Washington, DC: International Monetary Fund.

International Monetary Fund (IMF) (2010b). *Iraq: Staff Report for the 2009 Article IV Consultation and Request for Stand-By Arrangement.* Washington, DC: International Monetary Fund.

International Monetary Fund (IMF) (2010c). *Annual Report on Exchange Arrangements and Exchange Restrictions: 2010.* Washington, DC: International Monetary Fund.

International Monetary Fund (IMF) (2011a). *Iraq: Second Review Under the Stand-By Arrangment, Requests for Waiver of Applicability, Extension of the Arrangement, and Rephasing of Access.* IMF Country Report No. 11/75. Washington, DC: International Monetary Fund. March.

International Monetary Fund (IMF) (2011b). *Iraq IMF Country Report.* No. 11/7. Washington, DC: International Monetary Fund.

Iraq, Government of (2005a). Constitution. At: http://www.uniraq.org/documents/iraqi.constitution.pdf.

Iraq, Government of (2005b). *National Development Strategy: 2005–2007.* Baghdad: Government of Iraq.

Iraq, Government of (2007). *National Development Strategy: 2007–2010.* Baghdad: Government of Iraq.

Iraq, Government of (2010). *National Development Plan: 2010–2014.* Baghdad: Government of Iraq.

Iraq Partners Forum (2010). *The Iraq Briefing Book.* Washington, DC: Iraq Partners Forum. December.

Iraq Stock Exchange (ISX) (2012). Subscribed Shares and Closing Price, Market Capitalization, and Turnover Ratio for the Listed Companies in ISX. At: http://www.isx-iq.net/isxportal/portal/sectors Details.html.

Issawi, Charles (1966). *The Economic History of the Middle East: 1800–1914.* Chicago: University of Chicago Press.

Issawi, Charles (1982). *An Economic History of the Middle East and North Africa.* New York: Columbia University Press.

Issawi, Charles (1988). *The Fertile Crescent: 1800–1914.* New York: Oxford University Press.

Jawari, Hadeel al- (2009). Iraq Government Hit by Graft: 4,000 Forged University Degrees Uncovered. *Azzaman.* At: http://www.assaman. com.

Johnson, Kirk A. (2007). Understanding the Unemployment and Underemployment Situation in Iraq (unpublished).

Jurewitz (1987). The Deregulation of Electricity. Working Paper.

Kami, Aseel and Yara Bayoumy (2012). Banks that Can't Cash a Cheque Slow Iraqi Economy. *Reuters.* March 7.

Kami, Aseel and Serena Chaudhry (2011). Iraqi Banks Struggle with Limited Services, Capital. *Reuters.* July 20.

Kane, Sean (2010). Iraq's Oil Politics: Where Agreement Might Be Found. *Peaceworks.* No. 64. January.

Kaufmann, Daniel, Aart Kraay, and Massimo Mastruzzi (2003). Governance Matters III: Governance Indicators for 1996–2002. *World Bank Policy Research Working Paper No. 3106.* Washington, DC: World Bank.

Khaleej Times Online (2011). Iraq Cancels Direct Cash Purchases of Food Items. May 30. At: http://iraqdailytimes.com/iraq-cancels-direct-cash-buying-of-essential-food.

Khaleej Times Online (2012). Iraq Seeks DED Expertise. June 27. At: http://www.khaleejtimes.com/biz/inside.asp?xfile=/data/bankingfin ance/2012/June/bankingfinance_june24.xm/&section=bankingfinance.

Kirzner, I.M. (1979). *Perception, Opportunity, and Profit.* Chicago: University of Chicago Press.

Klein, Matthias S. (2006). Development of the Iraqi Public Pension System. *Global Action on Aging.* September 8. At: http://www.globalag-ing.org/pensions/world/2006/iraqenglish.htm.

Klitgaard, Robert (1988). *Controlling Corruption.* Berkley, CA: University of California Press.

Knack, Stephen and Philip Keefer (1995). Institutions and Economic

Performance: Cross-Country Tests Using Alternative Institutional Measures. *Economics and Politics*, 7(3): 207–27.

Knight, Frank H. ([1921] 1971). *Risk, Uncertainty and Profit*. Chicago: University of Chicago Press.

Krueger, Anne (1974). The Political Economy of the Rent Seeking Society. *American Economic Review*, 64(3): 291–302.

Kuran, Timur (2004). *Islam and Mammon: The Economic Predicaments of Islamism*. Princeton, NJ: Princeton University Press.

Kuran, Timur (2010). The Scale of Entrepreneurship in Middle Eastern History: Inhibitive Roles of Islamic Institutions. In David S. Landis, Joel Mokyr, and William J. Baumol (eds), *The Invention of Enterprise*. Princeton, NJ: Princeton University Press, pp. 62–87.

Kuran, Timur (2011). *The Long Divergence: How Islamic Law Held Back the Middle East*. Princeton, NJ: Princeton University Press.

La Porta, Rafael, Florencio Lopez-de-Silanes, Andrei Shleifer, and Robert Vishny (1999). The Quality of Government. *Journal of Law, Economics and Organization*, 15(1): 222–79.

Lambsdorff, Johann G. (2006). Causes and Consequences of Corruption: What do we Know from a Cross-Section of Countries? In Susan Rose-Ackerman (ed.), *International Handbook on the Economics of Corruption*. Cheltenham, UK and Northampton, MA, USA: Edward Elgar, pp. 3–51.

Landes, David (1998). *The Wealth and Poverty of Nations*. New York: W.W. Norton.

Lawless, R.I. (1972). Iraq: Changing Population Patterns. In J.I. Clark and W.B. Fisher (eds), *Populations of the Middle East and North Africa*. New York: Africana Publishing Corporation, pp. 97–129.

Leite, C. and J. Weidemann (1999). Does Mother Nature Corrupt? Natural Resources, Corruption and Economic Growth. International Monetary Fund Working Paper, 99/85. July.

Lewis, Bernard (2002). *What Went Wrong?* New York: Oxford University Press.

Lingelbach, David, Lynda de la Viña, and Paul Asel (2005). What's Distinctive About Growth-Oriented Entrepreneurship in Developing Countries? At: http://papers.ssrn.com/sol3/papers.cfm?abstract_id= 742605.

Looney, Robert E. (2006). Economic Consequences of Conflict: The Rise of Iraq's Informal Economy. *Journal of Economic Issues*, 60(4): 991–1007.

Looney, Robert E. (2008). Reconstruction and Peacebuilding Under Extreme Adversity: The Problem of Pervasive Corruption in Iraq. *International Peacekeeping*, 15(3): 424–40.

Machiavelli, Niccolo (1988). *Florentine Histories.* Trans. Laura F. Banfield and Harvey C. Mansfield Jr. Princeton, NJ: Princeton University Press.

Maddison, Angus (2003). *The World Economy: Historical Statistics.* Paris: OECD.

Maddison, Angus (2007). *Contours of the World Economy, 1–2030 AD.* New York: Oxford University Press.

Mahdi, Kamil A. (2000). *State and Agriculture in Iraq: Modern Development, Stagnation and the Impact of Oil.* Reading, UK: Ithaca Press.

Mahdi, Kamil A. (ed.) (2002). *Iraq's Economic Predicament.* Reading, UK: Ithaca.

Mahdi, Kamil A. (2007). Iraq's Oil Law: Parsing the Fine Print. *World Policy Institute*, June, 11–23.

Marr, Phebe (2004). *The Modern History of Iraq.* Boulder, CO: Westview Press.

Mauro, Paolo (1995). Corruption and Growth. *Quarterly Journal of Economics*, 110(3): 681–712.

McMillan, John and Christopher Woodruff (2002). The Central Role of Entrepreneurs in Transition Economies. *Journal of Economic Perspectives*, 16(3): 153–70.

Meese, Michael J. (2007). Electrical Frequency and Underfrequency Load-Shedding. Working Paper. Baghdad, Iraq.

Megginson, William L. and Jeffrey M. Netter (2001). From State to Market: A Survey of Empirical Studies on Privatization. *Journal of Economic Literature*, June, 39: 321–89.

Merza, Ali (2008). Policies and Economic and Social Trends in Iraq: 2003–2007. Paper presented at International Association of Contemporary Iraqi Studies, July 16–17.

Mirza, Ali (2012). Budget 2012: Financial, Economic and Institutional Issues in Iraq. Memo. January 26.

Mookherjee, Dilip and I.P.L. Png (1995). Corruptible Law Enforcers: How Should They Be Compensated? *Economic Journal*, 105(428): 145–59.

Murphy, Kevin, Andrei Shleifer, and Robert V. Vishny (1993). Why is Rent Seeking So Costly to Growth? *American Economic Review*, 83(2): 409–14.

Nagl, John and Daniel Rice (2009). A Jump Start for Iraq's Private Sector. *Wall Street Journal.* July 7.

National Iraqi News Agency (2011). Telecommunications. March 15. At: http://www.ninanews.com/english.

National US-Arab Chamber of Commerce (NUSACC) (2011). US

Exports to the Arab World to Reach $117 Billion by 2013. February. At: www.nusacc.org/assets/library/12_trdln0211outlook13a.pdf.

Niqash (2011a). Iraq Gets Tough on Fake Qualifications, Up to 50,000 Jobs at Risk. April 11. At: www.niqash.org/articles/?id=2821.

Niqash (2011b). Basra's Big Business: Fake Building Contractors Defaulting on Jobs. July 20. At: www. niqash.org/articles/?id=2866.

Noland, Marcus and Howard Pack (2007). *The Arab Economies in a Changing World.* Washington, DC: Peterson Institute for International Economics.

North, Douglass C. (1990). *Institutions, Institutional Change and Economic Performance.* New York: Cambridge University Press.

Oil, Ministry of (2012). Crude Oil Exports and Domestic Consumption. Baghdad: Ministry of Oil. At: http://www.oil.gov.iq/moo/.

Olivier, G.A. (1988). Trade of Iraq, 1790s. In Charles Issawi (ed.), *The Fertile Crescent: 1800–1914.* New York: Oxford University Press, pp. 178–82.

Oman Tribune (2011). Iraq Begins Pumping Oil Through Al Ahdab. July 24. At: http://omantribune.com/index.php?page=new&id=97092&heading=news%20in%20detail.

Omer, Tara Mohamed Anwar (2011). Country Pasture/Forage Resource Profile. Rome, Italy: Food and Agricultural Organization of the UN.

Organization of Petroleum Exporting Countries (OPEC) (2009). *OPEC Annual Statistical Bulletin.* At: www.opec.org/opec_web/static_files_project/media/downloads/publications/ASB2009.pdf .

Owen, Roger and Şevket Pamuk (1999). *A History of Middle East Economies in the Twentieth Century.* Cambridge: Harvard University Press.

Ozlu, Onur (2006). *Iraqi Economic Reconstruction and Development.* Washington, DC: Center for Strategic and International Studies.

Parker, Ned and Usama Redha (2009). Last Minute Campaigning in Najaf. *Los Angeles Times.* January 31.

Parker, Simon C. (2009). *The Economics of Entrepreneurship.* New York: Cambridge University Press.

Parkinson, C. Northcote (1957). *Parkinson's Law and Other Studies in Administration.* London: Houghton Mifflin.

Patai, Raphael (2002). *The Arab Mind.* New York: Hatherleigh Press.

Pearson, Bryan (2009). Theater Groups Reappear in Iraq. *Variety.* January 7.

Persson, Torsten and Guido Tabellini (2004). Constitutions and Economic Policy. *Journal of Economic Perspectives*, 18(1): 75–98.

Pickthall, Marmaduke ([1930] 1992). *The Glorious Koran.* New York: Alfred A. Knopf.

Planning, Ministry of (2006). SOE's Economic Reform Commission. December 26.

Planning, Ministry of and Ministry of Finance (2004). Iraq Budget 2003, July–December, State-Owned Enterprises.

Pollack, Kenneth M. (2012), Reading Machiavelli in Iraq. *National Interest*. November/December. At: http://nationalinterest.org/article/reading-machiavelli-iraq-7611.

Previté-Orton, C.W. (1952). *The Shorter Cambridge Medieval History*, Vol. 2. London: Cambridge University Press.

Przeworski, Adam, Michael E. Alvarez, Jose Antonio Cheibub, and Fernando Limongi (2000). *Democracy and Development: Political Institutions and Well-Being in the World*. New York: Cambridge University Press.

Psacharopoulos, G. (1991). *The Economic Impact of Education: Lessons for Policymakers*. San Francisco, CA: ICS Press.

Psacharopoulos, George (2005). Economic Impact of Education. In Gerald M. Meier and James E. Rauch (eds), *Leading Issues in Economic Development*. New York: Oxford University Press, pp. 189–92.

Psacharopoulos, George and Harry Anthony Patrinos (2002). Returns to Education: A Further Update. World Bank Policy Research Working Paper 2881. September.

Qian, Yingi (2003). How Reform Worked in China. In Dani Rodrick (ed.), *In Search of Prosperity*. Princeton, NJ: Princeton University Press, pp. 297–333.

Rahdi, Rahdi Hamza al- (2007). Testimony to the House Committee on Oversight and Government Reform on the Status of Corruption in the Iraqi Government. October 4.

Rauch, James E. and Peter B. Evans (2000). Bureaucratic Structure and Bureaucratic Performance in Less Developed Countries. *Journal of Public Economics*, 75(1): 49–62.

Reuters (2011a). Iraqi Banks Struggle with Limited Services, Capital. July 20.

Reuters (2011b). Iraq Names Trade Bank President. July 17.

Reuters (2011c). Baghdad Subsidizes Electricity. February 13.

Reuters (2012). Iraq Approves $100.5 Bln Budget for 2012. February 23.

Richards, Alan and John Waterbury (2008). *A Political Economy of the Middle East*. Boulder, CO: Westview Press.

Rivlin, Paul (2009). *Arab Economies in the Twenty-First Century*. Cambridge: Cambridge University Press.

Robinson, Linda (2008). *Tell Me How This Ends: General David Petraeus and the Search for a Way Out of Iraq*. New York: Public Affairs.

Rose-Ackerman, Susan (1999). *Corruption and Government: Causes, Consequences and Reform.* New York: Cambridge University Press.

Rousseau, J.B. (1966). Description du Pachalik de Baghdad. In Charles Issawi (ed.), *The Economic History of the Middle East: 1800–1914.* Chicago, IL: University of Chicago Press, pp. 135–6.

Rubin, Alissa J. (2008). Iraqi Trade Officials Ousted in Corruption Sweep. *New York Times.* September 24.

Salter, Lord and S.W. Payton (1955). *The Development of Iraq: A Plan of Action.* London: Iraq Development Board.

Sattar, Omer (2012). Integrity Committee to Investigate Corruption in Iraqi Ministries. *Al-Monitor.* July 7.

Savello, Paul A. (2009a). Water Issues in Iraq: Water Availability and Its Usage. Paper#1. Baghdad: Iraq Transition Assistance Office.

Savello, Paul A. (2009b). Water Issues in Iraq: Future Water Projections. Paper #2. Baghdad: Iraq Transition Assistance Office.

Schoon, Natalie (2008). *Islamic Banking and Finance.* London: Spiramus Press.

Schumpeter, Joseph A. (1911). *Theory of Economic Development.* Cambridge: Harvard University Press.

Smith, Adam (1776). *An Inquiry into the Nature and Causes of the Wealth of Nations.* New York: Modern Library.

Special Inspector General for Iraq Reconstruction (SIGIR) (2009a). Full Impact of Department of Defense Program to Restart State-Owned Enterprises Difficult to Estimate. SIGIR-09-09. January 30.

Special Inspector General for Iraq Reconstruction (SIGIR) (2009b). *Hard Lessons: The Iraq Reconstruction Experience.* Washington, DC: US Government Printing Office.

Special Inspector General for Iraq Reconstruction (SIGIR) (2009c). Cost, Outcome, and Oversight of Iraq Oil Reconstruction Contract with Kellogg Brown & Root Services, Inc. SIGIR-09-008. January 13.

Special Inspector General for Iraq Reconstruction (SIGIR) (2010). *Quarterly Report to the United States Congress.* Washington, DC: SIGIR, July 30.

Special Inspector General for Iraq Reconstruction (SIGIR) (2012). *Quarterly Report to the United States Congress.* Washington, DC: SIGIR. April 30.

Speville, Bertrand de (1997). *Hong Kong: Policy Initiatives Against Corruption.* Paris: Development Center of OECD.

Springborg, Robert (2007). *Oil and Democracy in Iraq.* London: SAQI.

Stallings, Barbara and Wilson Peres (2000). *Growth, Employment and Equity: the Impact of Economic Reforms in Latin America and the Caribbean.* Washington, DC: Brookings Institution.

Stansfield, Gareth and Hashem Ahmadzadeh (2008). Kurdish or Kurdistanis? Conceptualizing Regionalism in the North of Iraq. In Reidar Visser and Gareth Stansfield (eds), *An Iraq of Its Regions: Cornerstones of a Federal Democracy?* New York: Columbia University Press, pp. 123–49.

Stevenson, Lois (2010). *Private Sector and Enterprise Development.* Cheltenham, UK and Northampton, MA, USA: Edward Elgar.

Stiglitz, Joseph E. (1987). Some Theoretical Aspects of Agricultural Policies. *World Bank Research Observer*, 2(1): 43–60.

Sundahl, Mark J. (2007). Iraq Secured Transactions and the Promise of Islamic Law. *Vanderbilt Journal of Transnational Law*, 1302–43.

Svensson, Jakob (2005). Eight Questions about Corruption. *Journal of Economic Perspectives*, 19(3): 19–42.

Szirmai, Adam (2005). *The Dynamics of Socio-Economic Development: An Introduction.* New York: Cambridge University Press.

Tanzi, V. (1998). Corruption around the world: Causes, Consequences, Scope and Cures. *IMF Staff Papers*, 45: 559–94.

Task Force for Business and Stability Operations (TFBSO) (2011). Iraq Final Impact Summary. Washington, DC: Task Force for Business and Stability Operations.

Thede, Susanna and Nils-Åke Gustafson (2010). The Multifaceted Impact of Corruption on International Trade. Mimeo.

Timmer, C. Peter. (1988). The Agricultural Transformation. In H. Chenery and T.N. Srinivasan (eds), *Handbook of Development Economics.* Amsterdam: Elsevier Science Publishers, pp. 321–8.

Timmer, C. Peter. (2002). Agriculture and Economic Development. In Bruce L. Gardner and Gordon C. Rausser (eds), *Handbook of Agricultural Economics.* Amsterdam: Elsevier Science Publishers, pp. 1520–1524.

Timmer, C. Peter (2005). Agricultural Development Strategies. In Gerald M. Meier and James E. Rauch (eds), *Leading Issues in Economic Development.* New York: Oxford University Press, pp. 394–6.

Toynbee, Arnold (1972). *A Study of History.* New York: Barnes and Noble Books.

Transparency International (2011). Corruption Perceptions Index. At: http://www.transparency.org/identity#IRQ.

Treisman, Daniel (2000). The Causes of Corruption: A Cross-National Study. *Journal of Public Economics*, 76(3): 399–457.

Tripp, Charles (2000). *A History of Iraq.* Cambridge: Cambridge University Press.

Tullock, Gordon (1967). The Welfare Costs of Tarrifs, Monopolies, and Theft. *Western Economic Journal*, 5: 224–32.

Tullock, Gordon (1986). Industrial Organization and Rent Seeking in Dictatorships. *Journal of Institutional and Theoretical Economics*, 142: 4–15.

Tullock, Gordon (2005a). Rent Seeking: the Problem of Definition. In Charles K. Rowley (ed.), *The Rent Seeking Society.* Indianapolis: Liberty Fund, pp. 3–10.

Tullock, Gordon (2005b). Rent Seeking. In Charles K. Rowley (ed.), *The Rent Seeking Society.* Indianapolis: Liberty Fund, pp. 11–81.

UNCT Iraq (2010). *United Nations Development Assistance Framework for Iraq 2011–2014.* New York: United Nations.

UNDP (2003). *Arab Human Development Report.* New York: United Nations.

United Nations (2004). *Convention Against Corruption.* New York: United Nations.

United Nations (2012). Population Divison. At: http://esa.un.org/unpd/wpp/documentation/publications.htm.

United Nations and World Bank (2003). Joint Needs Assessment: State-Owned Enterprises. Working Paper. October.

United Nations Industrial Development Organization (UNIDO) (2010). UNIDO Supports Iraq's Efforts to Rehabilitate State-Owned Enterprises. March 22. At: http://www.unido.org/index.php?id=7881&tx_ttnews%5Btt_news%5D=457&cHash=5f0eb07d6c.

United Nations International Children's Emergency Fund (UNICEF) (2012). Iraq Statistics. At: http://www.unicef.org/infobycountry/iraq_statistics.html.

United Press International (UPI) (2012). Iraq Oil Exports Rise But Problems Remain. May 9. At: http://www.upi.com/Business_News/Energy-Resources/2012/05/09/Iraq-oil-exports-rise-but-problems-remain/UPI-20161336580985/#axzz2CwsqPBDr.

United States Agency for International Development (USAID) (2006a). A Presentation on Privatization. Baghdad: USAID, October 29.

United States Agency for International Development (USAID) (2006b). *Agricultural Reconstruction and Development Program for Iraq: Assessment of Rangelands in Iraq.* Preliminary Report. February. Baghdad: USAID.

United States Agency for International Development (USAID) (2006c). *Excess Employment in State Owned Enterprises.* Iraq Private Sector Growth and Employment Generation Series. June. Washington, DC: USAID.

United States Agency for International Development (USAID) (2006d). *Iraq Competitiveness Analysis.* Iraq Private Sector Growth and Employment Generation Series. Washington, DC: USAID.

United States Agency for International Development (USAID) (2007a). *An Overview of the Iraqi Banking System*. Washington, DC: USAID.

United States Agency for International Development (USAID) (2007b). *An Overview of the Iraq Cement Industry*. Iraq Private Sector Growth and Employment Generation Series. November 25. Washington, DC: USAID.

United States Agency for International Development (USAID) (2009). *Iraq: Economic Recovery Assessment*. February. Washington, DC: USAID.

United States Agency for International Development (USAID) (2011). *State of Iraq's Microfinance Industry*. Washington, DC: USAID.

Urdal, Henrik (2012). Youth Bulges and Violence. In Jack A. Goldstone, Eric P. Kaufmann, and Monica Duffy Toft (eds), *Political Demography: How Population Changes are Reshaping International Security and National Politics*. Boulder, CO: Paradigm Publishers, pp. 117–32.

US Army (2006). *Counterinsurgency Field Manual*. US Army Field Manual 3-24, Marine Corps Warfighting Publication No. 3-33.5.

US Census (2012). International Database. At: http://www.census.gov/population/international/data/idb/.

US Central Intelligence Agency (US CIA) (2012). *Fact Book: Iraq*. At: https://www.cia.gov/library/publications/the-world-factbook/geos/iz.html.

US Congress (2004). Review Iraqi Agriculture: From Oil for Food to the Future of Iraqi Production, Agriculture and Trade. Testimony before Committee on Agriculture, House of Representatives. Serial No. 108-33. June 16.

US Department of State (2006). Iraq Railroads. Mimeo.

US Department of State (2008). Iraqi Government Charges More than 300 Officials with Corruption in 2008. News Release. November 26.

US Department of Treasury (2009). Iraqi Banking System: An Overview. Washington, DC: Department of Treasury.

US Government Accountability Office (US GAO) (2007). Rebuilding Iraq: Integrated Strategic Plan Needed to Help Restore Iraq's Oil and Electricity Sectors. Washington, DC: GAO.

US News and World Report (2007). Islam and Science. September 10.

Visser, Hans (2009). *Islamic Finance: Principles and Practice*. Cheltenham, UK and Northampton, MA, USA: Edward Elgar.

Visser, Reidar (2008). Introduction. In Reidar Visser and Gareth Stansfield (eds), *An Iraq of Its Regions: Cornerstones of a Federal Democracy?* New York: Columbia University Press, pp. 1–26.

Visser, Reidar (2011). Anti-Corruption Measure Sparks Constitutional Confusion in Iraq. May 10. At: http://gulfanalysis.

wordpress.com/2011/05/10/anti-corruption-measure-sparks-constitutio
nal-confusion-in-iraq/.

Visser, Reidar and Gareth Stansfield (eds) (2008). *An Iraq of Its Regions: Cornerstones of a Federal Democracy?* New York: Columbia University Press.

Voltaire (2010). *La Begueule, Conte Moral (1772)*. Whitefish, MT: Kessinger Publishing.

Wall Street Journal (2011). Crude Oil: All Barrels are Equal, but some are More Equal Than Others. April 9–10, A6.

Walters, Alan A. (1968). *The Economics of Road User Charges.* Baltimore, MD: Johns Hopkins University Press.

Walters, Alan A. and Steve H. Hanke (1992). Currency Boards. In Peter Newman, Murray Milgate, and John Eatwell (eds), *The New Palgrave Dictionary of Money and Finance.* New York: Stockton Press, pp. 558–61.

Warren, Count Edward de (1966). European Interests in Railways in the Valley of the Euphates. In Charles Issawi (ed.), *The Economic History of the Middle East, 1800–1914.* Chicago: University of Chicago Press, pp. 137–45.

Weber, Max ([1920] 2002). *The Protestant Ethic and the Spirit of Capitalism.* Los Angeles, CA: Roxbury Publishing Company.

Weiss, Martin A. (2009). Iraq's Debt Relief: Procedure and Potential Implications for International Debt Relief. Congressional Research Service, 7-5700. January 26.

White, Thomas E., Robert C. Kelly, John M. Cape, and Denise Youngblood Coleman (2003). *Reconstructing Eden.* Houston, TX: Country Watch Inc.

World Bank (1995). *Bureaucrats in Business.* New York: Oxford University Press.

World Bank (2004). State Owned Enterprises Reform in Iraq. Reconstructing Iraq Working Paper No. 2. Washington, DC: World Bank.

World Bank (2005). *Pensions in Iraq: Issues, General Guidelines for Reform, and Potential Fiscal Implications.* Washington, DC: World Bank.

World Bank (2006a). Rebuilding Iraq: Economic Reform and Transition. Report No. 35141-IQ. Washington, DC: World Bank.

World Bank (2006b). Iraq Country Water Resource Assistance Strategy. Report No. 36297-IQ. Washington, DC: World Bank.

World Bank (2009). *Doing Business in the Arab World.* Washington, DC: World Bank.

World Bank (2010). *World Development Indicators.* Washington, DC: World Bank.

World Bank (2011a). *Financial Sector Review: Republic of Iraq.* Washington, DC: World Bank.

World Bank (2011b). *Accelerating Reform Within Iraq's National Board of Pensions.* MENA Quick Note. Washington, DC: World Bank.

World Bank (2011c). *Ease of Doing Business 2011.* Washington, DC: World Bank.

World Bank (2011d). *Confronting Poverty in Iraq.* Washington, DC: World Bank

World Bank (2011e). *Doing Business in the Arab World: 2011.* Washington, DC: World Bank.

World Bank (2012a). *Economy Profile: Iraq.* Doing Business Series 2012. Washington, DC: World Bank

World Bank (2012b). *World Development Indicators 2012.* Washington, DC: World Bank.

World Food Program (WFP) (2010). Capacity Development to Reform the Public Distribution System (PDS) and Strengthen Social Safety Nets for Vulnerable Groups in Iraq. World Food Program Development Project Iraq 200104.

World Health Organization (WHO) and United Nations International Children's Emergency Fund (UNICEF) (2006). Meeting the MDG drinking-water and sanitation target: the urban and rural challenge of the decade. At: http://www.who.int/water_sanitation_health/monitor ing/jmp2006/en/index.html.

Wunsch, Cornelia (2010). Neo-Babylonian Entrepreneurs. In David S. Landis, Joel Mokyr, and William J. Baumol (eds), *The Invention of Enterprise.* Princeton, NJ: Princeton University Press, pp. 40–61.

Yilmaz, Mehsmet (2003). The War that Never Happened: The Sharing of Euphrates – Tigris Rivers' Water between Turkey, Syria and Iraq. Naval Postgraduate Thesis, June.

Zulfikar, Yavuz Fahir (2012). Do Muslims Believe More in Protestant Work Ethic than Christians? Comparison of People with Different Religious Background Living in the U.S. *Journal of Business Ethics*, 105(4): 489–502.

Zedalis, Rex J. (2009). *The Legal Dimensions of Oil and Gas in Iraq.* New York: Cambridge University Press.

Zulal, Shwan (2012). The Battle for Iraqi Oil: Can There Ever Be a Winner? *Niqash.* At: http://www.niqash.org/articles/?id=3043.

Index